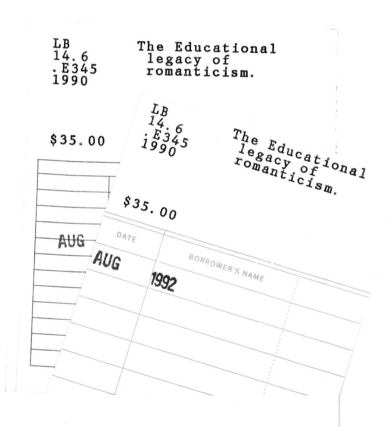

THE EDUCATIONAL LEGACY OF ROMANTICISM

Edited by

John Willinsky

This international collection of essays by leading authorities in literature and education presents the first comprehensive view of the impact of Romanticism on education over the course of the last two centuries. Romanticism's reconception of self, nature, writing and the imagination forms a chapter of intellectual history that has led to a number of innovative programs in the schools. The book returns to the educational thinking of key figures from the time — Rousseau, Wordsworth, Mary Shelley and Coleridge — before charting their influence on such historical and contemporary developments as Montessori schools, art education, free schools and current writing programs. The contributors tend to challenge common assumptions concerning Romanticism and do not shy away from its darker side; their work encompasses both theoretical considerations of Romantic and post-modern conceptions of the self and practical concerns with Romanticism's potential for the school curriculum. *The Educational Legacy of Romanticism* represents a multi-disciplinary inquiry into the continuing influence which cultural endeavours can have on the social practices of society.

John Willinsky is Associate Professor of Education and Director of The Centre for the Study of Curriculum and Instruction, The University of British Columbia.

™ᴱEducational
Legacy ᴼꜰ
Romanticism

^{THE}Educational
Legacy $_{OF}$
Romanticism

Edited by

John Willinsky

Essays by

Aubrey Rosenberg
Ann E. Berthoff
Clarence J. Karier
Diana Korzenik
Edgar Z. Friedenberg
Johan Lyall Aitken
Richard L. Butt

John Willinsky
Anne McWhir
Max van Manen
Jane Roland Martin
Madeleine R. Grumet
Deborah A. Dooley
Kieran Egan

Published by
Wilfrid Laurier University Press
for
The Calgary Institute for the Humanities

Canadian Cataloguing in Publication Data

Main entry under title:
The Educational legacy of romanticism

Papers presented at a meeting held Oct. 13-16, 1988
at the Calgary Institute for the Humanities.
Includes bibliographical references and index.
ISBN 0-88920-996-0

1. Education – Philosophy – Congresses.
2. Romanticism – Congresses.   3. Education in
literature – Congresses.   I. Willinsky, John M.
II. Rosenberg, Aubrey, 1928-   .   III. Calgary
Institute for the Humanities.

LB1025.2.E38 1990   370'.12   C90-094898-1

Copyright © 1990
Wilfrid Laurier University Press
Waterloo, Ontario, Canada
N2L 3C5

Cover design by Leslie Macredie

Printed in Canada

The Educational Legacy of Romanticism has been produced from a manuscript
supplied in camera-ready form by The Calgary Institute for the Humanities.

In memory of J. M. W. and A. I. W.

TABLE OF CONTENTS

FROM THE DIRECTOR

Established in 1976, the Calgary Institute for the Humanities has as its aim the fostering of advanced study and research in all areas of the humanities. Apart from supporting work in the traditional "arts" disciplines such as philosophy, history, ancient and modern languages and literatures, it also promotes research into the philosophical and historical aspects of the sciences, social sciences, fine arts, and the various "professional" disciplines.

The Institute's programs in support of advanced study attempt to provide scholars with time to carry out their work. In addition, the Institute sponsors formal and informal gatherings among people who share common interests, in order to promote intellectual dialogue and discussion. Recently, the Institute has moved to foster the application of humanistic knowledge to contemporary social problems.

The seminar *The Educational Legacy of Romanticism*, October 13-16, 1988, brought together scholars of education, literature, philosophy, composition and modern languages to examine the impact that Romanticism has had upon Education. This study has theoretical importance for our understanding of how the great figures of the Romantic movement have influenced our educational experience.

We wish to record here our gratitude to the Social Sciences and Humanities Research Council of Canada; The University of Calgary Conference Grant Committee; the Faculties of Humanities and Education, and the Departments of English and Educational Curriculum and Instruction at The University of Calgary. Without the careful attention of Gerry Dyer, the Institute Administrator, the seminar would not have been the success that it was. Gerry Dyer and Cindy Atkinson both deserve thanks for their careful preparation of the manuscript in camera-ready form which made possible the publication of this book.

H. G. Coward
Director
The Calgary Institute
for the Humanities

ABOUT THE AUTHORS

Johan L. Aitken, Professor, The Joint Centre for Teacher Development, University of Toronto/O.I.S.E., is the author of numerous books and articles in literary theory and literature including *Masques of Morality: Females in Fiction.*

Ann E. Berthoff, Professor Emeritus, University of Massachusetts at Boston and the Randolph Distinguished Visiting Professor at Vassar College, 1989-90, is the author of *Forming/Thinking/ Writing, The Making of Meaning,* and an anthology, *Reclaiming the Imagination: Philosophical Perspectives for Writers and Writing Teachers.* She is completing an anthology of I. A. Richards' essays which are of special interest to teachers of composition, *Richards on Rhetoric.* In 1981, she directed an NEH Summer Seminar at the University of Massachusetts, Boston, "Philosophy and the Composing Process." Professor Berthoff has also written on the philosophy of language and Renaissance poetics. She is the author of *The Resolved Soul: A Study of Marvell's Major Poems.*

Richard L. Butt, Professor of Education at The University of Lethbridge, is interested in curriculum praxis, professional development, classroom change, science education and multiculturalism. Within these different areas he exercises a commitment to emancipatory forms of education and research. Currently, he uses autobiographical inquiry in understanding the sources, evolution, and nature of teachers' knowledge. He is also developing classroom materials that help reduce racism and prejudice.

Deborah Dooley, Associate Professor of English at Nazareth College of Rochester, has teaching interests in Victorian literature, women's studies and rhetoric. She has written and given presentations on teaching learning disabled students, on women's literature, and on feminist theory and the teaching of writing, and has a book in progress on the relationship of these last three topics.

Kieran Egan, Professor of Education at Simon Fraser University, is the author of *Teaching as Storytelling* and *Primary Understanding,* and a number of other books on educational topics.

Edgar Z. Friedenberg, Professor Emeritus at Dalhousie University, is the author of six books, from *The Vanishing Adolescent* to *Deference to Authority: the Case of Canada.* An American, he has lived in Canada for 20 years — a feat that he hopes to repeat, if possible.

Madeleine R. Grumet, Professor and Dean of the School of Education of Brooklyn College, City University of New York, is the author of *Bitter Milk: Women and Teaching* and editor of the series on Feminist Theory in Education for the State University of New

York Press. A curriculum theorist, specializing in humanities education, she writes often about teacher education, the use of autobiography in teaching and educational research, and theatre in education.

Clarence J. Karier, Professor of History and Education and Head of the Department of Educational Policy Studies at the University of Illinois at Urbana-Champaign, is the author of *Scientists of the Mind: Intellectual Founders of Modern Psychology* and *The Individual Society and Education: A History of American Educational Ideas.* He is also author of *Shaping the Educational State: 1900 to the Present* and is co-author of *Roots of Crisis: American Education in the Twentieth Century.*

Diana Korzenik, Professor of Art Education at Massachusetts College of Art, is author of *Drawn to Art: A Nineteenth Century American Dream.* She has contributed chapters to *Art Education Here, Art & Cognition, Art & Back to Basics, American Play.*

Max van Manen is Professor of Education in the Department of Secondary Education, University of Alberta. He is founding editor of the human science journal *Phenomenology + Pedagogy*, author of *The Tone of Teaching, Researching Lived Experience for an Action Sensitive Pedagogy*, and numerous articles and translated works on hermeneutic phenomenology and pedagogy.

Jane Roland Martin, Professor of Philosophy at the University of Massachusetts, Boston is a past president of the Philosophy of Education Society and the author of many articles on education and philosophy. Her most recent book is *Reclaiming a Conversation: The Ideal of the Educated Woman.*

Anne McWhir, Associate Professor at the University of Calgary, has taught literature at junior high school as well as at university and has published articles on several eighteenth-century and Romantic writers.

Aubrey Rosenberg, Professor of French at the University of Toronto, is the author of *Tyssot de Patot and his Work, Nicolas Gueudeville and his Work*, and *Jean-Jacques Rousseau and Providence.*

John Willinsky, Associate Professor and director of the Centre for the Study of Curriculum and Instruction at the University of British Columbia, is the author of *The New Literacy* and *The Well-Tempered Tongue.*

INTRODUCTION

Romanticism needs no introduction and is, for that reason, all the more difficult to introduce. As a cultural movement, its formative years were the closing decades of the eighteenth century and the opening ones of the nineteenth, a troubled time in European history that fell between the Enlightenment's cult of reason and the brutal triumph of industrialization, a time rocked by the American and French Revolutions and torn by the Napoleonic Wars. We might say, then, that Romanticism is a child of social ferment and reaction born of a revolutionary age. For artist and poet, musician and critic, the period proved an astonishingly creative *fin de siècle* that produced lasting artistic works in many fields. These Romantic spirits sought to revise the language of experience and expression, and the results of this experiment have gradually seeped into our cultural makeup. This collection of essays on the educational legacy of Romanticism focuses on the process of intellectual transfer, as various elements within the spirit of Romanticism have influenced educational thinking and practice. In another sense, this book is about the infrequent meeting of poets and educators.

It may well seem, at first glance, that Romanticism's gift to education is neatly circumscribed in the high school poetry anthology. It is true that students are annually asked to read and appreciate Romantic standards by Blake, Wordsworth, Coleridge, Keats, Shelley, and Byron. But as chapter after chapter of this book makes clear, this is but a small aspect of the Romantic influence on the education of the young. For the true weight of Romanticism on the schools is not found in even the best literature classes that students might receive on Romantic poetry. Rather, when this greater influence of Romanticism is present, it is as an unnamed force shaping the very form of schooling. For as Romantics revered childhood and celebrated the imagination, they provided an inspiring vision and vocabulary out of which more than a few educators have created this century's major educational alternative to traditional patterns of rote-learning and skill-and-drill exercises.

The results of this influence are scattered across more than a century of educational innovation. I first came upon it in Ruth Fletcher's classroom of six- and seven-year-olds as the students happily found their way to literacy through stacks of blank paper in a rural Ontario school (the details and Romantic roots of which I have described in *The New Literacy*). But to begin to grasp the extent of this influence one need only think of various programs that have taken on Wordsworthian goals of self-realization for the child. This book documents the Romantic roots in such educational enterprises as child-centred curriculum projects, expressive language programs, Montessori schools and the alternative school movement. How, then, does this influence operate? Although undoubtedly leading theorists of such Romantically inclined organizations as the Progressive Education Association read the Romantics as part of their own education, there is little direct quotation of Wordsworth or Coleridge in their educational work. It suggests that insofar as their work bears traces of Romantic influences, the actual process of influence is a subtle one of cultural infusion, lost to sight for the most part.

One reason for this obscuring of origins is the diffuse nature of the literary and artistic phenomenon known as Romanticism. It is based on the work of highly individualistic *artistes*, and the sum of their parts cannot be readily named except to say that they were Romantics, alive to that period and to each other's work. It can seem that beyond that, whatever is said about Romanticism fails to hold. The tendency among scholars has been to treat the term as either inexhaustible or, for that reason, exhausted. There is the sizeable *'Romantic' and Its Cognates: The European History of a Word*, edited by Hans Eicher, that in its 500 pages does not claim to have fully covered the word. Jacques Barzun in *Classic, Romantic and Modern* is blunt enough about the problem, dismissing such typically Romantic attributes as "a love of the exotic, a revolt from reason, an exaggeration of individualism, a liberation of the unconscious" by pointing out that Romanticism "is not any of these things for the simple reason that none of them can be found uniformly among the great Romantics." Exasperated by this illusiveness and the continuing frequency of use, Arthur Lovejoy felt obliged a good number of years ago to write Romanticism's semantic obituary in his essay "On the Discrimination of Romanticisms": "The word 'Romantic' has come to mean so many things that, by itself, it means nothing. It has ceased to perform the function of a verbal sign." But, of course, it goes on functioning, especially in educational circles, where "Romantic" continues to perform as a verbal sign, principally on the order of a pejorative adjective. The term has slipped to this maledictive level because its roots have been obscured; we have lost sight of the wealth of ideas and inspiration that first launched the original array of Romantic visions.

Thus, this book sets out to recover the Romantic roots of various educational concepts to facilitate a fair evaluation of their original promise and their subsequent development. It does so without making the mistake of imagining that somewhere deep down there lies *the* root of Romanticism, for the term did not begin with a single meaning. While themes of self-expression, for example, seem to persist through a number of chapters, the only sustained thread or spirit linking these works is the interest in reconsidering the Romantic influence on education, in all its diversity. As Romanticism remains a diffuse and obscured semantic object, some of the essays gathered in this volume take delight in offering examples of the treasures buried deep within the term while others are cautious about the implications of Romantic dispositions. In either case, this collection would undermine that simple-minded labelling of an educational program or innovation as "Romantic" by way of dismissing it as out of touch with the hard reality of the world or, for want of greater academic discipline, as tainted with a certain anti-intellectualism. This book challenges such facile judgements and misconceptions through its careful examination of complex intellectual traditions influenced by Romanticism. It tracks the strands of this influence through the work of Emerson and Thoreau in the nineteenth century and follows it into the twentieth with Richards, Montessori, Jung, Sartre, Gadamer, Trilling, Kristeva, to name a few of those who figure in this volume.

A second, more specific reason for the subterranean nature of this intellectual transfer from literary movement to educational practice is that the Romantics gave little enough of their enormous creative energies to the practical concerns of schooling the young. While Blake and Wordsworth, for example, thought a good deal about childhood and the ways of learning, they left an open-ended legacy that has invited a good deal of imaginative interpretation and skillful implementation to bring its brightest aspects into the classroom. Even Rousseau's extensive treatise, *Emile, or On Education*, was by no means a useful guide for public schooling, if it was in any literal sense about educational methods at all. When the powerful Committee on Public Instruction set out to implement the ideas of Rousseau in French schools during the height of the French Revolution, their program relied on a *catéchisme français républicain* to replace Catholic lessons. Such innovations fell considerably short of Rousseau's educational vision. Or consider that Wordsworth's reflections on his own best educational moments in his long autobiographical poem, *The Prelude*, spoke principally in favor of lessons out of school. He and Coleridge declined the superintendency of a

Nursery of Genius, as proposed to them by Thomas Wedgwood in 1797, with its program of systematic instruction. Nonetheless, over the course of time the spirit of these Romantic philosophers and poets, however divergent their views, crept into the language of educational discourse. This process in itself demonstrates an article of Romantic faith as it points to the transformative powers of the imagination; the aesthetic reckoning of the world by Romanticism has come to shape, in some instances, the organization of teachers' and children's lives. Yet this educational legacy has had to be earned and worked rather than simply received as an outright gift.

Although the work of many progressive educators can be shown to possess the unmistakable mark of a Romantic understanding, it is not, I am suggesting, because lines from Wordsworth or epigrams from Rousseau spring readily to their lips. The original literary and historical contexts which gave rise to these ideas have settled out of the language, and this form of thinking which invests a landscape with transcendental qualities, for example, becomes a commonplace in a society such as ours, seemingly without root or origin. The fourteen contributors to this book dig into the layers of this obscured sediment for aspects of Romanticism which have continued to inform conceptions of learning and schooling. At this point, these pervasive ideas about the nature of our humanity play too important a role in the hotly debated question of how best to educate the young for them to go unexamined in their origins and in their transformation over time and place. The work gathered together in this volume represents a meeting of intellectual, literary and social history as it is realized through the schools. Although the schools are seldom reckoned as test sites for the viability of philosophical systems of thought, this book seeks to demonstrate the ways in which education systems do, in fact, reflect the history and culture of the society they serve. The school provides a strong instance of how ideas as diverse and literary as those represented by Romanticism can eventually become the stuff of such practical matters as how to set up a school and conduct a lesson with young children.

One distinct and intriguing feature of this educational legacy is the way in which ideas can move across forms of discourse, from the intricacies of a traditional verse form to the pragmatics of a teacher's lesson plan, in under two centuries. And thus it can seem that Wordsworth's "Immortality Ode" might form a leaf in a progressive teacher's daybook filled with lessons that would have students burn like the sun rising over the horizon of the commonplace, filling the sky with their own display:

> Shades of the prison-house begin to close
> > Upon the growing Boy,
> > > But he beholds the light, and whence it flows,
> > He sees in it his joy;
> The Youth, who daily farther from the east
> > Must travel, still is Nature's Priest,
> > And by the vision splendid
> > Is on his way attended;
> At length the Man perceives it die away,
> And fade into the light of common day.

But just as the process of transfer and implementation has been complex, the legacy itself is not a straightforward one. This idealizing tendency, this appeal to the romance of Romanticism against "the light of common day," also has its intimations of a darker side. The simple centring of the curriculum on the child as Nature's Priest is no guarantee against worshipping false gods. Wordsworth's insightful if troubled manner of looking back on the world requires a critical vigilance, lest it prove a poor and misleading basis for educating the young about the world that has long ceased to exist. It is as if the growing ambivalence that comes with the "years that bring the philosophic mind" needs to be kept in sight along with the promise of light—"Whither is fled the visionary gleam? / Where is it now, the glory and the dream?"

The lingering tension here is endemic to an education bearing the marks of Romanticism. It emerges from what we would have of the young and what they are, between Wordsworth's vision of this youthful splendor—"thou best philosopher"—and where the young might wander in their "unconscious intercourse with beauty." How does the educator encourage and assist without intervening and interfering in this unfolding? For Wordsworth, the best thing for a teacher was "to manage books, and things, and make them work / Gently on infant minds, as does the sun / Upon a flower," rather than following the path of those who, after Rousseau, "in their prescience would control / All accidents, and to the very road / Which they have fashion'd confine us down, / Like engines." Yet Wordsworth did not really wrestle with this dilemma of educational responsibility, as Rousseau did, if only by having Emile's tutor work hard to bring the child's desire and interest in line with the educator's project. If Rousseau appears to have gone too far in manipulating Emile's educational experiences for the child's own good, it does nothing to deny that a line must still be drawn between directing an education and allowing students to find their own course. In this book, we find a variety of responses to how this fine line can be maintained and such a course set out, specifically in the contributions of Richard Butt, Deborah Dooley, Kieran Egan, and Madeleine Grumet, who each in their own way have entered into the careful fashioning of a curriculum that bears a Romantic legacy, that wrestles with the Romantic's vision and the educator's responsibility.

But I would at this point introduce a little more fully the contents and organization of this work. The first eight essays bring a historical perspective to the question of Romanticism's educational legacy, while the remaining six essays work with it in a contemporary setting. More specifically, the book begins with chapters on key figures in Romanticism — Rousseau, Wordsworth, Coleridge and Mary Shelley — whose work contains the basis of a Romantic re-vision of education. Aubrey Rosenberg in "Rousseau's *Emile*: The Nature and the Purpose of Education" sets the groundwork for situating the seminal ideas of this proto-Romantic by treating the misconceptions and the distinctiveness of Rousseau's educational experiment. My own contribution to this volume, "Lessons from the Wordsworths and the Domestic Scene of Writing," explores for its current implications the collaborative writing process by which Wordsworth draws on and overwrites the place of his sister in his poetry. Ann Berthoff in "Coleridge, I. A. Richards, and the Imagination" traces the productive movement of imagination, as a foremost concept in Romanticism, in the process of becoming a complex vehicle for grasping how we come to meaning in the world. Anne McWhir in "Teaching the Monster to Read: Mary Shelley, Education and Frankenstein" pulls from the books found in the monster's pockets her own reading of the subversive Romantic education that Mary Shelley introduced into the novel.

In another set of four essays, the book then examines a number of prominent historical figures who were first to feel the sway of Romanticism as an influence on their educational thinking. In "Nineteenth-Century Romantic and Neo-Romantic Thought and Some Disturbing Twentieth-Century Applications," Clarence Karier contrasts the Romanticism that gained a voice in Emerson's essays and verse with a second, troubling strand of Romantic influence that found expression in the racial thinking of Stanley Hall, Carl Jung, and Herman Hesse. Max van Manen in "Romantic Roots of Human Science in Education" explores how in Europe there developed a hermeneutical and phenomenological treatment of pedagogy that grew out of Romantic interests. Dealing more specifically with the work of a single educator, Diana Korzenik in "The Artist as Model Learner" examines the Romantic roots of Francis Parker who bravely fashioned and implemented a new scheme for education in nineteenth-century America that took the realm of art as a model for the entire curriculum. Jane Roland Martin also deals with a single, highly influential figure in "Romanticism Domesticated: Maria Montessori and the Casa dei Bambini," as she inquires into the nature of Romanticism that infused Montessori's "children's home" and what was lost and preserved in the transfer of her thinking to America.

With the historical starting points and earlier progenitors in place, the book takes up more recent applications of Romanticism to the educational scene. Edgar Friedenberg in "Romanticism and Alternatives in Schooling" reflects on his involvement in the blossoming of "free" schools and examines the inherent limitations in their conceptions of the child and of education which guided their best hopes. Madeleine Grumet in "The Theory of Subjectivity in Contemporary Curriculum Thought" brings a broad analysis of this crucial Romantic question of the self to her own work in fostering the autobiographical reflections of her students. Johan Aitken completes this set with "An Education in Romanticism for Our Time" that makes critical sense of an otherwise overwhelming myriad of Romantic influences that suffuse this not-so-post-Romantic culture.

The final three essays report on educational programs that have been wisely and carefully informed by Romanticism. Deborah Dooley in "Women's Writing and the Recovery of the Romantic Project: Lessons for Contemporary Writing Pedagogy" rethinks Romanticism through her own work with women's writing and her teaching experience with women who are learning to trust the page in their own writing. Richard Butt also tells of his teaching and learning experiences in "Autobiographic Praxis and Self-Education: From Alienation to Authenticity" as he advances the pedagogical usefulness of teachers telling their own story by demonstrating its value through an explication of his own educational tale. In the concluding chapter, Kieran Egan presents a curricular rationale in "Recapitulating Romanticism in Education" that would offer adolescent students an education in an understanding of the world informed by a Romanticism of literacy and engagement.

This coverage of the educational legacy of Romanticism is by no means complete but is powerfully suggestive of how diverse and complex the influence of Romanticism has been. The idea is not that educators owe a certain fidelity to the "original" or "true nature" of Romanticism. The very theme in Romanticism of irrevocable loss of an earlier time marked by innocence and insight, speaks against recovering the spirit of Romanticism for purposes of improving the state of education today. Yet to see how those ideas have evolved and been adapted to fit the times, how parts have been overlooked and others highlighted, offers a fresh perspective on the ideas competing for support in the schools. This collection of essays moves behind the scenes and Romantic commonplaces in our thinking; it traces the transitions and distortions which constitute a significant portion of our educational legacy. Its hope is that we can not only learn about the currents of thought that influence educational programs and positions from a re-examination of the past, but that we can use this renewed understanding to build a more thoughtful future for the education of the young.

*   *   *

I cannot introduce this book fairly without referring to one important event in its production. These essays are not the proceedings of a conference gathered together in the typical fashion. Yet the writers, carefully selected to provide a broad and expert coverage of the topic, did have the opportunity of sitting down together and discussing their work, due largely to the foresight and assistance of Harold Coward, director of the Calgary Institute for the Humanities, and his staff. It turned out to be a more auspicious and affecting meeting than any of us would have guessed. One October day we assembled at Nakoda Lodge on the Morley Indian Reserve in Alberta. The Rocky Mountains towered around us, and the weather that weekend was to alternate among sunshine, snow, and rain in a manner that reflected our fortunes. The meeting began in the spirit of the enlightenment with the writers sitting around a large conference table attending to each presentation in turn. However, not long into the conference, a backhoe intent on excavating a new path through the wilderness around us inadvertently cut off the lodge's power and water supply, lifeblood of our post-Romantic civilization. We found ourselves dislodged and packing. The fourteen of us boarded two station wagons and drove off in search of a suitable alpine cabin or mountain crag with, of course, the full complement of facilities, that we might carry on our weighty Romantic discoursing.

As we wound our way through mountains gracefully carrying the first snowfall of the season, we passed a yellow school bus pulled over by the side of the road. The teacher and children appeared to be intently searching the rock-cut for fossil traces from the oceanic past of this mountain range. It seemed to me as we drove by them that in our conference for this book we were doing no less than those schoolchildren, only with the archaeological traces of Romanticism in the educational record. To take the instance at hand, the children's school trip into the mountains was one form of proof of that Romantic legacy, as was our very ability to be moved by the sublime beauty of the mountains that morning.

In re-routing our meeting, we were also to find the sort of friendships occasioned by adversity in travel that Coleridge and the Wordsworths, Byron and the Shelleys, had found in their visits to Germany and the Alps. Fortunately, we found accommodation and had a chance to discuss the remaining chapters of this book comfortably ensconced in a motel room by a mountain stream. This sequence of events had gone as no one had expected, and yet seemed to be no less than was called for in tracing the Romantic threads in educational practice:

> Winter like a well-tamed lion walks,
> Descending from the mountain to make sport
> Among the cottages by beds and flowers.
> Whate'er in this wide circuit we beheld,
> Or heard, we fitted to our unripe state
> Of intellect and heart. With such a book
> Before our eyes, we could not choose but read
> A frequent lesson of sound tenderness,
> And universal reason of mankind,
> The truths of young and old.
> (Wordsworth, *Prelude*, 1850 6.538-547)

In light of what a book such as this has afforded, I wish to express my sincere appreciation to those who participated in its making, as well as to The Calgary Institute for the Humanities for the sponsorship of this work and in particular to its director, Harold Coward, executive assistant, Gerry Dyer, and secretary, Cindy Atkinson. I also thank Angela Héroux for her editorial services, as well as Robert Graham, Muriel Hamilton, and LaDonna MacRae for their contribution to the symposium. The Social Sciences and Humanities Research Council of Canada, the Faculties of Education and Humanities at the University of Calgary, the University of Illinois and Simon Fraser University have all been generous with their support. The Educational Legacy of Romanticism was one of a series of events which were affiliated with the "William Wordsworth and the Age of English Romanticism" project organized by the

Department of English at Rutgers University and the Wordsworth Trust. Linda Schulze, assistant director of the Rutgers project, deserves a credit for prompting the original idea of this book, and the Spencer Foundation has earned my appreciation for affording me some measure of time to devote to this rewarding endeavor.

John Willinsky

Chapter 1

ROUSSEAU'S *EMILE*:
THE NATURE AND PURPOSE OF EDUCATION

Aubrey Rosenberg

When I was invited to address Rousseau's philosophy of education in the context of "The Educational Legacy of Romanticism," and discovered that the symposium was affiliated with the project called "William Wordsworth and the Age of Romanticism," it seemed a good idea to examine the relationship between Wordsworth's pedagogical ideas and those of Rousseau.[1] It soon became apparent, however, that there was no agreement as to the extent of Wordsworth's debt to Rousseau if, indeed, there was any. Legouis, for example, termed Rousseau's influence on Wordsworth as "more powerful, perhaps, than any other to which he was subjected, all the more profound because, instead of manifesting itself in any particular portion of his work or at any special period of his life, it permeates the whole" (57). De Selincourt, on the other hand, thought that though Wordsworth "had certainly read *Emile.* . . he based his views solely on his own experience, and only seems to refer to Rousseau when he differs from him" (*The Prelude* 266-67). Voisine doubts that the poet had any first-hand knowledge of Rousseau and states that, even if he did read the *Emile*, it is still not possible to identify a direct influence. Morkan interprets Wordsworth's comments on education as a bitter attack on the methods proposed in the *Emile*: "Rousseau's educational theory, camouflaging an elaborate set of controls beneath a surface appearance of freedom and spontaneity, would have appeared to Wordsworth the most subtle and insidious of plans. . . . This authoritarianism clashed with Wordsworth's creative individualism" (251). Sewall, by contrast, sees in the treatment of man, nature, religion and morality, very close analogies between the *Emile* and some of Wordsworth's poems. She finds these similarities "too numerous and too striking to be simply a coincidence. The thematic parallels. . . suggest the existence of a close intellectual relationship between Rousseau and Wordsworth" (174). More recently, Sabin has proposed that we should abandon the attempt to look for influences and even be wary of speaking of affinities when dealing with two such different traditions as English and French Romanticism. But this advice has not found favor with James Chandler, who contends that "Wordsworth's early knowledge and use of Rousseau are greater than has been assumed," and that "the five-book *Prelude* relates to Rousseau. . . . His *Emile*, probably the period's most widely influential book on education, must acquire a new relevance to Wordsworth's project when *both* works can be described as quasi-philosophical arguments in five books that cover the stages of a child's natural education from infancy to early manhood" (xxii, 95).

During the course of compiling this daunting array of contradictions, of which I have given only a sample, I found not only that there was no meeting of the minds over the Rousseau/Wordsworth question, but also that there was a wide divergence of opinion about the significance of the *Emile* itself as a treatise on education. Now few would deny the enormous contribution Rousseau made as a pioneer in the field of child psychology. The theory and practice of such notables as Montessori, Pestalozzi, Froebel, Dewey, and others, are a testimony to the influential role played by Rousseau's delineation of the different stages of child development, the importance of physical training, sense experience, learning through play and field trips, as well as a host of other features now regarded as the fundamental elements of a sound education.

The disagreement is not so much about the legacy of ideas from the *Emile*, but rather about the intentions underlying those ideas and the methods Rousseau proposed for implementing them. Interpretations of the meaning of the *Emile* vary according to whether the interpreter is a political theorist, pedagogue, theologian, philosopher or psychologist, to name but a few of the kinds of readers who have commented on the book. Moreover, the interpretations differ markedly depending on the particular school of thought to which the critic subscribes.[2]

Apart from the general question of the validity of any book on education written by someone who abandoned all his children at their birth,[3] and whose own brief career as a teacher was hardly a resounding success,[4] there are more fundamental problems involved in understanding the *Emile*. For example, Rousseau sometimes seems unclear about his own intentions and occasionally appears to contradict himself. He never defines what he means by "Nature," a term he uses constantly and in a variety of ways to apply to the exterior world, to human nature, and to providence. In the preface, he claims to be setting down only general principles based on his observations of human nature while, later on, he maintains that his "reasonings are founded less on principles than on facts" (110). Yet the whole basis of his educational philosophy is founded on a view of the state of Nature that derives, as he explains in the *Discourse on Inequality*, not from facts but from a purely hypothetical premise.[5]

Rousseau attributes some of his more blatant contradictions to the difficulty of expressing his ideas with sufficient precision "in the poverty of our language."[6] But he also claims at another point that such contradictions are part and parcel of the intellectual process: "Common readers, pardon me my paradoxes. When one reflects, they are necessary and, whatever you may say, I prefer to be a paradoxical man than a prejudiced one" (93).[7] In the light of all the misunderstandings, misinterpretations, and disagreements outlined above, it seemed that the most useful task I could perform would be to put aside the Rousseau/Wordsworth question and, instead, try to clarify as objectively as possible what Rousseau himself has to say about his educational philosophy and the ways of realizing it.

A logical way to begin is by examining to what extent the *Emile* is a work on education, and what kind of education it is about. We should not take at face value the title, *Emile or On Education*, since titles are quite often ambiguous or misleading, sometimes intentionally so. The second book of More's *Utopia*, for example, purports to describe a *real* place of happiness but the name of the country also indicates that it is to be found nowhere. Erasmus' *In Praise of Folly* is really in praise of good sense. Voltaire's *Candide or Optimism* is often interpreted as an expression of deep pessimism, and there are few readers today who find no irony in Huxley's *Brave New World*.

Rousseau himself was very guarded, if not ambivalent, in his references to the *Emile* as a work on education. Two years before its publication in 1762, he characterized it in a letter to Vernes as "a kind of treatise on education, full of my usual rêveries" (November 29, 1760). In the preface to the *Emile*, predicting that he will be attacked for the "systematic part" of the book, he allows that such attacks might be justified since the *Emile* will appear to be "less an educational treatise than a visionary's dreams about education" (34).

Rousseau makes it quite plain from the outset that, although he will offer advice about bringing up children, his intention is to be general rather than specific.[8] His book will be directed towards the understanding of the nature of the child and, consequently, of what is central to human nature. That is the goal, and the way it will be achieved is of secondary importance: "Childhood is unknown.... The wisest men. . . are always seeking the man in the child without thinking what he is before being a man. This is the study to which I have most applied myself, so that even though my entire method were chimerical and false, my observations could still be of profit" (33-34). Since every system of education will vary according to the accidents of place, birth, and the temperament of the individual, Rousseau's statement of principles, based on observations, is applicable to mankind in general.[9] It is for this reason that, throughout the *Emile*, there are reminders of Rousseau's basic tenet that the main purpose of education is to produce not a scholar, not a specialist, but a man for all seasons, adaptable and independent, a philosopher who earns his living with his hands.[10]

However, despite Rousseau's insistence on the abstract nature of his treatise and on the inapplicability of his methods to specific cases, when the Prince of Wurtemberg writes of his intention to raise his newborn daughter according to the methods prescribed in the *Emile*, Rousseau is delighted to participate in the process by sending letters of encouragement and guidance.[11] On the other hand, when a bourgeois from Strasbourg claims to be educating his son on Rousseauean lines, Jean-Jacques retorts: "So much the worse, sir, for you and your son, so much the worse."[12] Replying to someone who considered his system utopian, Rousseau explains: "You are quite right to say it is impossible to create an Emile; but do you really think that was my intention and that the book that bears this title is truly a treatise on education? It is a quite philosophical work based on the principle, advanced by the author in other writings, that man is naturally good" (Letter to P. Cramer, October 13, 1764). And, in a similar vein, he writes as follows to another correspondent: "If it is true that you have adopted the plan I tried to sketch in the *Emile*, I admire your courage; for you are too intelligent not to see that, in such a system, it is all or nothing" (Letter to the abbé de Monquin, February 18, 1770).

In his *Letter to Christophe de Beaumont*, archbishop of Paris, Rousseau makes explicit the extent to which his ideas on education are founded on his overall view of the human condition: "The fundamental principle of all morality, on which I have argued in all my writings, and that I have developed in this latest [the *Emile*] with all the clarity I was capable of, is that man is a being who is naturally good, loving justice and order, that there is no original perversity in the human heart, and that the first movements of nature are always right" (*O.C.* IV.935-936). He goes on to say that men become wicked because of society, and that he wrote the *Emile* in order to show what has to be done to prevent man's degradation. The fact that, in the *Emile* itself, he refers to Plato's *Republic*, normally regarded as a political work dealing with the foundation of the just society, as "the most beautiful educational treatise ever written" (40), should provide us with a key to the understanding of what he had in mind when he called the *Emile* a treatise on education.

It is so in the way that Plato's dialogues are works of education in the broadest sense. They are enquiries into the nature of man, the relationship between the individual and society, morality, justice, and all the big unanswered and unanswerable questions. It should always be kept in mind that the principal ideas of the *Social Contract* are summarized in the fifth book of the *Emile* (458-69), and that Rousseau himself wrote to Duchesne that his "treatise on the Social Contract . . . being cited several times and even summarized in the treatise on education must be considered as a sort of appendix to it, and . . . the two together make a complete whole" (May 23, 1762).

The *Emile*, then, as Rousseau describes it in the *Dialogues*, is his *summa*.[13] It is the most complete and mature expression of all his ideas on religion, politics, society, culture, civilization and, of course, education which is the key factor in all of the aforementioned. For this reason, it is important not to be misled by the abundance of details about the child's upbringing since each detail, however trivial or seemingly insignificant, is directly related to, and in the service of, the higher goals outlined.[14] It should be added that the *Emile* is also a highly polemical work in that it attacks, sometimes explicitly but more often by implication, some of the fundamental tenets of the country in which he lived, not least the principles of Jesuit education that had dominated the French system for over two centuries.[15]

What is especially confusing about the *Emile* is that it combines, in the same work, elements that Plato kept separate. The *Republic* is essentially a theoretical work. If we want the practical details of the education of the citizen from birth, we are obliged to turn to the *Laws*, where advice of all kinds is given on the rearing and education of young children even from the time they are still in the womb, an approach that has been carried much further in our day by R. D. Laing.[16] The *Emile* is a combination of the *Republic* and the *Laws* in that it contains both the theory and the practice in a somewhat disconcerting fashion as, for example, when Rousseau passes quite unconcernedly from a detailed discussion of the baby's diet and hygiene (56-59) to a disquisition on sensationalism (61-65). But the practical side is always incidental to the main goal of designing a new kind of man who one day might be called upon to lead men away from the paths of corruption that they daily tread: "go and live in their midst, cultivate their friendship in sweet association, be their benefactor and their model. Your example will serve them better than all our books, and the good they see you do will touch them more than all our vain speeches" (474). The main object of Emile's education, then, is to prepare him for an independent, self-sufficient life in a society in which he will act as a role model for the purpose of reforming his fellow men.

Since no one before Rousseau had ever attempted to portray such a model and the way in which such an end might be achieved, his thesis was bound to be hypothetical and his methods experimental. In fact, the *Emile* is a kind of laboratory experiment of which the conclusions require testing in the field, in a multitude of places, climates, political systems, etc., in order to verify Rousseau's methods and their implications. Rousseau focused his attention on what is common to all societies. In order to do this, he chose an ideal specimen to be brought up in ideal circumstances. This is why Emile is an imaginary child, without a family, without any individual characteristics. This is also why Emile is brought up in isolation by an equally imaginary tutor who bears some resemblance to Saint-Preux in *La Nouvelle Héloïse* and, of course, to Rousseau himself. It is pointless, then, to accuse Rousseau of creating a thoroughly impractical system when he himself draws explicit attention to the idealistic nature of the enterprise. In order for others to be able to adapt his ideas to a particular place, time, and set of beliefs, Emile's religion, like his education, will be natural and universal: It is essential that the model be brought up, as it were, out of space and time, without family or friends other than the tutor or governor. The idealism of the *Emile* is explained near the beginning of Book I:

> I have. . . chosen to give myself an imaginary pupil, to hypothesize that I have the age, health, kinds of knowledge, and all the talent suitable for working at his education. . . . This method appears to me useful to prevent an author who distrusts himself from getting lost in visions; for when he deviates from ordinary practice, he has only to make a test of his own practice on his pupil. . . . In order not to fatten the book uselessly, I have been content with setting down the principles whose truth everyone should sense. But as for the rules which might need proofs, I have applied them all to my Emile or to other examples; and I have shown in very extensive detail how what I have established could be put into practice. . . . I do not speak at all here of a good governor's

qualities; I take them for granted, and I take for granted that I myself am endowed with all these qualities. (50-51)

Emile and his upbringing, then, will be the standard against which all other children and all other educational systems may be compared, in the way that the political regime of the *Social Contract* or the domestic government of Clarens in *La Nouvelle Héloïse* provide ideal models towards which one might aspire. Whether or not Rousseau believed his essentially tutorial system could be adapted to the exigencies of public education is not made clear. Presumably, this is for others to decide. His intention was to lay the foundations on which others could build. The key to his system is to obey the dictates of Nature, to follow a prescribed order that must be adhered to if one wants to succeed in producing, from an ignorant and helpless baby, a wholly authentic and self-sufficient human being.

Nature, in the *Emile*, bears only marginal similarities to its counterpart portrayed in the *Confessions* and the *Rêveries* where it is presented in lyrical and quasi-mystical terms. This is not to say that there are no hymns to Nature in the *Emile*. In the introduction to the *Profession of Faith of the Savoyard Vicar*, for example, Rousseau describes the magnificent setting in which the Vicar expounds his philosophy of natural religion. But this evocation of a splendid sunrise is purely for the benefit of the reader and not for Emile to whom the Vicar's credo is not addressed.[17] Earlier on, Rousseau uses the occasion of another sunrise to demonstrate that the poetic view of Nature has absolutely no meaning for children. When the tutor and his pupil are out early in the countryside for a practical lesson in cosmography, they witness a spectacular dawn. The tutor, overwhelmed by the beauties of the landscape that is described in the most lyrical terms, wants the young boy to share his emotions:

> He believes he moves the child by making him attentive to the sensations by which he, the master, is himself moved. Pure stupidity! It is in man's heart that the life of nature's spectacle exists. To see it, one must feel it. The child perceives the objects, but he cannot perceive the relations linking them; he cannot hear the sweet harmony of their concord. For that is needed experience he has not acquired.... If he has not long roamed arid plains, if burning sands have not scorched his feet, if the suffocating reflections of stones struck by the sun have never oppressed him, how will he enjoy the cool air of a fine morning? How will the fragrances of the flowers, the charm of the verdure,

the humid vapors of the dew, and the soft and gentle touch of the grass underfoot enchant his senses? How will the song of the birds cause a voluptuous emotion in him, if the accents of love and pleasure are still unknown to him? . . . how can he be touched by the beauty of nature's spectacle, if he does not know the hand responsible for adorning it? (168-69)

Nature for the young Emile, when he notices it at all, for the natural order of things makes him largely unaware of his environment, is simply necessity and, most often, unpleasant necessity. Even the healthiest baby experiences the pains of growing teeth, just as the infant and the child bear their share of bumps and bruises, all of which, according to Rousseau, must be met with Spartan fortitude and Stoic indifference: "To suffer is the first thing he ought to learn and the thing he will most need to know" (78).[18]   Pain and eventual death are natural and, therefore, inevitable. Similarly, the authority of the tutor must be made to appear as absolute as the physical laws of Nature, and his word accepted as necessity:

> Emile is an orphan. It makes no difference whether he has his father and mother. Charged with their duties, I inherit all their rights. He ought to honor his parents, but he ought to obey only me. That is my first, or rather, my sole condition. I ought to add the following one, which is only a consequence of the other, that we never be taken from one another without our consent. This clause is essential, and I would even want the pupil and the governor to regard themselves as so inseparable that the lot of each in life is always a common object for them. (52-53)

This is part of the contract and also a result of the fact that, in the early years of life, the infant is little more than a helpless animal that has to be cared for. The child may be the father of the man but, in Rousseau's book, he trails no clouds of glory at his birth. Weak and ignorant, he is at the mercy of the tutor on whose protection he depends for his very life.

In the second of the two letters on education in *La Nouvelle Héloïse*, Julie recounts an event that admirably clarifies Rousseau's view of will presented as necessity. The older of the two children in Julie's household takes a drum from the younger who cries. The servant in charge of the children says nothing, but an hour later when the older one is distracted, she retakes the drum and refuses to return it despite the boy's protests and tears. She points out that he took the drum by force and that she is now doing the same. It is the law of the strongest that prevails. But when she wants to return the drum to the younger child, Julie stops her on the grounds that this would be interfering with the laws of Nature and that the younger child must learn to accept "the harsh law of necessity" (*O. C.* II.578-79).

Rousseau's view of human nature is equally unromantic in his attitude to the development of curiosity and imagination. The former is not to be encouraged too early while the latter is to be long suppressed. Rousseau does not even consider the question of curiosity until the child is aged twelve or thirteen.[19] His reasoning is that human intelligence has its limits and that it is never too soon to teach the child that we waste our time in being curious about things above our needs and beyond our grasp. *Instinctive* curiosity is to be cultivated because it is always in proportion to our ability to satisfy it; *intellectual* curiosity is to be disdained because it is based solely on *amour-propre*.

Related to curiosity is imagination, the premature exercise of which, according to the *Emile*, is not only useless but positively dangerous. In the *Confessions*, Rousseau deals with the question of imagination from the point of view of the isolated, persecuted artist who uses his imaginative powers to escape from the real and unpleasant world, and who, in the process, transmutes the base metal of experience into gold. It was from this sort of sublimation that *La Nouvelle Héloïse* was born:

> The impossibility of reaching real beings threw me into the land of fantasies, and seeing nothing in existence that was worthy of my delirium, I nourished it in an ideal world, that my creative imagination had soon peopled with beings after my own heart. . . . In my continual ecstasies I became overwhelmingly intoxicated with the most delightful feelings that have ever entered a man's heart. (*O. C.* I.427)

Rousseau's ideal pupil, because of his education and the purpose for which it is designed, will have a different destiny from which the creative imagination is excluded as inimical. For this reason, the *Emile* is full of warnings against the use of the imagination that encourages the child to have dreams and desires far beyond his capacity to realize them, a predicament experienced, of course, not only by children but by adults as well: "The real world has its limits; the imaginary world is infinite. Unable to enlarge the one, let us restrict the other, for it is from the difference between the two alone that are born all the pains which make us truly unhappy" (81). Imagination fuels the nascent passions transforming them into vices so that one becomes a slave to one's emotions. This is particularly the case for the sexual passion, the most powerful of all: "Nature's instruction is late and slow; men's is almost always premature. In the former case the senses wake the imagination;

in the latter the imagination wakes the senses; it gives them a precocious activity which cannot fail to enervate and weaken individuals first and in the long run the species itself" (215). Towards the beginning of Book 4, Rousseau gives an astonishing example he claims to have heard from a mother who wished to curb the curiosity and imagination of her young son who wanted to know where babies come from. "My child," answered the mother without hesitation, "women piss them out with pains which sometimes cost them their lives" (218).

It is because of the perils of imagination that Rousseau long delays the introduction of books into the educational process. Having expressed his hatred of all books, Rousseau makes an exception in favor of *Robinson Crusoe* that he regards as a manual for living according to Nature and, therefore, most appropriate to Emile's development:

> Robinson Crusoe on his island, alone, deprived of the assistance of his kind and of the instruments of all the arts, providing nevertheless for his subsistence, for his preservation, and even procuring for himself a kind of well-being—this is an object interesting for every age and one which can be made agreeable to children in countless ways. . . . this state, I agree, is not that of social man; very likely it is not going to be that of Emile. But it is on the basis of this very state that he ought to appraise all the others. The surest means of raising oneself above is to put oneself in the place of an isolated man and to judge everything as this man himself ought to judge of it with respect to his own utility. (185)

When it comes to the question of who might be suitable for this kind of education, Rousseau proves himself to be very much a man of his age who, though railing against class distinctions and the privileges of birth and wealth, nonetheless excludes the common people from participating in the movement of enlightenment, although they will eventually benefit from it. In the meantime, he subscribes to the idea of a chain of being whereby every element of Nature, including man, has its place in the grand design (83). In the same way, human society necessarily has its own hierarchy based not simply on privilege but on economic realities. In an agricultural economy, for example, there have to be workers and managers. In the ideal world, Emile would perform both functions but, until that time, the only hope of reform in the real world is through educating the children of the rich and powerful, much as Fénelon, whom Rousseau greatly admired, tried to instill into the duc de Bourgogne, heir to the throne of France, the ideals of justice and truth.[20] For this reason, Rousseau chooses his imaginary child from the ranks of the privileged:

The poor man does not need to be educated. His station gives him a compulsory education. He could have no other. On the contrary, the education the rich man receives from his station is that which suits him least, from both his own point of view and that of society. Besides, the natural education ought to make a man fit for all human conditions. Now, it is less reasonable to raise a poor man to be rich than a rich man to be poor, for, in proportion to the number of those in the two stations, there are more men who fall than ones who rise. Let us, then, choose a rich man. We will at least be sure we have made one more man, while a poor person can become a man by himself. (52)

Rousseau has been criticized, notably by Karl Marx, for his fundamentally bourgeois solutions to the ills of society (Lecercle). But the aspect of the *Emile* that has provoked the greatest unease and that, because of similar elements said to be found in *La Nouvelle Héloïse* and the *Social Contract*, has led to his being described as a fascist, a totalitarian and the like, is the method proposed for ensuring that Emile will grow up according to the natural order as identified by the tutor. One of the underlying principles of Emile's education is that he be totally unaware that any educational process is going on. He must always have the feeling of being completely independent and free to do whatever he wants, when he wants, within the bounds of his capacities to do so. The many ruses and stratagems employed by the tutor to make sure that the right conditions prevail for bringing up such a child have caused several critics to judge the process and the end product somewhat harshly. Martin Rang, for example, refers to Emile as a "child without emotions, without affection, without pity, even without loves.... thoroughly enclosed within himself, in short, a child without a soul, reasonable certainly, but cold and insensitive and who—let us admit it frankly—if we met him in real life, would make us shudder" (196-97). Lester Crocker similarly terms him "a puppet whose strings are pulled by his tutor-guide" (164).

There is a good deal in the *Emile* to give grounds for these sorts of attacks. Rousseau's insistence on the tutor's absolute control of his charge from birth is not so different from the Jesuit philosophy of indoctrination of the child for the first few years of his life except that, in the latter case, the child soon becomes aware of the process involved. Rousseau, as I shall show, is much more devious. His method of bringing up children is to treat them as a gardener treats his plants. Indeed, the dominant imagery of the opening pages of the *Emile* is that of horticulture, and, as is well known, the concept of the kindergarten is one of the striking legacies of Rousseau's system. The mother for whom the *Emile* was supposedly written is exhorted to "cultivate and water the young plant before it dies. Its fruits will one day be your delights. . . . Plants are shaped by cultivation, and men by education" (38).[21] You may interfere with the natural growth of plants, but Nature will eventually and inevitably take over again. And so it is with us. Therefore, education should be according to Nature.

It turns out, however, that in order to train children to grow up according to Nature, a great deal of artifice is required to keep Nature under control, especially if children are to be prepared to take their place in a society which itself is unnatural. Rousseau's method is best understood by reference to the description in *La Nouvelle Héloïse* of Julie's garden in which Saint-Preux can find no evidence of human handiwork: "It is true," replies Julie, "that Nature has done everything, but under my direction, and there is nothing here that I have not arranged" (*O. C.* II. 472). In the same way, there is nothing in Emile's upbringing that the tutor has not arranged in advance by trickery and deception for the purpose of ensuring that the child will never feel he is doing anything against his will or even be aware that he is being educated:

> Command him nothing, whatever in the world it might be. Do not even allow him to imagine that you might pretend to have any authority over him. . . . let him always believe he is the master, and let it always be you who are. . . . Doubtless he ought to do only what he wants; but he ought to want only what you want him to do. He ought not to make a step without your having foreseen it; he ought not to open his mouth without your knowing what he is going to say. . . . Thus, not seeing your eager to oppose him, not distrusting you, with nothing to hide from you, he will not deceive you, he will not lie to you, he will fearlessly show himself precisely as he is. You will be able to study him at your complete ease and arrange all around him the lessons you want to give him without his ever thinking he is receiving any. (91, 120)

Those most critical of this educational strategy see Rousseau as having anticipated the theories of behavioral modification and engineering pioneered by J. B. Watson and further developed by B. F. Skinner who proposed applying to human beings methods effectively used for the training of animals. Just as Rousseau wrote his "novel"[22] the *Emile*, to show how, under experimental conditions, one could outline a science of education by which it might be possible to reform society, so Skinner incorporated his ideas on behavioral science into a novel,

Walden Two, in which he described how a small isolated community, under experimental conditions, might eventually become the nucleus for a new kind of society. As Skinner wrote in a new preface to the second edition of *Walden Two*: "What is needed is not a new political leader or a new kind of government but further knowledge about human behavior and new ways of applying that knowledge to the design of cultural practices"(xvi).

It is true that there are superficial similarities between the ways in which Rousseau and Skinner proposed raising their children. The minimal clothing to allow for unrestricted movement, the absence of punishment, the constant supervision, the education tailored to the capacities of the individual, are some of the more notable features in common. As Frazier, the leader of the Walden community, points out:

> Here the child advances as rapidly as he likes in any field. No time is wasted in forcing him to participate in or be bored by activities he has outgrown.... We also don't require all our children to develop the same abilities or skills.... But they've all developed as rapidly as advisable, and they're well educated in any useful respects. By the same token we don't waste time in teaching the unteachable. (110)

But whatever similarities there are on the surface, there is a profound gulf that divides the philosophies of Rousseau and Skinner.

In the first place, Skinner believes that, if properly conditioned, children can achieve responsible behavior and absorb an enormous amount of material at a very early age. His great fear, as revealed in the above quotation, is that time will be wasted. Rousseau, by contrast, is all in favor of wasting time, for this is the principle of his passive or negative education that allows Nature to do its work as the child's physical powers develop. One has to be a child first:

> Dare I expose the greatest, the most important, the most useful rule of all education? It is not to gain time but to lose it.... The most dangerous period of human life is that from birth to the age of twelve. This is the time when errors and vices germinate without one's yet having any instrument for destroying them.... Thus, the first education ought to be purely negative. It consists not at all in teaching virtue or truth but in securing the heart from vice and the mind from error.... You know, you say, the value of time and do not want to waste any of it. You do not see that using time badly wastes time far more than doing nothing with it.... You are alarmed to see him consume his early years in doing nothing. What? Is it nothing to be happy? Is it nothing to jump,

play, and run all day? He will never be so busy in his life. (93, 107)

Moreover, infant mortality, in Rousseau's day, took a heavy toll, so that living for the moment, and enjoying childhood seemed to him far more important and worthwhile than sacrificing the present for some dubious future.[23]

In the second place, and here is the crucial difference between the two systems, apart from the help a baby and an infant need to sustain life, Rousseau's child is kept completely unaware that any human agency is involved in his acquisition of knowledge, whether practical, intellectual, or moral. One of Rousseau's golden rules is that there must never be a clash of wills between the tutor and his pupil, for once the child realizes his life is governed by forces other than that of neutral necessity, his illusory sense of freedom is destroyed and all is lost. Skinner's pupils, by contrast, are quite aware of the rigorous and man-made nature of their situation.

Rousseau would have been appalled at the ethical training imposed on the young children in *Walden Two*, a training designed to be completed by the age of six when Emile has hardly progressed beyond the animal stage. In Skinner's program, children of the age of three or four are taught self-control by being given lollipops that they are not allowed to eat until later in the day, or by being forced to wait for a meal that is in full view (98-100). Such a policy would spell disaster for Rousseau's system in which the pupil must always be kept absolutely unaware of the fact that the tutor has anything to do with the trials he undergoes. When, for example, the tutor wants to teach Emile the notion of private property, he concocts with Robert the gardener an elaborate scheme whereby the child learns that land belongs to the one who first works it. When Emile is distraught on discovering he has planted his beans in Robert's garden and that the supposedly enraged Robert has dug them up, the tutor identifies himself with the boy as though he, too, had been thoughtless: "Excuse us, my poor Robert. You had put your labor, your effort there. I see clearly what we did wrong in ruining your work. . . . And we will never again work the land before knowing whether someone has put his hand to it before us" (99). When the tutor wants to show Emile the stupidity and the danger of *amour-propre*, he devises a plan in which the boy, thinking incorrectly that he has discovered the secret of a magician's trick, is humiliated in public. But it is the tutor whom the magician pretends to rebuke:

"I willingly excuse," he says to me, "this child. He has sinned only from ignorance. But you, monsieur, who ought to know his mistake, why did you let him make it? Since you live together, as the elder you owe him your care and your counsel; your experience is the authority which ought to guide him. . ." He departs leaving us both very embarrassed. I blame myself for my soft easygoingness. I promise the child to sacrifice it to his interest the next time and to warn him of his mistakes before he makes them. (174-75)

When the tutor wants to reinforce Emile's knowledge of cosmography, he arranges for Emile and himself to get lost in the woods.

In short, then, as far as Emile is concerned, nothing happens because the tutor wants it to. On the few occasions the tutor finds himself unable to avoid imposing his will, he must do it with all the force of natural and inflexible necessity:

Let all your refusals be irrevocable; let no importunity shake you; let "no," once pronounced, be a wall of bronze against which the child will have to exhaust his strength at most five or six times in order to abandon any further attempts to overturn it. It is thus that you will make him patient, steady, resigned, calm, even when he has not got what he wanted, for it is in the nature of man to endure patiently the necessity of things but not the ill will of others. The phrase "There is no more" is a response against which no child has ever rebelled unless he believed that it was a lie. (91)

Of course, Emile cannot be forever kept in the dark about the role of the tutor nor can the tutor keep on treating the growing boy as a child. Inevitably, the nature of the relationship must change as Emile matures and has to be prepared to deal with the world outside the narrow confines of his isolated existence. But Rousseau assures us that by the time Emile is old enough to understand something of how his education has been conducted, he will be so completely under the influence of the tutor that he will have no desire to change the pattern of his life. On the contrary, he will want it to continue:

You cannot imagine how Emile can be docile at twenty? How differently we think! I cannot conceive how he could have been docile at ten, for what hold did I have on him at that age? It has taken fifteen years of care to contrive this hold for myself. I did not educate him then; I prepared him to be educated. He is now sufficiently prepared to be docile. . . . It is true that I leave the appearance of independence, but he was never better subjected to me; for now he is subjected because he wants to be. As long as

> I was unable to make myself master of his will, I remained master
> of his person; I was never a step away from him. Now I
> sometimes leave him to himself, because I govern him always.
> (332)

The secret of Rousseau's method, then, is to allow the child to do
what he wants but to ensure that what he wants to do is what he ought to
do at any given moment, according to the natural order of development.
This is the only way to arrive at the goal of the wholly authentic adult:
"The truly free man wants only what he can do and does what he pleases.
That is my fundamental maxim. It need only be applied to childhood for
all the rules of education to flow from it" (84). To those who would
object that Rousseau's approach is even more inhumane than that of
Skinner who, at least in some respects, invites the participation of the
child in the educational process, Rousseau would reply that the concept
of freedom he wished to inculcate cannot be acquired by any means
other than instilling in the unaware child the idea that freedom is
responsibility and that responsibility is a matter of *impersonal* necessity:

> There are two sorts of dependence: dependence on things, which
> is from nature; dependence on men, which is from society.
> Dependence on things, since it has no morality, is in no way
> detrimental to freedom and engenders no vices. Dependence on
> men... engenders all the vices.... If the laws of nations could,
> like those of nature, have an inflexibility that no human force
> could ever conquer, dependence on men would then become
> dependence on things again; in the republic all the advantages of
> the natural state would be united with those of the civil state, and
> freedom which keeps man exempt from vices would be joined to
> morality which raises him to virtue. (85)

For Rousseau, this noble end justifies the means that have been so
severely criticized, a criticism that is directed not only at the means but
also at the premise on which the whole project is based, namely, that
everything natural is, *ipso facto*, good. Rousseau holds that God and
Providence have so arranged the world that, if we resign ourselves to the
dictates of Nature and Necessity, all is destined to turn out for the best.
The *Emile*, like the *Discourse on Inequality*, is, in a sense, a rewriting of
the book of Genesis. In the *Discourse*, Rousseau gives to the account of
the fall of man, and his subsequent banishment from the garden of Eden,
a social and economic interpretation. In the *Emile*, the child grows up in
a new garden of Eden, but subject to no temptations or injunctions
before he is ready to deal with them. In the Biblical story, God
established the order of events that culminated in the creation of Adam

and Eve. Then he rested from his labors. At the end of the *Emile*, when the new Adam is married to his Eve, born not out of his rib but from his heart and an imagination carefully prepared, this divine Rousseau looks on his work, sees that it is good, and rests:

> How many times, as I contemplate my work in them.... How many times I join their hands in mine while blessing providence.... A few months later Emile...says, "As long as I live, I shall need you. I need you more than ever now that my functions as a man begin. You have fulfilled yours. Guide me so that I can imitate you. And take your rest. It is time." (480)[24]

The conclusion is inescapable that Rousseau's *Emile* is a vast project that far transcends the preoccupations of modern pedagogy. Our educators today, if they think about the problem at all, can only hope that, as a by-product of the educational process, students will somehow emerge from the primary and secondary levels as potentially responsible citizens. The idea that the sole purpose of education should be precisely to achieve that end, and that, once it is achieved, the next goal should be radical transformation of the social order, could not be more alien to what we, in the Western world, understand by the principles and practice of education in a democratic society. We have learned a lot from Rousseau, and several of his proposals are now part and parcel of our educational philosophy. But the most important aspect of the *Emile*, its very *raison d'être*, the search for a new, ideal order, has been largely discarded. Perhaps it is because we do not share Rousseau's conviction that humanity is fundamentally good. If this is the case, the need to have and to promote new ideals, in this pragmatic age, is more urgent than ever.

NOTES

1. All quotations from the *Emile* are taken from the translation by Allan Bloom. Other Rousseau quotations are from the *Oeuvres complètes* (hereafter *O. C.*). References to the correspondence are taken from the *Correspondance complète*. The translations from these two editions are my own.

2. Of the many interpretations of the *Emile*, I include a small selection in the list of works cited. There is also a variety of interpretations in the introductions and commentaries found in the different editions of the *Emile* referred to in the list.

3. In the *Confessions* and the *Correspondance*, Rousseau offers a variety of reasons for sending his five illegitimate children to an orphanage. Among the explanations are that everyone did it, that he could not afford to keep them, that he was following Plato's opposition to family life, and that the children would have had no future in a class-ridden society. Nevertheless, he was stricken with remorse and frequently refers to his children right up to his last work, the *Rêveries du promeneur solitaire* (*O. C.* I.1087). In the *Emile* itself, he makes a veiled reference to his guilt. Speaking of the duties of a father towards his children, he says: "He who cannot fulfill the duties of a father has no right to become one. Neither poverty nor labors nor concern for public opinion exempts him from feeding his children and raising them himself. Readers, you can believe me. I predict to whoever has vitals and neglects such holy duties that he will long shed bitter tears for his offense and will never find consolation for it" (49). In the *Confessions*, commenting on this passage, Rousseau writes: "The remorse finally became so keen that it almost forced out of me a public confession of my fault at the beginning of the *Emile*, and the allusion itself is so clear that, after such a passage, it is surprising that anyone can have had the courage to reproach me" (*O. C.* I.594). For a full discussion of the question of Rousseau's children see the notes to 344-345 of the *Confessions*.

4. During 1740-1741 Rousseau, aged 28, acted as tutor, in Lyon, to the two sons of M. de Mably for whom he wrote down his ideas on education under the title, *Projet pour l'éducation de Monsieur de Sainte-Marie*. In the *Confessions* he describes his experiences in the Mably household: "I had more or less the knowledge necessary for a tutor and I thought I had the talent. During the year I spent at M. de Mably's I had the time to disabuse myself. My gentle disposition would have made me suitable for that profession if my bad temper had not interfered. As long as everything was going well and I could see that my unsparing attention and efforts were succeeding, I was an angel. When things went awry I was a devil. When my pupils did not understand me I went wild and when they misbehaved I could have killed them. . . . With patience and calm I might perhaps have succeeded; but having neither I did nothing worthwhile and my pupils turned out very badly. . . . I could see all my faults. . . but what good was it to see the evil without knowing how to remedy it? While seeing through everything I prevented nothing, I succeeded in nothing, and everything I did was precisely what ought not to have been done (267-68)."

5. "Let my readers not imagine, then, that I dare flatter myself that I have seen what seems to me so difficult to see. I have begun some arguments, I have hazarded some conjectures, less in the hope of resolving the question than with the intention of clarifying it and reducing it to its true state. Others will easily be able to go further along the same road, without it being easy for anyone to reach the end. For it is not a light undertaking to disentangle what is original and what is artificial in the present nature of man, and to know properly a state that no longer exists, that perhaps has not existed, that probably never will exist and yet of which it is necessary to have exact notions in order to judge properly our present state" (*O. C.* III.123).

6. "I have a hundred times in writing made the reflection that it is impossible in a long work always to give the same meaning to the same words. There is no language rich enough to furnish as many terms, turns, and phrases as our ideas can have modifications. The method of defining all the terms and constantly substituting the definition in the place of the defined is

fine but impracticable, for how can a circle be avoided? In spite of that, I am persuaded that one can be clear, even in the poverty of our language, not by always giving the same meanings to the same words, but by arranging it so that as often as each word is used, the meaning given it be sufficiently determined by the ideas related to it, and that each period where the word is found serves it, so to speak, as a definition. One time I say children are incapable of reasoning; another time I make them reason quite keenly. I do not believe that with that I contradict myself in my ideas; but I cannot gainsay that I often contradict myself in my expressions" (*O. C.* III.108, author's note).

7. The translator annotates this remark by observing that "paradox means *apparent* contradiction, or contradiction of *common opinion*, not self-contradiction."

8. As far as the physical education of babies is concerned, Rousseau seems to make no distinction between boys and girls. The real difference begins in infancy as is clear from the discussion of Sophie's education in Book 5. In my paper, although I have used the words "child" and "children" indiscriminately, Rousseau's main preoccupation is with boys and, specifically, with Emile. I do not deal with the education of girls since for Rousseau their future role in the political process is negligible.

9. "My examples, good perhaps for one pupil, will be bad for countless others. If one catches the spirit of these examples, one will surely know how to vary them according to need. The choice depends on the genius peculiar to each pupil, and the study of that genius depends on the occasions one offers each to reveal himself." (*Emile* 192)

10. "If I have made myself understood up to now, one should conceive how I imperceptibly give my pupil, with the habit of exercising his body and of manual labor, the taste for reflection and meditation. This counterbalances in him the idleness which would result from his indifference to men's judgements and from the calm of his passions. He must work like a peasant and think like a philosopher so as not to be as lazy as a savage. The great secret of education is to make the exercises of the body and those of the mind always serve as relaxations from one another." (202)

11. See letters 2955, 2976, 2983, 3017, 3066, 3092, 3116, 3128, 3220 and 3222 of the *Correspondance complète*. The fact that Rousseau was delighted to participate in the girl's upbringing confirms the idea that the very early education of girls would differ little from that of boys.

12. Quoted in the introduction to the Garnier edition of the *Emile*, xxxvii-xxxviii.

13. "I had perceived from my very first reading that these writings proceeded in a certain order that it was necessary to find in order to follow the chain of their contents. I believed I had seen that this order was the reverse of their order of publication and that the Author, ascending from principle to principle, had reached the first only in his last writings. It was necessary, therefore, in order to proceed by synthesis, to begin by these last, and that is what I did by devoting myself first to the *Emile* by which he finished.... In this second reading, better organized and more considered than the first, following as best as I could the thread of his meditations, I saw everywhere the development of his great principle that nature has made man happy and good but that society depraves him and makes him miserable. The *Emile* in particular, this book so much read, so little understood and so badly appreciated, is nothing but a treatise on the original goodness of man..." (*O. C.* I.933-934).

14. "From these tears what we might think so little worthy of attention is born man's first relation to all that surrounds him; here is formed the first link in that long chain of which the social order is formed" (p. 65).

15. For further details see the comments of J.-L. Lecercle in the Editions Sociales edition of the *Emile*, op. cit., 61-79.

16. ATHENIAN: And isn't it precisely when a body is getting most nourishment that it needs most exercise?
CLEINIAS: Good Heavens, sir, are we going to demand such a thing of newborn babies and little children?
ATHENIAN: No - I mean even earlier, when they're getting nourishment in their mother's body.
CLEINIAS: What's that you say? My dear sir! Do you really mean in the womb?
ATHENIAN: Yes, I do. But it's hardly surprising you haven't heard of these athletics of the embryo.... All bodies find it helpful and invigorating to be shaken by movements and joltings of all kinds, whether the motion is due to their own efforts or they are carried on a vehicle or boat or horse or any other mode of conveyance. All this enables the body to assimilate its solid and liquid food, so that we grow healthy and handsome and strong into the bargain.... A pregnant woman should go for walks... and all young children, especially tiny infants, benefit both physically and mentally from being nursed and kept in motion, as far as practicable, throughout the day and night...." (From the Penguin translation of the *Laws*, 789-790).

17. The *Profession of Faith* is based on one of several autobiographical incidents in the book. On this occasion, Rousseau recalls the advice given to him when, as a feckless youth, he was rescued from a purposeless life by the care and understanding of the abbés Gaime and Gâtier on whom the Savoyard Vicar is modelled. See the *Confessions (O. C.* I.91, 119).

18. "The fate of man is to suffer at all times. The very care of his preservation is connected with pain. Lucky to know only physical ills in his childhood – ills far less cruel, far less painful than are the other kinds of ills and which far more rarely make us renounce life than do the others!" (48).

19. "To the activity of the body, which seeks development, succeeds the activity of the mind, which seeks instruction. At first, children are only restless; then they are curious; and that curiosity, well directed, is the motive of the age we have now reached. Let us always distinguish between the inclinations which come from nature and those which come from opinion. There is an ardor to know which is founded only on the desire to be esteemed as learned; there is another ardor which is born of a curiosity natural to man concerning all that might have a connection, close or distant, with his interests" (167).

20. Although Rousseau owed many of his ideas on education to Plato, Montaigne and Locke, he was also greatly indebted, especially for Book 5 of the *Emile*, to François de Salignac de La Mothe-Fénelon (1651-1715). See the *Emile* (369, 404-405, 410, 414-415, 424, 450, 467).

21. Mme de Chenonceaux, the daughter-in-law of Mme Dupin for whom Rousseau worked as a secretary in the years immediately preceding the publication of his *First Discourse*.

22. In Book 5 of the *Emile*, commenting on the education of Sophie and her relationship with Emile, Rousseau writes: "If I have been able to make these essays useful in some respect, it is especially by having expanded at great length on this essential part.... It makes very little difference to me if I have written a novel. A fair novel it is indeed, the novel of human nature. If it is to be found only in this writing, is that my fault? This ought to be the history of my species. You who deprave it, it is you who make a novel of my book" (416). Bloom translates "roman" as "romance" but I think Rousseau intended the more general term here. Mme de Créqui wrote to Rousseau: "I have read your novel on education; I call it so because it seems to me impossible to realize your method..." (June 2, 1762).

23. For bibliographical references to infant mortality, see the article of Nancy Senior.

24. For a detailed discussion of this aspect of Rousseau's philosophy, see my *Jean-Jacques Rousseau and Providence*.

Works Cited

Bloom, Allan. "The Education of Democratic Man: *Emile.*" *Daedalus* (Summer 1978): 135-53.

Boyd, William. *The Educational Theory of Jean-Jacques Rousseau.* London: Longmans, Green & Co., 1911.

_____. *Emile for Today.* London: Heinemann, 1956.

Chandler, James K. *Wordsworth's Second Nature.* Chicago: University of Chicago Press, 1984.

Château, Jean. *Jean-Jacques Rousseau, sa philosophie de l'éducation.* Paris: Vrin, 1962.

Crocker, Lester G. *Jean-Jacques Rousseau. The Prophetic Voice (1758-1778).* New York: Macmillan, 1973.

Jimack, Peter D. *La Genèse et la rédaction de l'Emile.* Geneva: Institut et musée Voltaire, 1960.

Laing, Ronald D. *The Facts of Life.* New York: Pantheon Books, 1976.

Lawrence, Nathaniel. *The Encyclopedia of Education.* Ed. Lee C. Deighton. New York: Macmillan, 1971.

Lecercle, J. -L. "Rousseau et Marx." *Rousseau After Two Hundred Years.* Ed. Ralph A. Leigh. Cambridge: Cambridge University Press, 1982. 67-86.

Lecoq, J. -P. "Rousseau's System of Education in the Light of Modern Research." *Educational Forum* 9 (1945): 289-98.

Legouis, Emile H. *The Early Life of William Wordsworth 1770-1798.* London: Dent, 1921.

Martin, J. Roland. *Reclaiming a Conversation: The Ideal of the Educated Woman.* New Haven: Yale University Press, 1985.

Meyer, Paul H. "The Individual and Society in Rousseau's *Emile.*" *Modern Language Quarterly* 19 (1958): 99-114.

Morkan, Joel. "Structure and Meaning in *The Prelude*, Book V." *PMLA* 87 (1972): 246-254.

Patterson, Sylvia W. *Rousseau's "Emile" and Early Children's Literature.* New Jersey: Scarecrow Press, 1971.

Plato. *Laws.* Trans. by Trevor J. Saunders. Penguin Books, 1970.

Rang, Martin. "Le Dualisme anthropologique dans l'*Emile*," in *Jean-Jacques Rousseau et son oeuvre.* Paris: Klincksieck, 1964.

Ravier, André. *L'Education de l'homme nouveau.* Issoudun: Edition SPES, 1941.

Rosenberg, Aubrey. *Jean-Jacques Rousseau and Providence: An Interpretive Essay.* Sherbrooke: Naaman, 1987.

Rousseau, Jean-Jacques. *Emile or On Education.* Trans. by Allan Bloom. New York: Basic Books, 1979.

_____. *Emile.* Eds. Henri Wallon and J.-L. Lecercle. Paris: Editions Sociales, 1958.

_____. *Emile*. Eds. François and Pierre Richard. Paris: Garnier, 1964.

_____. *Oeuvres complètes*. 4 vols. Paris: Gallimard, 1959-1969.

_____. *Correspondance complète de Jean-Jacques Rousseau*. Ed. Ralph A. Leigh. Oxford: The Voltaire Foundation, 1965-199-.

Sabin, Margery. *English Romanticism and the French Tradition*. Cambridge: Harvard University Press, 1976.

Senior, Nancy. "Aspects of Infant Feeding in Eighteenth-Century France." *Eighteenth-Century Studies* (Summer 1983): 367-88.

Sewall, Bronwen D. "The Similarity between Rousseau's *Emile* and the Early Poetry of Wordsworth." *Studies on Voltaire and the Eighteenth Century* 106 (1973): 157-74.

Skinner, B. F. *Walden Two*. 2nd ed. New York: Macmillan, 1976.

Voisine, Jacques. *J. -J. Rousseau en Angleterre à l'époque romantique*. Paris: Didier, 1956.

Wordsworth, William. *The Prelude*. Ed. E. de Selincourt. London: Oxford University Press, 1933.

Chapter 2

LESSONS FROM THE WORDSWORTHS
AND THE DOMESTIC SCENE OF WRITING

John Willinsky

My sister! ('tis a wish of mine)
Now that our morning meal is done,
Make haste, your morning task resign;
Come forth and feel the sun.

William Wordsworth, "To My Sister"

With her many cares and fears for her helpless Family she must at that time have mingled some bitter self-reproaches for her boldness in venturing over the Mountains.

Dorothy Wordsworth, *George and Sarah Green*

The historical and literary territory that I would span in this essay begins with Dorothy Wordsworth's *Grasmere Journal,* which she started in 1800, and stretches to Donald Graves' *Writing: Children and Teachers at Work,* which he published in 1984. It is not the first time I have made such a leap. I have argued in an earlier paper that Graves' work is part of a latter-day manifestation of Romanticism in the teaching of writing and reading. In brief, advocates of this "New Literacy," as I have begun to term it, encourage students to take greater charge of their own literacy, in selecting their own books for class, for example, and giving expression to their impressions of them. The New Literacy programs also treat young students as writers and editors by setting up writing workshops and publishing ventures in the classroom. These programs certainly have their immediate roots in the educational experimentation of the 1960s and, before that, in certain strands of progressive education and the work of John Dewey. But I hold that the New Literacy also resonates with intellectual and artistic currents which were given great cultural currency by the Romantics. To put it another way, Wordsworth's celebration of himself as a child learning from the natural world has found another form of expression in the students' search for their own voice through the teacher's New Literacy program. I would go after these earlier layers of meaning and context not simply for the pleasure of digging the ground from under the feet of these educational innovators — ground that I also stand on in my teaching — but because I think the Romantics offer fascinating and instructive examples about living out literary ideals, and they offer those lessons in a poetic form larger than life.

In that earlier essay, I attempted to demonstrate that the New Literacy has taken more than a few of its best ideas about children, learning, and literacy from the Romanticism of Wordsworth and — with a debt to the scholarship of Ann Berthoff — Coleridge.[1] After dealing with the conceptual parallels between Romanticism and the New Literacy in this earlier work, it seemed a worthwhile extension of my project to examine the actual composition processes of the Romantics. This manner of composing forms a natural point of inquiry because it is the "writing process" which the New Literacy has introduced into the classroom, and because it has attempted to model its program on the methods of successful writers. As the New Literacy is working from a conception of the child much in accord with Wordsworth's view, it seems especially worthwhile to examine aspects of the poet's writing process for how it might compare to the work in contemporary classrooms and, more generally, add to our understanding of literacy.

In turning to the situation of Wordsworth's writing for this purpose, I have been struck by one unusual and pertinent element over all others in his successful composition process, and that is the presence of his younger sister, Dorothy. In brief, she tirelessly served his writing as researcher, audience, inspiration, copyist, secretary, housekeeper and babysitter for his children. At first blush, this sibling support, if worth investigating on its own merits, may still seem removed from the New Literacy's interest in reordering the relationship between students and teachers in learning to read and write. Yet at the heart of this reordering in the classroom is what could be termed the *domestic relations of the writing process*, for the teacher is now to nurture the growth of the child as a writer rather than offer instruction in the subject. In light of this shift, brother William and his sister Dorothy have much to teach about the underplayed sociability of literary production. This may well seem an odd twist in the Romantic legacy. Romanticism has given a good deal to the image of the writer as a solitary figure, struggling alone with troubling thoughts on the mountainside, by a mist-shrouded lake, or bent over a desk in a seedy garret. This ostensible celebration of solitary anguish may be misleading the New Literacy about the writing process, but may also be misleading it in a more profound way about the urge to expression and the very need to write which underlies both Romanticism and the New Literacy.

The introduction of domestic concerns into educational settings which I am proposing borrows a good deal from the investigations of feminist scholarship, and especially the work of Madeleine Grumet, on the sense which women have made of their calling in teaching. For in examining the relationship between Dorothy and William Wordsworth, as a domestic unit of literary production, it quickly becomes apparent that Dorothy's service forms something of a model for the New Literacy teacher of the young writer. Yet it is a form of service that educators must approach cautiously. Grumet warns in her book *Bitter Milk* that women drawn to teaching have often felt a degree of alienation and denial of integrity as they learn to move "children out of intimacy and knowledge of the family into the categorical and public world" (57). As we shall see in this essay, Dorothy assisted William in no less a fashion — "she lived his life to the full," as Elizabeth Hardwick cleverly notes (150) — while affording him the domestic support and encouragement for making the most of his original childhood intimacy and knowledge of the world. Likewise, the New Literacy is an attempt to rewrite the nature of the teacher's relationship with children by restructuring the work processes involved in reading and writing. That children find their own voice and take a greater degree of control over their learning is nothing less than Wordsworthian in its aspirations. And in a spirit to match Dorothy's pride in William's accomplishment, it also offers teachers a return on their investment of energy in helping the children tell their own stories.

But Dorothy's example raises an unresolvable question which this essay would also pose to the New Literacy: How sure can we be that this vicarious pleasure in helping another gain a public hearing was all that Dorothy wanted, or that this might be all that teachers would have today? Could the New Literacy be leading teachers to again deny themselves in their work? In this regard, Grumet calls for teachers to reclaim aspects of the teaching profession which have betrayed them: "I call upon teachers to make a place for themselves where they can find the silence that will permit them to draw their experience and understanding into expression" (88). In support of finding the silence that might result in expression on the teachers' and the children's parts, it seems especially appropriate to examine those social relations in Romanticism which made the poetic expression of these educational ideals possible. But it also seems important to question the forms of expression that are granted legitimacy. What does it mean to suggest that Dorothy's life constituted an act of "repression" or "resistance to poethood," as literary critics Susan Levin and Margaret Homans have portrayed it? Are we assuming that this need, not simply to expression, but to poethood, to an accomplished profession in writing, is somehow essential to our nature, and thus a proper foundation for an educational program? With these questions of process and expression in mind, I would turn to the lessons offered by the Wordsworths.

Not surprisingly, the wealth of critical attention paid to William Wordsworth tends to keep our eye focused on his poetry, with occasional illuminating glances at the man and the times. Christopher Caudwell is the critical exception in a number of ways, not least of which is that he begins with the Romantic processes of literary production, if somewhat abrasively. In *Illusion and Reality*, Caudwell gives little enough to Wordsworth's poetic accomplishment, except to acknowledge its proud declaration of bourgeois individualism. Caudwell takes specific issue with Romanticism's denial of the class basis of literary production: "the poet increasingly regards himself as a man removed from society, as an individualist realizing only the instincts of his heart and not responsible to society's demands—whether expressed in the duties of a citizen, a fearer of God or a faithful servant of Mammon" (101). Caudwell brings his own form of Marxist cultural materialism to bear as he accuses Wordsworth of attempting an escape from "the specific social relations of industrialism, while still retaining the products, the freedom, which these relations alone make possible" (107). But if Caudwell draws our attention to the economic organization of society that supports Romantic poetry, he misses another set of social relations which Wordsworth depended upon for launching this vivid form of bourgeois individualism. Wordsworth was indeed removed from much of the business that engaged a rising middle class, while offering it a redemptive poetry of great power, subjectivity, and nostalgia. But in this service, he was able to utilize the existing patriarchal mechanism of the middle-class family to organize a successful cottage industry around the reproduction of his literary work, with Dorothy—journal, iron, and rolling pin in hand—playing a variety of supporting roles in this writing process.

If the poet and his sister working together in a domestic literary process do not first come to mind in thinking about "The Daffodils," or, more generally, if the domestic scene seems removed from the popular conception of the poet, we have Wordsworth to thank in part. In a theme that came to dominate Romantic poetry, Wordsworth set the poet apart, as a genius among commonness, and closer to the primal forces of nature, childhood, and society's outsiders, such as the beggar and the idiot, than to the family and hearth.[2] The poet's distinction was made to seem, at times, an oracular burden of knowing what others could not perceive. But the aura of isolation was taken farther than the remote landscape in the creation of a Romantic subjectivity. The orphan Wordsworth held to his self-birth as something that left him seemingly unbound to anyone or anything but his own life: "The Child is father of the Man" ("My Heart Leaps Up"). Marilyn Butler identifies exactly how far this poetic separation can carry the determined poet away from others: "Wordsworth from 1797-8 ceases to see others as social phenomena; they are objects for contemplation, images of apparent alienation which the poet's imagination translates into private emblems of his troubled communion with nature" (67). He distances the others, including those who facilitated his creative work, to foreground his own poetic distinction, even as he, following the manifesto of the Preface to the *Lyrical Ballads*, "chose incidents and situations from common life" (71).

The sense of detachment which his poetry conveys — most often in the opening of the poem, as the Poet wanders alone, grows up alone, looks out alone — sets behind him the domestic scene marked by the onlooking figure of his sister. Yet with the close of the eighteenth century, his ability to become absorbed in a oneness with nature and his ability to convey it in his poetry was unmistakably underwritten by her support. I therefore find it more than a little ironic when Charles Rzepka, in his recent book on vision and identity in the Romantics, concludes that "domesticity" was an element in William's rather dramatic poetic decline (99). Rather, it was the very thing that allowed him to produce and sustain his heroic self-image as poet, if only for that productive decade beginning in 1798 with his life with Dorothy at Grasmere Vale.[3] Without going so far as to contend that his poetry depended on Dorothy's health, it does add to this domestic picture to note that shortly after William's most fruitful period, Dorothy gradually slipped into what has since been diagnosed as pre-senile dementia (Gibson in Gittings and Manton 282-283).

Wordsworth's representation of this apartness as a time of inspiration and humaneness is for us a quintessential moment in Romanticism. For the most part, then and now, it amounts to day-trips away from the situation at home, in a slight episode of stand-offishness by the lake as the sun goes down. Although Wordsworth had planned to title his great autobiographical poem *The Recluse*, of which he finished only *The Prelude*, it was a limited reclusion at best, removed from London as much as anything. His retreat from the world into nature retains that domestic element of a secure return, of not venturing beyond the bounds of the home that will always take you in. This is part of what Caudwell saw in Wordsworth's service to the construction of a bourgeois individualism that found in literature a setting of itself apart in its sensitivity—"a greater promptness to think and feel" was how Wordsworth described the Poet's qualities in the Preface of 1802. This detachment within bounds is also, I would suggest, part of the Romantic posture of progressive education, as it imagines itself going against, in Wordsworth's words, "the light of common day" and "the shades of the prison house" for the sake of powers in childhood too precious to waste. In such a spirit, teachers take students out of the fluorescent classroom for an afternoon's field trip, or transform the classroom into a workshop, as if to restore a connection with natural world of light and work. It temporarily dispels from sight the commonplace without recklessly undoing it.

The element of displacement in Wordsworth's poetry has been the subject of much critical notice, but the attention has been more often paid to the fading of the revolutionary and political light in his work. Critics have seen it as their duty to track his poetic posturing toward the French Revolution and other public events. As it is, the question of where he stood politically at any given point is hardly to be agreed upon. Butler allows that "he succumbed to the conservative intellectual tide so much more slowly than Coleridge" (66), while James Chandler mounts a substantial argument in favor of a persistent Burkean influence that can be traced back to Wordsworth's earliest verse. In an attack on Wordsworth's political evasiveness that is relevant to our theme, Jerome McGann accuses Wordsworth of being "interested in preventing—in actively countering"—social and economic conditions in such works as the "Ruined Cottage" (84). Wordsworth's youthful interest in revolution and political change are displaced, even as the poet continues to draw on a subject that is not removed from the social unrest of his day: "We are not permitted," McGann points out, "to remember 1793 and the turmoil of the French revolution, neither its 1793 hopes nor—what is more to the point for Wordsworth—the subsequent ruin of those hopes. Wordsworth displaces all that into a spiritual economy. . ." (88). Here McGann finds the kernel of a "Romantic ideology" which he also cannot help but noting "has been incorporated into our academic programs": "The idea that poetry, or even consciousness, can set one free from the ruins of history and culture is the grand illusion of every Romantic poet" (91).

Yet if the ideology in these literary acts is indicated by its silences — "that abyss over which ideology is built," as Pierre Macherey proposes in his theory of literary production — then the displaced political in Wordsworth is also the missing depth of the domestic life which forms a part of what his poetry only mentions in passing, even as it draws so directly from it. This from a poet with "a disposition to be affected more than other men by absent things as if they were present," as Wordsworth put it in the 1802 Preface (78). Yet I feel that in another sense William labored to create a place in his work that was deliberately, rather than deceptively, free from the ruins of culture and history which were no less personal than political. The Romantic ideology which William worked was built over a domestic abyss he was not ready to fully explore.

On first turning to Dorothy's life and journals, I looked for signs of the silencing, of her frustrated aspirations to find a public voice, as she might be William's mute and moribund Lucy, or his solitary reaper — "Reaping and singing by herself. . . . Will no one tell me what she sings?" But I soon realized that her situation could not be simply cast as unwarranted suppression. She gave herself to the literary process of William's work and appears to have sought nothing except a place in her brother's life. But the nature of that relationship, as is common to the domestic scene, was hardly straightforward and may well be ultimately unfathomable. Her life with her brother has been the subject of rather maudlin accounts that would redeem her poetic contribution; Amanda Ellis, to take one example, attempts to show "how much of Wordsworth's, for example, and Coleridge's poetry grew out of Dorothy Wordsworth's observations" while also freely speculating on her romantic fate: "The fact that she suppressed her love [for Coleridge] accounts, in part, I believe, for her premature senility" (xii).

Yet rather than her association with the man she did address on occasion as "Dear Dear Coleridge" (letter, 27 February 1799), I found Dorothy's attachment to her brother a source of pathos and wonder. It forms the emotional heart of her journal which she kept "because I shall give William pleasure by it" (11). Their sibling relationship emerges most poignantly in the 1802 entry on the wedding of William and Dorothy's good friend Mary Hutchinson: "I gave him the wedding-ring — with how deep a blessing! I took it from my forefinger where I had worn it the whole of the night before — he slipped it again onto my finger, and blessed me fervently" (167). Her life with William, after a good deal of childhood separation, began in 1794 at the age of 23 and was rarely interrupted, certainly not by his honeymoon with Dorothy's good friend Mary Hutchinson, until his death in 1850. Her life is marked by her selfless, troubled devotion to William and his understated attachment to her as her journal captures with only partial frankness in this 1801 entry: "I was melancholy and could not talk, but at least eased my heart by weeping—nervous blubbering says William. It is not so. O how many, many reasons have I to be anxious for him" (67). Yet rather than explore the psycho-sexual depth of those "many, many reasons" in this paper, I want to keep them in the background of the literary process which William found in this domestic situation.

If we return again to the parallel that might be drawn with the New Literacy, we might ask what were the constituent parts of this productive writing process that verged at times on outright collaboration. In some very important instances, including William's poems "Resolution and Independence," "Beggars," " 'I wandered lonely as a cloud' " and a half dozen others, we have a sequence which appears to begin with an entry in Dorothy's journal and ends in William's poem. As a second method, John Hayden, in his edition of William's poems, has pointed to a number of poems that were composed on the same day as Dorothy's journal entry, as with "Hambleton Hills," for which Hayden reports that "it is now thought that the poem and journal entry probably derive from the conversation during the time in question" (997). Such collective, tranquil recollection or as we would have it in these more inclement times, "brainstorming," is certainly an effective technique. It points to an otherwise undocumented role which Dorothy played in this process as collaborator and initial audience.[4]

For the poem, "Resolution and Independence," which deals with an old man who gathers leeches, the poetic process consisted of William either taking what Dorothy diligently recorded shortly after witnessing it, or at least discussing with her in some detail what she had witnessed. He gives the situation not only a blank verse rendering, but a certain metaphysical sheen by insinuating himself and his fearful thoughts into a poetic picture of what was a passing incident and chat on the road. In this fashion, a collaborative literary process took place and in what Dorothy plainly noted in her journal, Wordsworth found his poetic voice:

> He was of Scot parents but had been born in the army. He had a wife "and a good woman and it pleased God to bless us with ten children." All these were dead but one of whom he had not heard for many years, a sailor. His trade was to gather leeches, but now leeches were scarce and he had not the strength for it. He lived by

begging and as making his way to Carlisle where he should buy a few godly books to sell. (*Journal* 44-45)

My former thoughts returned: the fear that kills;
And hope that is unwilling to be fed;
Cold pain, and labor, and all fleshy ills;
And mighty poets in their misery dead.
— Perplexed, and longing to be comforted,
My question eagerly did I renew,
"How is it that you live, and what is it you do?"
 ("Resolution and Independence" 113-119)

However, only a small part of Dorothy's *Journal* is filled with such suitable material for William's use. It is more often taken up with short entries about the endless rounds of domestic and secretarial labors in the home. One simply wonders at the sections which William skipped over in favor of the more colorful incidents with leech gatherers and beggars which acted as catalysts for his poetry:

A rainy morning. I ironed till dinner time — sewed till dark — then pulled a basket of peas, and afterwards boiled and picked gooseberries. William came home from Keswick at eleven o'clock. A very fine night. (35)

The journals reveal that a good many of Dorothy's nights ended in headaches, although a few consisted of long walks with William and with Coleridge that were important times for her. Certainly, my initial reaction to reading about incident after incident of this pathetic and laborious devotion was to speak out on her behalf as a martyr to William's poetry. But on reflection, that began to seem the ultimate unfairness to her life, as she clearly wanted to give as much to this end, having wished for it for some time. In 1793, and the year before she moved in with William, she wrote to a friend of a daydream about a "little Parsonage" inhabited by a clerical William:

When our refreshment is ended I produce our Work, and William brings his book to our Table and contributes at once to our Instruction and amusement, and at Intervals we lay aside the Book and each hazard our observations upon what has been read without Fear of Ridicule or Censure. (qtd. in Homans 45)

And if it didn't work out in precisely this fashion, Dorothy and William did achieve an idyllic harmony at Dove Cottage, and they did have a life together, a description of which Dorothy noted in her journal without fear of ridicule or censure:

I made pies in the morning. Wm went into the wood and altered his poems. In the evening it was so very warm that I was too tired to walk. (33)

The journal entries give an expression to "incidents and situations from common life" that still forcefully speaks in a domestic rather than poetic way to Romantic concerns about drawing strength from nature. If this is an early version of the domestic Romanticism which Jane Roland Martin also comes to consider in this volume, it remains a record of William's life, too, as another version of the Romanticism which he lived in Grasmere. The journals were not private, but were along with William's poetry an integral element in the domestic life of the Wordsworths, and a self-contained life it was between the two of them during the years of the Grasmere journal. In their biography of Dorothy Wordsworth, Gittings and Manton point out that she began the journal about the same time as the Wordsworths' attendance at church fell off and "orthodox devotions are never mentioned in her Dorset letters" (58). She stopped keeping a regular journal shortly after William's marriage to Mary Hutchinson in 1802, although she kept a record during their travels, which formed an album to share with her family. Dorothy's journals are a form of self-expression that stands in marked contrast to the self-presentation in William's poetry. The entries have a directness, guilelessness, that can be abrupt and cryptic at times, which makes them seem at times like snapshots that have caught Dorothy unawares.

Yet I would not want to be so naïve as to regard them as completely frank or profoundly honest. But taken as a whole, they offer this double vision, as scenes from Grasmere's striking beauty and poverty break up the entries about her own routines and health. In one sense, they mock the Romanticism of the poetry which they served so well; Dorothy's despondency appears to have less of William's spiritual aspirations to it, rooted as it is in the daily toil and physical suffering of herself and others. It is worth noting that one contemporary reader of William's poetry, Anna Seward, did not hesitate to denounce him as an "egotistic manufacturer of metaphysic importance on trivial themes" (qtd. in Hartman, "Wordsworth" 8). In comparing the handful of Dorothy's journal entries that actually fed William's poems, it does seem that Seward has put her finger on the very manufacturing process. William adds exactly that metaphysical element, removing from the leech-gatherer some of the class and ecological woe, while adding considerable reflections to the poem of his own state of mind. The metaphysical revaluations of everyday rural life are indeed a part of William's poetic contribution. While William made it the privilege of genius to realize the metaphysical, Dorothy made it the purview of the diarist to rest happily with the unworked reflection and unadorned notes of the day.

In seeking the pedagogical parallels in this only half-buried literary process, there emerges a sense of the nurturing bond in which the teacher makes possible the poetry of another by so willingly serving as the Other, who provides the reason to speak, to connect, and who acts as partner in the dialogue that will shape the flow of language. In the earlier case, Dorothy did not *teach* William, and the neo-Romantic teacher of the New Literacy does not *teach* the student. They provide an initial reason for giving voice, in the same way that Dorothy's life with William might be said to be exemplary for the teacher intent on Dorothy-ing these young Williams, whether they are male or female. In terms of the contemporary production practices of the New Literacy, the Wordsworths offer a perverse instance of collaboration on the pre-writing/re-writing model which seems to undo the purer, deeper aspects of Romantic individuality in the literacy act. After all, Dorothy's journals constitute a perfect instance of "pre-writing," and, in a sense, William followed through with the re-drafting and polishing that was needed to prepare the daffodils, the leech gatherer, the solitary reaper, and Westminster bridge, for public consumption as poetry. While the idea of a teacher making notes, in Dorothy's fashion, for the students to rework may seem far-fetched, in fact, many teachers do offer writing prompts for the students with field trips, pictures or model texts from which the students are to draw their inspiration.

But more importantly, the instance of this collaboration in creation speaks to three lessons in literary production which Romanticism has done its part to write over: a) the social relations that make writing possible and which in this case form an inextricable blend of domestic and literate processes; b) the tendency in writing to sweep the table (the tablet) clear of any trace of this sociable enterprise; and, finally, c) the extent to which this process elevates the literary work into a primary form of human expression. Here we have, perhaps, the metaphysical conceit that links the impulse of Romanticism with the New Literacy program: To assume that the literary work establishes the truth of ourselves, which we would not otherwise know, and with this truth as our goal, the literary life is our natural and rightful calling. Out of largely Romantic admiration for the art and accomplishment of writing, the New Literacy advocate may over-invest in this singular measure of life's worth. The critical judgements of Dorothy, as either an important prop for William or as a repressed poet, seemed based on such an assumption. Elizabeth Hardwick stands alone in concluding that Dorothy's "conquest" of a "quiet country life with her brother" was "lucky, safe, and interesting" (153), as if Dorothy had more than a partial life outside of assisting her brother's work or finding publication for herself. We may want to keep this in mind in considering the fact that a number of students have *not* leapt at the New Literacy possibilities of writing out their stories in classrooms when they have been faced with that option in contemporary British schools (Barnes and Barnes).

While I have up to this point focused on Dorothy's journal, her literary efforts did include the writing of poetry. Susan Levin has been able to assemble 27 poems and fragments which Dorothy is thought to have written; William was good enough to include five of the poems with credit to Dorothy in various collections of his works. But for the most part these poems, too, appear to be intended for domestic circulation, as in "Lines Intended for My Niece's Album":

But why should *I* inscribe my name,
No Poet I — no longer young?
The ambition of a loving heart
Makes garrulous the tongue.

Dorothy appears much more *at home* in the journals, although such judgements are tenuous at best. The evidence pertaining to Dorothy's feelings about authorhood is of little help, except to suggest that she did indeed resist the encouragement she received. In a letter to Lady Beaumont, who was one of William's patrons, Dorothy puts off the kind woman's encouragement for her to write for a wider audience: "And you would persuade *me* that I am capable of writing poems that might give pleasure to others besides my own particular friends!! Indeed, indeed you do not know me thoroughly" (76). As if that might not convince, she goes on to say, as one might to a patron, that she has tried several more poems as Lady Beaumont had requested, but she states that nothing came of them and is finally reduced to saying that she had "been obliged to give it up in despair; and looking into my mind I find nothing there" (77). I suspect that she did not despair and certainly able proof exists in letter, journal and subsequent poetry that she had a good deal in mind. The journals were intended for William and the family; they constituted a form of domestic publication that clearly gave her pleasure. William did make the most of her journals in a manner that must have comforted her. These domestic works demonstrate an initial function of writing as a record that verifies a life in a series of selected moments felt to constitute a life, a walk at sunset, a headache after a long day.

Yet the journal had been used as a literary vehicle prior to this period, most notably by Defoe, Boswell, and Sterne; Wordsworth himself later expressed it as a "wish long entertained" (see note 4) that Dorothy's and his wife's journals be published. However, the separation of the spheres — of women's workaday lives and literary discourse — made it unlikely that Dorothy would think of her domestic life as literary material except as it could move in a disguised form through her brother's office as poet. The distance between these voices, domestic and public, was to be increasingly bridged by the resurgence of feminism in the 1960s, with such instances as Doris Lessing's *The Golden Notebook* and Anais Nin's multi-volume *Diary*. That Dorothy's use of the journal strikes us as limited and curtailed is a credit to this contemporary movement which has successfully created a public place for the personal voice of women (that this creation constitutes, in fact, a contemporary and valuable extension of the Romantic project is Deborah Dooley's argument in this book).

In comparing the writing of sister and brother, Homans points out that William identifies Dorothy with natural forces, as he does of the feminine generally in his work, an identification which Dorothy, for her part, avoids even as she is given to the most acute perception of the natural. Wordsworth patronizingly noted her indiscriminate eye as a form of innocent, untroubled connection to nature:

She welcomed what was given, and craved no more;
Whatever scene was present to her eyes,
That was the best, to that she was attuned
Through her humility and lowliness,
And through a perfect happiness of soul,

(*Prelude*, 1805 11.207-211)

If it denied her the disquieting thoughtfulness of the Poet, it was still an eye for detail and incident — Coleridge speaks of "her eye watchful in minutest observation of nature" (qtd. in Homans 103) — that could serve William's poetry. In Dorothy's poem "Thoughts on My Sickbed," she refers to her "busy eyes" (qtd. in Levin 219) stressing her sense of industry as well as this bodily breakdown of the writing process that leaves her the eyes for their thoughtful minds, the *camera lucida* for their *camera obscura*. Although she would turn the lens of record on herself ("We walked upon the platform as dizzy as if we had been on the deck of a ship in a storm"; qtd. in Homans 93), she would not allow herself to fall into what Hartman has identified as Wordsworth's "vortex of self-consciousness" which is to be finally transcended through nature ("Antiself" 293). She was there to take in what was given, rather than to draw out what could be imagined to lie beyond it. It was as if she did not find it in her power to seek out those poetic insights into the world, but was satisfied to support her brother's literary process of producing them as if they had struck him like lightning—"when the light of sense / Goes out in flashes that have shewn us / The invisible world" (*Prelude*, 1805 6.534-536).

However, I would not slight the constrained possibilities she did face as a woman. As Homans notes, Dorothy's formal education fell considerably short of William's Cambridge University days. Although Dorothy read and listened to a good deal of literature around the hearth, she missed that further institutional warrant for assuming that additional voice in presuming to speak to the world. Yet the picture of women and literature that continues to emerge from feminist scholarship is still a complex one. During the Romantic period, the majority of English novelists were, in fact, women (Tuchman), and Mary Shelley along with her mother before her found life with a writer a productive if disquieting one in terms of published work. Women were seeking public expression for their work by the close of the eighteenth century, although some of these writers still shied away from the mantle of authorship: "The magazines of the time, for example, print anonymous poems, many of them by women readers, which leads to the feeling that a submerged class is struggling for its *voice*" (Hartman, "Romantic" 279-280, original emphasis). It was by no means a level playing field for women who wanted to write, and they went as much without encouragement as opportunity.

Dorothy does not address the issue in her journal and indicates only an interest in a local and immediate readership for her work. Her journal entries slip easily into lyrical descriptions of local scenes, but they are more often a recording of who, what and where—health and welfare notes—in the domestic circulation of labor and warmth among her family and friends. She did not employ the written word to establish a self-conscious vision or identity for herself. This was the "literary" space which William had created for himself almost directly, at times, out of her initial work. Of course, had she chosen to pursue a literary place of her own, she might have gone in other directions than William's. Certainly, one thing she lacked in considering a literary career was the domestic structure, a cottage industry of one's own, by which William so benefited. If she had not the physical support of time and space to labor at authorship—she was busy providing for others—she also wasn't about to find encouragement in the work she copied for her brother, and it is that treatment of Dorothy in William's work that I would now turn to in concluding to demonstrate this Romantic treatment of the domestic scene of writing.

In William's poetry, Homans finds a fatal vision of the feminine nature, which would offer little comfort for the woman imagining herself as a poet: "Each Wordsworthian landscape contains the buried presence of a maternal or feminine figure, whether she is figurative maternal quality diffused through nature, or a more literal figure who once lived. The woman's death is lamented but made inevitable by the character of Wordsworth's project" (25). William, for his part, was happy enough to inspire Coleridge to great poetic accomplishments; he was also pleased to have his sister play her backroom muse-ical role, which preserved him in his daily trip to the office of Poet:

                    and then it was
That the beloved Woman in whose sight
Those days were passed, now speaking in a voice
Of sudden admonition—like a brook
That does but *cross* a lonely road, and now
Seen, heard and felt, and caught at every turn,
Companion never lost through many a league—
Maintained for me a saving intercourse
With my true self; for, though impaired and changed
Much, as it seemed, I was no further changed
Than as a clouded, not a waning moon:
She, in the midst of all, preserved me still
A Poet, made me seek beneath that name
My office upon earth, and nowhere else;
                    (*Prelude*, 1805 10.908-921)[5]

William grants Dorothy a slight voice, a whispered reassurance, in that necessary encouragement a writer requires. In a number of his poems, William acknowledges his debt to Dorothy, and perhaps most movingly in "Tintern Abbey." As one who traces expressions of poetic debt with a great avidity, Harold Bloom finds that Wordsworth's failure to fully recognize the anxiety of influence becomes a telling "scene of instruction" in "Tintern Abbey." However, from Bloom's perspective of the literary heritage, Milton is the unacknowledged source of this composition process ("Wordsworth"). Undoubtedly, Wordsworth wrote for Milton and out of Milton; yet equally so, the scene of instruction in this poem is also forged out of Wordsworth's more immediate and local history as he attempted to tell it and as he was told by it. His heart-felt recognition of Dorothy in "Tintern Abbey" attempts to describe Dorothy's part and in his understanding attempts to draw the line around the boundaries of this influence:

> For thou art with me here upon the banks
> Of this fair river; thou my dearest Friend,
> My dear, dear Friend; and in thy voice I catch
> The language of my former heart, and read
> My former pleasures in the shooting lights
> Of thy wild eyes. Oh! yet a little while
> May I behold in thee what I was once,
> My dear, dear Sister! and this prayer I make,
> Knowing that Nature never did betray
> The heart that loved her;

(114-123)

Dorothy is almost the object of love here, playing second to Nature. Although she is five-times dear in this passage, it is for something that is more unconsciously hers than anything she deliberately intends, and she remains somewhat removed from the intimacy Wordsworth claims in his relationship with Nature. For immediately prior to these lines, he makes it clear that it is "nature and the language of sense" which have "thus taught" him and provided "The anchor of my purest thoughts, the nurse, / The guide, the guardian of my heart, and soul / Of all my moral being" (109-11). Dorothy would restore him like a tonic to the "former heart" that is central to William's poetic process. He comes closest in the culminating lines of the poem to acknowledging her power to affect this poetic transformation: "And this green pastoral landscape, were to me / More dear, both themselves and for thy sake" (158-159). When it comes to his summative statement in *The Prelude*, William grants that the debt has been repaid through this earlier poetic work:

> Child of my parents! Sister of my Soul!
> Thanks in sincerest verse have been elsewhere
> Poured out for all the earliest tenderness
> Which I from thee imbibed;

(1805 14.232-235)

But such personal debts always amount to more than "thanks" can say. A return to this "sincerest verse. . . poured out" for Dorothy reveals the limits of acknowledgement for this important source of influence and support. Whatever Dorothy may have wanted from her life and William's poetry, to our way of thinking she seems to deserve greater credit just as he needed to represent more of the domestic scene of the poetic process that was so often his topic. I can hardly resist pointing out that with William's penchant for explicit and literal titles—such as "Written with a Slate Pencil upon a Stone, the Largest of a Heap. . ."—we might have expected in all fairness at some point in his work something like "Lines Inspired and Images Lifted with Gratitude from a Journal Entry of a Beloved Sister."

To return to the historical parallel which this paper is attempting, Dorothy's domestic enabling of William's poetry has something in common with the New Literacy's interest in turning the teacher from an instructor of writing methods to a facilitator of a writing process. In encouraging the young to write, the teacher is in a position to take students "over the Mountains," to recall my epigraph and the bold move which Dorothy feared would be the source of approbation for one such as herself, from her story *A Narrative Concerning George and Sarah Green* (qtd. in Homans 62). But if the young will find expression in these new programs, Dorothy's apprehensions for her heroine strike me as both encouragement and warning for the teacher. Although it would seem that Dorothy was not unhappy with her role and that she found an important outlet for her need to connect, it also appears that she did not consider that the office of Poet was open to her. She had to look to her domestic situation first and foremost. For the teacher, of course, things are somewhat different.

The New Literacy would restructure the domestic setting of child and adult as it opts for the nurturing of the child's story in workshop and family-room settings over the traditional classroom/insurance-office model of educational architecture. Teachers, in taking hold of the authority invested in them and sharing it with the students as writers and readers, need to remain curious about how these domestic relations become part of the literary production process. They need to ask if they are to foster only the expression of others, in this domestic sense, or is the classroom to become a vehicle for teachers, as well, in the literary process of exploring what writing can do, not as an exercise or skill, but as a voice in the world. They need to imagine a wide variety of opportunities for articulation and connection for their students and themselves. Finally, they also have to watch how this composition process continues to mask itself in an ideology of individual achievement that is not likely to be otherwise fully spoken. Writing has to be realized as a social process of support and belief, even as it tends to represent itself, in the Romantic spirit, as the lone striving of the solitary poet.

As it was with William and Dorothy, the social relations of literacy—in who writes and who is written—reflect the social order of the larger world. To alter those relations, as the New Literacy proposes, in the first and formative instance, may be to shift them irrevocably for the life of the classroom. The challenge of a New Literacy extends beyond education and poetry; it shares a populist urge with William Wordsworth. The New Literacy might do well, then, to query how what is written covers over what has yet to be said about power and intention. It needs to address the future that might be imagined for these outspoken students and empowered teachers. It is the old question of "literacy for what?" and the New Literacy seems poised to give it a fresh answer. But in this composition process it remains important, as Grumet has pointed out, that teachers create a space for themselves as well as their young authors to consider the possibilities of expression. Taking a lesson from the Wordsworths, teachers would be well advised to reflect on how these processes can be openly explored and become themselves the subject of expression and inquiry.

Notes

1.   I am not alone in this effort to give the New Literacy its historical bearings as Knoblauch and Brannon have brought the history of rhetoric and composition to bear in a defence of the New Literacy at the college level.

2.   It might be noted, as an aside, that this posture is the root of the writer's seemingly "spectator role" which has become an important posture in British writing programs which partake of the New Literacy (Britton).

3.   Coleridge, on the other hand, at least privately acknowledges this domestic contribution with great generosity in his notebook when he arrives at the formula:

W + D + MW + SH + HDSC = STC
= Ego contemplans.

Which is to say that William plus Dorothy plus Mary Wordsworth plus Sara Hutchinson plus Hartley, Derwent, Sara Coleridge (his children) add up to Samuel Taylor Coleridge and personal identity (cited from Coleridge's *Notebooks* by Rzepka 102).

4.   One danger here is that the role in this literary process of William's wife, Mary, is lost to sight. In William's notes to Isabel Fenwick on "Memorials of a Tour on the Continent, 1820," he gives credit to both his wife's and sister's journals: "Details in the spirit of the sonnets are given both in Mrs. Wordsworth's Journals and my Sister's, and re-perusal of them has strengthened a wish long entertained that somebody would put together, as in one work, the notices contained in them, omitting particulars that were written down merely to aid our memory, and bringing the whole into as small a compass as is consistent with the general interests belonging to the scenes, circumstances, and objects touched on in each writer" (*The Poems*, 2.998). Note that more than details in "spirit" found their way into his poetry and that Wordsworth would have those borrowed literary details removed from the journals prior to publication.

5.   It is worth noting that in the 1850 revision to this passage, "beloved Woman" is changed to "beloved Sister"; the importance of this more specific naming becomes apparent in the later disagreement among critics as, for example, J.C. Maxwell believes that the "She welcom'd what was given" lines, cited above, refer to William's wife, Mary Hutchinson (in his notes to *The Prelude*; 562), compared to Homans' assumption that this is Dorothy (102). Dorothy (no less than Mary) toiled in obscurity, but is finally designated as "beloved Sister," as in this attachment she happily trailed alongside his thoroughfare. In the later revisions to this passage, William also added the line "She whispered still that brightness would return."

Works Cited

Barnes, Douglas and Dorothy Barnes. *Versions of English*, with S. Clark. London: Heinemann, 1984.

Berthoff, Ann. "The Intelligent Hand and the Thinking Eye." *The Writer's Mind: Writing as a Mode of Thinking*. Ed. J. Hays et al. Urbana: National Council of Teachers of English, 1983. 191-196

Bloom, Harold. "Wordsworth and the Scene of Instruction." *Poetry and Repression: Revisionism from Blake to Stevens*. New Haven: Yale University Press 1976. 52-82

Britton, James. *Language and Learning*. Harmondsworth, UK: Penguin, 1972.

Butler, Marilyn. *Romantic, Rebels, and Reactionaries: English Literature and its Background 1760-1830*. New York: Oxford University Press, 1982.

Caudwell, Christopher. *Illusion and Reality: A Study of the Sources of Poetry*. New York: International, 1937.

Chandler, James K. *Wordsworth's Second Nature: A Study of Poetry and Politics*. Chicago: University of Chicago Press, 1984.

Ellis, Amanda M. *Rebels and Conservatives: Dorothy and William Wordsworth and their Circle*. Bloomington: Indiana University Press, 1967.

Gittings, Robert, and Jo Manton. *Dorothy Wordsworth*. Oxford: Clarendon Press, 1985.

Graves, Donald. *Writing: Teachers and Children at Work*. Portsmouth: Heinemann, 1982.

Grumet, Madeleine R. *Bitter Milk: Women and Teaching*. Amherst: University of Massachusetts Press, 1988.

Hardwick, Elizabeth. "Dorothy Wordsworth." *Seduction and Betrayal: Women and Literature*. New York: Vintage. 149-163.

Hartman, Geoffrey H. "On the Theory of Romanticism." *The Fate of Reading and Other Essays*. Chicago: University of Chicago Press, 1975. 277-283.

_____. "Romanticism and Anti-Selfconsciousness." *Romanticism: Points of View*. Eds. Robert F. Gleckner and Gerald E. Enscoe. 2nd Ed. Detroit: Wayne State University Press, 1970. 286-297.

_____. "Wordsworth Revisited." *The Unremarkable Wordsworth*. Minneapolis: University of Minnesota Press, 1987. 3-17.

Homans, Margaret. *Women Writers and Poetic Identity: Dorothy Wordsworth, Emily Bronte, and Emily Dickinson*. Princeton: Princeton University Press, 1980.

Knoblauch, C. H. and Lil Branon. *Rhetorical Trends and the Teaching of Writing*. Upper Montclair: Boynton/Cook, 1984.

Lessing, Doris. *The Golden Notebook*. New York: Ballantine, 1962.

Levin, Susan M. *Dorothy Wordsworth and Romanticism*. New Brunswick: Rutgers, 1987.

Macherey, Pierre. *A Theory of Literary Production.* Trans. Geoffrey Wall. London: Routledge and Kegan Paul, 1978.

McGann, Jerome J. *The Romantic Ideology: A Critical Investigation.* Chicago: University of Chicago Press, 1983.

McGavran, James Holt. "Dorothy Wordsworth's Journals: Putting Herself Down." *Private Self: Theory and Practice of Women's Autobiographical Writing.* Ed. Shari Benstock. Chapel Hill: University of North Carolina Press, 1988. 230-253.

Nin, Anais. *The Diary of Anais Nin.* 7 vols. New York: Harcourt Brace Jovanovich, 1966-1981.

Rzepka, Charles J. *The Self as Mind: Vision and Identity in Wordsworth, Coleridge, and Keats.* Cambridge: Harvard University Press, 1986.

Tuchman, Gaye. *Edging Out Women: Victorian Novelists, Publishers, and Social Change.* New Haven: Yale University Press, 1989.

Willinsky, John. "The Seldom-Spoken Roots of Curriculum: Romanticism and the New Literacy." *Curriculum Inquiry* 17.3 (1987): 269-291.

Wordsworth, Dorothy. *The Grasmere Journal.* Intro. Jonathan Wordsworth. London: Michael Joseph, 1987.

_____. *The Letters of Dorothy Wordsworth: A Selection.* Ed. Alan G. Hill. Oxford: Clarendon, 1981.

Wordsworth, William. *The Poems*, ed. John O. Hayden. 2 volumes. New Haven: Yale University Press, 1977.

_____. *The Prelude: A Parallel Text.* Ed. J. C. Maxwell. New Haven: Yale University Press, 1971.

_____. "Preface and Appendix to *Lyrical Ballads* (1800, 1802)." *Wordsworth's Literary Criticism.* Ed. W. J. B. Owen. London: Routledge and Kegan Paul, 1974. 68-95.

Chapter 3

COLERIDGE, I. A. RICHARDS,
AND THE IMAGINATION

Ann E. Berthoff

To apprehend the fact that all children are not alike is not revolutionary, but to have recognized its pertinence to education probably was. To hold that one or another personality has its own inclinations and that a sensible thing would be to ease the path of its development is an expression of Romanticism's faith in Nature. George Ticknor, credited with inventing the idea of the American university, visited Walter Scott in 1819 and heard about his application of this education principle. Let it stand as representative of this aspect of a Romantic theory of education:

> Mr. Scott gave me an odd account of the education of the whole family. His great object has always been not to overeducate, and to follow the natural indications of character, rather than to form other traits. The strongest instance is his son Walter, a young man with little talent; "and so," said Mr. Scott, "I gave him as much schooling as I thought could do him good, and taught him to ride well, and shoot well, and tell the truth; and I think now that he will make a good soldier, and serve his country well, instead of a poor scholar or advocate, doing no good to himself or anybody else." (284)

But an equally important aspect of Romantic theories of education is the idea that all children *are* alike, that there are certain universal powers which we all share in some measure. This tenet expresses a Romantic faith in human nature and is rooted in freshly apprehended ideas of the powers of perception and language, especially as they were developed in German Romanticism. In visiting the leading German philosophers and philologists, Ticknor unfortunately missed meeting Friedrich Schleiermacher, a friend of Herder's and a noted scholar and theologian, known to us as the father of hermeneutics. He was also, as a Protestant, intensely interested in literacy (for each individual to have access to the Word of the Lord would assure his freedom from priests), and he founded his pedagogy, as well as his hermeneutics, on a principle which he identified as his "highest intuition":

> Each man is meant to represent humanity in his own way, combining its elements uniquely, so that it may reveal itself in every mode, and all that can issue from its womb be made actual in the fullness of unending space and time.[1]

That each person is at once individual and representative is a mythic apprehension as old as language itself; indeed, it depends on the power of language to name and classify simultaneously, to identify by differentiating and to gather by sorting. It was the great contribution of German Romanticism to develop the argument that power of language is inseparable from imagination, which Coleridge called "the prime agent of all human perception," the capacity not just to see but to *see as*. Imagination, as it is the prime agent of both recognition and envisagement, thus creates our humanity. The commonalty of Imagination makes it possible to speak of "the all-in-each of human nature."

The phrase comes from Coleridge who was, of course, the chief conduit for the ideas of German Romanticism and his interpretations and transformations are essential to an understanding of the philosophy of language and the theory of imagination which evolved in English Romanticism. To appreciate the legacy of Romanticism in education requires that we consider certain changing conceptions of individual powers and talents and their relationship to society and God, to Nature and History. I propose that Coleridge's theory of imagination and its influence on I. A. Richards offers a focus for such a study.

Romanticism as a protest on behalf of the organic view of nature, in Whitehead's famous definition (138), meant the recognition of process and the need for methods of inquiry which could take it into account. The move beyond taxonomy to observation and experiment had been a phenomenon of the seventeenth century; the contribution of Romanticism was a deepened understanding of the appropriateness of organic metaphors in the description and apprehension of human affairs, especially in history and art. Thus *form*, conceived of in terms of growth and development, supplanted *structure* and *order*, conceived taxonomically.

In the case of Coleridge, it would be misleading to speak of "organic metaphors" if we should take that to mean that he simply dressed up his ideas of the active mind in figurative language. Entailed in his organic metaphors are organic conceptions otherwise virtually inexpressible. In

Coleridge's theory, imagination is not *like* a natural, organic power: "the living principle" can only be conceived in those terms. He speaks of imagination's power of semination, its germinal power, and we are meant to take this not as a figurative descriptor but as a logically accurate definition of function.

For Coleridge, "the *rules* of the IMAGINATION are themselves the very powers of growth and production" (*Biographia* 2:84). Development should suggest an unfolding of what in some sense is already there, a process of growth which is determined by habit and tendency, with intention and plan in dialectic with environment, context, alternate purposes and other constraints—whatever the forces of recalcitrance might be. The Imagination is the power which apprehends and articulates the relationships which are our means of making meaning and it does so by seizing upon forms, hearing the concords. If we think of Imagination as the forming power, the import of the organic metaphors by which it is expressed is clarified.

The defining characteristic of Imagination is that it is alive: "To know is in its very essence a verb active" (*Biographia*, 1:264). The function of the active mind is to organize both experience and knowledge. Coleridge considered that his ideas of imagination provided the keys to the great LOCK, as he was fond of putting it. He declared that "the pith of my system is to make the senses out of the mind, not the mind out of the senses," as Locke had done. This principle is crucial to an understanding of what Coleridge meant by Imagination. The following passage from Coleridge's *Aids to Reflection* offers further explanation:

> The dependence of the Understanding on the representations of the senses, and its consequent posteriority thereto, as contrasted with the independence and antecedency of Reason are strikingly exemplified in the Ptolemaic system (that truly wonderful product and highest boast of the faculty judging according to the senses!) compared with the Newtonian, as the offspring of a yet higher power, arranging, correcting, and annulling the representations of the senses according to its own inherent laws and constitutive ideas. (155-56)

This differentiation of Reason and Understanding is analogous to what Coleridge labored to establish between Imagination and Fancy. The activity by which the Imagination breaks down and builds up as it brings about the reconciliation of opposites is contrasted with the work of Fancy, which neither discovers nor creates; it puts things together and manipulates the arrangement. Fancy is not despicable; indeed, it is necessary for certain purposes, but what it does is radically different from the work of Imagination.

If one pole of Coleridge's theory of the active mind is Imagination, at the other we find Symbol: neither is conceivable without the other. The reason for speaking in terms of polarity and polar oppositions is provided by the Coleridgean doctrine that oppositions are expressions of one and the same force. In considering the symbol, it would be very easy to get lost in the thickets of German metaphysical forests, but one aspect of the symbol is especially important in considering its role in Coleridge's theory of imagination; the symbol *partakes* of the reality it represents. Coleridge also uses metaphors of translucence and incarnation, but communion is perhaps the master trope. It is not meant to signify a mystical power, but to represent the idea that the Imagination creates in symbols the reality we know:

> A symbol always partakes of the Reality which it renders intelligible; and while it enunciates the whole, abides itself as a living part in that Unity of which it is the representative. (Coburn 76)

The polarity of Imagination and Symbol is dynamic, not static: the function of polar opposites is to turn on that opposition. In this case, the wheeling is an organic process of growth and development of forming and transforming, a process best modelled by language. Because it is an organic form, language provides the means by which the mind can act according to its nature. This is what Coleridge means when he states, as he continually does, that knowledge proceeds from within:

> Alas! how many examples are now present to my memory, of young men the most anxiously and expensively be-school-mastered, be-tutored, anything but *educated*; who have received arms and ammunition, instead of skill, strength, and courage; varnished rather than polished; perilously over-civilized, and most pitiably uncultivated! And all from inattention to the method dictated by nature herself, to the simple truth, that as the forms in all organized existence, so must all true and living knowledge proceed from within; that it may be trained, supported, fed, excited, but can never be infused or impressed. (Coburn 55)

The metaphor of interiority expresses an essential character of natural process, namely, that what develops is in a sense already there. (This idea has been sloganized in the phenomenologists' "always already.")

All natural processes take time, a point necessarily of interest in education. Coleridge notes the root *educere* in education and declares that the extended consciousness by which the mind is educed is achieved by a "reflective attention." After observing how difficult it is to know what we mean by such terms as *organ, consciousness, mind, will, habit,* etc., he then asks himself: "Know?   Ay. . .but do you know your knowledge?" (Coburn 206). Reflection, the *polar opposite* of activity, is a natural process and natural processes take time; they demand patience of learner and teacher alike.   In the following observation, Coleridge makes a familiar distinction between the natural process that takes time and the seemingly efficient shortcut:

> In all the processes of the Understanding the shortest way will be discovered the last and this, perhaps, while it constitutes the great advantage of having a teacher to put us on the shortest road at the first, yet sometimes occasions a difficulty in the comprehension, in as much as the longest way is more near to the existing state of the mind, nearer to what, if left to myself on starting the thought, I should have thought next.   The shortest way gives me the knowledge best; the longest way makes me more knowing. (*Notebooks* #3023)

Analogous to the natural dialectic of linguistic activity and reflection is the instrumentality of language; we find the same kind of dynamic reciprocity in its power of symbol-making: "Words are no passive tools, but organized Instruments, reacting upon the power which inspirits them" (Coburn 7).   Recognition of this dialectic leads Coleridge to conclude that the way we learn language initially offers the best guidance for the way we should go about learning anything:

> We shall learn to value earnestly and with a practical seriousness, a means, already prepared for us by nature and society, of teaching the young mind to think well and wisely by the same never forgotten results, as those by which it is taught to speak and converse. (*Biographia* 2:144)

Thus in Coleridge's theory of imagination, mind and language share with nature an organic character — an essentially active, growing, developing, transforming power.   Thought and discourse can be described in organic terms because they are natural processes, motivated or inspirited by a "living principle" which is never single, never isolated, never passive, never merely concrete or merely abstract.   It is, rather, dialectical: in Coleridgean terms, the living principle brings about a reconciliation of opposites.   This dynamic polarity of Nature, Mind, and Language is discernible in Life, Thought, and Discourse, which are all created by it.   In all, we find an interinanimation by which the individual embodies the universal and the universal inspirits the individual, the part representing the whole by partaking of it.   Nature/Life has its being in a dynamic interaction of structure and function; Mind/Thought subsists in a coalescence of subjective and objective; Language/Discourse — what we say and what we mean — determine one another, "words. . .reacting upon the power which inspirits them."

What answers to this dynamic polarity — the organic process by which forms find forms, as meanings provide the means of making meaning — is *method*, in Coleridge's theory of Imagination. His method has both a semiotic and a hermeneutic dimension, as we can see from the following aphorisms:

> Life is known only in its product and beholds itself only insofar as it is visible in its offspring.

> There is no way of arriving at any sciential End but by finding it at every step. (Coburn 301, 114)

The metaphor of the *way* is embedded in the word *method*, as Coleridge does not fail to note. As the active mind makes sense of the world, it does not see things but relations of things. Thus there is, Coleridge writes in his *Treatise on Method*, "immediate need of some path or way of transit from one to the other of the things related; there must be some law of agreement or of contrast between them; there must be some mode of comparison; in short, there must be method" (*Method* 3). The realizing principle is natural; the mind's activity is natural; the process of learning is natural — but that does not mean that everything will happen by itself. The process of growth and development means keeping the options open, but that is not the same as not choosing. Coleridge believed that "man begins to be free when he begins to examine" (Coburn 68). Discretion, however, must not be presupposed. Coleridge tells of a conversation with his friend John Thelwall:

> Thelwall thought it unfair to influence a child's mind by inculcating any opinions before it should have come to years of discretion, and be able to choose for itself. I showed him my garden, and told him it was my botanical garden. "How so?" said he, "it is covered with weeds." — "Oh," I replied, "*that* is only because it has not yet come to its age of discretion and choice. The weeds, you see, have taken the liberty to grow, and I thought it was unfair in me to prejudice the soil towards roses and strawberries." (Coburn 54)

Natural processes take time and, in early stages, chaos must be tolerated and direction must not be settled on: it is the longest way which will make the learner more knowing of his knowledge. Choice is the ground of freedom, but without discretion, a sense of what the choices are, Reason will be mocked. For Coleridge, the process of education must assure that that does not happen.

To suggest the importance Coleridge's conceptions of language and imagination have for education, I want now to turn to I. A. Richards, one of the most influential teachers and critics of the century.[2] Early and late, Coleridge was a presence in Richards' work: it was in Coleridge's criticism that he found his principal "speculative instruments," the concepts we think with. Richards' pragmatism led him to emphasize that his concern was not to determine "what Coleridge thought" but to discover what we might do with what he thought, to describe how Coleridge's ideas could help us think about education and the human future.

I. A. Richards' greatest importance for us is that he was able to see the pedagogical implications of certain organic conceptions of language and thought as they were set forth in Coleridge's theory of imagination. He certainly assented to Whitehead's claim that Romanticism was a protest on behalf of the organic, recognizing the centrality of ideas of mediation and activity, of growth and development. For Richards, *Imagination* named the active mind, the mind in action construing and constructing, dissolving and recreating, making sense, making meaning. He is following out the Romantic idea that thought is a process whereby an inner form is made manifest when he declares that interpretation is a branch of biology and that "we shall do better to think of meaning as though it were a plant that has grown, not a can that has been filled or a lump of clay that has been moulded" (*Rhetoric* 12).

Richards' philosophy of rhetoric and his "practical criticism" — he reclaimed both the phrase and the idea from Coleridge — emerge as a confluence of his reading of Coleridge, his study of translation, and his lifelong interest in semiotics. Richards preferred to speak of signs rather than of *symbols*, probably because of the heavy mystic overlay borne by the word *symbol* and because he believed in a scientific study of meaning: in *The Meaning of Meaning*, he and Ogden had called for a science of signs. In any case, Richards held from the first that a philosophy of rhetoric would have to be able to account *for* meaning in order to give an account *of* meanings. It was his way of insisting that theory and practice are interdependent. As he developed his own account of meaning, which he eventually called a theory of comprehending, he was involved continually with hermeneutics (a word he never used and would have found suspect, insofar as it suggests secret knowledge); that is to say, he was pursuing the art and science of interpretation. Both the semiotic and the hermeneutic dimensions are represented in Richards' definition of rhetoric which included both a study of "how words work" and a study of "misunderstandings and their remedies." His philosophy of rhetoric, his theory of comprehending, and his programs to assure the centrality of interpretation in learning and teaching can best be understood by considering what he learned from C. S. Peirce who, along with Plato and Coleridge, was a chief influence on his thinking. Here, briefly, is what Richards took from Peirce.

Peirce's semiotics — he reclaimed the word, spelling it *semeiotics* — predates Saussure's semiology by thirty-five years and differs from it crucially.[3] The Saussurian sign is dyadic: there is a signifier and a signified. For Peirce, however, the sign is three-valued. The third value is interpretation itself: there is no sign without it. Peirce did not speak of interpreters but of the *interpretant*, the idea held by the interpreter. Interpretation is not a psychological additive but the logical condition of signification. In *The Meaning of the Meaning*, Ogden and Richards represented Peirce's triadic conception of the sign by a triangle with a dotted base line. A symbol (left hand corner) stands for an object (right hand corner), but there is no direct route from one to the other; we must get there by way of the interpretant which is found at the apex of the triangle. All that we know is mediated by what we already know; we make meaning by means of other meanings.

What Richards called Peirce's "revolutionary doctrine of the Interpretant" certainly guided him in formulating his theory of comprehending, which has a dual origin in his ideas about translation and in his critique of information (or communication) theory. Translation is not a dyadic operation in which one word is substituted for another; it is a process whereby *what is meant* is represented by a continuing transformation of *what is said*, by means of multiple definition and interpretive paraphrase. Translation is a matter of developing contexts from which the original message can be generated anew. What Richards intended in formulating a theory of comprehending in terms other than those offered by information theory was analogous to what Coleridge intended in differentiating Imagination and Fancy. Indeed, I think we could say that the positivist psycholinguistics against which Richards argued for forty years proceeds from exactly the same conceptions of meaning and language as those Coleridge associated with Fancy.

Richards saw the consequences of triadicity by the light of Coleridge's conception of the dialectic of imagination and symbol, the polarity of mind and nature. Paradoxically, triadicity is consonant with polarity; but it is only an apparent paradox since polarity is not actually a dyadic conception. There is a Third in all polar oppositions: the axle turns and there is in that wheeling something new—in Coleridge's terms, a reconciliation of opposites, an activity which is the work of Imagination. Both Peirce's semiotics and Coleridge's theory of imagination give a central role to the mind's activity. Peirce always stresses the process of determination as we represent our recognitions; the process of symbol-making he called *semiosis*. Here is Richards' resounding echo of this fundamental idea:

> All activity (ACT-EEV-ITY, I'd like to say...), all acteevity depends on, and is made into acteevity by, feed-forward.... We do not find anything unless we know, in some sense, what we are looking for. (*Instruments* 119)

Information theory—Fancy—is all feedback, stimulus-response, mere recollection. But Imagination is the power not only of recognition, of analogy and hypothesis; it is also the power of envisagement and thus of discovery and creation.

Richards' critique of information theory as the basis for accounting for meaning is concentrated on what he calls "the problem of initial terms." Richards' point of departure is the observation that what is found between the addressor and the addressee is not *message* but *signal*. Messages are not of a sort with the binary code on which the signal depends; they are generated by contexts; they are created by "purposing" and are dependent on other messages. Messages are meanings which must always be mediated by means of other meanings. If *message* is the initial term, that means that we cannot set meaning aside, studying syntactic structures without reference to "semantics." The consequences of making message primary are that ends must be presupposed; propositions must be hypothetical; determination must be recognized as an ongoing process. And, of course, interpretation must itself be interpreted. At this point, Peirce's *pragmatism* is entirely consonant with Coleridge's *method*, which features the dialectic of creation and recreation, of activity and reflection.

Richards' pragmatism sharpened his recognition of what Coleridge's practical criticism could model. His philosophy of rhetoric would be useless if there weren't practical consequences; indeed, we can't really understand any theory without looking back on it from the perspective of the practice it produces: "How we use a theorem best tells us what a theorem is" (*Rhetoric* 27). Richards wanted to know how a theory would change practice and he submitted all his designs to the test of the pragmatic maxim: If we hold such and such. . . if we put it this way. . . if we proceed along these lines, what difference would it make to our practice?

The different practice Richards was trying to develop was a procedure which would rescue learners from bewilderment and give them a way of proceeding other than guessing. Richards saw more clearly than most that the errors and inadequacies teachers face — when they are not, indeed, artifacts of the teacher's practice — are in large part due to students' lack of practice in developing procedures for taking control. He urges that distracting illustrations, exemplifications, explanations be cleared away so that "the partially parallel task" (*Instruments* 96), when it comes along, can be recognized, and the warrant for this discarding of additions is found in the conviction that everybody likes to think, if they think they can. It is "the lure of the task itself" that motivates and not any "adventitious jollying up" (*Design* 25).

Remembering that the Imagination was for Coleridge "the prime agent of all human perception" can clarify the reason for Richards' reliance on visual analogs and perception exercises; indeed, most of his practical criticism can be characterized as exercises in looking — and looking again. He believed that audio-visual aids to learning could and should be "aids to reflection," in Coleridge's phrase. And Richards continually takes as his point of departure the comparative power of mind and language: *sames* and *differents* he saw as analogous to Socrates' divisions, as dialectical and heuristic — heuristic because dialectical. These comparisons and differentiations constitute what he called "speculative instruments," the means by which we discern and create meanings. "There is no study," he wrote, "which is not a language study, concerned with the speculative instruments it employs" (*Instruments* 116). Each discipline has centrally important ideas with which those who practice it think and with which formulations can be amended and corrected. Richards defined *dialectic* as a continuing audit of meaning. We aim for balance — the love of balance was for Coleridge a defining characteristic of our species — and achieving it is a natural process. *Audit* suggests arrangements *a posteriori*, the work of Understanding — and so it is; but as the arranging creates new possibilities, it is, as well, the work of Imagination.

Richards was committed to the idea of a conjunction of organic conceptions and scientific inquiry and he continually cites from Coleridge passages attesting to the commonalties of science and poetry. Coleridge saw methodological parallels between them and Richards tried in his theory and practice to define what they share and how they differ. "Poetry as an instrument of research" was a favorite idea. A poem offers the best opportunity for studying how words work, and since all studies are language studies, all can benefit from the study of poetry, and from close reading generally, treating all texts with as much care as one would a poem. In his conception of the classroom as a philosophic laboratory, Richards sees the dialectic of experiment and experience as the chief source of heuristic. He returned twice – in 1935 and 1970 – to a little book first published as *Science and Poetry* in 1926. He continued to defend his assertion that poetry makes "pseudo-statements," an unfortunate attempt to solve the perennial problem of how to differentiate ways of knowing and modes of representation, while exploring the implications of the change he made in the title, *Poetries and Sciences*. But of all the ways of finding the commonalty between science and poetry as "modes of intellectual energy" (*Biographia* 2:144), it was the concept of imagination which allowed him to focus most sharply on the powers of the active mind.

The scientist and the poet – both learners – lead their minds out; they both meet the world of Nature with inner powers; both are dependent on speculative instruments to mediate their experience of the world. Scientists and poets alike are guided in the task of interpretation by what Coleridge called "the fore-thoughtful query"; no formulation of the idea that meanings are our means of making meaning was more useful to Richards than this Coleridgean version of Peirce's doctrine of the Interpretant. On occasion, Richards could invent fantastical terms for procedures and instrumentalities, principles and working concepts, but when it came to method, he deliberately stayed with the simplest possible terms. He spoke of instruction as a matter of offering "assisted invitations" to students to look at "what they are doing and discovering thereby how to do it" (*Design* 111). Getting the *how* from the *what* is matched by his description of scientific method as a matter of observing *what* varies with *what*. In all his experiments with multiple definition and interpretive paraphrase – developed as techniques out of the theory of translation set forth in *Mencius on the Mind* – Richards continually asks "How would it change the meaning if we put it this way?" Practice in controlling *sames* and *differents*, accomplished by the process Coleridge called "desynonymizing," was a procedure Richards recommended for students learning a second language, as well as for the teachers in his seminars at the Harvard Graduate School of Education and the undergraduates in his Humanities courses. An exam question was likely to be a selected short passage and the question: *"What* is going on *here?"*

It is not, I think, that Richards took one or another idea from Coleridge and put it into practice, but that he found support there for educational designs which derived from his own practice and from his lifelong study of Plato and his always renewed understanding of Peirce. Richards' designs were all intended to clear the path so that the mind could be led out by the learner himself. The aim was to realize purpose, to exercise intelligent choice. The choices of words as the discourse unfolded could become the model for a "theory of all choice" (*Rhetoric* 86). The Coleridgean ideal of moral improvement through clear thinking was one he embraced from the start. What seems a simple-minded Utopianism to skeptics and problem solvers is actually a conviction deeply rooted in the Romantic tradition. Richards' benevolent rhetoric and his hopeful pedagogy are theoretical that they might be practical; this Romantic visionary was always dreaming of what might more readily be seen to make a difference. All his teaching was based on a conception of mind empowered by language to act and reflect. Thinking about our thinking, "arranging our techniques for arranging," "comprehending our comprehensions more comprehensively": it is consciousness of consciousness which constitutes method. The intellectual energy which inspirits his practical criticism derives from a theory of imagination as the forming power — and what it forms is symbol. Every line of a poem, every student response, every perceptual exercise is representative of a principle or a question; just so, "the simplest scrap or pulse of learning and the grandest flight of speculation share a common pattern" (*Read* 106).

Expectably, there is an important political significance in virtually everything Richards wrote, from *Mencius on the Mind* and *Coleridge on Imagination* to *Design for Escape*, which is his meditation on literacy education as an escape from global catastrophe. The deepest conviction — that it is the all-in-each of human nature which makes learning possible — is at once a metaphysical idea, an epistemological theorem, and a political manifesto. Like the great Romantics before him, I. A. Richards believed in universal science and the brotherhood of man.

It is certainly true that we must earn our heritage. In this instance, there are, I believe, two tasks. One is to expose the false conceptions of "Romanticism," the false consciousness of its liberatory power; the other is to reclaim imagination as the forming power of the active mind. Both tasks, as I have been claiming, require the support of a triadic semiotics.

It is a misconception to see Romanticism as a philosophy which preaches the supremacy of the merely subjective, thus legitimizing the selfish and uncritical attitudes vulgarly excoriated as "relativism." It is a false Romanticism which debases method to a matter of procedure and then dismisses it as anti-pedagogical, which considers theory as being antithetical to practice and therefore *im*practical.   Romanticism is misconceived when it is taken as support for the doctrines that feeling is antithetical to thought or that feeling is primary and therefore superior: both attitudes are fostered by the killer dichotomy of an affective and cognitive domain.   A dichotomy is a logical device essential in establishing one or another universe of discourse, but any and all dichotomies are dangerous when they are mistaken as representative of real or actual divisions in nature or society. In that case, dichotomies act to halt the process of interpreting our interpretations.

Dyadic formulations forestall that necessary reflection and they cannot account for the process by which oppositions are reconciled. Nor is the corrosive effect of the old hierarchies and dichotomies diminished by re-naming them, one of the strategies of positivist ideologies which so often advance under the cover of "Romanticism."   For instance, the various "new rhetorics" in rejecting the old so-called "modes of discourse" — narrative, description, compare-contrast, definition, and so forth — are off to a good start, but there is no real advance if what happens is that creative/expressive/private uses of language are seen as antithetical to critical/transactional/public uses. If "what is happening" is "real" but what is said about it is not, then Thirdness has been forgotten and interpretation has been reduced to "opinion," which is right back where we started from. If a teacher says, "I don't care about what you think, tell me how you feel," that is no improvement on True/False quizzes, "objective" term papers, or fill-in-the-slot workbooks.

Concepts rather new to educational theory — gender, the life-world, praxis, de-schooling, voice, women's ways of knowing and the like — will be powerless to help us unless they are entertained in a triadic perspective. What that means is that we must be able to see what constitutes them, how they work, the kind of process entailed as they are seen as activities, actualities. New concepts can't serve as speculative instruments unless they further critical inquiry and, triadically speaking, that means that an idea without a method is powerless.

The impulse to reductionist, essentialist, foundationist thinking often sounds "Romantic": opting for simplicity, often seen as a Romantic concept, can be seen as an appealing alternative to the complexities involved in thinking about our thinking and interpreting our interpretations. If we "romantically" cut praxis loose from theory, it will be directionless – or, more likely, will be directed by a theory inaccessible to review. "Voice," separated from the making of meaning, from purpose and intent, has no heuristic power. In the absence of conceptions of purpose and action, "the life-world" will not generate method and is likely to degenerate into a pseudo-concept in Vygotsky's sense – a grab bag in which no differences are to be discerned – and it will therefore have no power to guide our understanding of what we think we are doing. If gender theory takes the male-female dichotomy in a dyadic perspective, deploying it in other than biological contexts, there will be no way found for a healing reconciliation of opposites to be realized. If we forget the Third, any identification we make will be powerless to guide our reflections and any opposition we make will rigidify. Dyadic formulations create killer dichotomies and they bring the interpretation of interpretation to a halt.

Just so, mythic ideation, when it is cut loose from the reflective moment provided in poetic discourse, is dangerous because it conflates symbol and object, identifies part and whole, confounding cause and effect, concrete particular and abstract universal. Mythic ideation is not pre-logical, but it is, by definition, pre-judicial. Thus when "Romanticism" is identified with "myth," it can be blamed for all the evils of the nineteenth and twentieth centuries. This false conception of Romanticism leads to the claim that certain myths spawned fascism, whereas what actually happened was that National Socialism fostered an uncritical, unreflective dependence on mythic ideation in order to create certain interpretive communities whose purpose was to invent Aryan purity and the Final Solution.

If we forget the Third, even Imagination will be powerless to guide our philosophy of education: dyadically conceived, imagination remains the antithesis of reason, method, science, intellectual enterprises of all sorts, seriousness, the Real World. Kidnapped and sequestered in the Affective Domain, Imagination is in chains. William Blake's great metaphors and images are devoted to representing the fate of Imagination when we forget that it is "the living principle," and "the prime agent of all human perception."

Reclaimed as the forming power of the active mind and understood in the triadic perspective which assures interpretation as constitutive of the sign, Imagination could serve as our most valuable speculative instrument in the enterprise of developing what Paulo Freire calls "a pedagogy of knowing." Imagination reclaimed could help us rethink the *organic*, to see it not as an undirected or directionless process but as a dialectical determination. *Personal* expression would be understood not as a private game, uncritical and unreflective, but as the expression of attitude, itself dependent on an interdependence of perspective and context. *Expressive* uses of language would be defined not as non-social or anti-social exercises but as a dialogue with the self and others — and *dialogue* would be seen not as debate but as a dialectic "encounter between people to name the world," in Freire's memorable phrase.

Dialogue, it should be noted, is not dyadic; like the reconciliation of polar opposites, it creates a Third — discourse — which, as it is created by interpretation, is subject to interpretation. Such a dialectical understanding of dialogue reminds us, further, that language is not a "communication medium" but the great heuristic: the syntactic and semantic resources it offers are our means of discovering and inventing knowledge. Imagination, taken triadically, reminds us that each active mind requires other active minds; semiosis is a process necessarily social. As Peirce observed, in a very Coleridgean vein, Man is a Sign. Since each sign requires another for its interpretation, it is clear that each Human-Sign requires other Human-Signs. And society — this community of Human Signs — Peirce saw as "a loosely compacted person."

For Coleridge, for Peirce, for Richards, language is at once personal and social, a biologically innate capacity which is realized in society. Language is at once formal and cultural, just as we are at once individuals and members of society; just as "each man represents humanity in his own way," as Schleiermacher saw. Romanticism gave us an understanding of the heuristic power of language, a theory of interpretation, and a critical method. What we must ask of it now is the wherewithal for a philosophy of language which can guide an understanding that personal knowledge and the social construction of knowledge are interdependent, necessarily so, and that the making of meaning is the recognition and representation of purposes, which are never merely personal. Imagination reclaimed offers the best hope that we will remember the Third, thus assuring that interpretation will have a central place in our educational theory and practice and that we will be more likely to recognize the all-in-each of human nature and the universal capacity to interpret interpretations.

Notes

1. This passage comes from the *Monologen*, but the idea is articulated over and again in sermons, lectures, and letters. The most illuminating commentary on Schleiermacher comes not, in my opinion, from literary critics and historians but from theologicans who have actually read him. I have found Karl Barth's essay on Schleiermacher especially useful, and the most instructive and interesting examination I know of is provided by Richard E. Niebuhr.

2. I have offered a general account of Richards' importance for the study of composition and rhetoric, noting especially his pedagogical innovations, in a chapter contributed to *Traditions of Inquiry* edited by John C. Brereton. For an analysis of Richards' critique of misguided attempts to deploy information theory in semiotics, see my "I. A. Richards and the Audit of Meaning."

3. Peirce's theories are not always accessible, because of his style and habits of mind. The best point of entry is by way of the letters to Lady Welby, passages from which first appeared as an appendix to Ogden and Richards' *The Meaning of Meaning*. They are now available in an excellent volume edited by Charles Hardwick.

Works Cited

Barth, Karl. *Protestant Thought from Rousseau to Ritschel.* New York: Harper & Row, 1959.

Berthoff, Ann E. "I. A. Richards and the Audit of Meaning." *New Literary History* 14 (1982): 63-79.

_____. "I. A. Richards," in *Traditions of Inquiry.* Ed. John C. Brereton. Oxford: Oxford University Press, 1985.

Coburn, Kathleen. *Inquiring Spirit: A New Presentation of Coleridge from his Published and Unpublished Prose Writings.* New York: Pantheon, 1951.

Coleridge, Samuel Taylor. *Aids to Reflection.* London: George Bell & Sons, 1893.

_____. *Biographia Literaria.* Vol. 7 of *The Collected Works of Samuel Taylor Coleridge.* Ed. James Engell and W. Jackson Bate. Princeton: Princeton University Press, 1983.

_____. *The Notebooks of Samuel Taylor Coleridge.* Ed. Kathleen Coburn. London: Routledge and Kegan Paul, 1962.

_____. *Table Talk.* Vol. 14 of *The Collected Works of Samuel Taylor Coleridge.*

_____. *Treatise on Method.* Ed. Alice Snyder. London: Constable, 1934.

Hardwick, Charles S., ed. *Semiotics and Significs: The Correspondence between Charles S. Peirce and Victoria Lady Welby.* Bloomington: University of Indiana Press, 1967.

Niebuhr, Richard E. *Schleiermacher on Christ and Religion.* New York: Scribner, 1964.

Ogden, C. K. and I. A. Richards. *The Meaning of Meaning: A Study of the Influence of Language upon Thought and the Science of Symbolism.* London: Routledge and Kegan Paul, 1923.

Richards, I. A. *Design for Escape: World Education Through Modern Media.* New York: Harcourt, 1968.

_____. *How to Read a Page: A Course in Efficient Reading, with an Introduction to a Hundred Great Words.* New York: W. W. Norton, 1942.

_____. *The Philosophy of Rhetoric.* New York: Oxford University Press, 1936.

_____. *Speculative Instruments.* Chicago: University of Chicago Press, 1955.

Schleiermacher, E. *Monologen. Schleiermacher's Soliloquies.* Trans. H. L. Friess. Chicago: Open court, 1926.

Ticknor, George. *Life, Letters, and Journals.* Vol. 1. Boston: Houghton Mifflin, 1909.

Whitehead, Alfred North. *Science and the Modern World.* New York: Macmillan, 1947.

Chapter 4

TEACHING THE MONSTER TO READ:

MARY SHELLEY, EDUCATION

AND *FRANKENSTEIN*

Anne McWhir

If the time should ever come when what is now called science, ... familiarized to men, shall be ready to put on, as it were, a form of flesh and blood, the Poet will lend his divine spirit to aid the transfiguration, and will welcome the Being thus produced, as a dear and genuine inmate of the household of man. (Wordsworth, Preface to *Lyrical Ballads*, 1802)

[T]o be mistaught is worse than to be untaught; and no perverseness equals that which is supported by system, no errors are so difficult to root out as those which the understanding has pledged its credit to uphold. (Wordsworth, "Essay Supplementary to the Preface," 1815)

In the late eighteenth century, Samuel Stanhope Smith reports, a native Indian student at the College of New Jersey was made almost white by his education (107-08). Smith intends to demonstrate that racial difference is merely superficial; but, of course, for him white is normative, and education means submission to paternalistic Anglo-American values. About the same time in England, the double effect of chap-books by such writers as Hannah More, which both "perpetuat[ed] literacy" in the 1790s and also "advocat[ed] quiet obedience" illustrates a similar point about the controlling effects of education (Olivia Smith 90). These versions of a familiar story may help us to understand Frankenstein's monster, who suffers because, unlike Samuel Stanhope Smith's native student, he cannot pass for white: he is trapped in the abyss between the ideology his education teaches and his own experience of a rejecting world. Educated to reiterate lessons of submission, dependence, and assimilation, the monster in *Frankenstein* replicates the transformation of repression into oppression. In the process he may teach us something not only about the political context of Mary Shelley's novel, but also about our own situation as teachers and as students.

Without regarding ourselves as Indians or colonizers, monsters or monster-makers, most of us — both as students and as teachers — have experienced in the classroom the problem of a doubtful authority. Our intellectual parents have taught us to read, designed our curricula, and even written the books that shaped the way we think. But if we are to be made intellectually and politically conscious, we eventually need to choose our own books and read them for ourselves, going on to teach lessons that do not merely replicate the lessons we were taught, and thus becoming more than parodies or caricatures of our own teachers. Denying that our teachers have formed us altogether, we must resist in turn the temptation to impose our own image on our students. But Victor Frankenstein's monster, deformed as much by the texts that teach him as by his "creator," constructs his own sense of self only to discover that he has no right to exist. Through the books he reads, he discovers, or perhaps constructs, his intellectual parents — only to realize that their lessons have formed him for a world that will not accept him. In a sense he is twice made — first through Frankenstein's macabre piecing together of fragments from the grave, then through the textual construction of his own sense of self. His attempt to discover and to make sense of the father is thus both biological and literary. But, I will argue, he is more trapped by the textual values he assimilates (ideology, mythology, symbolism) than he ever was by biology. Either he reads the wrong books or, more probably, Mary Shelley (as author and teacher) denies him the ability to read them critically.

In 1815 Mary Wollstonecraft Godwin — not yet Mary Shelley — was living with Percy Bysshe Shelley in England, estranged from her father after her elopement the previous year.[1] A girl of eighteen, she had already, in March, given birth to a baby which had died. Here, and not only at Villa Diodati the next year, we can find the genesis of *Frankenstein*. Mary Shelley's reading list for 1815 — for she kept such lists for herself and Shelley from 1814 until 1820 — includes three of the books the monster reads: Goethe's *Werther*, Milton's *Paradise Lost* and Plutarch's *Lives*.[2] It also contains, among a wide variety of others, works by Rousseau and Holbach's *System of Nature*. These books are also present in *Frankenstein*, though not explicitly, for Rousseau, Holbach, Godwin and numerous others are as important in the formation of the creature as Plutarch and Milton. The general relationship of Rousseau to *Frankenstein* is quite obvious: indeed, Frankenstein's confession begins like a revision of Rousseau's — "I am by birth a Genevese" — and goes on to develop an idealized version of Rousseau's guilty confusion between the mother and the lover.[3] In *Frankenstein*, Safie, the Arab girl who marries Felix De Lacey, is perhaps a corrective revision of Sophie in *Emile*, with whose education Mary Wollstonecraft took issue in her *Vindication of the Rights of Woman* (77-92; Scott 174). Even more obviously, Frankenstein's monster is a parodic version of Rousseau's child of nature, whose education in the ways of society can either make or break him.

But, as Frankenstein learns to his horror, the creature is more than the sum of his parts, literary or biological. The text of *Frankenstein* is also more than the sum of its parts: put together out of fragments of reading and a wide variety of ideas and influences, it perplexes the reader with its intertextual complexity. Reading *Frankenstein*, the reader is both like the monster, who is also a reader, and unlike the monster, who is deconstructed by being read. The monster in *Frankenstein* is badly educated, deformed by his social and literary experience. But who is this educable — and educative — monster? What can we learn from reading him as a literary patchwork, sewn together out of fragments not only of corpses but of texts, even as he constructs himself out of similar, but not always identical, fragments? The question is unanswerable without compiling one's own list of fragments, for Mary Shelley's creative process is no more recoverable than Frankenstein's. I can merely attempt to piece together part of an intellectual and literary context, hoping that it may help to explain the limitations of the monster's education.

Rousseau — whom Mary Shelley reads but to whom she does not give her creature access — claims (notoriously) that misery and degradation are not natural but are ills contracted through socialization. In the *Discourse on the Origin and Foundations of Inequality Among Men*, for example, he describes natural man "satisfying his hunger under an oak, quenching his thirst at the first stream, finding his bed at the foot of the same tree that furnished his meal; and therewith his needs are satisfied" (105). For Rousseau, reason is a means of achieving happiness only for those who have long ago left the primeval state of nature for civilization. The implications of Rousseau's myth of natural man for a reading of *Frankenstein* are clear in the *Discourse on Inequality*: "Nothing. . . would have been so miserable as savage man dazzled by enlightenment, tormented by passions, and reasoning about a state different from his own" (127).

The monster in *Frankenstein* is, in part, natural man dazzled by enlightenment, tormented by loneliness and desire, reasoning about a social state in which he can never find a place. Because of his ugliness, he cannot hope to be treated like Victor the wild boy of Aveyron, who wandered out of the forest in 1799 and was brought to Paris to be educated.[4] He is no Emile, raised from the cradle as a citizen of the world. He is an educable child of nature denied perfectibility within a social context and thus doomed to perversity: a literate Caliban. He is given no Rousseau to read—and he comes to believe in the anti-Rousseau position that man is weak *without* society. Godwin's golden age follows the abolition of government rather than preceding its institution; but Godwin's lesson, like Rousseau's, might have reconciled the creature to his condition: "He is the most perfect man, to whom society is not a necessary of life, but a luxury, innocent and enviable, in which he joyfully indulges" (Godwin 302).

But others, including Jean Marc Gaspard Itard, who undertook to educate the wild boy, regarded society as essential to human happiness, and even to survival. Although the monster is explicitly *not* "one of the feeblest and least intelligent of animals" (Itard v), he achieves less than Godwinian perfection because he assumes that his self-sufficiency must be a sign of inferiority. For him, the De Laceys are the model of perfection. But they are the worst possible model, we discover, because they teach the creature certain values they themselves cannot rise to when tested. Describing himself as "more agile than [man]," able to "subsist upon coarser diet," and able to withstand extreme temperatures, the creature concludes that he is "not even of the same nature as man," "a monster, a blot upon the earth" (115-16), rather than realizing that he is simply different from the De Laceys in ways that might have made him their equal or even their superior, rather than their inferior. He believes that he *needs* to be accepted by the De Laceys and, since he cannot be, he demands our sympathy even when he is most criminal.

But Rousseau might have regarded the De Laceys not as the monster's connection with a beneficent, if flawed, social world, but as the unwitting means of his corruption. The blind De Lacey—unknowingly and ironically—succeeds in educating the monster only for misery and hatred. Education can make a monster into a human being by socializing him; but it may offer only a false enlightenment, worse than blindness, degrading natural man into a monster by raising desires and aspirations that nature cannot and society will not satisfy. Obviously, Frankenstein's creature can be educated as a human being only if society is willing to accept him as such (even if such acceptance goes no further than giving him a monstrous companion). Otherwise, he can be educated only to know the full extent of his exclusion, denied social identity by the very society he longs to join.[5]

One difficulty in reading *Frankenstein* is the familiar problem of nature and nurture: is the monster intrinsically evil, perhaps because of the circumstances of his creation, or is he made evil by bad treatment, as he himself claims in his conversations with Frankenstein? I consider him to be amoral in the beginning, radically natural in a sense that Mary Shelley might have understood from her reading of Holbach's *System of Nature*. Holbach, like other radical free-thinkers of his day (including Volney, whose *Ruins of Empires* the monster does read), regards Nature as all that can be known: whatever may lie behind or beyond her—causes, universal necessity—is unknown and unknowable. To all intents and purposes, then, Nature is parthenogenic, a female principle whose laws govern man's being and who sends him out into the world "naked and destitute" (Holbach 11). According to Nature's laws, "matter acts by its own peculiar energy, and needs not any exterior impulse to set it in motion":

> If filings of iron, sulphur and water be mixed together, these bodies thus capacitated to act on each other, are heated by degrees, and ultimately produce a violent combustion. If flour be wetted with water, and the mixture closed up, it will be found, after some little lapse of time, by the aid of a microscope, to have produced organized beings that enjoy life, of which the water and the flour were believed incapable: it is thus that inanimate matter can pass into life, or animate matter, which is in itself only an assemblage of motion. Reasoning from analogy, the production of a man, independent of the ordinary means, would not be more marvellous than that of an insect with flour and water. Fermentation and putrefaction evidently produce living animals. We have here the principle; and with proper materials, principles can always be brought into action. (20)

The creature in *Frankenstein* is, if one accepts Holbach's argument, a child of nature—not an artificial man or even the monster his "creator" thinks he is. In his origin he is neither good nor evil, though he is capable of becoming either. From such a point of view, moreover, Frankenstein is not a god-like creator at all: he is simply a man who understands and employs a principle of nature. Holbach's insects produced with flour and water are not created by the man who puts the materials in a jar. They grow according to natural principles, and the word "creation" is thus inappropriate to the scientist's activity. Nature herself produces life, a statement suggesting two conclusions. First, the monster is no monster;

in Holbach's words, "there can be neither monsters nor prodigies, wonders nor miracles in nature: those which are designated as *monsters* are certain combinations with which the eyes of man are not familiarized, but which are not less the necessary effects of the natural causes" (35).[6] It is Victor Frankenstein, insisting on his own creative power, who calls his creature a "monster"—"the miserable monster whom I had created"(53). Second, the creature (for want of a better word) learns a mythology or ideology that must destroy him when accepted as truth: convinced that happiness is possible only in society and only through a loving relationship with his creator-God, convinced of his need for romantic love, the creature is destroyed by his discovery of civilized human wants and desires. The question of identity is a matter of ideology, and, unfortunately, the monster either reads the wrong books or learns to read them badly.

Natural man is an ideological construct, as Rousseau admits.[7] Artificial in his radical naturalness, the philosopher's natural man cannot be liberated from the text: he is read. To teach him to read is either to destroy him by making him aware of his alienation, or to undertake to accept him as a member of civil society, a subject whose rights can be asserted. Significantly, Mary Shelley's creature reads neither Rousseau nor Holbach, Godwin nor Wollstonecraft. Rousseau might have taught him a positive way of looking at his role as natural man—but, of course, by then it would have been too late: natural man is not a reader. But Rousseau, like Godwin, is present in *Frankenstein* not as a text the creature reads, but as a component of the creature himself, as Milton, Plutarch, Volney and Goethe also are: if the creature is Mary Shelley's version of herself in relation to Godwin as suggested by Knoepflmacher, of her own stillborn child or dead baby as proposed by Moers, if he is Milton's Adam, or the dream/nightmare of contemporary science, he is also Mary Shelley's comment on Rousseau's natural man. Thus, if Frankenstein the self-deluded creator puts together his creature out of fragments salvaged from the grave, Mary Shelley forms her "hideous progeny" out of fragments of her reading as well as her experience.[8] His deformity is partly that of parody; if, as the creature thinks, language is a compensation for deformity, that is because language seems to offer secure contexts and constructs.

But the deformity persists, tripping up any reader who approaches *Frankenstein* expecting the vindication of an ideological position. Is the text radical, conservative, feminist, patriarchal? Godwinian in its critique of Rousseau, anti-Godwinian in its rejection of perfectibility? If the text/creature analogy stands, is Frankenstein a surrogate for the writer or for the writer's father? Does Mary Shelley stand with Frankenstein or in opposition to him? Instead of trying to answer such questions as these directly, I will attempt to show what effect the creature's education has in his formation or deformation and how the creature's role as reader intersects with his other role as textual construct. The strain between the pastoral and apocalyptic in the monster's account of his education — now a vegetarian of the Golden Age, now an outcast demon — emphasizes the incompatibility of the different views of self he is given by his reading.[9] While he reads Plutarch and Goethe and Milton, while he listens to Felix reading Volney to Safie, we continue to put the pieces of a still unfinished creature together and come up with an uncritical reader, a confused curriculum, and an inconsistent reading.

Yet the creature in *Frankenstein* is competent as natural man from the moment of his animation. Or perhaps he is an amusing distortion of natural man. He gets dressed — thus demonstrating remarkable fine-motor control and a natural modesty unknown to infants, wild men, and Rousseau's man in a state of nature — and he goes outside, walking without help or example. He can even choose his own food, and when he sees the moon he feels awe resembling Volney's description of primitive religious feeling.[10]

Perhaps the moon is a kind of primeval female presence for the creature, who lacks a mother but who is the hideous progeny of a woman writer and, in Holbach's sense, the child of female Nature. Reading Volney — no supporter of Rousseau, but a skeptic like Holbach — should have suggested to the creature such a way of understanding his own origin, for Volney's Genius makes man a child of nature and puts these words into the mouth of the mother:

> Feeble work of my hands, I owe thee nothing, and I give thee life; the world wherein I placed thee was not made for thee, yet I give thee the use of it; thou wilt find in it a mixture of good and evil; it is for thee to distinguish them; for thee to guide thy footsteps in a path containing thorns as well as roses. Be the arbiter of thine own fate; I put thy destiny into thine own hands! (21)

These challenging words may recall in another context Mary Wollstonecraft's assertion of the moral advantages of independence: "it is a farce to call any being virtuous whose virtues do not result from the exercise of its own reason" (21). Against this, the creature's words to Frankenstein, "Make me happy, and I will again be virtuous" (95), strike a note of whining dependence, for the creature cannot take responsibility for his own actions or destiny, choosing Milton's patriarchal myth of creation instead.[11]   Mary Shelley makes her creature competent — prodigiously competent; but the patriarchal message of his education and the political and social context in which he receives it sap this native power and strength. He is made dependent and horrific, but, except in his taskmaster's eye, he does not come into the world so. Translating this into feminist terms, he suffers the fate of an educated young woman persuaded that beauty and submission are all she has to offer and equally convinced that she is too ugly ever to take up this only possible role. She, like the creature, misunderstands the problem, which is not lack of beauty, but acceptance of an oppressive ideology.

The creature thus has something in common with other anomalous, marginalized creatures of controversial human status: black people, wild men, idiots, orangutans, women (who, according to Mary Wollstonecraft's ironic account of Safie's father's religion, do not possess souls; *Rights of Woman* 19).[12] Political analysis must depend on some judgement of the creature's status, especially in the context of a novel written by the child of the authors of *Political Justice* and *A Vindication of the Rights of Woman*. In one place, Godwin seems to imply that virtue and educability have nothing to do with physical configuration: "Those moral causes that awaken the mind, that inspire sensibility, imagination and perseverance, are distributed without distinction to the tall or the dwarfish, the graceful or the deformed, the lynx-eyed or the blind" (1.4.33-34). Yet in another place, writing of perfectibility, he remarks, "every perfection or excellence that human beings are competent to conceive, human beings, *unless in cases that are palpably and unequivocally excluded by the structure of their frame*, are competent to attain" (1.5.59, emphasis added). It is tempting to regard the creature in *Frankenstein* as a handicapped person in today's terms, marginalized because of "the structure of [his] frame"; yet his deficiency, if we can call it that, is clearly not an intellectual one. The creature's dilemma is that he can be educated as "civil man" but that he cannot be accepted as such by society — or even by himself once he has learned certain social attitudes.[13]   The social skills he acquires, including knowledge of language, can lead only to consciousness of exclusion. He is therefore the victim of a compelling ethnocentrism, a revulsion based on recognition of something sufficiently like one's self to be disturbing. Significantly, the creature does not shrink from his own image until *after* he has accepted the "perfect forms of [his] cottagers" (109) as normative.

The monster moves from his creator's "work-shop of filthy creation" (50) to begin his life in nature, but, if we can accept Walton's account of

Frankenstein's confession, his relationship to nature is anomalous. He has been assembled by an obsessive, solitary, male scientist out of debris from the grave and knowledge wrested from Nature's secret recesses. Thus, while he is as natural as any other living thing in the conformity of his being to Holbachian natural principles, he is the child of rape, snatched without birth from the tomb/womb of Nature and rejected by his father. Seeking unconsciously to return to maternal Nature, he sleeps in the forest and feeds himself on berries, enlightened and comforted by the moon and frightening himself with his own inarticulate cries. His salvation lies in flight from the father, in his growing familiarity with his place in nature.

But he also has the capacity to learn as the rest of us learn, or as mankind might have learned in the slow progress or fall from a state of nature to one of civilization: he distinguishes objects from one another, learns the nature and use of fire, and discovers the pleasures of shelter and society. In Rousseau's terms, he discovers wants that, in the perplexity of his first awakening, he had never dreamed of. Learning from his observations of the De Laceys, he comes to attach names to objects, he models his speech and behavior on human examples, and at last he learns to read. In doing all these things he learns that he is both like a human being and unlike a human being. He has neither father nor mother to teach him who he is, and so the particular books that the De Laceys – and Mary Shelley – make available to him are crucial in forming his sense of identity.

There is no clear political or social conclusion to be drawn from the creature's reading, for all of it (except Volney's *The Ruins of Empires*, which is quite explicitly radical) may be and has been given more than one interpretation, and Volney explicitly treats the problem of a multiplicity of ideas and beliefs. The presence of *Paradise Lost* in the monster's reading list and in the novel as a whole is an obvious example of this point, for there is more than one reading of Milton even in *Frankenstein* itself, as the creature identifies himself now with Adam, now with "the fallen angel, whom [Frankenstein drives] from joy for no misdeed" (95), and as he regards his "creator" now as divine, now as demonic. The monster cannot at the same time be both innocent, virtuous, vegetarian, natural man *and* be a demonic outcast.[14] Yet he considers himself to be both, and is destroyed by the same perplexities that confuse the reader.

In *A Vindication of the Rights of Woman* Mary Wollstonecraft attacks Milton for insisting on Eve's subservience to Adam. This attack provides an obvious precedent for a subversive treatment of Milton in *Frankenstein*. And the very presence of an epigraph from *Paradise Lost* —

> Did I request thee, Maker, from my clay
> To mould me man? Did I solicit thee
> From darkness to promote me?
>
> (10.743-745)

— next to Mary Shelley's dedication of her novel to Godwin indicates that she was aware of the ambivalence of devotion and reproach in the relation of children to fathers or creatures to Creator: Adam's complaining stance is balanced by Mary Shelley's own dutiful acknowledgement of the respect she owes to her father.[15] I see subversion in the effects of the creature's initial, conservative reading of Milton's text. In spite of the influence of Volney, which might have made him scorn Milton's religion and his domestic authoritarianism, in spite of what most critics see as the salutary example of the De Lacey family, with their sexual equality and radical political ideas, the monster reads *Paradise Lost* as an interpretation of his own condition:

> It moved every feeling of wonder and awe, that the picture of an omnipotent God warring with his creatures was capable of exciting.... [Adam] had come forth from the hands of God a perfect creature, happy and prosperous, guarded by the especial care of his Creator; he was allowed to converse with, and acquire knowledge from beings of a superior nature: but I was wretched, helpless, and alone. Many times I considered Satan as the fitter emblem of my condition.... (125)

Amazingly, having drawn these analogies between his own condition and that of Milton's characters, the creature continues to believe everything he reads — even though his texts clash with one another continually. Constructing his sense of self and his theory of origin, the creature reads rewritings of the book of Genesis and collaborates in a conservative reading of an authorized version.[16]

Other scholars have shown how the word "monster" is used by both parties during the revolutionary period in a way that recalls Blake's play with the words "angel" and "devil" and his reading of *Paradise Lost* in *The Marriage of Heaven and Hell*.[17] Radical philosophers like Mary Wollstonecraft make the monster a despot, an "artificial monster" made so "by the station in which he was born" (*A Vindication of the Rights of Men* 73). The conservative, on the other hand, makes the monster a mob and idealizes the ruler, as Burke idealizes Louis XVI and Marie

Antoinette in his *Reflections on the Revolution in France* (90-92).[18] These two versions of the story of power are incompatible with each other.

But the monster in *Frankenstein* reads books that have incompatible views of the nature of power, and he claims to accept them all as true histories. His fascination with the content of *Paradise Lost* reinforces his tendency to treat text as revelation. Accepting *Paradise Lost* as a true history, he will obviously accept Frankenstein's journal entry—his creator's revelation of the creative act—as a parody or perhaps an antitype of Milton's account of creation. "You, doubtless, recollect these papers," he tells Frankenstein, "Here they are. Every thing is related in them which bears reference to my accursed origin" (126).[19] Believing in revelation, he is assured of his own powerlessness.

He might, however, have adopted some alternative to Milton's myth of origin. Volney writes vividly about the races of mankind: "A race of men now rejected from society for their *sable skin and frizzled hair*, founded on the study of the laws of nature, those civil and religious systems which still govern the universe" (17). It never seems to occur to the creature to take pride in his difference, regarding it as a source of strength; but *Frankenstein* was banned in South Africa in 1955, a fact that underlines the racial implications of the conversation between the creature and De Lacey, with its repetition of forms of the word "prejudice" and its emphasis on De Lacey's physical blindness (O'Flinn 196). Other plausible analogues to the creature are found in texts that haunt the fringes of the narrative—other versions of Genesis in a variety of eighteenth-century works on race, society, and the nature of man.[20]

But the creature believes the convenient account of his own creation he finds in a pocket of his clothes (125-26). This text (inaccessible to all other readers) at the heart of interlocking texts becomes a kind of conservative backlash against any of the liberating or radicalizing effects of the creature's education—as revelation repeatedly is for conservative thinkers of the revolutionary period. For Samuel Horsley, for example, "the Christian is possessed of a written rule of conduct, delivered from on high." Horsley's answer to all challenges of authority is God's word, which refutes the possibility of a natural state except as a miserable fall from a divinely ordained social order:

> The Providence of God was careful to give a beginning to the Human Race in that particular way, which might for ever bar the existence of the whole, or of any large portion as of mankind, in that state which hath been called the State of Nature. Mankind, from the beginning never existed otherwise, than in Society, and under Government. (143)

For the monster who has learned to read, Frankenstein's journal entry with its account of his origin becomes all-too-scriptural, proof of his weak and dependent status. On the face of it, this is just clumsy plotting. But documentary evidence and the claims of the written word are important subjects in the novel, and the author's relation to *her* authorities is as important as the authority she imposes on the creature. Mary Shelley identifies with her hideous progeny at the same time as she collaborates in the misconstruction of his identity.

The creature accepts only those ideas that contribute to his dependent status. Mary Shelley, however, is a better reader than the creature: she adopts such ideas as suit her fiction—Rousseau's or Volney's child of nature, radical critiques of oppression and despotism, ideas (including those of both her parents) about the importance of education as a social tool. Thus she acknowledges a debt to her parents and admits her intellectual heritage. But her mother, Mary Wollstonecraft, insists on a woman's right to a life free from patriarchal oppression; Mary Shelley, as if in reply, shows that her creature is oppressed and dependent in ways similar to those described in *A Vindication of the Rights of Woman*. Mary Wollstonecraft condemns Milton for his treatment of Eve; Mary Shelley shows how the creature's treatment by his creator is also destructively condescending. Mary Wollstonecraft attacks Rousseau's prescription for Sophie's education; Mary Shelley transforms Sophie into Safie, whose mother had taught her well, though—in her rejection of the creature, her fellow-alien—perhaps not well enough.

Thus, indirectly and often silently, the mother's teaching is restored to *Frankenstein*, partly to reinforce the father's word and partly to challenge it. But it is not restored to the creature's experience. Knowing how to read far better than her creature does, Mary Shelley still identifies with his trapped, frustrated condition. If the creature is Mary Shelley's "hideous progeny," as the woman writer identifies in part with the pseudo-creative role of Frankenstein, he is also her other self, the outcast dependent on the father who has rejected him/her. Continually pointing to the suppressed but life-giving mother (Holbach's nature, Mary Shelley herself), and to the educative mother conspicuous by her absence (Mary Wollstonecraft), both creature and text resist definitive interpretation, suggesting more ambivalence than they admit directly.

Provided with texts that might have promoted an independent view of self, the creature is assured of his dependence. Given a curriculum that might have taught him that belief is enslavement, he chooses to worship or to war with his creator. Provided with sufficient information to distrust his father, he collaborates with the father/creator he half creates and, in doing so, distorts the role of the mother. Like Rousseau in the *Confessions* and like Frankenstein in his relationship with Elizabeth, the creature confuses the mother with the lover. His reading offers him precedents for doing so: Eve may be the mother of the human race, but she is more centrally the lovely, incompletely submissive object of male desire; Lotte (in *Werther*) is the mother-sister of a brood of children, evidently an ideal of romantic/maternal love for the creature as well as an influence on Mary Shelley's depiction of Elizabeth. When the creature bends over the body of William (139), he is filled with the murderous rage of fruitless desire by a miniature of Frankenstein's *mother* — not of Elizabeth, with whom she is confused even by Frankenstein himself.

Mary Shelley knows (perhaps from her own experience) that education goes wrong when the mother is missing or when her relation to the child is distorted. In *Frankenstein*, the De Laceys have no mother — and the word "daughter" is also missing from the monster's list of words pertaining to relationships (107-08). The omission is a familiar one: in *Emile*, Rousseau addresses the "[t]ender, anxious mother" (5) who ought to exert an important role in the education of the child, and then takes over all such responsibility himself; in his *The Law of Nature* — in spite of a long footnote to *The Ruins of Empires* attacking patriarchy (33-34) — Volney defines paternal love, conjugal love, filial love, and fraternal love, but ignores maternal love completely, as if it is either insignificant or obvious (199-200).

Mary Shelley thus identifies with the creature's search for his origins even while, in her role as author (identifying with Frankenstein as creator and with Milton as teacher), she herself forms and deforms the hideous progeny. The creature in *Frankenstein* is given little access to the mother through his education. Although his attempt to make contact with his benevolent foster-father, De Lacey, is frustrated, he has learned a myth of fatherhood that leads him to assign to Frankenstein the role of divine creator. His relation to Frankenstein is ambivalent rather as Mary Shelley's relation to Godwin is ambivalent, a mixture of devotion and resentment.

The romantic hero — Werther-like lover of Elizabeth, man of virtue and sensibility, Mary Shelley's idealized version of Shelley — replaces the white-haired old man who rejects the creature and who shakes his faith in the benevolence of fatherhood. Mary Shelley responds ambivalently to her own father's words because Godwin is both the oppressive personal tyrant whom she has left behind and also the radical philosopher, enemy of oppression and tyranny, her own biological parent and Percy Bysshe Shelley's intellectual father. It is tempting to speculate that, in her identification with the creature, she is ambivalent not only to Godwin/De Lacey (father) but also to Shelley himself, the model for the creature's idealizing construction of Frankenstein. Held together by the (inadequate) Miltonic archetype of the father/creator and the (equally inadequate) Romantic archetype of the hero of sensibility, the male figures in *Frankenstein* construct in spite of themselves a world based on tyranny, not love.

I began this essay with two quotations from Wordsworth, whose role as intellectual parent is more obvious and far more often celebrated than Godwin's in forming the second generation of English Romantic writers.[21] Wordsworth imagines (in the 1802 Preface to *Lyrical Ballads*) a humanized science, transfigured by the power of poetry—a power associated with love, as it is by Percy Bysshe Shelley in *Prometheus Unbound*. Elsewhere, in the Essay Supplementary to the Preface (1815), Wordsworth shows that he understands the general problem of overcoming a conservative but inadequate education: the "mistaught" conspire in perpetuating their own errors because they are formed by such errors. Denied through an ideology of patriarchal power the alternative humanizing power of love, and unable to construct a self adequate to the world of his experience, the creature in *Frankenstein* is doomed as much by his education as by his origin. In denying his place in nature, in denying his independence as a child of nature, in giving him as teachers no nurse but *only* figures of authority and power (De Lacey, Frankenstein, Milton), Mary Shelley denies her creature education in the sense of nurture.[22] Surrogate self or neglected child, the creature moves us because he can resemble in an extreme and exaggerated way the victim of any social, political or educational system—which is to say the one most dependent on system. Taught to read, he is taught to know his rights and to recognize that, in the world of things as they are, such rights are illusory. We might think that it would have been better for him had he never learned to read; but in doing so we join the ranks of those who reject him and would wish the unmaking of all misfits. In discovering how inconsistent are the fragments that make him up, and in understanding the incompatibility between benevolent theory and Safie's fainting revulsion when she glimpses him, the reader as teacher and as former student can perhaps share the writer's ambivalence by recognizing her own role as oppressor—manipulating texts for authoritarian ends—as well as her own sympathy, even identity, with the perplexity of the oppressed and dependent.

Notes

1. Shelley and Mary Godwin married on 30 December 1816, following Harriet Shelley's suicide earlier that month (*Journal* 71).

2. The reading lists are in Mary Shelley's *Journal*, 1815 (47-49). There is no list for 1819.

3. I am thinking of Rousseau's ambivalence in the *Confessions* to his relationship with Mme de Warens: "I felt as if I had committed incest" (189); "I had a tender mother, a dear friend; but I needed a mistress. In my imagination I put one in Mamma's place, endowing her with a thousand shapes in order to deceive myself" (210). In *Frankenstein* not only is the sister/lover (Elizabeth) confused with the mother – in Frankenstein's macabre dream on the night of the monster's animation – but both are confused through associations of death with the creature constructed out of fragments from the grave. The following passage from Paine's *Common Sense* suggests a political context for the horror created by such confusion: "This new world [America] hath been the asylum for the persecuted lovers of civil and religious liberty from *every part* of Europe. Hither have they fled, not from the tender embraces of the mother, but from the cruelty of the monster..." (19).

4. It is interesting that Victor Frankenstein, whether by chance or design, has the wild boy's name.

5. He gets a middle-class education by chance, and it is tempting to think that he would have been better off without it. But Tom Paine's *Rights of Man* provides food for thought: "A nation under a well regulated government should permit none to remain uninstructed. It is monarchical and aristocratical governments only, that require ignorance for their support" (*The Complete Writings* 428).

6. Diderot's definition of "monstre" might also exclude Frankenstein's creature. According to the *Encyclopédie*, a monster is an "animal qui naît... avec une structure de parties très différentes de celles qui caractérisent l'espèce des animaux dont il sort," an animal "bizarre par la grandeur disproportionnée" (166). Frankenstein's creature is ugly and disgusting, but he has all the attributes of a human being and Frankenstein claims, "His limbs were in proportion, and I had selected his features as beautiful" (52).

7. "It did not even enter the minds of most of our philosophers to doubt that the state of nature had existed, even though it is evident from reading the Holy Scriptures that the first man, having received enlightenment and precepts directly from God, was not himself in that state" (*Discourse on Inequality* 102-03).

8. Mary Shelley's Introduction to the Third Edition (1831), in *Frankenstein* 229.

9. The monster ascribes to the example of the De Laceys his preference for "peaceable lawgivers" (124) in the early *Lives* of Plutarch over more warlike heroes. But he understands that in different circumstances he could admire the exploits of a bloodier heroism.

10. Volney insists that religious dogma originates in apprehension of "the physical powers of the universe," and that "the idea of God has not been a miraculous revelation of invisible beings, but a natural offspring of the human intellect" (113). The creature begins by responding to the powers of the natural world, but his education soon teaches him to substitute belief in external, authoritative revelation.

11. The connection between happiness and virtue is, of course, commonplace. But Holbach has it the other way round: "The virtuous man is always happy" (349).

12. The status of orangutans was a matter of debate in the eighteenth century. See Rousseau's notes to the *Discourse on Inequality*: "Without ceremony our travelers take for beasts, under the names *pongos, mandrills, orangutans*, the same beings that the ancients, under the names

satyrs, fauns, sylvans, took for divinities. Perhaps, after more precise research, it will be found that they are neither animals nor gods, but men" (209). According to James Burnet, Lord Monboddo (1.187-88), they were in fact members of the human species. Monboddo argues this on the basis of their educability and their presumed capacity for speech. For a good discussion of the literature on this subject, see Aarsleff.

13. This is another way in which he is different from a "monster," for Diderot shows that such creatures are entitled to legal rights and protections and are thus members of civil society.

14. Such confusion about his own nature and role is apparent in the following passage: "[The hut] presented to me then as exquisite and divine a retreat as Pandemonium appeared to the daemons of hell after their sufferings in the lake of fire. I greedily devoured the remnants of the shepherd's breakfast, which consisted of bread, cheese, milk, and wine; the latter, however, I did not like" (101).

15. Godwin writes crisply and dryly about the limitations of "parental and filial affection": "I must take care not so to love, or so to obey my love to my parent or child, as to entrench upon an important and paramount public good" ("Thoughts Occasioned by the Perusal of Dr. Parr's Spital Sermon, Preached at Christ Church, April 15, 1800," *Enquiry* 323). But this utilitarian attitude, considered together with Godwin's atheism, must be balanced against his description of Milton as "the most advantageous specimen that can be produced of the English nation" *(Lives of Edward and John Philips, Nephews and Pupils of Milton*, quoted in Marshall 312). Mary Shelley's dedication of *Frankenstein* to her father reads as follows: "To WILLIAM GODWIN / Author of Political Justice, Caleb Williams & c. / These Volumes / Are respectfully inscribed / by / The Author."

16. The creature is, of course, denied some texts — such as *Emile* and the *Discourse on Inequality* — that are, as Professor Aubrey Rosenberg points out in this volume, "rewriting[s] of the book of Genesis." But constructing and revising theories and myths of origin — political, personal, linguistic — is perhaps the central project of the enlightenment. I simply argue that the creature gives up too soon.

17. Angels are conventional moralizers; energy, passion, and imagination belong in hell with all the interesting people. Milton, in Blake's famous phrase in *The Marriage of Heaven and Hell*, was "of the Devils party without knowing it" (Plate 5). Blake assumes that the energy and power of *Paradise Lost* are in the scenes of hell, and that the reader's attention is engaged most strongly not by the scenes in heaven, but by Satan. Who is the monster in *Paradise Lost*? a punishing tyrant-God, or a justified rebel? The same question can obviously apply to *Frankenstein* and to many other revolutionary and Romantic texts.

18. See also Sterrenburg, which sees a shift in the use of language in Frankenstein from the political to the psychological, and O'Flinn, which makes political issues central again.

19. A less theological, more scientific creature might have regarded these journal entries as a blueprint for constructing his *own* female counterpart. The fact that this possibility never seems to occur to anyone indicates how unquestioningly reader and characters accept the given patriarchal mythology.

20. In Rousseau's *Discourse on the Sciences and Arts*, he tells a story about Prometheus to emphasize his point about the ambivalence of knowledge: "'The satyr,' an ancient fable relates, 'wanted to kiss and embrace fire the first time he saw it; but Prometheus cried out to him: Satyr, you will mourn the beard on your chin, for fire burns when one touches it'" (48 n.). This story, the subject of the frontispiece to Rousseau's discourse, suggests one role for the creature in *Frankenstein*: see his description of his first experience with fire, 99-100. Accounts of first experiences with fire are prominent in many contemporary accounts of savages and their relation to civilized society.

21. In addition to the more general influence of Wordsworth on the language of *Frankenstein*, Mary Shelley twice quotes substantially from poems in *Lyrical Ballads*: "The Rime of the Ancient Mariner" (54), and "Tintern Abbey" (154).

22. Rousseau quotes a useful distinction from Varro (though Rousseau attempts to reunite the different functions): "'Educit obstetrix,' says Varro. *'Educat nutrix*, instituit paedagogus, docet magister'" (*Emile* 9-10; emphasis added).

Works Cited

Aarsleff, Hans. "An Outline of Language-Origins Theory since the Renaissance," *From Locke to Saussure: Essays on the Study of Language and Intellectual History*. Minneapolis: University of Minnesota Press, 1982. 278-92.

Burke, Edmund. *Reflections on the Revolution in France*. Ed. William B. Todd. New York: Holt Rinehart, 1959.

Burnet, James, Lord Monboddo. *The Origin and Progress of Language*, 6 vols. Edinburgh, 1773-1792.

Butler, Marilyn, ed. *Burke, Paine, Godwin, and the Revolution Controversy*. Cambridge: Cambridge University Press, 1984.

Diderot, Denis. "Monstre." *Encyclopédie, ou Dictionnaire Raisonné des sciences, des arts et des métiers*. Geneva, 1778. XXII, 166-70.

Godwin, William. *Enquiry Concerning Political Justice, with selections from Godwin's other writings*. Abridged and ed. K. Codell Carter. Oxford: Clarendon, 1971.

Goethe, Johann Wolfgang von. *The Sorrows of Young Werther and Selected Writings*. Trans. Catherine Hutter. Foreword by Hermann J. Weigand. New York: New American Library, 1962.

Holbach, Paul Heinrich Dietrich, Baron d'. *The System of Nature, or Laws of the Moral and Physical World*. Trans. H. D. Robinson. New York: Franklin, n.d.

Horsley, Samuel. "A Sermon Preached Before the Lords Spiritual and Temporal. . . on. . . January 30, 1793." Butler 142-44.

Itard, Jean Marc Gaspard. *The Wild Boy of Aveyron*. New York: Appleton-Century-Crofts, 1962.

Knoepflmacher, U.C. "Thoughts on the Aggression of Daughters." Levine and Knoepflmacher 88-119.

Levine, George and U. C. Knoepflmacher, eds. *The Endurance of Frankenstein: Essays on Mary Shelley's Novel*. Berkeley: University of California Press, 1979.

Marshall, Peter H. *William Godwin*. New Haven: Yale University Press, 1984.

Milton, John. *Paradise Lost. John Milton: Complete Poems and Major Prose*. Ed. Merritt Y. Hughes. Indianapolis: Bobbs-Merrill, 1957.

Moers, Ellen. "Female Gothic." Levine and Knoepflmacher 77-87.

O'Flinn, Paul. "Production and Reproduction: the case of *Frankenstein*." *Popular Fictions: Essays in Literature and History*. Ed. Peter Humm, Paul Stigant and Peter Widdowson. London: Methuen, 1986. 196-221.

Paine, Thomas. *The Complete Writings of Thomas Paine*. Ed. Philip S. Foner. New York: Citadel, 1945.

Plutarch. *Lives*. Vol. I: Theseus and Romulus, Lycurgus and Numa, Solon and Publicola. Trans. Bernadette Perrin. London: Heinemann, 1959.

Rousseau, Jean-Jacques. *Emile*. Trans. Barbara Foxley. Introd. André Boutet de Monvel. London: Dent, 1911.

Rousseau, Jean-Jacques. *The Confessions*. Trans. J. M. Cohen. Harmondsworth: Penguin, 1953.

Rousseau, Jean-Jacques. *The First and Second Discourses (Discourse on the Sciences and Arts* and *Discourse on the Origin and Foundations of Inequality Among Men)*. Trans. Roger D. and Judith R. Masters. Ed. Roger D. Masters. New York: St. Martin's, 1964.

Scott, Peter Dale. "Vital Artifice." Levine and Knoepflmacher 172-202.

Shelley, Mary. *Frankenstein, or, The Modern Prometheus. The 1818 Text*. Ed. James Rieger. Indianapolis and New York: Bobbs-Merrill, 1974.

Shelley, Mary. *Mary Shelley's Journal*. Ed. Frederick L. Jones. Norman: University of Oklahoma Press, 1947.

Smith, Olivia. *The Politics of Language 1791-1819*. Oxford: Clarendon, 1984.

Smith, Samuel Stanhope. *An Essay on the Causes of the Variety of Complexion and Figure in the Human Species*. Enlarged ed. 1810 Cambridge, MA: Belknap, 1965.

Sterrenburg, Lee. "Mary Shelley's Monster: Politics and Psyche in *Frankenstein*." Levine and Knoepflmacher 143-71.

Volney, C. F. *The Ruins, or, Meditations on the Revolutions of Empires: and The Law of Nature*. New York: Truth Seeker, 1950.

Wollstonecraft, Mary. *A Vindication of the Rights of Woman*. Ed. Carol H. Poston. New York and London: Norton, 1988.

Wollstonecraft, Mary. *A Vindication of the Rights of Men* [1790]. Butler 72-74.

Wordsworth, William. *The Prose Works of William Wordsworth*. Ed. W. J. B. Owen and J. W. Smyser. 3 vols. Oxford: Clarendon, 1974.

Chapter 5

NINETEENTH-CENTURY ROMANTIC AND NEO-ROMANTIC THOUGHT AND SOME DISTURBING TWENTIETH-CENTURY APPLICATIONS

Clarence J. Karier

In the film *Cabaret* there is a dramatic scene in a rural German cafe in which a small group of young people are singing a song which portrays a quiet, highly romanticized pastoral scene. Peace and tranquillity abound, signifying sleep. However, within a few short lines the image is broken as the child is awakened to his future destiny, a destiny made clear by his fatherland. The camera sweeps the cafe and the young people are all standing singing louder and louder in unison with uniformed Hitler youth, swastikas and all. The words may help recall that scene:

The sun on the meadow is summery warm
The stag in the forest runs free
But gathered together to greet the sun
Tomorrow belongs to me
The branch of the linden
is sleepy and green
The Rhine gives its glow to the sea
But somewhere a glory
awaits unseen
Tomorrow belongs to me
The babe in his cradle
is closing his eyes
The blossoms embrace the bees
But soon there's a whisper
Arise, arise
Tomorrow belongs to me
Oh Fatherland, Fatherland, show us a sign
Your children have waited to see
The morning will come when the world is mine
Tomorrow belongs

Tomorrow belongs
Tomorrow belongs to me.[1]

This scene captures and foreshadows the ominous spirit of National Socialist youth emerging from a *volkish* background.[2] The pastoral symbols of forest, river, blossoms and bees, along with a babe in the cradle, all set the Romantic mood from which youth must be awakened to claim their world. Romanticism abounds here. It is, of course, a peculiar Romanticism and, some might argue, a very distorted kind. Nevertheless, in retrospect, it is clear that certain Romantic ideas, conceptions, values and views of reality helped fuel the flames that seared the world in the first half of this century. The relatively benign Romantic movement that swept European thought in the early nineteenth century was by the end of that century well within the darker, more virulent shadows of the primitive unconscious. The world of Wordsworth, Goethe, and Emerson was a very different world from that of Schopenhauer, Nietzsche, Wagner, or Jung and yet the later thought emerged from the former. While the road from Weimar to Buchenwald is geographically short, symbolically it is a considerable distance.

In this essay I will briefly examine selected ideas of Jean-Jacques Rousseau and turn quickly to the thought of Ralph Waldo Emerson as an early nineteenth-century American romantic, and then by way of contrast consider some of the ideas of G. Stanley Hall as a later American neo-romantic. Lastly, I will consider how some of these ideas found their way into the psychotherapy of Carl Jung and the literature of Hermann Hesse which proved so popular among German youth during the National Socialist era.

Traditionally, most educators have pointed to Jean-Jacques Rousseau's *Emile* as the cornerstone of educational Romanticism. Rousseau introduced the age of the child in his call for an education according to the nature of the child. This education usually was interpreted as highly individualistic and child-centred, offering a considerable degree of freedom. However, since World War II a growing number of thinkers have pointed to the fact that the education of *Emile* can be interpreted to mean just the opposite.[3] In the end when Emile begs his tutor not to leave him, it would seem to indicate that Emile is not a free person nor is his spouse, Sophie. Both appear to be enslaved by their tutor who manages to control their entire environment and ultimately their very will as persons. Many who take this tack also point to the fact that this interpretation of the *Emile* fits better with Rousseau's other writings such as the *Social Contract* wherein the general will rules supreme and one may be forced to be free. More important still was his *Consideration on the Government of Poland*, where he fashioned what amounts to a totalitarian system of education in which the fatherland is supreme:

> It is education that must give the souls of the people a national form, and so shape their opinions and their tastes that they become patriots as much by inclination and passion as by necessity. A child ought to look upon his fatherland as soon as his eyes open to the light, and should continue to do so till the day of his death. Every true patriot sucks in the love of country with his mother's milk. This love is his whole existence. He thinks of nothing but his country. He lives only for his country. Take him by himself, and he counts for nothing. If his country ceases to exist, so also does he. If not dead, he is worse than dead. (97)

While Alexander von Humbolt, in *Limits of State Action*, detailed the dangers of a state-imposed education and John Stuart Mill followed suit, Johann Gottlieb Fichte in his *Addresses to the German Nation* heeded Rousseau and established a blueprint of the educational state. It was that system of education which, when once implemented, managed to produce such great reverence for fatherland and state. German Romanticism, whether it appeared in the highly rationalized philosophic idealism of Hegel lecturing at the university or the nursery rhymes of the kindergarten, permeated German culture and German rationalism in all its aspects. The person who best represented that culture was a poet rather than a philosopher. As Emerson put it, Goethe was the "representative man" of German culture. It was Goethe who led so many into the exploration of the unconscious. Goethe's Faust remained a recurring German dream, touching the soul of the German nation.

Ralph Waldo Emerson

On the nineteenth century American cultural stage, it was Ralph Waldo Emerson, son of a Unitarian minister, who emerged as the representative figure. Surrounded by the remnants of his not-too-distant Puritan past, Emerson shook loose from his immediate Unitarianism to espouse his own highly Romanticized transcendental view of the world. Forced to give up the pulpit because of those views, he went on to become one of America's most popular speakers during the mid-century. While people would not listen to what he had to say on Sunday, they were interested every other day of the week. He became, in a way, America's minister-at-large. Emerson preached his moral lessons to a new frontier nation, a nation that successfully rationalized killing Indians in the name of "free land" and enslaved black people while cultivating a national self image as a land of opportunity and freedom for all the weak and downtrodden of the earth.

America was a land of extreme contradictions, of regional, sectarian and ethnic differences unified in one principle – the unabashed pursuit of wealth. It was to that nation that Emerson became teacher, preacher, and in many ways its conscience. Repeatedly, he reminded his countrymen that life was more important than the material things they sought:

> When I heard the Earth-song,
> I was no longer brave;
> My avarice cooled
> Like lust in the chill of the grave. *(Works* 87)

He insisted there was more to life than building railroads, canals, and bridges, and conquering a wilderness. Although he loved the solitude of his study, he was forever being drawn out into the world of action that he knew enslaved mankind:

> The horseman serves the horse,
> The neatherd serves the neat,
> The merchant serves the purse,
> The eater serves the meat;
> 'Tis the day of the chattel,
> Web to weave, and corn to grind;
> Things are in the saddle,
> And ride mankind. *(Works* 73)

Looking out on a hurried, bustling America bent on becoming the most materialistic nation of the world he reminded his fellows:

> There are two laws discrete,
> Not reconciled, –
> Law for man, and law for thing;
> The last builds town and fleet,
> But it runs wild,
> And doth the man unking. *(Works* 73)

Although "things were in the saddle and appeared to ride mankind," Emerson insisted the law for man represented the higher law. It was that law which mirrored the spark of the divine that existed in all souls, and under such circumstances he urged his countrymen to look into their own souls to find the secrets of all souls. Humanity, he believed, was linked to all living souls in the form of an "Over-Soul" in which all participated. Having carefully studied Plotinus, Porphyry and Iamblichus, Emerson was at home with the neo-platonists who saw their world through mystical eyes. Emerson, too, had such a vision:

I become a transparent eyeball; I am nothing; I see all; the currents of the Universal Being circulate through me; I am part or parcel of God. The name of the nearest friend sounds then foreign and occidental: to be brothers, to be acquaintances, master or servant, is then a trifle and a disturbance. I am the lover of uncontained and immortal beauty. In the wilderness, I find something more dear and connate than in streets or villages. In the tranquil landscape, and especially in the distant line of the horizon, man beholds somewhat as beautiful as his own nature. (*Five Essays* 4)

Emerson found his God in nature and the beauty of the human soul. His God was a loving, benign God that reflected the beauty of the universe. The child born into this universe came forth as something new and different with a spark of the divine mission:

Trust thyself: every heart vibrates to that iron string. Accept the place the divine providence has found for you, the society of your contemporaries, the connection of events. (*Complete Writings* 138)

Every individual is a unique identity which must find expression:

There is a time in every man's education when he arrives at the conviction that envy is ignorance; that imitation is suicide; that he must take himself for better for worse as his portion. The power which resides in him is new in nature, and none but he knows what this is which he can do, nor does he know until he has tried. (138)

He insisted that one must listen to the voice within and not mistake the compromises one makes in daily life for that which is truly sacred:

Society everywhere is in conspiracy against the manhood of every one of its members. Society is a joint-stock company in which the members agree, for the better securing of his bread to each shareholder, to surrender the liberty and culture of the eater. The virtue in most requests is conformity. Self reliance is its aversion. It loves not realities and creators, but names and customs. Who so would be a man, must be a nonconformist . . . . Nothing is at last sacred but the integrity of your own mind. (139)

Emerson pitted himself against every form of constraint including that of the mind itself. To those who were constrained by the mental lash of consistency he offered a warning:

A foolish consistency is the hobgoblin of little minds, adored by little statesmen and philosophers and divines. With consistency a great soul has simply nothing to do. (141-142)

To those who feared to speak lest they be misunderstood, he pointed to the historical fact that Socrates, Jesus, Luther, and Galileo were all misunderstood and therefore concluded: "To be great is to be misunderstood" (142). Emerson was essentially saying what William Shakespeare had previously said, "to thine own self be true."

In the end it was his frequent house guest, gardener, and close friend, Henry David Thoreau, who in his famous essay on "Civil Disobedience" defined the limits of individualism. Shedding the last restraint, Thoreau argued long before Franklin Delano Roosevelt plagiarized his work: "we have nothing to fear but fear itself" (468). American transcendentalism defined and called forth an American individualism bordering, some would argue, on near anarchy. To Emerson it was not anarchy. He knew that within the soul of every individual was a part of the Over-Soul which served as a guiding spirit for each person.

It was this kind of belief system which laid the foundation for Emerson's classic essay "Education." In it he advised teachers in a Romantic vein:

> The great object of education should be to inspire the youthful man with an interest in himself; with a curiosity touching his own nature; to acquaint himself with the resources of his mind, and to teach him that there is all his strength. (*Writings* 986)

Because the child has a destiny all its own to fulfill, Emerson implored the would-be educator to take heed:

> Nature, when she sends a new mind into the world, fills it beforehand with a desire for that which she wishes it to know and do. Let us wait and see what is this new creation, of what new organ the great Spirit had need when it incarnated this new Will. A new Adam in the garden, he is to name all beasts in the field, all the gods in the sky. (988)

The new Adam was to be realized in that next generation not by teachers shaping and molding new minds, but rather by assisting those minds in coming into their own. Emerson gave his most important advice to teachers when he said:

> I believe that our own experience instructs us that the secret of Education lies in respecting the pupil. It is not for you to choose what he shall know, what he shall do. It is chosen and foreordained, and he only holds the key to his own secret. By your tampering and thwarting and too much governing he may be hindered from his end and kept out of his own. Respect the child. Wait and see the new product of Nature. Nature loves analogies,

but not repetitions. Respect the child. Be not too much his parent. Trespass not on his solitude. (991)

Repeatedly he cautioned against trying to make the student over into the image of the teacher. To those would-be tyrants of the mind he complained: "You are trying to make that man another you. One's enough" (991). At the very heart of Emerson's philosophy of education was a belief in a divine spirit which was to be realized in each living soul.

These beliefs were not easily derived and adopted solely in the sunshine of life, but for Emerson they were tested and developed through the darker corridors of life's tragedies as well. The first great tragedy of his life came with the death of his first wife, Ellen, whom he deeply loved. Grieved by his loss, Emerson struggled with the meaning of death and longed to make contact with her soul. Just ten months after her death he quoted in his journal Ellen's poem, "The Violet":

When winter reigned I'd close my eye, but wake with bursting spring
And live with living Nature, a pure rejoicing thing.

(qtd. in Allen 178)

Emerson wrote in his journal:

O friend, that said these words, are you conscious of this thought and this winter? I would not ask any other consolation than to be assured by one sign that the heart never plays false to itself when in its scope it requires by a necessity the permanence of the soul. (qtd. in Allen 178)

He was struggling with death as the eternal dividing line between spirit and matter. A few days later he wrote: "How we come out of silence into this sounding world is the wonder of wonders. All other marvels are less" (qtd. in Allen 178). By January he was struggling with his dreams: "Dreams and beasts are two keys by which we are to find out the secrets of our own nature. All mystics use them. They are like comparative anatomy. They are test objects" (qtd. in Allen 183). Just a few months later on March 29, 1832 after having visited Ellen's tomb daily for over a year Emerson wrote in his journal: "I visited Ellen's tomb and opened the coffin" (qtd. in Allen 182). No further entries regarding Ellen follow. The following year he resigned his pastorate and travelled to Europe, meeting Coleridge, Carlyle and Wordsworth, then returned to America as one of its leading cultural scholars and teachers.

In the depth of despair, Emerson had explored his unconscious in search of spiritual eternity. Like Goethe and Freud who followed later, Emerson said:

> Dreams have a poetic integrity and truth. Their extravagance
> from nature is yet within a higher nature. They seem to suggest an
> abundance and fluency of thought not familiar to the waking
> experience. (*Writings* 950)

Emerson had probed the limits of sanity and touched the secrets of the
unconscious world of time and space especially in his discussion of the
"Over-Soul:"

> The influence of the senses has in most men overpowered the
> mind to that degree that the walls of time and space have come to
> look real and unsurmountable; and to speak with levity of these
> limits is, in the world, the sign of insanity. Yet time and space are
> but inverse measures of the force of the soul. The spirit sports
> with time,
>> Can crowd eternity into an hour,
>> or shelter an hour to eternity.   (207)

Emerson had indeed walked on the darker side of life and explored its
shadows. He had considered the demonological and disagreed with
Goethe and others who invested so much in its mysteries (952). The
world of devilish forces, the occult and the "monstrous proverb" of
"nobody against God but God" were but human creations (952).
Emerson concluded: "The demonologic is only a fine name for egotism;
an exaggeration namely of the individual, whom it is Nature's settled
purpose to postpone" (952).

Emerson would not invest demonology with supernatural powers as
Goethe had done and Jung would do in the twentieth century:
"Demonology is the shadow of theology. The whole world is an omen
and a sign. Why look so wistfully in a corner? Man is the Image of God"
(955). Emerson saw Goethe as the representative man of German
culture. Goethe was, he insisted, "the soul of his century" (405). While
giving him such an accolade, he still withheld his full endorsement, and in
the end he disagreed with him. He felt Goethe had lost sight of man as
an end. Culture had become the end. Goethe, Emerson surmised,
believed: "That a man exists for culture; not for what he can accomplish,
but for what can be accomplished in him. The reaction of things on the
man is the only noteworthy result" (*Representative* 208). Thus Emerson
insisted: "Goethe can never be dear to man. His is not even the
devotion to pure truth; but to truth for the sake of culture" (206).
Perhaps, as if in premonition of things to come when people would be
seen as existing for the state rather than the state for the people,
Emerson found what he believed was a fatal flaw in the thinking of this
most representative German cultural leader.

Although Emerson had not lost sight of the fact that the law for men must govern the law for things, his philosophy was not that of the cloister. He was intrigued by the building and bustle of a new nation, and he personally loved to ride the trains. Emerson lived through the very birth of American imperialism, and while he resisted it, he was in some ways very much a part of it. The belief in a unique American destiny, a destiny which would conquer the West, was present in Emerson's mind when he wrote in his journal:

> The question of the annexation of Texas is one of those which look very differently to the centuries and to the years. It is very certain that the strong British race which has now overrun much of this continent, must also overrun that tract, and Mexico and Oregon also, and it will in the course of ages be of small import by what particular occasions and methods it was done. It is a secular question. It is quite necessary and true to our New England character that we should consider the question in its local and temporary bearings, and resist the annexation with tooth and nail. (qtd. in Allen 444)

The destiny of America was being achieved by theft, plunder and slaughter over the protests of a troubled New England conscience. While Thoreau, Emerson and others vigorously protested the Mexican War and pointed to the New Englander's desire for profit which undergirded our expansionist policies, the law for things prevailed and an American empire was built. The methods by which the continent was won, however, proved to be more than a "secular question." It was an important lesson, one devoid of moral restrictions, which was learned and relearned by succeeding generations and repeatedly applied in building the American worldwide empire of the twentieth century. The end, in this case the frontier, always justified whatever means were necessary to achieve it. The frontier mythos was the thread out of which much of America's twentieth century ideological fabric was woven.

Emerson clearly saw America's long-range destiny because he had such faith in the superiority of the Anglo-Saxon race. He believed that the blue-eyed race gave rise to the "love of truth," "fine sensibility," and "poetic construction." Emerson argued that the fair "Saxon Man" "is not the wood out of which cannibal, or inquisitor, or assassin is made, but he is moulded for law, lawful trade, civility, marriage, the nurture of children, for colleges, churches, charities, and colonies" (Burns 201). Here is the Americans' view of themselves on the frontier, bringing civilization to the uncivilized. Emerson insisted that it was the superiority of the Anglo-Saxon race which put "the hundred millions of India under the domination of a remote island in the north of Europe" (qtd. in Burns 190). So, too, he believed it was the Jewish "race" which "accounted for their keeping 'the same character and employments'" (qtd. in Burns 190). Although Emerson's vision of America's destiny included a belief in the superiority of the Anglo-Saxon race, his New England conscience nevertheless bothered him as he actively argued against America's conquest of Mexican territory, and early on he supported John Brown and the abolitionist movement. Nor was he squeamish about drawing blood for a just cause. In the midst of the Civil War, Emerson exulted, "Slavery is broken irretrievably." For such a gain he thought, "one generation might well be sacrificed" (qtd. in Burns 240).

Running throughout Emerson's philosophy and life as he lived it, through those crucial years of American history, are all the tensions and contradictions between the ideal and the real. More important was the practice of placing the destiny of the nation out of reach of moral strictures and the control of his generation. This, of course, was not Emerson's problem alone, rather it was an American problem. In many ways Emerson had become a "representative American."

G. Stanley Hall

As a young college student, G. Stanley Hall heard Emerson lecture in the village hall at Williamstown, Massachusetts, whereupon he obtained an interview with him in his hotel room:

> I even ventured to call upon the great man in his room at the hotel, and although I had nothing to say and remember nothing he said at the interview I felt that I had come into personal contact with the greatest living mind. I doubt if he was ever alluded to by the faculty in the classroom, for his ultra-Unitarianism was thought to be a very subtle and dangerous thing. (*Life* 163)

As a seminary student, Hall also courted "dangerous" ideas. Having entered Union Theological Seminary in 1867, Hall recounted the following experience:

> The president, Skinner, was very old and taught us homiletics and pastoral theology. After preaching our trial sermon before the institution we visited the president for criticisms. When I entered his study for this purpose, instead of discussing my sermon with me he at once knelt and prayed that I might be shown the true light and saved from mortal errors of doctrine, and then excused me without a word. (178)

President Skinner's prayers were never answered. G. Stanley Hall was not "shown the true light and saved from mortal errors of doctrine," which President Skinner had espoused. However, Hall went on to minister to the spiritual needs of thousands of young students and professors in the newly developing science of the soul — psychology. To Hall this new science was a religion in the making (Karier, *Scientists* 140). Just as Emerson moved away from traditional views of human nature and developed his own perspective of the Over-Soul, so was Hall also to move from his traditional faith and develop his own neo-romantic perspective of what he termed "Mansoul." He too became, like Emerson, a travelling teacher and preacher. Hall was particularly influential in shaping the field of child psychology. Through the thousands of students he taught, the many journals he founded, the institutions he created, his eleven books, hundreds of articles and over 2,500 lectures in some forty states, Hall left his mark on the field. He was the first person to receive a Ph.D. in psychology in America (taken under William James). He founded Clark University, the American Psychological Association, and a number of journals, including the *American Journal of Psychology*, *Pedagogical Seminary*, *The Journal of Religious Psychology*, and *The Journal of Applied Psychology*. Perhaps Hall's most important work came in 1904, when he helped shape America's conception of adolescence with his massive work *Adolescence, Its Psychology and Its Relations to Psychology, Anthropology, Sociology, Sex, Crime, Religion and Education*. Over 25,000 copies of this 1,337 page text were sold (Karier, *Scientists* 161). While shaping the field of psychology of the adolescent, his effect on his students was both charismatic and legendary. As one of his students reflected on his experience at Clark University, "I only touched the hem of his garment, and yet it was a healing touch. I would not give the months I spent at Clark for any other period of my life" (Pruette 7).

Both Emerson and Hall were deeply impressed with Plato and the neo-Platonist view of reality; both were Romantics concerned with the alienation of the soul, and both called attention to the unity within the unconscious soul. There were, however, major differences. Emerson had learned about evolution from Louis Agassiz, while Hall studied it and made it a crucial part of his belief system while studying in Germany (Allen 572-575). Although Emerson had explored the unconscious, he was still more a child of the traditional faith which saw the divine beyond man. He turned away from the darker more primitive side of man and insisted that "man was made into the image of God." Hall, on the other hand, seemed to relish the exploration of the darker side. On that darker side he found the primitive animal nature of man at the very root of human existence. The biologically sensual being fully evolved was the only divinity. Hall insisted "man is the only divinity, or at least God is only a collective term for man" (Eddyism 14). The child, he believed, is the genetic product of the racial past, and as he matures he passes in an abbreviated form through the major experiences of its racial history. While some might get fixated along the way in their individual development and remain at the savage or barbarian stage, others would become civilized, and a few might make it to the next higher stage of civilization which is that of the superman.[4] Hall knew what that stage was like. It was the stage of the scientist who passed beyond good and evil and who scanned the whole spectrum of humanity as he had done. Hall called that complete spectrum "Mansoul." Hall's "Mansoul" was a long way from Emerson's "Over-Soul." "Mansoul" was a collective term for the entire spectrum of humanity, including its complete genetic history. "Mansoul" embodied the only divinity. The true scientist as a psychologist, or as he put it, "heart former," constantly searched for the truth and eventually would produce a faith worthy of the superman who had passed beyond good and evil. Hall insisted that "when psychology has expelled the last vestige of magic from religion and taken its place, then only shall we have a psychotherapy that is true to its name" (Eddyism 21). Hall saw himself as a prophet of this new faith in "Mansoul." Going beyond good and evil, the psychologists would do more than help adjust people to their existence but would, as scientists, know the truth which exists behind the veil of appearances and become a midwife to the new therapeutic society:

> The true psychologist born and bred, yearns with all his heart for a
> deeper understanding of man and of all his psychic life, past and
> present, normal and morbid, good and bad, at all stages of his
> life. . . . He feels a peculiar urge to be intensely human, to glimpse,
> feel, or strive in his own brief little life for everything possible to
> man's estate . . . . Thus he is called today to be a sort of high
> priest of souls as in an earlier age the great religious founders,
> reformers and creators of cults and laws used to be, for the day of
> great leadership in these fields seems to have passed. (*Life* 436)

In Hall one begins to sense what it means to think with one's blood. The key to understanding humanity and its progress was to be found in its evolutionary history. Hall believed the genetic history of the race, from the slime of the sea to the temple of the superman, held its highest knowledge. The secrets of the race history lay hidden in childhood, for as he put it: "Childhood is the paradise of the race from which adult life is a fall. Childhood is far more generic in body and soul than even woman, just as she is more so than adult man" ("Notes" 496). The scientist, however, would more than know that history; he would have felt it, experienced it:

> Genetic sense or the vitalistic category of *werden* [becoming] is, in men of true sympathy, so strong that they have to believe not only in anthropomorphization but in animism, if not, indeed, in hylozoism. This gives us a new orientation toward both origins and destinies and shows us that the highest knowledge of anything is a description of its evolutionary stage. (*Life* 461)

Hall was a believer in hylozoism (the doctrine that matter is animated by the spirit). To Hall the authentic spirit lay in the soil of his childhood. He believed one had to return to mother nature, to his family farm where he could once again feel the spirit of his ancestry. Hall stayed in touch with that ancestry. Even as the fifty-five-year-old president of Clark University he would periodically return to his family farm and walk the hills and dales of his childhood, strip off all his clothes as the last vestiges of civilization and roll down the hillside in the nude:

> I finally several times enjoyed the great luxury of being in complete undress, and of feeling pricked, caressed, bitten and stung all over, reverting to savagery as I had often done as a boy by putting off civilization with all clothes and their philosophy. It was a curious experience of lightness and closeness to nature. ("Notes" 504)

Hall had tuned into the cosmic landscape of "Mansoul" by touching the spiritual qualities in the soil of his youth. Hall had drunk deeply from that strange neo-Romantic well of primitive German Volk culture, from which Wagner and later Hitler would draw, and had applied it fully to his own New England countryside (Karier, *Scientist* 180-181). Hall argued that if we truly listened to the voice within, we would each find our true place and our true calling and then be the very best we can be. His was a complete, totalitarian ideal in which: "For most of us the best education is that which makes us the best and most obedient servants" ("Education" 321-322). Hall's estimate "for most of us" is strangely similar to that of another charismatic leader later in the century – Adolf Hitler. A decade after Hall died, Hitler took the public stage in Germany, listened to the voice within and announced: "Providence has ordained that I should be the greatest liberator of humanity. I am freeing man from the demands of a freedom and personal independence that only a few can sustain" (qtd. in Muller 36).

Both men propounded a doctrine of the superman rooted in the soil and both saw the bulk of humanity eager and willing to escape the burden of freedom. They both intuitively sensed the underlying yearning for security which engulfed the Western mind as it suffered the alienating effects of both industrialization and secularization of the culture. Both Hall and Hitler were intuitively aware of the kinds of symbolic uses of the past that could satisfy that yearning.

Hall was convinced that through a process of genetic psychological planning, selective breeding, and a tightly controlled educational system, the super state might emerge in the near future. Hall preached a new religion, a totalitarian naturalistic faith in which he intuitively touched the future. Hall was not long in his grave when Westerners began to hear those strange themes of back to nature, soil, fatherland, hearth and home, health, strength through joy, agrarian virtue, world order, new order, charismatic leadership, superhumans and super-race, ancestral calling, thinking with one's blood and ultimately that voice from "within" echoing off those cold gray walls of the sports colossus at Nuremberg. Hall had touched the symbolic structure that the National Socialists would use to wield Germany into an ironclad soul of "obedient servants" (Karier, *Scientist* 185-186). Hall's biographer, Dorothy Ross, makes note of the number of people who find Hall's ideas about Mansoul similar to those of Carl Jung's notions of the collective unconscious (408). She also correctly notes Hall's reservations about Jung's mysticism. What seems clear is that both men had reacted to the alienation of the modern person in Western culture, and both created their religious beliefs as ways of overcoming that alienation. Both were neo-Romantics, and both came to believe in a volkish set of beliefs which found spiritual qualities in the soil. At this point, however, each man differed.

Carl Jung

Carl Jung had mystical experiences which lead him to found his own school of psychology. His father was a minister who had lost his faith and died a broken man. His father's lack of faith and death affected him deeply. Spiritually called to be a "doctor of the soul," Jung propounded a very ancient pre-Christian Gnostic theology. In his concept of a collective unconscious, Jung found not only the God of goodness, which was basic to the Judeo-Christian tradition, but he also found the God of evil. For Jung, evil was not — as most Christians define it — an absence of good. In contrast to Emerson, who chided those who invested the darker side of the unconscious with supernatural powers, Carl Jung did just that. For Jung, the God of the universe was not the God of good and light alone but of evil and darkness as well. A significant part of Jung's therapeutic psychology included a process by which men and women could come to accept the evil that was in their "shadow" as well as in their God. Through a therapeutic process men and women would overcome their alienation by becoming reunited to their true selves properly rooted in the mystical archetypes of the cosmic universe. The universe he envisioned was Gnostic and neo-Platonic (Karier, "Ethics"; Buber).

Jung's Gnosticism repeatedly raises the basic moral question: How can one be held responsible for acting out the evil will of God? Obviously one cannot. Evil must be allowed to burn itself out; the shadow in each person must be allowed to find expression. In this sense it is important to be authentic, true to one's self, even if that self is evil. When the darker side of the collective unconscious expresses itself, there is no stopping it. For example, Jung thought he saw in the unconscious of the youthful bands marching across Europe the spirit of Wotan. The catastrophe was coming and he knew it. Nothing could stop it. In 1918 he foresaw the terror that was yet to come:

> As the Christian view of the world loses its authority, the more menacingly will the "blond beast" be heard prowling about in its underground prison, ready at any moment to burst out with devastating consequences. When this happens in the individual it brings about a psychological revolution, but it can also take a social form. (*Civilization* 10:13)

Jung's Gnostic faith carried him into witnessing the rise of National Socialism as virtually an act of God. The "blond beast" had broken from its cage, and Adolf Hitler spoke for that beast. Hitler spoke for the darker, deeper needs of the German people. His power, Jung insisted, was not political but "magic." Hitler was a "true" leader, a charismatic leader who spoke with a divine force, albeit demonic authority of the Gnostic God which lived in the collective unconscious of the German people. As Jung analyzed it:

> Now the secret of Hitler's power is not that Hitler has an unconscious more plentifully stored than yours or mine. Hitler's secret is twofold: first, that his unconscious has exceptional access to his consciousness and, second, that he allows himself to be moved by it. He is like a man who listens intently to a stream of suggestions in a whispered voice from a mysterious source and then acts upon them. In our case, even if occasionally our unconscious does reach us as through dreams, we have too much rationality, too much cerebrum to obey it. This is doubtless the

case with Chamberlain, but Hitler listens and obeys. The true
leader is always led. (qtd. in Knickerbocker 116)

According to Jung, Hitler was the "true" leader who listened to the
voice within. "Hitler's unconscious knew—it didn't guess or feel, it knew
(qtd. in Knickerbocker 116). Hitler thus followed the voice of the
demonic divine as part and parcel of his destiny. Jung, too, followed his
destiny by taking over an Aryanized psychoanalytical journal in Germany
and "scientifically" stereotyping Jews within the context of the holocaust
itself (Karier, "Ethics"). Jung's neo-Romantic-Gnostic beliefs led him
into rationalizing the greatest evil of the century.

The acceptance of evil was structurally a functional part of Jung's
philosophy of therapy.[5] The shadow must be accepted for what it
represents as part of the collective unconscious, and the inner voice of
evil must be heard. Shortly after undergoing more than a year of Jungian
therapy, Hermann Hesse wrote a book titled, *Demian*, (1919) which
captured the hearts and minds of many German youth. The book is a
not-too-fictitious rendition of Hesse's own therapy.[5] It is a story about a
young boy named Sinclair who struggles to "live in accord with the
promptings which came from his own self." The story exemplifies the
Jungian process of individuation. The young Sinclair struggles to free
himself from the "persona," or social roles that he is expected to play
within a middle-class culture. In time, and with the assistance of
Pistorius, Sinclair confronts his "shadow" and finds the evil in his soul
which is sparked by Abraxas, the Gnostic God of good and evil. As
Pistorius put it, "Sinclair, our God's name is Abraxas and he is God and
Satan and he contains both the luminous and dark world" (115-116).

Young Sinclair is thus led to believe he is one of those children of
Cain who murdered his brother because he was destined by God to do so.
One must be true to what he or she is and thus accept evil and follow
through on his or her appointed destiny. The world of Sinclair is an
empty shell of unauthentic beliefs waiting to be smashed so a new order
could emerge. The children of Cain will play a vital role in smashing that
order. Looking to the future, Hesse, like Jung before him, sensed the
trouble to come:

> The soul of Europe is a beast that has lain fettered for an
> infinitely long time. And when it's free its first movements won't
> be the gentlest. But the means are unimportant if only the real
> needs of the soul—which has for so long been repeatedly stunted
> and anesthetized—come to light. (124)

The unauthentic, alienated world of Sinclair's urbanized middle class must be destroyed to make way for a new order, a more authentic order which would take its place. The children of Cain will listen to the voice within and be ready and willing to carry forth, violently if necessary, the evil deed. Destiny must be fulfilled:

> Then our day will come, then we will be needed. Not as leaders and lawgivers — we won't be there to see the new laws — but rather as those who are willing, as men who are ready to go forth and stand prepared wherever fate may need them. Look, all men are prepared to accomplish the incredible if their ideals are threatened. But no one is ready when a new ideal, a new and perhaps dangerous and ominous impulse, makes itself felt. The few who will be ready at that time and who will go forth — will be us. That is why we are marked — as Cain was — to arouse fear and hatred and drive men out of a confining idyl into more dangerous reaches. (124)

The future belonged to the children of Cain who were ready and willing to bloody themselves and others for the new ideal, the new order yet to be born. Hesse had found his destiny, his inner voice, his "master." Hesse also had found his therapeutic salvation in a nihilistic world of World War I by listening to his inner voice echoing from the dark unconscious world which determined his fate. God really hadn't died after all. He had been rediscovered in the darker recesses of the unconscious. He was different, however, from the Judeo-Christian God. He was as Jung also had found him, a Gnostic god of both good and evil (Karier, "Ethics" 129). Just two decades later German youth received the sign for which many of them had waited. In the uniform of the S.S. they ushered in the new ideal — the new order.

Conclusion

From Emerson to Hesse we have gone from "the sun on the meadow is summery warm" to "tomorrow belongs to me." Within that century Romantics and neo-Romantics reacted to the alienating effects of an emerging secularized industrial civilization and in the process rediscovered the unconscious where the place of nature, God, and human destiny were transformed. The tragic aspect of this transformation could be found in the very effort to find meaning in life. Where rationality was abandoned, the groundwork for manipulation of the emotions in the service of a totalitarian ideal often emerged. In such a world human beings sought the security of their collective illusions rather than face the disconcerting truths of their real world. As the search for security took precedent over the search for truth the ground for catastrophe was established. To be sure, the Romantics and the neo-Romantics did not cause the catastrophe of the twentieth century which followed. They themselves, as a rule, were not fascists. They were, however, very much a part of the ideational palette that went into it.

More disturbing is the fact that many of these ideas show signs of rebirth in post-World War II America which is built on a mythologized frontier past repeatedly employed to justify the most arrogant uses of imperialistic power. Within such a context America's current longing for a reactionary past, simplistic easy answers, charismatic leadership, the rise of health cults, religious cults, back to the soil and nature movements, a quest for mystical roots and meaning in the simple virtues of "manhood," "womanhood," "motherhood," and "family" may all stand for veiled warnings of things to come. More depressing still, it may well be that such an ideological combination of yearnings in conjunction with the growth of American militarism in the atomic age may be the spark that lights the path to an even greater, if not final, catastrophe.

Notes

In writing this chapter I have incurred a debt to Timothy Glander for his research assistance.

1. "Tomorrow Belongs to Me," from the original sound track of *Cabaret*, conducted by Ralph Burns, ABC Records, Inc., Los Angeles, CA, 1972.

2. Throughout this essay I am using the term "Volkish" as defined by George Mosse. As Mosse said: "'Volk' is one of those perplexing German terms which connotes far more than its specific meaning. 'Volk' is a much more comprehensive term than 'people,' for to German thinkers ever since the birth of German romanticism in the late eighteenth century 'Volk' signified the union of a group of people with a transcendental 'essence.' This 'essence' might be called 'nature' or 'cosmos' or 'mythos,' but in each instance it was fused to man's innermost nature, and represented the source of his creativity, his depth of feeling, his individuality, and his unity with other members of the Volk" (4).

3. See Coates, White and Shapiro (287-289), as well as Blackburn. For an excellent discussion of Sophie see chapter 3 in Martin.

4. As Hall put it, "all doctrines of another life are thus but symbols and tropes in mythic terms of the superman as he will be upon this earth" ("Thantophobia").

5. Most literary authorities agree that Sinclair was Hesse and Pistorius his Jungian therapist.

Works Cited

Allen, Gay Wilson. *Waldo Emerson*. New York: Viking, 1981.

Blackburn, Gilmer W. *Education in the Third Reich*. Albany: State University of New York Press, 1985.

Buber, Martin. *Eclipse of God*. New York: Torchbook, 1952.

Burns, Edward McNall. *The American Idea of Mission*. New Brunswick: Rutgers University Press, 1957.

Coates, Willson H., White, Hayden V., and J. Salwyn Schapiro. *The Emergence of Liberal Humanism*. New York: McGraw Hill, 1966.

Emerson, Ralph Waldo. *Emerson's Complete Works*. Vol. 9. Cambridge: Riverside Press, 1867.

_____. *Five Essays on Man and Nature*. New York: Appleton and Century Crofts, 1954.

_____. *The Complete Writings of Ralph Waldo Emerson*. New York: Wm. H. Wise, 1875.

_____. *Representative Men*. New York: Hurst, n.d.

Hall, G. Stanley. *Life and Confessions of a Psychologist*. New York: Appleton, 1923.

_____. "Eddyism and Emanuelism." May 1909, 14, Clark University Archives, Hall Papers, Box 28, Folder No. 1, 14.

_____. "Thantophobia and Immortality." *The American Journal of Psychology* 26 (1917):610-611.

_____. "Notes on Early Memories." *The Pedagogical Seminary* 6 (1898-99): 496.

Hesse, Herman. *Demian*. New York: Bantam, 1970.

Jung, C. G. *Civilization in Transition*. 10 vols. London: Routledge and Kegan Paul, 1964.

Karier, Clarence J. *Scientists of the Mind: Intellectual Founders of Modern Psychology*. Urbana and Chicago: University of Illinois Press, 1986.

_____. "The Ethics of a Therapeutic Man: C. G. Jung." *The Psychoanalytic Review* 63 (1976): 115-46.

Knickerbocker, H. R. "Diagnosing the Dictators." *Hearst's International Cosmopolitan* (January 1939): 116-118.

Martin, Jane Roland. *Reclaiming a Conversation: The Ideal of the Educated Woman*. New Haven: Yale University Press, 1985.

Mosse, George. *The Crisis of German Ideology*. New York: Grosset & Dunlap, 1964.

Muller, Herbert J. *Issues of Freedom*. New York: Harper & Row, 1960.

Pruette, Lorine. *G. Stanley Hall*. New York: Appleton, 1926.

Ross, Dorothy. *G. Stanley Hall: The Psychologist as Prophet*. Chicago: University of Chicago Press, 1972.

Rousseau, Jean-Jacques. *The Minor Writings of Jean-Jacques Rousseau*. Ed. William Boyd. New York: Columbia University Press, 1962.

Thoreau, Henry David. *The Journal of Henry D. Thoreau*. Ed. Bradford Torrey and Francis H. Allen. Cambridge: Riverside Press, 1949.

Chapter 6

ROMANTIC ROOTS OF HUMAN SCIENCE
IN EDUCATION

Max van Manen

Modern human science in education is animated by an unsuspected complex of Romantic impulses. To say this, however, is to employ the notion of Romanticism in a broad but not necessarily pejorative fashion (which may be against the grain of our modern sensibility). These Romantic impulses are spurred by social forces which originate in continental historical events. Of course, our North American and European cultures are infused with the values and spirit of various intellectual epochs and movements that anteceded it and that gave rise to it: scientific empiricism, classicism, existentialism, pragmatism, and the "isms" associated with the various confessional and political movements. But in North American educational thought the roots of Romanticism in the human sciences are largely obscured by the discontinuity between the earlier human science tradition of continental Europe and the modern and postmodern applications of human science (ethnography, hermeneutics, phenomenology, critical theory, semiotics) to educational research in North America. Yet, romantic concepts and sensibilities pervade our present-day search for a new realism which aims to supplant the representational reality of empirical or positivistic social science and the performative demands of technological rationality. This sensibility is evident in the renewed interest in the concrete features of the lifeworld, in the ethnographies of childhood, as well as in the postmodern nostalgia for the unattainable, the ineffable, the unpresentable, the indeterminable. But more than a search for a new realism the romantic impulse has given rise to a quest for methodological technologies which would ground educational research in more meaning-centred, discourse-based, culture-sensitive, narrative-mediated, and politically engaged epistemologies.

In this essay, I wish to examine some of the fundamental categories of the human science tradition in German and Dutch pedagogical theory.

They were the consequences of the Romantic reaction to the enlightenment rationalism of previous periods in continental thought. Interestingly, in Germany, this reaction was in this century foremost a pedagogic movement. However, the relevance of my discussion here is not to trace the cultural determinants of current North American educational thought. As suggested above, there is an obvious lack of influence in current human-science-in-education research from the continental traditions. And yet, in spite of obvious differences, both share interests and both seem animated, in part at least, by common Romantic themes. My intent with this examination of some Romanticist aspects of the German and Dutch human science tradition in education is to provide a backdrop for contemporary North American human science efforts in education. I do this not to criticize, from the sidelines as it were, earlier or later conceptions of human science research for their Romantic errings. In fact, the attempt to search for roots and for possible redemptive conciliations or integrations between the old and the new is itself a Romantic gesture.

More so than in England, where Romanticism was largely an aesthetic movement, and in France where it was first of all a reaction against social conventions, Romanticism in Germany began as an aesthetic movement but quickly became a general cultural perspective or life-philosophy. In education this perspective, modified by anti-Romantic themes, became known as the *Geisteswissenschaftliche Pädagogik* (Human Science Pedagogy) which had its antecedents in what has been called "the German Movement" (Hintjes; Danner; Imelman) of the eighteenth century. From approximately 1910 to the late 1950s in Germany, and from the end of the second world war to the middle 1960s in the Netherlands, several generations of educational scholars participated in a human science tradition. In Germany the first major proponents of the *Geisteswissenschaftliche* tradition in education were Herman Nohl (1879-1960) and his contemporaries Theodor Litt (1880-1962), Eduard Spranger (1882-1963), Max Frischeisen-Kohler (1878-1923), and somewhat independently Peter Petersen (1884-1952). Nohl was a student of Wilhelm Dilthey (1833-1911). He was largely responsible for working out a first human-science oriented pedagogical theory on the basis of Diltheyan starting-points and formulations. To the second generation belong especially Nohl's students such as Erich Weniger (1894-1961), Wilhelm Flitner (1889-), Otto Friedrich Bollnow (1903-), as well as Josef Derbolav (1912-), Theodor Ballauf (1911-) and Klaus Schaller (1925-). The thinking and the theoretical corpus of this group became known as the Dilthey-Nohl School. I will discuss the German and Dutch traditions partly in methodological terms, but it is important to realize that this movement was primarily substantive in nature. It was oriented to explicating the meaning of pedagogy in human life. Pedagogy was first of all a notion that the *Geisteswissenschaftliche Pädagogik* approached on the basis of two modes of manifestation: pedagogy as a primordial human phenomenon and pedagogy as a cultural phenomenon. Methodologically speaking, the predominant epistemology of this tradition was hermeneutic or interpretive in nature, influenced strongly, but not only, by the *Verstehende* human science of Dilthey and his predecessor Friedrich Schleiermacher. Hermeneutics was not understood here in the sense of translating/interpreting and understanding linguistic documents, but as Flitner says, "in a metaphorical sense: as the interpretation of lived life, as the self-confidence of concrete thinking which enlightens itself about the situation in which it finds itself" (*Gegenwart* 24). Actually Flitner elaborates on the more complex philosophic, hermeneutic and pragmatic structure of educational theorizing. As a variation of this hermeneutic thrust by Nohl, Spranger, Litt, and Flitner, the writings of Derbolav and Bollnow have more pronounced phenomenological leanings. Especially in Bollnow's work there is noticeable the influence of the existential phenomenology of Heidegger and others. During the 1960s Weniger directed the *Geisteswissenschaftliche* tradition into a more critical direction. To the Weniger Schule belong his students Klaus Mollenhauer and the influential critical theorist Wolfgang Klafki (1927-), both of whom oriented their pedagogical thinking strongly to the work of Jürgen Habermas and his predecessors at the University of Frankfurt. In the Netherlands the most important figures in education were Martinus Jan Langeveld (1905-), Stephan Strasser (1905-), and Nicolas Beets (1915-), and more recently Ton Beekman (1926-). Langeveld was influenced by Nohl, Flitner, and especially by the work of Litt and by the more phenomenological writings of his contemporary Bollnow. Langeveld developed an approach to pedagogy which was phenomenological in a less philosophical sense than Bollnow and which aimed particularly to minister to the practical requirements of our educational lives at home and at school. In contrast, Strasser, whose philosophical work is better known in North America, mostly engaged in more theoretical writing about phenomenology and education (*Opvoedingswetenschap* 1963). The work of Langeveld, Beets and their colleagues Frederick Buytendijk (1887-), Jan Linschoten, D. J. van Lennep, and E. E. A. Vermeer, in psychology, and Henricus Rümke and Jan Hendrik van den Berg, in psychiatry, at the University of Utrecht, became known as the Utrecht School (van Manen, 1979) in the Netherlands during the 1950s and early 1960s (van Manen, "Utrecht").

I would like to provide a brief discussion of some main features of the German and Dutch human science movements in education by articulating a few of their Romanticist themes. The early initiator of the German tradition, Nohl (*Pädagogik*; *Bewegung*; see especially Hintjes), has provided an account of the cultural dynamics of the developments that culminated in the twentieth century pedagogical tradition. According to Nohl, the German Movement, which lasted from about 1770-1920, swept through four phases. The phases are structured in couplings, each in a polar relation to its predecessors: one rupturing and breaking with past rationalities and the next giving shape or form to its impulse (Hintjes).

The first phase Nohl considers the *Sturm und Drang* (1770-1800) period to which belonged Herder, the young Goethe, Jacobi and the educator Pestalozzi. Characteristic of *Sturm und Drang* is the protest against enlightenment rationalism and the urge to interpret life meaningfully and purposively from the midst of life and from the whole of life. Thus, Pestalozzi argued for a holistic education that is concerned with "the development of the head, the heart, and the hand," while he observed that "the affairs of reason often remain dominated by the affairs of the heart." According to Nohl, *Sturm und Drang* found a gradual transition to the Classical period (1800-1830) to which belong Humboldt, Schiller, and Fichte. Classicism aimed to arrive at more disciplined conceptualizations of ideas of the earlier period. For education Humboldt developed the concept of *Bildung*, the formative growth of the whole person, and this led to an interest in the notion of the *gebildete*, well-rounded, well-developed person. In time there grew a sense of discomfort with the formalist tendencies of this phase, which expressed itself in a new rupturing impulse, that of Romanticism (1830-70). Representatives of this movement are Schleiermacher, Novalis, Hegel, Schelling, and the educator Froebel. Characteristic of this phase of Romanticism, according to Nohl, is the realization that humans live subjectively within the envelopes of larger objective realities such as the community, the church and the state. It included a commitment to articulating the living meaning and living sentiments of life, and a questioning of and striving for higher purposes in life. In education, too, there is the strongly felt idea of the individual's intense connectedness to the wider cosmos or life context, as in Froebel's notion of *Lebensereinigung* or life community. For example, in play (*Spielgaben*) children are seen by Froebel to develop an harmonious relation with the encompassing reality of larger life-forms.

The reaction to this romantic impulse is, in Nohl's scheme, found in the fourth more formative movement, that of Culture Criticism (1870-1900), as represented in the work of Nietzsche, Lagarde and Hildebrandt. The notion of the larger culture as an harmonious entity simply sounded too naïve and unrealistic to these social commentators. Rather, life was seen to be characterized by conflicting, antinomous, or polar elements and forces that require a dialectical hermeneutic for its understanding. And Nohl mentions especially the formative work of Dilthey in this regard. Dilthey not only aimed to develop a hermeneutic approach to the study of culture and life, he also worked at describing the unfolding sense of the German Movement itself. In the view of Culture Criticism, the idealistic thrust of Romanticism failed to succeed in bridging the gap between the reality of everyday life and the higher spiritual values of the culture. Nohl argues that, interestingly, around the turn of the century the German Movement became primarily a pedagogic movement. At this time there was a flurry of reform movements noticeable in educational practices in the shape of a variety of experimental schools and new school types. Nohl too became involved in co-founding a new Public High School in Jena in 1919.

In Germany this pedagogic movement then became known as the tradition of the *Geisteswissenschaftliche Pädagogik* (Human Science Pedagogy) which, in the words of Nohl, saw as the primary task of theory of education (*Bildung*) "to determine the autonomous position of the work and form of life of education in the context of the larger culture, and to show what is the essence of pedagogy and its place within the whole" (*Bewegung* 124). Especially until the second world war, and as part of its general program, the *Geisteswissenschaftliche Pädagogik* aimed to bring into a higher relation the developing individual and the developing culture. Dilthey too contributed to the pedagogical thinking of this emerging Human Science Pedagogy tradition. In the school curriculum this interest in bringing the individual in contact with the higher spiritual values and relevant contents of life (and of German culture in particular) was expressed in the prominent place of German Studies. Understandably, after the second world war, there was clearly a diminishing preoccupation with the notion of German Spirit and with the thrust of the German Historical Movement. And while certain historical aspects of the German Movement arguably seemed to have played in the hands of the ideology of national socialism or fascism in Germany, apparently there were great discrepancies between the *Geisteswissenschaftliche* pedagogy of the Dilthey/Nohl School and the national-socialistic pedagogy of early twentieth-century Germany. One such fundamental discrepancy resides in the collectivistic ideology of national socialism which stands at cross-purposes with the radical subject-orientation of the starting point of the *Geisteswissenschaftliche* tradition. Although Nohl and many other proponents of the *Geisteswissenschaftliche* pedagogy movement, before and after the Hitler period, had been critical of authoritarian and fascist trends in education (Spranger seemed to have been an unfortunate exception in this regard), nevertheless, the *Geisteswissenschaftliche* tradition eventually was effectively accused by its own proponents (Klafki) that it too easily identified with bourgeois and conservative forces in society.

In the Netherlands, and at first largely as a consequence of the productive influence of Langeveld, the pedagogical interest was strongly oriented to the experiential meaning of the lifeworld of children. Langeveld wrote extensively in the area of pedagogical psychology, clinical psychology especially concerning children with learning and behavior difficulties, and theoretical pedagogy especially for professional educators and child care professionals (*Beknopte*; *Scholen*). And Langeveld has contributed to the pedagogic literature with child-sensitive life world studies ("Secret Place"; "Stillness"; "Things"; "Father"). More so than the German pedagogical scholars, Langeveld, Beets, Vermeer, and Perquin developed a phenomenological pedagogical program that has a practical intent. As Dutch scholars they were interested in insights into pedagogy provided by the German scholars but the Dutch proponents manifestly severed the interest in questions of a cultural pedagogy, the question of *Bildung*, or in the aims of the German historical movement.

The term *Geisteswissenschaften* itself has roots in the Romantic period (as Nohl distinguishes it). It probably traces back to 1824, when it was coined by J. R. Werven, who was a member of the circle around the Romantic philosopher Schelling. We now translate *Geisteswissenschaften* with "human sciences," which does not do justice, however, to its Romanticist flavor. The word *Geist* translates as "mind," but the term *Geist* refers to an aspect of our humanness that includes a quality of inwardness, spiritual refinement — clearly Romantic themes. The English term "mind," in contrast, has cognitive overtones and more pragmatic connotations. In keeping with the vitalistic and transcendental sentiment of the Romantic movement, the word *Geist* has complex and rich meanings which can be gleaned from expressions such as *Zeitgeist* which means the "spirit of the age"; *der Heilige Geist* which translates as the "Holy Spirit"; *geistig* which means witty in a refined or more intellectual sort of way; *geistig* can also refer to the emotional or moral atmosphere that may reign in a home, a school, or such lived space. Betraying such enduring Romantic perspectives, Bollnow points out, in a more contemporary article (1974), that in the human sciences knowledge is not a matter of the formal intellect alone. But knowledge as understanding is *geistig*, a matter of the depth of the soul, of living human purpose, of spirit and sentiment, of embodied meaning and being.

There is the further Romantic complication that the notion of *Geist* has individual and objective, cultural and historical, dimensions. Thus there is a reaching back to Hegel here. The objective aspect of *Geist* becomes self-evident for Nohl and his contemporaries when we consider how the meaningful experience of the world has a shared and historical character. And Dilthey, too, has shown how human beings express their experience of the world through art, science, law, medicine, architecture, and especially through language. In this language they also discover a world that is already meaningfully constituted. The *Geisteswissen-schaftliche* tradition did not think of objective *Geist* as some absolute notion or quality; rather, objective *Geist* was itself considered a dynamic human life phenomenon: it tells us who we are but it is also ongoingly formed by us in a self-forming process. So *Geist* is also the expression of our oriented becoming, answering the question of where are we and where are we going? Through language people always simultaneously make and re-make themselves and thus they make and re-make the shared world in which people live together.

So, we might ask, what is meant and implied by the term *Geist* in the context of a human science pedagogy? It means that the human being, and so the child, is seen and studied as a "person" in the full sense of that word, a person who is a meaning-maker in a deeply moral, emotional, intellectual and embodied sense. The human being is a person who signifies — gives and derives meaning to and from the "things" of the world. In other words the "things" of the world are meaningfully experienced and on that basis these "things" are then approached and dealt with in a phenomenological sense. The *Geisteswissenschaftliche* pedagogy in Germany and the *Fenomenologische* pedagogy in the Netherlands share this distinguishing characteristic, that they wished to develop pedagogical theory on the basis of our lived or concrete educational reality.   Herein lies the difference between the *Geisteswissenschaftliche Pädagogik* and their contemporary Neo-Kantian pedagogy, in that the former aimed to take its point of departure in the concrete reality of pedagogic life, while the latter saw pedagogy predominantly as applied philosophy that started from normative ideals and theoretical principles. All representatives of the European human science tradition have this in common, that they always want to find their starting point in the educational reality as it is meaningfully and purposively experienced in everyday interactions, relations and situations (Hintjes).

It may be helpful to add as well that the German word *Wissenschaft* cannot properly be translated into English, since in North America the word "science" immediately is associated with the attitude of the methodology of the natural, physical, and behavioral sciences. Thus to speak of the "human sciences" is actually a misnomer if one is not aware of the broadened set of connotations that the word "sciences" should evoke in this coupling.   For Nohl and his contemporaries *Geisteswissenschaften* (human science) then refers to any kind of disciplined research that aims at knowledge in the more hermeneutic sense. The proper subject matter for the *Geisteswissenschaften* is the human world characterized by *Geist* — thoughts, values, feelings, actions, purposes which find their objectifications in languages, beliefs, arts, and institutions. There is a broadened sense of rationality involved in this epistemology. Here again we see the Romanticist theme of favoring the rationality of *Vernunft* (or deep, broad, and rich meaningful understanding) over *Verstand* (or logical, more purely intellectual knowing).

An immediate consequence of this Romantic theme of the broadened rationality of the *Geisteswissenschaftliche* scholarship, is the tendency to reunite the arts, literature, and poetry with philosophy and with social science. For the Romantic scholar, art and literature are sources of truth. And it is striking how in the name index of his *Ausgewählte pädagogische Abhandlungen* (Selected Pedagogical Writings, dating from 1914-54), Nohl makes as many references (13) to the poet Goethe as to the educator Froebel. And in addition to frequent citations from Dilthey, Plato, Heidegger, Pestalozzi, Herbart and other educators and philosophers, he refers to Beethoven, Cervantes, Chaplin, Gide, Holderlin, Kafka, Rilke and many other figures from the arts and literature. This is a typical methodological feature of the hermeneutic and phenomenological inquiry by representatives of the human science tradition in education in Germany and in the Netherlands. And in the child-sensitive lifeworld studies of, for example, Bollnow, Langeveld and Beets, this tendency to approach pedagogical concerns with literary resources has also consequences for the formative dimension of "style" of their textual work. This has led some critics (for example, Strasser, *Opvoedingswetenschap*) to apply to this work less flattering, critical labels, such as "phenomenological impressionism" and "literarized phenomenology." What Strasser and like-minded critics may have failed to see, however, is that the aesthetic character of the scholarship of someone such as Langeveld is only the consequence of a pervasive Romanticist insistence that truth is also aesthetic and needs to be brought to language by means of literary and aesthetic resources. Significantly, this breaking down of the barriers between literature, the arts, and philosophy finds a romanticist continuity from the work of Nietzsche and Heidegger to the recent writings by postmodernistists such as Foucault and Derrida.

Another feature of the *Geisteswissenschaftliche Pädagogik* is the conception of its proponents of how the notion of theory and research is to be related to the practice of living. In contrast to the more positivist and behavioral social sciences, human science does not see theory as something that stands *before* practice in order to inform it technically, as it were. Rather theory "enlightens" and gives moral purpose to practice. Practice (or life) always comes first and theory comes later as a result of reflection. "The integrity of praxis does not depend on theory," said Schleiermacher, "but praxis can become more aware of itself by means of theory" (40). And he points out, "In and of itself theory does not control praxis; the theory of any science of education comes always later. Theory can only make room for itself once praxis has settled" (41). Discussions bearing on the question of the relation between knowledge and life, theory and practice, understanding and experience, often were directed to the elaboration of the German notion of *Bildung*, which was referred to above.

For many North Americans this *Geisteswissenschaftliche* understanding of the meaning of theorizing and praxis is hard to accept or comprehend. Even the earlier Herbartian view of the theory-practice relation sounds more amenable to the modern ear. With Herbart, pedagogy is theory *for the purpose of* practice. Pedagogic practice, said Herbart, is artful. With pedagogic tact the educator who is practically involved with children bridges the abyss between science and artfulness (van Manen, "Discontinuities"). Herbart's formulation of the theory-practice relation was such that it permitted, especially in his North American followers, the elaboration of a kind of mechanistic system. Schleiermacher, in contrast, sees a less instrumental connection between knowledge and action. Knowledge enlightens practical life and can therefore be helpful for a more thoughtful practice, but this is a matter of increased awareness, sensitized consciousness, not of the more effective application of methods or techniques.

For the purpose of articulating some of the themes of European Human Science Pedagogy there follows a brief discussion of the following foundational principles — keeping in mind, however, that the works of the European authors are extremely complex so that this discussion is inevitably a simplification: a) the principle of pedagogy as an autonomous human science, b) the principle of pedagogy as the "self-reflection of life," c) the principle of the child as the starting point for pedagogy, d) the principle of antinomy in the pedagogic life-world.

Although the work of the prominent authors belonging to the German and Dutch traditions is complex and extensive in scope (each of the above mentioned figures has authored at least a dozen major texts), the above four principles are found over and again in several of their books. And although the synoptic literature, which reviews the hermeneutic and phenomenological pedagogical tradition, is rather scarce, these principles are identified, implicitly or explicitly, in the original works as well as in their critical reviews (Hintjes; Danner; Imelman).

The Principle of Pedagogy as an Autonomous Human Science
The idea that pedagogy is a domain of human life that cannot be reduced to other cultural forms or other life processes was already proposed by Dilthey in a text entitled: "On the Possibility of a General Pedagogical Science." In this notion we can spot the Romanticist desire to get back to the origin or essence of something. And in this process the notion of pedagogy was elevated to something more than a separate discourse. Pedagogy was seen to inhere in the very notion of life itself — life that constitutes for the human being the absolute ground, the final reality beyond which the human mind cannot proceed.

The church, the family, and the state are cultural institutions that shape an individual; just as religion, science, art are knowledge forms that contribute to the development of the individual human being. However, said Dilthey, the pedagogical impulse, which serves the process of the child's growth toward independence or mature adulthood, is not just the extension of any of these cultural institutions or knowledge forms. In fact, pedagogy must sometimes place itself in opposition to the demands and influences of the culture and its institutions. Pedagogy is that phenomenon or domain of human life that must understand the nature of the various influences that bear on a child's growth and development, and it must do this from its own unique vantage point. Nohl pointed out that Rousseau, too, had argued something like this in his request to respect the nature and natural development of the child and to protect it from the sometimes conflicting interest of the church or state.

The question of the autonomy of pedagogy, as it has been discussed in the German *Geisteswissenschaftliche* tradition, was, on the one hand, justified on the basis of a philosophical anthropology of human nature. A fundamental feature of human life is that humans cannot become human without the child-rearing or educative relation that newcomers develop with their parents and other caretakers. No matter what the cultural or historical context, children must be "educated," "brought up." Pestalozzi (1746-1827) has often been credited for describing the fundamental significance of the personal relation between educator and pupil, which for Pestalozzi was rooted in the primordial relation of mother and child. It is in this fundamental anthropological condition that the pedagogical relation is grounded. A human child cannot do without child-rearing or education: to develop into a healthy and mature adult a newborn child is fundamentally dependent upon adults. Most profoundly, what distinguishes the human being then is the principle of *homo-educandum*: the human being is a being who needs education in order to become human in the first place (Langeveld, *Beknopte*).

On the other hand, this anthropological principle of the educability of human beings led to the epistemological claim that, therefore, pedagogy cannot be reduced to psychology, sociology, theology, politics, and it cannot be seen to serve the interests that social, cultural, political, or social sectors of society may have in those various knowledge forms. It even means that pedagogy needs to defend itself against the interests and claims that other agencies (church, state, the industrial apparatus) may wish to make on its subject matter. Bollnow has summed up well the various arguments that were formulated by Nohl, Weniger, Litt, and others:

> The state, the parties, and other factions—all of these objective forces—would gladly take hold of the child, in order to use the child for their own purposes. For this reason they desire to prescribe for education, how and toward what ends it should

educate. Even with the parents, things are no different. In fact
they are often the worst enemies of a rational education, because
as a rule they have the economic progress of their children in
mind in a one-sided fashion. They want "things to go better" for
their children than they have for themselves, and thus they
emphasize the practical side of education and training, the so-
called "useful," and for this reason they thus often neglect the
deeper humane education of the child. Education, on the other
hand, must rebuff all of these demands which impinge on it from
without. It is primarily oriented to the child. It must assist this
child to his proper unfolding, and to this end must act as an
advocate for the child, and protect the child from the grip of any
objective societal powers. In this sense education must develop its
goals entirely from within itself, and on its own responsibility,
goals which cannot be overruled by any outside force. In this
fashion education serves not a single power or faction, but rather
life as a whole. (Bollnow 1966, 113, 114)

This line of defence asserts that first and last pedagogy finds its
significance and legitimacy in its own principle: the life, learning and
becoming of the child. Thus, in terms of its purpose and object of study
pedagogy differs from psychology, philosophy, sociology, and other social
sciences. Pedagogy is a unique way of reflecting on the way we live and
on the way we are to live with children. It involves a form of knowing
that is fundamentally normative, rather than empirical in an inductive or
deductive sense (Strasser, *Opvoedingswetenschap*). At the same time,
however, pedagogy does need to consider the insights and perspectives
which the empirical, sociological and psychological sciences can apply to
the pedagogic lifeworld. Therefore, as a discipline, pedagogy was seen to
exercise a "relative autonomy."

In this principle of pedagogy as a normative, autonomous science, lies
a crucial difference between the continental tradition of Human Science
Pedagogy and the modern North American human science developments
in education. Pedagogy in the earlier sense was considered to *be* a
human science, whereas the modern North American relation seems to
be a search for ways in which the various human sciences (such as
ethnography, ethnomethodology, symbolic interactionism, hermeneutics,
phenomenology, critical theory, gender theory, semiotics or
deconstruction) can function as *resources* or research perspectives for the
benefit of the educational enterprise. Moreover, when we compare our
present-day interest in the human sciences with the continental *Geisteswissenschaftliche Pädagogik*, then we may note how at present we value
method over matter: the overwhelming concern with the significance of

the human sciences in education seems to generate epistemological debates — such as the virtues of quantitative versus qualitative methodologies (Smith and Heshusius) — rather than concerns with substantive issues, such as the meaning of pedagogic phenomena themselves. If this interest in methodology is seen as a rationalist attempt to find criteria and standards for truth and validity outside of the genius of the individual scholar, then this increasing preoccupation with method and epistemology is a sign of strength of non-Romantic tendencies in contemporary North American and also in European society.

The Principle of Pedagogy as the Self-Reflection of Life

Within the original Human Science Pedagogy movement in Germany the idea of life's self-reflectivity has been elaborated in three related directions: (1) self-reflection as an ontological phenomenon, (2) self-reflection as a life-philosophy, and (3) self-reflection as a praxis concept.

Ontologically, self-reflection was seen as the fundamental way that human beings exist in the world and acquire living understanding of the world: not just by formal intellectual thinking but by reflectively living through the totality of emotional, aesthetic, moral, and intellectual dimensions of human reality. For Nohl, Flitner, and Weniger the essence of human life is self-reflectivity. And this means that through the human being life reflects on life. More pointedly, pedagogy is the medium by way of which life reflects on itself, comes to understand itself, and forms itself in purposeful becoming. The subject matter of pedagogy is pedagogy itself. This is what is meant by the notion of "life's self-reflectivity." Pedagogy holds a mirror to pedagogic reality in order to show it for what it is; and vice versa pedagogic reality always prompts us to reflect on the living meaning of concrete situations in order to gain greater insights into its complex and depthful nature. In these Diltheyan formulations we recognize that Human Science Pedagogy also offered itself as a life-philosophy, and not merely as a professional or practical discipline. To be an educator, parent or teacher, is to live a committed, rich, full, and deep pedagogic life with children.

The life-philosophic foundations of Human Science Pedagogy are rooted in the above mentioned Romantic sensibility of the German Movement — the deep interest in celebrating the fullness of life, including its mysterious, elusive, or irrational elements. This means that all pedagogical theorizing can only proceed from this principle of the primacy of life. Pedagogical theorizing should always start from lived life, or as Langeveld used to say "the home-kitchen-street reality" rather than from some abstracted or external source.

Practically speaking, pedagogy's task is to exercise an active self-reflection, a thoughtfulness, on the reality in which adults live with children in order to be able to offer those adults — parents, teachers, and other educators — insights or understandings that minister to their pedagogic praxis. Theory has thus the heretofore-mentioned peculiar relation to praxis. First there is the praxis of life, then there is the theoretical or reflective moment. Theory formation does not function as a solution to the problems of praxis — theory cannot be the source of praxis. Rather praxis is the source of theory — theory always reflects on, holds a mirror to, praxis in order to provide praxis with a more thoughtful understanding of its own active suppositions.

The Principle of the Child as the Starting Point
for Pedagogy

The human science perspective implicates the value of the primacy of life thoroughly, so that the aim of pedagogy as an autonomous discipline turns a main effort to a reflective explication of the phenomenon of pedagogy as it is experienced and lived through in everyday life. Whereas with earlier approaches to education, pedagogical recommendations were largely derived from and articulated on the basis of certain theological, confessional pedagogies and/or political, philosophical (Rousseau), or psychological (Herbart) premises, the human science view forced an acknowledgement of the importance of the subjective elements of the pedagogical experience. In modern terms, human science pedagogy wanted to reconstitute itself as theory of meaning.

Amongst the writings of the German and Dutch pedagogical theorists, one phrase from Schiller is often cited. It is from Schiller's *Briefe über die aestetische Erziehung des Menschen* (1795) in which he establishes a relation between aestheticism and human development. His famous phrase asserts that the importance of play to our humanity: *Der Mensch spielt nur, wo er in voller Bedeutung des Wortes Mensch ist, und er ist nur da ganz Mensch, wo er spielt* ("the human being only plays when he is human in the full sense of the term, and he is only really fully human when he plays"; qtd. in Noordam 73). According to Schiller, the world of the senses and the world of the intellect do not do justice to the fullness of our human nature, since the first one is too vitalistic and the second one is too abstract. The reconciliation is found in the in-between world of the aesthetic experience. It comprises both the content of the vitalistic domain and the form of the abstract realm. In other words, it forms a synthesis where form and content are one. Now, the creation of this world occurs in play; an open world in which the human being is truly free, truly human. And it is through this creative impulse of play that human beings develop cultural structures that ensure provisions of order, permanence, and belonging in an otherwise rootless existence.

In order to recover this human state of play and openness toward the world, Romanticism developed an anthropological interest in the world of childhood and youth where the playful impulse can be studied in its natural form. And it is partly because of this anthropological focus on childhood that the German Historical Movement expressed an interest in education or child-rearing (Noordam 20). Initially the interest in childhood and pedagogy served the conception of a full-fledged philosophical anthropology and cultural pedagogy. However, with Nohl, Litt, Spranger, and Flitner the cultural pedagogy soon became only the objective pole against the subjective pole of the study of the pedagogy of the child.

With the first generation of representatives of the German Human Science Pedagogy movement, the subjectivity of the child is largely a hermeneutic concern. However, the interest in the child's subjectivity was less for the purpose of recovering a primordial feeling of life or a sense of intuitive reason for the sake of an aesthetic form of knowledge, as it was for the English Romantic poets. Rather, the pedagogical thinkers wanted to recover a concrete form of knowledge for the sake of formulating a notion of growth for the child and purpose for the culture. In contrast, Wordsworth could ethereally refer to the young child as "Thou best philosopher. . .thou eye among the blind. . .haunted for ever by the eternal mind, — Mighty prophet! Seer blest!" someone who feels "the sentiment of Being spread / O'er all that moves and seemeth still." And Wordsworth could speak of the "infant sensibility, [as the] great birthright of our being"; "a master-light of all our seeing." There exists perhaps a certain irony in this Romantic search for a new realism through the recollection of childhood experience and the child's vision — since it expresses an obvious inability to see like a child any longer.

So, on the one hand, the English poet aimed for a form of knowledge which would serve the subjective examination of the poet's self and effect a Romantic reconciliation of the self with the whole. On the other hand, the German educator aimed for a form of knowledge which would serve the pedagogical understanding of the child's subjectivity and minister to the child's process of becoming, as well as the elevation of the larger culture.

Nohl elaborates the importance of understanding the child's own life aims as contrasted with the aims imposed or wished on the child's life by parents and teachers. The purpose of pedagogy lies in the child, says Nohl. And before one formulates educational aims in the name of any agency, one must understand this particular child and how the child is oriented in his or her subjective life. The secret of pedagogic acting lies in this principle of turning in the first instance to the child (Nohl, *Bewegung* 126, 127):

> The basic principle of modern pedagogy is characterized especially by the fact that it takes its starting point in the child [pupil or student]. This means that pedagogy feels that it is not in the position to act as the executive agent on behalf of certain independent interests associated with the state, church, or the judicial, with certain economic sectors or political parties, or with some denominational groups. Another characteristic is that pedagogy does not attempt to shape the child in accordance with predetermined objective aims but that the primary goal of pedagogy lies in the person and his or her physical and intellectual becoming. In this sense we speak of the notion of autonomy, which means that pedagogy can claim a standard which is independent of all other cultural systems and by means of which it can adopt a critical orientation toward those systems. (Nohl, *Pädagogik* 152)

The pedagogic task, according to Nohl, entails a determination of the child's aims in life. However, the notion of "aim," with Nohl, is caught up with the life-philosophical interest in entelechy — the romanticist concept of a self-formative inner dynamism that is associated with the notion of *Geist*. This innerly forming power is a force one can sense in the individual person (child) as well as in the social architecture of a particular culture. This innerly form has a teleological character, it sponsors a sense of who one is and where one is going in life as a unique person. A hermeneutic of individual life and of cultural life is needed to engage oneself pedagogically in the ministry of both. Thus, in the pedagogical writings of Dilthey and his students Nohl, Frischeisen-Kohler, and Litt, we see a constant striving to formulate a view of pedagogy that is able to resolve the polarity between the dynamic forces of the child's world and the creative elements immanent in the cultural world. Pedagogical reflection needs to do justice to this duality in the service of the task to help the child develop a personal, unique and full human life and at the same time fulfill the social possibilities of a cultural potential. For Litt this meant that the pedagogue is both a guardian of the child and a guardian of the culture. On the one hand, this reference to entelechy strikes us now as strange and outmoded, and yet we may, in everyday life, acknowledge that a certain inclination, a certain bend is characteristic of a person. Parents notice this when they compare one sibling to another. And sometimes this fuels educational optimism with a sense of frustration when, quite independent from influences of parents and teachers, a particular child follows his or her own orientation to life. And so we say that this child is really his or her "own person."

And yet, in spite of this attempt to make transparent the foundational elements of the lived pedagogical experience, the image of the child in the writings of Nohl, Spranger, Litt, Flitner, and Weniger is often remarkably abstract. One might say that, on the whole, the German movement of *Geisteswissenschaftliche Pädagogik* suffered from too much hermeneutics and too little attention to the phenomenology of life as it is actually lived and experienced by the individual. We can say then that the importance of understanding the meaning of the child's experience was initially mainly understood and elaborated hermeneutically and ontologically. One wished to know hermeneutically what being a child is like, how the child *is* in the world, what it means to stand in a pedagogical relation to the child, and what is the nature of pedagogic understanding. The themes of the nature of the pedagogical relation and the pedagogical situation occur repeatedly in the writings of German and Dutch scholars (see van Manen, *Researching*). The new pedagogical subdiscipline which arose out of this interest became known as pedagogical anthropology.

This tendency of too much hermeneutics and too little phenomenology in the German tradition of Human Science Pedagogy does not really reverse itself into a more balanced approach except for the work of the Dutch educator M. J. Langeveld and his co-workers at the University of Utrecht. For example, in Langeveld's widely read book *Concise Theoretical Pedagogy* we see a clear affinity with the German *Geisteswissenschaftliche Pädagogik*. But it is also in this text that he shows a sensitive understanding of the need to grasp the meaning of the lived experience of the child from the point of view of the child. It is this subjective factor, our need to understand the child's lifeworld, not only from some hermeneutic ontological perspective, but also in the sense of *the meaning as lived and experienced by the child*, that must be at the centre, according to Langeveld, of our pedagogic interest:

How often do we need to remind educators that the subjective experience of the child in a pedagogic situation (for example, the child says "my father at home does not care for me") does not necessarily match the so-called objective facts (for example, father appears incapable of communicating his feelings of deep affection for his child)? And so, how often do we have to remind educators that the subjective or personal lived experience of the child is more a decisive factor in pedagogic relations and situations than what was in all likelihood "objectively" well-intended? (169)

In his famous *Psychology of Adolescence* of 1924 Spranger had already raised the question of the meaning of what he called *emporbildendes Verstehen* — pedagogic understanding. It is a form of practical understanding that has a constant eye for the formative possibilities of the child. According to Spranger it requires that the educator often is able to understand the child better than the child understands himself or herself. And he provides the example of the peculiar adolescent inclination to experience an unexplained sense of longing. Although Spranger's study of adolescence became widely influential, it suffered nevertheless (at least from a contemporary point of view) from a certain abstraction, from an absence of the voices of the children themselves. Unlike Langeveld, Spranger lacked personal experience, personal contacts with children. So, Langeveld went further by suggesting that in order to come to an understanding of what is good for the child, what is educationally desirable, we must first be able to listen to the child in a manner that respects the child's subjectivity — the way the child experiences and perceives things.

The Principle of Antinomy in the Pedagogic Lifeworld

The pedagogic lifeworld is full of tensions and contradictions. The child wants to do something by himself or herself but the parent feels responsible to assist or restrain the child in order to avoid a dangerous or undesirable situation. A new parent or teacher has vowed never to say "no" to a child but finds it impossible to live up to the determination. A person struggles with the tension between what one would like to be and is able to do, and what one is and is capable of at present. A child wishes to have a father but no one assumes the responsibility. Supper is on the table but the child would rather eat junk food.

These are examples of the endless contradictions, conflicts, polarities, tensions, and oppositions that structure the reality of the pedagogical experience. Most parents or teachers know by experience the challenges that these antinomies pose to everyday practical acting and living with children. The notion of antinomies is so fundamental to pedagogic life (or to life in general for that matter) that Schleiermacher (*Ausgewählte*) uses a discussion of pedagogical antinomies as a starting point for elaborating his thoughts on education in his seminal *Vorlesung* lecture of 1826. Pedagogical antinomies do not only challenge us in the practice of daily living—they also require of us a theoretical response. No theory of pedagogy can be satisfying if it does not know how to offer a perspective on the antinomies of daily life.

Starting with Schleiermacher and Dilthey, many representatives of the *Geisteswissenschaftliche Pädagogik* have addressed the question of pedagogical antinomies at the level of ontology and praxis. By identifying and clarifying the meaning of the fundamental structural antinomies of the pedagogic lifeworld one hoped to provide a basis for a more thoughtful pedagogic praxis. Schleiermacher points at two grounding antinomies: (1) the polarity of individual versus social or universal ends of pedagogical acting, and (2) the duality of the positive and the negative, the Good and the Bad, in the process of encouraging, stimulating, restraining, and disciplining the child. For Schleiermacher the project of pedagogy involves these two contrasting but necessary tasks: to help the child in his or her uniquely individual becoming, and to place this personalistic process in the service of the great universal values. We see with him a working out of the dialectic of *Natur* and *Vernunft*, life and moral reason. Each individual, according to Schleiermacher, is called upon to find his or her way of participating in the moral community of the whole. This charge is deeply ethical, almost religious. The parent or educator needs to be oriented to awaken the Good, while suppressing evil or undesirable impulses in children growing up.

Amongst the representatives of the *Geisteswissenschaftliche Pädagogik* the grounding antinomies explicated by Schleiermacher have been a stimulation for a further detailed probing of the antinomous structure of the pedagogic lifeworld. For example, this interest gave rise to Litt's *Führen oder Wachsenlassen* which discusses the dialectic of giving active direction to a child's life while being sensitive to the requirements of letting go, or holding back. Litt saw these conflicting tendencies to be the expression of two types of guardianship: the desire to protect and further the life and quality of the culture, and the desire to protect and permit the child's becoming of a unique personal life. Litt's work is characterized by the endeavor to always reflect on the welding together of two contradictory notions, in order to expose the need to come to terms with polarities in concrete life and at the level of values and systematic thought. Hintjes identifies three main types of antinomies that recur in the works of especially Nohl and Litt, but also with Spranger, Weniger, Flitner, Bollnow, and the Dutch educator Langeveld. The three main principal antinomies discussed by Hintjes are: the antinomy of the subjective and the objective culture-world; the antinomy of freedom and discipline, or freedom and constraint; and the antinomy of the ideal and the real.

Nohl, Spranger and their contemporaries thought that the exercise of pedagogic responsibility required that the adult actively would know how to come to a resolve (*Aufhebung*) of the many contradictions and tensions that are implicated in living with children. However, "resolve" (*Aufhebung*) for them did not necessarily mean that one comes to a "solution" or a cancellation of the antinomies. Some contradictions and/or tensions may be resolved but others do remain and these are now better understood at increasingly reflective levels. Nohl and Spranger understood the process of reflection epistemologically as hermeneutic *Verstehen* of the polarities which are situated in the pedagogic life sphere. It was expected of the educator to think through these antinomies (theoretically) in order to ready himself or herself for being able to deal with the antinomies practically. Nohl talked in this context of a "praxis-theory-praxis" cycle. Praxis leads to reflection which readies for praxis, and so forth. Litt developed a more dialectical notion of reflectivity. The antinomies of pedagogic life stand in a dialectic relation to each other—for example, the experience of freedom is opposed to discipline and yet requires discipline to transpose itself into a higher form of freedom and vice versa for the experience of discipline. And Litt drew the conclusion that pedagogical theory—which is itself constituted of antinomies—therefore demands dialectical thinking and acting. Litt developed a complex theoretical framework around the notion of the primordial significance of the notions of "inner" and "outer": The inner and the outer world for understanding human existence and for giving expression to the relation between being and thinking, reality and reflectively. But he was effectively accused that this "polemical play with abstract and conceptualizations" had lost touch with the concrete reality of educational life (Hintjes).

The development of a dialectical pedagogy which Litt initiated, led already in the direction of a critical epistemology which Weniger and his student Klafki founded by orienting to the social philosophy of critical theory of the Frankfurt Schule. And this critical turn eventually led to the demise of the *Geisteswissenschaftliche Pädagogik*. It would not be wrong to say that the critical turn in educational thought on the continent was a reaction against the Romantic thrust of the *Geisteswissenschaftliche Pädagogik*. The critical theorists accused the hermeneutic tradition of failing to establish an adequate link between educational thought and culture. In North America it was a very different reaction. Critical theory became a critique of positivism in education. What the *Geisteswissenschaften* (hermeneutic theory) did for education in Germany, critical theory has done in North America: a critique of scientized rationality. Interestingly, the critical theory period in Europe peaked in the 1970s, and there are now attempts to recover and cast in a new form aspects of a phenomenological-hermeneutic based science of pedagogy and of the pedagogic life world (Waldenfels; Danner and Lippitz; Mollenhauer).

Works Cited

Barritt, L., A. J. Beekman, H. Bleeker, and K. Mulderij. "Analyzing phenomenological descriptions." *Phenomenology + Pedagogy* 2.1 (1983): pp. 1-17.

Beekman, A. J. *Dienstbaar Inzicht: Opvoedingswetenschap als Sociale Planwetenschap.* Groningen: H.D. Tjeenk Willink, 1975.

Beekman, A. J. en K. Mulderij. *Beleving en Ervaring: Werkboek Fenomenologie Voor de Sociale, Wetenschappen.* Amsterdam: Boom Meppel, 1977.

Beets, N. *Verstandhouding en Onderscheid.* Amersterdam: Boom Meppel, 1952.

Beets, N. *De Grote Jongen.* Utrecht: Erven J. Bijleveld, 1954.

Beets, N. *Volwassen Worden.* Utrecht: Erven J. Bijleveld, 1960.

Bollnow, O. F. *Crisis and New Beginning.* Pittsburgh: Duquesne University Press, 1966.

Bollnow, O. F. "Lived-space." *Universitas* 15.4 (1960): pp. 31-39.

Bollnow, O. F. "The Objectivity of the Humanities and the Essence of Truth." *Philosophy Today* 18.1/4 (1974): pp. 3-18.

Bollnow, O. F. "On Silence—Findings of Philosophico-Pedagogical Anthropology." *Universitas* 24.1 (1982).

Bollnow, O. F. "The Pedagogical Atmosphere—The Perspective of the Child." *Phenomenology + Pedagogy* 7.1 (1989): pp. 5-76.

Buytendijk, F. J. J. *Het Kennen van de Innerlijkheid.* Utrecht: N.V. Dekker & van de Vegt, 1947.

Buytendijk, F. J. J. *De Psychologie van de Roman: Studies Over Dostojevski.* Utrecht: Aula Boeken, 1962.

Buytendijk, F. J. J. "The First Smile of the Child." *Phenomenology + Pedagogy* 6.1 (1988): pp. 15-24.

Danner, H. *Methoden Geisteswissenschaftlicher Pädagogik.* Munchen: Ernst Reinhardt Verlag, 1979.

Danner, H. and W. Lippitz. *Beschreiben, Verstehen, Handeln.* Munchen: Gerhard Rotter Verlag, 1984.

Dilthey, W. *Dilthey: Selected Writings.* Ed. H. P. Rickman. Cambridge: Cambridge University Press, 1976.

Dilthey, W. *Selected Works. Poetry and Experience.* Vol. 5. Princeton: Princeton University Press, 1985.

Dilthey, W. *Introduction to the Human Sciences.* Toronto: Scholarly Book Services, 1987.

Flitner, A. *Allgemeine Pädagogik.* Ullstein: Klett-Cotta, 1950/80.

Flitner, A. "Educational Science and Educational Practice." *Education* 25 (1982): pp. 63-75.

Flitner, W. *Das Selbstverständnis der Erziehungswissenschaft in der Gegenwart.* Heidelberg: Quelle und Meyer, 1957/66.

Flitner, W. *Ausgewählte Pädagogische Abhandlungen.* Paderborn: Ferdinand Schöningh, 1967.

Flitner, W. und H. Scheuerl (Hrsg.). *Einführung in Pädagogisches Sehen und Denken.* Munchen: Piper, 1967/84.

Gadamer, H.-G. *Truth and Method.* New York: Seabury, 1975.

Gadamer, H.-G. *Philosophical Hermeneutics.* Berkeley: University of California Press, 1976.

Herbart, J. F. *Pädagogische Schriften.* Düsseldorf-München: Walter Asmus, 1964.

Hintjes, J. *Geesteswetenschappelijke Pedagogiek.* Amsterdam: Boom Meppel, 1981.

Imelman, J. D. *Filosofie van Opvoeding en Onderwijs.* Groningen: Wolters-Noordhoff, 1979.

Klafki, W. *Aspekte Kritisch-Konstruktiver Erziehungswissenschaft.* Weinheim und Basel: Beltz Verlag, 1976.

Langeveld, M. J. *Beknopte Theoretische Pedagogiek.* Groningen: Wolters-Noordhoff, 1943/79.

Langeveld, M. J. *Inleiding tot de Studie der Paedagogische Psychologie.* Groningen: J. B. Wolters, 1937.

Langeveld, M. J. *Studiën zur Anthropologie des Kindes.* Tübingen: Max Niemeyer Verlag, 1968.

Langeveld, M. J. *Elk Kind Is Er Een.* Nijkerk: Uitgeverij Callenbach, 1974.

Langeveld, M. J. *Intelligentie Leef Je Zelf.* Amsterdam: Boom Meppel, 1974.

Langeveld, M. J. *Scholen Maken Mensen.* Purmerend: J. Muusses, 1967.

Langeveld, M. J. *Erziehungskunde und Wirklichkeit.* Braunschweig: Georg Westermann Verlag, 1971.

Langeveld, M. J. "The Stillness of the Secret Place." *Phenomenology + Pedagogy* 1.1 (1983): pp. 11-17.

Langeveld, M. J. "The Secret Place in the Life of the Child." *Phenomenology + Pedagogy* 1.2 (1983): pp. 181-189.

Langeveld, M. J. "How Does the Child Experience the World of Things?" *Phenomenology + Pedagogy* 2.3 (1984): pp. 215-223.

Langeveld, M. J. "What is the Meaning of Being and Having a Father?" *Phenomenology + Pedagogy* 5.1 (1987): pp. 5-21.

Linschoten, J. "Aspecten van de Sexuele Incarnatie." *Persoon en Wereld.* Eds. J. H. Van den Berg and J. Linschoten. Utrecht: Erven J. Bijleveld, 1953.

Linschoten, J. "Nawoord." *Persoon en Wereld.* Eds. J. H. Van den Berg and J. Linschoten. Utrecht: Erven J. Bijleveld, 1953.

Litt, Th. *Führen oder Wachsenlassen.* Stuttgart: Ernst Klett Verlag, 1925/67.

Mollenhauer, K. *Vergessene Zusammenhänge.* Munchen: Juventa Verlag, 1983.

Mollenhauer, K. *Umwege: Über Bildung, Kunst und Interaktion*. München: Juventa Verlag, 1986.

Nicolin, F. (Hrsg.). *Pädagogik als Wissenschaft*. Darmstadt: Wissenschaftliche Buchgesellschaft, 1969.

Nohl, H. *Pädagogik aus Dreissig Jahren*. Frankfurt am Main: Schulte-Bulmke, 1949.

Nohl, H. *Ausgewahlte Pädagogische Abhandlungen*. Paderborn: Ferdinand Schoningh, 1967.

Nohl, H. *Die Pädagogische Bewegung in Deutschland und ihre Theorie*. Frankfurt am Main: Schulte-Bulmke, 1935/70.

Noordam, N. F. *Het Mensbeeld in de Opvoeding*. Groningen: Wolters-Noorhoff, 1977.

Perquin, N. *Pedagogiek*. Roermond: J.J. Romen en Zonen, 1964.

Pestalozzi, J. H. *Meine Nachforschungen*. Bad: Heilbrunn, 1968.

Petersen, Peter. *Van Didactiek Naar Onderwijspedagogiek*. Groningen: Wolters-Noordhoff, 1982.

Petersen, Peter. *Het Kleine Jenaplan*. Barendrecht: Uitgeverij Doorbraak, 1927/85.

Rousseau, J.-J. *Emile*. New York: Dutton, 1969.

Schleiermacher, F. E. D. *Hermeneutics: The Handwritten Manuscripts*. Missoula: Scholars Press, 1977.

Schleiermacher, F. E. D. *Ausgewählte Padagogische Schriften*. Paderborn: Ferdinand Schöningh, 1959/83.

Smith, J. and Heshusius, L. "Closing Down the Conversation: The End of the Quantitative-Qualitative Debate among Educational Inquirers." *Educational Researcher* 15 (1986): 4-12.

Spranger, E. *Psychologie des Jugendalters*. Heidelberg: Quelle & Meyer, 1924.

Strasser, S. *Opvoedingswetenschap en Opvoedingswijsheid*. Hertogenbosch: L. C. G. Malmberg, 1963.

Strasser, S. *Phenomenology and the Human Sciences*. Pittsburgh: Duquesne University Press, 1974.

Strasser, S. *Phenomenology of Feeling*. Pittsburgh: Duquesne University Press, 1977.

Strasser, S. *Understanding and Explanation*. Pittsburgh: Duquesne University Press, 1985.

Van den Berg, J. H. and J. Linschoten, eds. *Persoon en Wereld*. Utrecht: Erven J. Bijleveld, 1953.

Van den Berg, J. H. *A Different Existence*. Pittsburgh: Duquesne University Press, 1972.

Van Manen, M. "The Utrecht School: An Experiment in Educational Theorizing." *Interchange: A Journal of Educational Policy Studies*. Vol. 10, No. 1, 1979: pp. 48-66.

Van Manen, M. "The Phenomenology of Pedagogic Observation." *The Canadian Journal for Studies in Education* 4.1 (1979): pp. 5-16.

Van Manen, M. "Phenomenological Pedagogy." *Curriculum Inquiry* 12.3, (1982): pp. 283-299.

Van Manen, M. *The Tone of Teaching*. Richmond Hill, Ont.: Scholastic-TAB Publications, 1986.

Van Manen, M. "Pedagogic Thoughtfulness and Tact." *Human Science in Education Monograph*. Edmonton: Faculty of Education, University of Alberta, 1988.

Van Manen, M. "Discontinuities of Human Science Research in Education: The Hermeneutic and Phenomenological Traditions." *Human Science in Education Monograph*. Edmonton: Faculty of Education, University of Alberta, 1988.

Van Manen, M. *Researching Lived Experience: Human Science for an Action Sensitive Pedagogy*. London, Ontario: Althouse Press, 1989.

Vermeer, E. A. A. *Spel en Spelpaedagogische Problemen*. Utrecht: Erven J. Bijleveld, 1962.

Waldenfels, B. *In den Netzen der Lebenswelt*. Frankfurt am Main: Suhrkamp, 1985.

Wordsworth, W. *A Choice of Wordsworth's Verse*. Ed. R. S. Thomas. New York: Scott, Foresman, 1971.

Wordsworth, W. *The Prelude, or Growth of a Poet's Mind, an Autobiographical Poem*. Ed. Ernest de Selincourt. Oxford: Clarendon Press, 1959.

Chapter 7

THE ARTIST AS THE MODEL LEARNER

Diana Korzenik

Educators have always used art to solve a variety of different problems. In nineteenth-century America, the growth of art as a subject of study was fuelled by class mobility, industrialization, and the innovations in the reproductions of images and in changes in general in the popular press. The new media of lithography and boxwood engraving, and the need for illustration and advertising, encouraged young people to become artists and allowed them wide latitude for innovation. A whole new world was opening. The fascination and popularity of art, artists, of becoming an artist, led to the burgeoning of art publications, art schools, art museums, art collecting and art education in the schools (Korzenik).

Art also became vital to nineteenth-century education for quite another reason: the artist became a *type* of person useful to educational theorists. By type, I refer to that set of behaviors or traits people attributed to artists that Ernst Kris and Otto Kurz examined in their 1934 book, *Legend, Myth and Magic in The Image of The Artist*.[1] According to these authors, through history there is a recurrent "image of the artist," embodying both idealized and feared qualities. The "image" is that of a boy, blessed with inborn talent, discovered by a man of position, either a patron or a master artist; the boy has the good fortune to have been left untaught, in respect to art, and has the benefit of living close to nature because he is of the lower classes. The boy's artistic gift ultimately becomes his access to class mobility. With his discovered gift, he ultimately assumes the position of teachers of others.

"The image of the artist," I believe, entered nineteenth-century education particularly through the writings and teaching of one influential American educator: Francis Wayland Parker (1837-1902). He used the "image of the artist" to exemplify his ideal learner. Since education in the United States was marked, not by a stable set of goals which are the birthright of its citizens, but by rivalling efforts toward building a new country, new industries, and of forming new citizens, each innovative direction for teaching won support when the powers-that-be perceived that a particular practice offered a possible solution to a political, social or economic problem. In the ferment and search for new and better ideas in the latter half of the nineteenth century, it was Francis Wayland Parker, a non-art educator, who offered Americans the notion that the ideal learner is one who is at home with behaviors characteristic of artists. In this chapter, I examine the sources of his thinking about art and education, leaving until another time the interesting question of why Parker's vision had such appeal.

Nineteenth-Century Background

Farming parents of a hundred or more years ago would have noticed that their children learned most of what they know sensorily. By piling stones, children learned concepts of tall and short, learned about size and distance. Parents directed their children to remove the rocks, to clear the soil. Because families farmed together, everyone needed to recognize different leaves and buds and to distinguish effects of weather. Thus not only developmentally, but as members of an agricultural, pre-industrial society, children learned through substances and materials. But because everyone knew materials and made things, the knowledge they had, coming from sensory work with the eyes and the hands, was taken for granted. What people *wanted* to know was how to read and write. So with the development of the common schools, written language, both forming ideas in writing and absorbing others' ideas by reading, became "schooling."

Even so, art, the training of observation and hand skills, found a place within the early public schools. Educational leaders argued for art in terms of amazingly different objectives, each geared toward mastery of particular behaviors that people could accept within the school. To set Col. Francis Wayland Parker's approach in context, I'll review what I see as the four major objectives that were used to validate the allocation of time for art into the curriculum.

The utilitarian: Gathered within this tradition are lessons that both trained the student's attitude for work, taught him discipline and obedience, and/or taught specific skills, like drafting or bricklaying pattern-making. The aim of all these practices was preparation of young people for their future worklives. Educators believed that schools can and should anticipate the forms of work that society will need. Peter Schmidt's drawing method, for example, required students to observe prearranged blocks and then draw with their slate pencils the exact measured edges from one end of a block to another and from the corner of one block across the space to the corner of another. When Horace Mann recommended in an 1845 issue of *The Common School Journal* that children be taught according to Schmidt's drawing techniques, the reason he spent so much money having the illustrated plates engraved and describing his method in such detail, was because Schmidt's method promised precise, obedient, careful workers for growing New England industries. The advantages of disciplined drawing seemed worth the risk that worried Mann, that restless young hands and minds, left undirected with their slates, might allow drawing to deteriorate into mere picture making!

In the last quarter of the nineteenth century, the utilitarian approach dominated American schools. In my state, Massachusetts, The Drawing Act of 1870 was passed into law, mandating that not only art be taught in the schools, but that free evening drawing classes be offered at the public expense so those over the age of fifteen could improve their drawing skills and thus share in the employment opportunities in the burgeoning mills. Drawing would enable them to plan patterns for the new textiles, or draw parts for the new machines that needed to be fabricated to weave them. The economic consequences of a design-skilled citizenry seemed so self-evident in the 1880s and 1890s, that the U.S. Senate commissioned Isaac Edwards Clarke's four-volume report, a state by state survey of the public's access to art education in that century.

In time, one of the problems with the utilitarian objective was its narrowing appeal. With the growth of urbanization and office work, only a segregated, sub-set of the working class looked forward to work with their hands, and would benefit from art labor. As the century came to a close, the skills in industrial drawing diminished in prestige, acquired a trade school stigma. A wider definition of art study was sought.

The aesthetic/spiritual: By the end of the century, for public school art to serve all social classes a different, broader approach needed to be developed. The new art instruction was to be purifying, pleasing and morally uplifting, good for everyone and free of any associations with work. In art class, students didn't even have to make anything. It was enough just to look at art and talk about it. In this new vein, art was unabashedly for teaching good taste and making good children even better. Instruction frequently had religious overtones and the paintings selected for the students' contemplation often had religious content. A madonna in a classroom was believed to calm the children and provide a model of gentleness for the perturbed teacher as well. One of these turn-of-the-century trends, the "Picture Study" movement, reflected this aesthetic/spiritual orientation.

Community making: With the diversity of populations migrating to the United States, a third objective for teaching art emerged. Jane Addams and Ellen Gates Starr, among their many innovations at Hull House in Chicago, realized how the art and crafts of different cultures could weave a community of dissimilar people, lacking even a common language, common holiday rituals, or life cycle traditions. Through community making, people taught each other the practices of their native countries and exhibited the precious crafts they carried with them: their weaving, embroidery, and ceramics. Through the Butler Art Gallery, the Labor Museum, and art studio classes at Hull House, Addams and Starr honed an objective for teaching art that remains vigorous through our century.

The pedagogical: With this approach objective, art-making becomes a method of teaching across all subjects. Francis Wayland Parker, teaching from the end of the Civil War into the twentieth century, epitomizes this tradition.   For him, object making and thinking are inseparable processes. Art-making becomes the model for learning; students observe and extract features from the world and then make something out of their observations by drawing, painting, or modelling.

Art-Making as a Model for Learning

John Dewey had few apprehensions about awarding Francis Wayland Parker an eminent place in American educational history: "Col. Francis W. Parker, more nearly than any other one person, was the father of the Progressive Education movement, a fact all the more significant because he spent most of his educational life in public rather than private schools – first at Quincy, Mass. and then at Cook County Normal School in Chicago" (217). Even in the early days of his teaching career, Parker believed in what is unmistakably a Romantic education: "The child's preparation for reading is *not* reading. The preparation is the acquisition of ideas from the world by means of the senses" (qtd. in Partridge 27-28). Parker objected to school practices that prevented children from feeling any substances in their hands and using their observations from the farms. In his own Bedford, New Hampshire childhood, Parker remained on the farm longer than his age-mates. When he was eight, two years after his father died, he was indentured for most of the five years to farm work in nearby Goffstown. For those five years, between the ages of eight and thirteen, except for only a few weeks of wintertime schooling each year, he indeed felt the soil in his hands and used his observations.

After the age of thirteen, Parker's life changed. He entered private academies, first at Mount Vernon and later at Hopkinton. This young man, so wary of schools, soon became a teacher and remained one until he went off to the Civil War. In retrospect, Parker blessed his good fortune which took him from school and placed him on a farm, where he had the opportunity to study geography and all the sciences in a practical way.

After serving in the Fourth Regiment of the New Hampshire Infantry Volunteers, he came home as Col. Parker, a war hero. He returned to his preferred work, teaching, assuming responsibility as the master of a whole elementary school, North Grammar School, while also serving as its eighth grade teacher. At that time, in the 1860s, few children remained in school even through eighth grade, so when as early as November 1865, Manchester's *Daily Mirror & American* cheerfully boasted that "Great innovations have been made in schoolbooks, new methods of making students fascinated with their studies are yearly being adopted" (209), Parker was on his way to being recognized as a local treasure.

Parker saw education as essentially two processes: attention and expression. Attention was an act of the senses and the mind. Ideas came from looking, listening, smelling, tasting and touching. Attention was an act of will inhibiting all "foreign" activities from consciousness. By attending, one held the associations and made new connections. In this way, the self becomes active and, to use Parker's word, "imaginative." Parker saw the effect of attending as stimulating "intense acts of imagination" (*Talks* 161). Imagination was not some elusive, unrealistic fantasy; it was thinking. "Imagination" was the integration of new ideas and observations into one's current understanding: "All education consists of the development of thought and expression. The thought must precede the expression" (qtd. in Partridge 84).

The other process that the teacher was to promote was expression. Once thoughts were in the child's mind, the teacher's role was to help the child get them out, to help the child express, to give form to his own thoughts. All modes of expression were equally usable; the speaking voice, singing voice, written language, drawing, moulding, and moving the whole body as in gymnastics.

Parker's simple plan disguised a complex vision. Once he described the processes of input and output, what remained to be explained was his structure for the information the child must know. Parker posited two categories of knowledge: Sciences of Inorganic Matter, and Sciences of Organic Matter. Under Sciences of Inorganic Matter he included "the central subjects" such as geology and meterology, and under Sciences of Organic Matter he included "the central subjects" of Botany, Anatomy, Zoology, and History! Under each list of the central subjects were Laws that explained change within that domain. Parker believed that children were internally compelled to learn these disciplines: "The child instinctively begins all subjects known in the curriculum of the university. He begins them because he cannot help it; his very nature impels him. . . . These quiet persistent, powerful tendencies, we must examine and continue with the greatest care"(8). He saw the child inventing his own relationships to the subjects of geography, geology, minerology, botany, zoology, and anthropology.

Parker's pedagogy provided education's answer to Emerson's question: "Why should we not enjoy an original relation to the universe?" (1). Parker worked to develop methods that enabled students to enjoy their own "original relation to the universe." He believed that agricultural children like himself already had this relationship through a responsibility for acting on their own looking and noticing of differences. The art maker did too. Drawing, painting or modelling, indeed dancing and singing as well, like farming and gardening, required planning, looking, and creating things perceivable to others. Learning involved watching, and modifying the effects of one's actions. Parker found a route for the child to have an original relation to the universe in the artistic process, in which the child is the source of his own ideas and the agent of giving them form:

> Every child has the artist element born in him: he loves to model objects out of sand and clay. Give a child a piece of chalk, and its fancy runs riot: people, horses, houses, sheep, trees, birds, spring up in the brave confidence of childhood. In fact, all the modes of expression are simultaneously and persistently exercised by the child from the beginning except writing. It sings, it makes, it moulds, it paints, it draws, it expresses thought in all the forms of thought expression, except one. (*Talks* 22-23)

Parker's theory was based on a single metaphor. The learning child was the working artist.

Parker's Influences

Even before 1872, when Parker decided to interrupt his teaching to study in Europe, he was familiar with the theories of European educators. Newspaper reports tell of his North Grammar School days when he adapted Froebel's ideas, discovering that he could use not only language, but also athletic and military drill to teach concepts to his students. *The Daily Mirror & American* in November, 1913, quoted one of Parker's students reminiscing at a class reunion: "He was a pioneer in kindergarten methods of instruction and tried some of them out on us." The newspaper reporter went on in admiration: "The entire class of fifty pupils willingly remained overtime, so great was the esteem of the pupils for Mr. Parker. He introduced the military drill in the schools and it was at his suggestion that athletic exercises were indulged in, and a horizontal bar erected in the school yard (176)." I only wish this reporter had told more!

Parker's search for advanced ideas seems inevitable. He conceived himself as heir to the family's education tradition, hearing of his maternal grandfather's career as the first recorded teacher in Derryfield (now Manchester), New Hampshire, watching his mother in her role as teacher and having a renowned artist-uncle, John Goffe Rand, a National Academician, who was probably also a teacher. After seven years of success in experimentation as master in Manchester's North Grammar School, Parker was drawn to further study of new ideas for education.

In 1872 he set off for study in Europe where Romantic views on education were current. Rousseau, Wordsworth, Froebel were likely subjects of his study. Though I cannot yet verify his reading of the first two, their prestige and influence were such that it seems likely. Froebel's influence is acknowledged in newspaper reports in the *Daily Mirror & American* (36-37). Since "the image of the artist" is in the work of all three, whether Parker read them or interpretations of them by his contemporaries, it is clear that Rousseau, Wordsworth, and Froebel deserve our attention in understanding Parker's approach to education.

Before looking at the artist in texts of Rousseau, Wordsworth, Froebel, we should ask who was this "artist" that so intrigued Romantic writers? What was becoming so exciting about "being an artist"? The early nineteenth-century Romantic visual artist was a person who promised a whole new world in a visual language independent of tradition. Artists, through their individual consciousnesses, were believed to be able to create a natural symbolism that grew out of their contact with Nature and would release the significance hidden within Nature herself. The new landscape painting proved that nature could be the subject in and of itself. Painting forms of nature no longer needed justification as settings or background for historical scenes.

Between 1790 and 1825, Romantic art struggled to break away from the traditional; artists were revolutionaries opposing the dominant hierarchies. They attacked the concept of a high art opposed to a low art, and concepts of major and minor genres (history painting versus still life) and united the then segregated notions of the sublime in art and the ordinary feelings of people. As part of the dissolution of the old order, artists courted censure. In 1857, Flaubert ironically boasted of the assault against him after the publication of *Madame Bovary*: "Now I have been attacked by the government, the priests, by the newspapers. It is complete. Nothing is lacking for my success!" (qtd. in Rosen and Zerner 15). One thing was missing: the charge that he was a "child." Other artists were charged with behaving like a child! In 1864, soon after French Romantic artist Delacroix's death, the French Minister of Fine Art, Nieuwerkerke, rejected any notion of the government reproducing Delacroix's work by saying: "Well! A ten year old child at school who did that, we would throw him out. We only encourage high class works, and all this emanates from a demented mind" (qtd. in Rosen and Zerner 15).

In this era, the artist, a Romantic bad boy, opened a channel for a new kind of behavior. The artist promised to free society from the constraints of the past. Art historians Charles Rosen and Henri Zerner claim that, "The most extreme statements, where romantic doctrine finds its purest expression in the visual arts, were often made by amateurs, craftsmen, eccentrics, outside the accepted centres of professional activity" (35). Children too could be added to the list. For those reconsidering childhood and education, the image of the Romantic artist provided just what they needed.

Rousseau

Jean-Jacques Rousseau was the first and most influential promoter of the child, though the child as artmaker was only one of his many ideas for Emile. Even in the first sentence, artist/creators appear in *Emile*, but the prognosis isn't very good; there are two kinds of creators, the natural and the human: "Everything is good as it comes from the hands of the Creator; everything degenerates in the hands of man" (55).

Further into the text, Rousseau becomes more optimistic. He describes Emile's sensations as the raw materials of his ideas and training the senses as "the apprenticeship to learning" (82). "Apprenticeship" was an intriguing word choice. Through apprenticeship, one learned a craft. Rousseau provided one bridge that Parker needed to develop his notion of the artist/child. Via the metaphor of the disciplined crafts apprenticeship, the senses open the way to all forms of mastery, including school disciplines: "People of all ages, but children above all, wish to show signs of their power and activity by imitation, creation and production" (101). Drawing for Rousseau was an activity by which boys might learn to analyze and imitate what they see: "Children being great imitators, all try to draw. My pupil will study this art, not precisely for its own sake, but to give him a good eye and a supple hand" (133)

Mistakenly, I believe, Rousseau included the "laws of perspective" as laws of Nature. As such, his student must know perspective. Rousseau seemed unaware of the contradiction between this statement and what follows:

> I shall not send him to a drawing-master, who would only teach him to imitate imitations and to draw from copies. I wish him to have no other master than Nature, no other model than the objects themselves. He should have the original before his eyes, not the paper representing it; he should draw a house from a house, a tree from a tree, a man from a man. Thus he will be accustomed accurately to observe the appearances of bodies, and not to mistake false and conventional imitations, for genuine representations. I would even discourage his drawing from memory, till frequent observation had strongly impressed the true shape on his imagination; lest through the substitution of strange fantastic shapes for the reality, he should lose his sense of proportion and his taste for the beauties of Nature. (133)

Here Rousseau drew the battle lines that have split art study ever since. On one side, some say art should be learned directly from observation, that nature is the best teacher. On the other, people claim that pictures come mostly from other pictures, and therefore that copying and studying the art of others are prerequisites to original work. The Romantic artist disdained copying as inevitably reiterating dead traditions, preferring direct observation of nature because it offered the albeit awkward route to an independent new vision.

To Rousseau, the benefits were worth the loss of elegance. "I know this method will, for a long time, lead to unrecognizable daubs.... But by way of recompense, he will certainly acquire an accurate eye and a steadier hand; he will learn to know the true relations of size and shape between animals, plants and other natural objects" (133). In drawing, children differentiate and recognize features that arise in all domains of knowledge. From this attitude, Francis Wayland Parker may have gleaned his conviction about the value of art making as a tool for *general* learning. Rousseau wrote: "My intention is not so much that he should imitate objects as that he should know them; I should much prefer him to be able to show me an acanthus than to be adept in drawing the leaves on a capital" (134).

As Rousseau values the awkwardness in Emile's drawing, he anticipates a soon-to-be fashion for incompleteness, a pattern that Rosen and Zerner identify as endemic to Romanticism:

> For a number of years, early in the nineteenth century, there was a monstrous fashion for writing fragments; hundred of writers published thousands of little clever observations. The fashion of the fragment was related on one hand to the contemporary taste for ruins, and on the other to the growing appreciation for sketches and the sketchy finish, a finish that made visible and exploited the individual brushstrokes. The fragment in the visual arts is not the result of literary doctrine but actually precedes the literary fashion in time. (25)

Even if he were the most skilled artist of his time, he would pretend in front of Emile that he could do no better at drawing than his student: "I shall use it [drawing] as badly as my pupil. Though I were an Apelles, I would appear a mere dauber" (134). Rousseau continued to describe his method for working with Emile:

> My first sketches of a man will be like those which boys draw on the walls; a stroke for each arm, a stroke for each leg, and the fingers thicker than the arms. After some time, one of us will notice the want of proportion; we shall remark that a man's leg has a certain thickness, that the thickness varies. . . . In this progress I shall keep pace with him, or advance so little ahead that he can easily overtake me, sometimes surpass me. We shall have brushes and colors; we shall try to imitate appearance and color as well as shape. We shall color, paint, daub; but in all our daubings we shall never cease to watch nature. (134)

The art-making process, for Rousseau, externalized the child's growth and change. Rousseau told us that drawing is a metaphor, and "will pass into a proverb," for all learning. He explains the metaphor in how he would frame the glass-protected drawings:

> Our first rude daubs will need to be set off by fine gilt frames; as the drawings improve, and the imitation (*sic*) becomes more exact, I shall be content with plain black frames. The pictures no longer need extraneous ornament; it would be a pity if the attention due the picture were distracted by the frame. Hence we both aspire to the honor of a plain frame; and, when either of us wishes to disparage the performance of the other, he condemns it

to a gilt frame. Some day no doubt these gilt frames will pass into a proverb with us, and we shall be astonished to see how many people do themselves justice by a similar adornment of their own person. (135)

It should be clear that in Rousseau, Parker could well have found the ingredients that became essential to his pedagogy: drawing was useful as an index to the boy's progress in all learning; drawing showed how the boy makes subtler and subtler distinctions. "As drawing stands to seeing, so do speech and music to hearing" (Rousseau 137). Parker adopted Rousseau's creed that the boy's curiosity naturally leads him to geography, physical sciences and other subjects: "The earth is man's island and the sun his most striking spectacle. As soon as our ideas begin to extend beyond ourselves, our attention will necessarily be attracted to one or the other of these two objects" (148). Drawing was to prove one route to a better sense of geography: "Here you will see the difference between Emile's ignorance, and other boys' knowledge, they know maps, he makes them" (153).

Contrary to his opening sentence of *Emile*, Rousseau provides many examples suggesting that *not* "everything degenerates in the hands of man." Francis Wayland Parker incorporated many of Rousseau's more positive ideas about art-making in his own methods, which in turn survived into the twentieth century progressive movement.

Wordsworth

Although education was not his profession, education became one of Wordsworth's themes. Wordsworth was born in 1770, just seven years after Rousseau conceptualized the boy's new education in *Emile*. By his twenty-fifth year, in the autumn of 1795, Wordsworth literally applied Rousseau's "negative education," when he and his sister Dorothy, assumed responsibility for the upbringing of Basil Montague, a two-year-old whose mother had died: "We teach him nothing at present but what he learns from the evidence of his senses. He has an insatiable curiosity, which we are always careful to satisfy... directed to everything he sees; sky, fields, trees, shrubs, and corn.... Our grand study is to make him happy" (qtd. in Wordsworth, Jaye, and Woof 70-71). More consequential to Francis Wayland Parker than any facts of Basil's care was Wordsworth's *The Prelude*:

                              I began
My story — not misled, I trust,
By an infirmity of love for days
Disowned by memory.

                                                    (1.614-617)

In his proto-lay analysis, Wordsworth examined his own childhood looking for the seeds of his own later development. He celebrated the power of childhood and contrasted the stages of childhood that Rousseau previously delineated. Wordsworth attributed growth to the child's inherent attraction to sensory experience. Wordsworth's "poet of the future" anticipates Parker's child. Both envision growth born of pursuit of the child's "soul unsubdued," born of the child's pursuit of its natural bent, its own attention and curiosity directed toward the sensory world.

In 1802, in the Preface to the *Lyrical Ballads*, Wordsworth foresees the poet of the future who "will be ready to follow the steps of the man of science — carrying sensation into the midst of objects of the science itself. The remotest discoveries of the chemist, the botanist, or the mineralogist, will be as proper objects of the poets art as any" (qtd. in Wordsworth, Jaye, and Woof 63). As Parker saw it, the child was best seen as a natural student: "The child instinctively begins all subjects known in the curriculum of the university. He begins them because he cannot help it; his very nature impels him" (*Pedagogics* 23). Wordsworth recalled his own childhood when "The earth/ And common face of Nature spake to me/ Rememberable things...." (1.586-588). Both Rousseau and Wordsworth would have confirmed for Parker what he already abhorred in most schoolrooms. Wordsworth regretted the impoverishment of the child who

... knows the policies of foreign lands,
Can string you names of districts, cities and towns,
The whole world over tight as beads of dew
Upon a Gossamer thread.

                    (qtd. in Wordsworth, Jaye, and Woof 84)

All three, across time, shared feelings about the liveliness of children's sensation and curiousity and the deadliness of rote learning.

But where in Wordsworth's work is Parker's ideal of the artist/creator? When a writer's subject is autobiography, his whole life *as* an artist is his subject. In *The Prelude*, Wordsworth explored and gave form to how a young child metamorphosed into the adult artist whose lines we read.

Frail creature as he is, helpless as frail,
An inmate of this active universe:
For feeling has to him imparted power
That through the growing faculties of sense
Doth like an agent of the one great Mind
Create, creator and receiver both,
Working but in alliance with the works
Which it beholds — Such, verily, is the first
Poetic spirit of our human life.

(2.255ff.)

By 1802, Wordsworth, admiring the nesting of his childhood feelings and his current ones, wrote the poem that begins: "My heart leaps up when I behold a rainbow in the sky" which shows clearly the influence of Rousseau and seems to anticipate Freud. Wordsworth notes how childhood experience is both the treasure trove and a tyranny over the life developing from it: "The Child is father of the Man." *The Prelude* offers another variation on that power:

Our simple childhood, sits upon a throne
That hath more power than all the elements.

(5.508-509)

Francis Wayland Parker, the teacher looking for ideas he could use, couldn't help but notice that Wordsworth too had looked for and found ideas in others' work. He must have read in Wordsworth echoes of Rousseau: that childhood feelings survive into adult life; transitions are linked; stages must be lived for what they are not only as preparation for what one will become; our past, present and future have critical interconnections; and the processes by which we learn begin from sensory and imaginative responses to Nature.

We can imagine Parker in a dialogue across time with Rousseau and Wordsworth. From Parker's own works, we can expect he resonated with sympathy reading Wordsworth's images of learning apart from schooling:

When I began to enquire,
To watch and question those I met, and speak
Without reserve to them, the lonely roads
Were open schools in which I daily read
With most delight the passions of mankind,
Whether by words, looks, sighs, or tears, revealed;
. . . .
And — now convinced at heart
How little those formalities, to which
With overweening trust alone we give

The name of Education, have to do
With real feeling and just sense.

(13.160ff.)

Even as he was sympathetic with Wordsworth's and indeed Rousseau's distrust of schools, Parker was likely to have been uncomfortable with this sentiment. After all, Parker, the headmaster and superintendent-to-be, was committed to schools. He was looking for ideas for curriculum. Conflict was inevitable.

Not only did Parker have differences with his precessors, but he would have noted their differences between one another. Concerning the image of the artist, particularly in how art-making becomes a model for education, as Parker read Rousseau and Wordsworth I imagine him wrestling with and trying to reconcile their differences. They differed in their emphasis. Rousseau stressed the importance of the child's tactile physical curiosity and tactile response. Wordsworth's concern was for the child's capacity for feeling and forming an emotional response. Rousseau emphasized that every learner had senses, hands, feet and a self to move in space, while Wordsworth showed how human emotion matters and how every human being has what it takes to feel. Parker did take what was useful from both Rousseau and Wordsworth, but what he needed to come home satisfied was a theorist with a program for schooling. For the transition to curriculum itself, he needed a theory in which the image of the artist could enter school practice Parker needed Friedrich Froebel.

Friedrich Froebel

In Froebel's theory of the kindergarten, Parker found the artist as the model for the young school boy. The kindergarten was a virtual children's art academy, just as Elizabeth Palmer Peabody, the American kindergarten advocate, had said it should be.

When Parker read Froebel, he must have felt as if he were cavesdropping on yet an even larger conversation. He could recognize in Froebel, ideas he'd just read in Wordsworth. One example is Froebel's *The Education of Man* of 1826. "This is seen in the child, man as a whole. . ." (36) is a restatement of Wordsworth's compressed complex vision written twenty-four years before, "The Child is father of the Man." Froebel himself was intrigued by Rousseau. One notion directly from Rousseau was that children were nourished by satisfying their own curiosity, creating their "self-activity." Froebel saw child's work as finding "inner connections," finding and pursuing what is personally attractive: "To have found one fourth of the answer by his own effort is of more value and importance to the child than it is to half hear and half understand it in the words of another" (86). In all this dialogue, the artist is the recurrent theme. In Froebel, the artist is evident:

> God created man in his own image; therefore, man should create and bring forth like God. His spirit, the spirit of man, should hover over the shapeless, and move it that it may take shape and form, a distinct being and a life of its own. . . . We become truly godlike in diligence and industry, in working and doing, which are accompanied by the clear perception or even by the vaguest feeling that thereby we represent the inner in the outer. (31)

The artist produces something external from inner motives: precisely Froebel's prescription for the child. Froebel observed in child play the behavior of the sketching artist or the clay-modelling sculptor.

Beyond the child/God analogy in which both are creators, Froebel is concrete on the specific evolution of drawing and of its relation to language:

> For the word and the drawing are always mutually explanatory and complementary, for neither one is, by itself, exhaustive and sufficient with reference to the object represented. . . . The faculty of drawing is, therefore, as much innate in the child, in man, as is the faculty of speech, and it demands its development and cultivation as imperatively as the latter. (79)

Here in Froebel we meet the theme first introduced by Rousseau, that through art-making processes, the child assimilates all knowledge across subjects: "The representation of objects by and in drawing induces and implies clear perception, e.g. two eyes, and two arms, five fingers and five toes. . . . Thus the drawing of the object leads to the discovery of number" (80). Froebel continues on the role of art making in general education:

> There is in art. . . a side where it touches mathematics, understanding; another where it touches the world of language, reason; a third, where — although itself clearly a representation of the inner — it coincides with religion. Yet all these relationships will have to be disregarded . . . in order to lead him to an appreciation of art. Here art will be considered only in its ultimate unity as the pure representation of the inner. (226-27)

Froebel's notion of education posits a boy who is a container for "the inner" experience. But those inner experiences only serve a purpose when the child gives them form: "Man is developed and cultured toward the fulfillment of his destiny and mission and is to be valued. . . by what he puts out and unfolds from himself" (270).

Conclusion

Ironically, Francis Wayland Parker, the professional educator, drew his ideas from those least attracted to schools — the Romantics. In the dialogue that engaged him, throughout his reading and in his development of his theories and practices for schooling, I see him drawn to make the most of ideas from precisely those writers who themselves idealized education *apart* from schools. The very "image of the artist," with which I began this discussion, was a wanderer in the fields, a loner discovered drawing out on his own. In the process of his incorporation of "image of the artist," Parker became enmeshed in a paradox. He institutionalized assumptions about human nature that, according to the pervasive myth of the artist, belonged *outside* of institutions. Nevertheless, engaged with the ancient myth, Parker tapped a concept originally invented and reinvented to account for the exceptional childhood experience of individual artistic geniuses, and generalized it to apply to *all children in schools*. His institutionalization of the image of the artist was a major alteration of the myth.

Parker actually preserved and transformed the myth. In his adaptation, he preserved the figure of the patron, by assigning that function to the school teacher. The classroom teacher becomes the discoverer of the children's talents. Poverty, too, is preserved from the original myth. The artist, in the myth, was some variant of the impoverished, innocent shepherd boy. Lacking money, he must practise his drawing with a stick in the dry soil or scratch a stone on the surface of larger rock. In poverty, Parker saw the child growing close to nature. Being close to nature itself became a condition of privilege. How adaptive, and basically democratic, it must have been for educators facing the ever widening classes of children who attended public schools, to believe that intelligence was as likely, or even more likely, to bloom among the poorest of children as among those more well to do.

Parker returned home from his European sojourn having captured, via the myth, the elusive butterfly, "the artist." He carried it back home, as it were, in a bottle, to open it inside American schools where it could fly free. With this far stretch of the artist myth, Parker used the Romantics to transform schools into laboratories where genius/creativity could become the rule. Education language has reflected this change well into our century.

Note

1. The authors discussed here write of boys. I have continued the use of the pronoun "he" keeping in mind its specific reference to males.

Works Cited

Archer, R. L. *Jean-Jacques Rousseau: His Educational Theories Selected from Emile, Julie and Other Writings*. New York: Barrons Educational Series, 1964.

Daily Mirror & American (Manchester, NH). Manchester, NH: Manchester Public Library Scrapbook.

Dewey, John. "How Much Freedom in New Schools?" *Education Today*, ed. Joseph Ratner. New York: G. P. Putnam's Sons, 1940. 216-223.

Emerson, Ralph Waldo. *Nature*. Boston: James Monroe, 1836.

Froebel, Friedrich. *The Education of Man*. New York: D. Appleton & Co., 1887.

Korzenik, Diana. *Drawn To Art: A Nineteenth Century American Dream*. Hanover: University Press of New England, 1986.

Parker, Francis Wayland. *Talks on Pedagogics*. New York: E. L. Kellogg, 1884.

Partridge, Lelia E. *Notes of Talks on Teaching Given by F. W. Parker at the Martha's Vineyard Summer Institute July 17-August 19, 1882*. New York: E. L. Kellogg, 1883.

Rosen, Charles and Zerner, Henri. *Romanticism and Realism: The Mythology of Nineteenth Century Art* New York: W.W. Norton, 1984.

Schmidt, Peter. *The Common School Drawing Master Containing Schmidt's Practical Perspective*. Boston: E. P. Peabody. 1846.

Wordsworth, Jonathan, Michael C. Jaye, and Robert William Woof. *Wordsworth and The Age of English Romanticism*. New Brunswick: Rutgers University Press, 1987.

Wordsworth, William. *Selected Poetry*. New York: Modern Library, 1950.

Chapter 8

ROMANTICISM DOMESTICATED:

MARIA MONTESSORI

AND THE CASA DEI BAMBINI

Jane Roland Martin

My heart leaps up when I behold
   A rainbow in the sky:
So was it when my life began,
So is it now I am a man,
So be it when I shall grow old,
   Or let me die!
The Child is father of the Man;
And I could wish my days to be
Bound each to each by natural piety.

(Wordsworth, "My Heart Leaps Up")

Heaven lies about us in our infancy!
Shades of the prison-house begin to close
   Upon the growing Boy,
But he beholds the light, and whence it flows,
   He sees it in his joy;
The Youth, who daily farther from the east
   Must travel, still is Nature's priest,
      And by the vision splendid
      Is on his way attended;
At length the man perceives it die away
And fade into the light of common day.

(Wordsworth, "Ode: Intimations of Immortality")

In tracing Maria Montessori's intellectual lineage to "the Rousseau-Pestalozzi-Froebel group" critics and admirers alike place her squarely in the Romantic tradition of educational thought (Kilpatrick; *cf.* Rusk). This characterization seems apt given Montessori's emphasis on the child, her faith in its inherent capacities, her belief that the educational process should follow the child's natural development, her commitment to the child's freedom and self-expression, and her insistence on the

159

importance in a child's education of direct sense experience. When one notices the allusions to Wordsworth in her writings, it appears to be all the more fitting. Yet when the Casa dei Bambini is added to the equation, Montessori's standing as a Romantic becomes problematic.

Speaking in 1907 at the opening of a Casa dei Bambini in Rome, Montessori said: "We Italians have elevated our word 'casa' to the almost sacred significance of the English word 'home,' the enclosed temple of domestic affection, accessible only to dear ones" (*Method* 53). Notwithstanding this emphasis on "home," from the beginning her term for school has been rendered in English as "The House of Childhood" or "The Children's House." Indeed, in 1912 the speech containing her cautionary note was published as chapter 3 of the first English language edition of *The Montessori Method* under the title "Inaugural Address Delivered on the Occasion of the Opening of One of the 'Children's Houses.'"

Read "casa" as house and one's attention is drawn to the child-size furniture, the exercises in dressing and washing, and perhaps the extended day. Read "casa" as home and one discovers a moral and social dimension to her theory that belies the Romantic label. Moreover, just as the designation of Montessori as a Romantic theorist of education is cast in question by a rereading of her accounts of the Casa dei Bambini, the interpretations that have been placed on her theory lose their initial plausibility. When it is understood that Montessori thought of school on the model of home, the elements of her system take on a different configuration. Where once small individuals were seen busily manipulating materials designed especially for learning, a domestic scene now emerges with its own special form of social life and education. In addition, her theory acquires an uncanny relevance to our own time and place.

The Casa dei Bambini

The Casa dei Bambini was designed for poor children whose mothers worked each day outside their own homes. In *A Montessori Mother*, written in 1912 for mothers, Dorothy Canfield Fisher noted that enterprises like laundry and baking, which had once been undertaken by women in the home, were now being carried on outside. Prophesying that the education of children under six would soon follow suit, she wrote: "At some time in the future, society will certainly recognize this close harmony of the successful Casa dei Bambini with the rest of the tendencies of our times" (236-237). If anything, Fisher's metaphor of harmony underestimates the significance for today of Montessori's idea of school.

I cannot help thinking that Canfield's prescience stemmed at least in part from the fact that she read "Casa dei Bambini" as Montessori meant it. "The phrase Casa dei Bambini is being translated everywhere nowadays by English-speaking people as 'The House of Childhood,'" Fisher wrote, "whereas its real meaning, both linguistic and spiritual, is, 'The Children's Home'" (31). "I feel like insisting upon this rendering, which gives us so much more idea of the character of the institution," she added (33).

Subtract the Children's Home from Montessori's system and her method sounds like a recipe for those British and North American open classrooms of the 1960s and 1970s to which the Romantic label is so often attached.[1] Her emphasis on children learning rather than teachers teaching, on the child's manipulation of concrete materials, on freedom and the absence of compulsion in the schoolroom were commonplaces of open classrooms. To be sure, advocates of open education undoubtedly considered the apparatus Montessori prescribed for learning too confining and, had they known of it, they would have thought that her conceptualization of the child's activities in school as *exercises* reflected an unfortunate rigidity as to the way skills are both acquired and put into practice. She, in turn, would probably have frowned upon the use of one and the same object for different purposes and would certainly have disapproved of what would have seemed to her the haphazard way in which concepts were learned and skills acquired in open classrooms. Still, the open-classroom teacher like the Montessori Directress was not supposed to take centre stage. Nor was that teacher supposed to tell children the answer as opposed to helping them figure things out. Moreover, the distinction between work and play was as blurred in open classrooms as it is in Montessori's theory and the location of both in time and place was as fluid.

The open-classroom movement did not share Montessori's conception of school, however. Rejecting the features of traditional schools that had led critics to characterize them as prisons, open classroom advocates were determined to remove the barriers between school and world. Allowing children to cross the threshold into the out-of-doors, bringing materials from the "outside" world into the classroom, inviting members of the community into school to demonstrate their skills, they saw school more as a replica in miniature of the world than as a home. Indeed, the very presence in many open classrooms of a "family *corner"* indicated that whatever the rest of school was seen as, it was not seen as home. One homelike area does not transform a school or even a classroom into a home.

In any event, it is not the furniture that makes the Casa dei Bambini a child's surrogate home. In *Education for Peace,* a collection of lectures Montessori delivered in the 1930s, she distinguished a negative concept of peace, as merely the cessation of war, from a positive one. Introducing an analogy to good health which, she said, is not simply a matter of the absence of disease but is based on a strong well-developed body relatively resistant to infection, she argued that positive or genuine peace requires a transformation of moral life. Peace, wrote Montessori, is not "a partial truce between separate nations, but a permanent way of life for all mankind" (*Peace* 70). How is this to be achieved? The child must be the starting point for the transformation since "the hope of altering adults is vain" (*Mind* 73).

Calling the child a "spiritual embryo," Montessori drew upon Wordsworth in her later writings as she had in her earliest. In the last paragraph of *The Montessori Method* she had said:

> I understand how the great English poet Wordsworth, enamored as he was of nature, demanded the secret of all her peace and beauty. It was at least revealed to him — the secret of all nature lies in the soul of a little child. He holds there the true meaning of that life which exists throughout humanity. But this beauty which "lies about us in our infancy" becomes obscured; "shades of the prison house, begin to close about the growing boy. . . at last the man perceives it die away, and fade into the light of common day." (*Method* 376)

More than two decades later Montessori told European audiences that the child "must no longer be considered as the son of man, but rather as the creator and the father of man" (*Peace* 104).

The spiritual embryo's promise will only be fulfilled if the child is allowed to develop normally, Montessori insisted. Since its psychic life begins at birth, the problem of peace becomes, then, one of educating young children. Just as the physical embryo derives its nutriments from the womb, the spiritual embryo absorbs them from its surroundings. Put children in the wrong environment, their development will be abnormal and they will become the deviated adults we now know. Create the right environment for them and their characters will develop normally. The "second womb" is what she called the young child's proper environment. From perhaps the age of two the Casa dei Bambini is that second womb.

If Montessori's own words in her Inaugural Lecture that "casa" means "home" are not convincing, these references to a child's very first home should be decisive. What is the character of the institution called home? One dwells in a house. One feels secure, loved, at ease — that is, "at home" — in a home, at least in the kind of home envisioned by Montessori.

Let there be no misunderstanding. Montessori did not model her school on just any home. Maintaining in her Inaugural Address that the Casa dei Bambini "is not simply a place where the children are kept, not just an *asylum*, but a true school for their education" (*Method* 62), she indicated that even its home-likeness was to be educative. Montessori reminded her audience that the Casa dei Bambini then opening was located in buildings in which, until they had been renovated, the poor had been living in unspeakable conditions. Upon completion of the project, the authorities had found themselves faced with an unexpected problem: the children under school age living in the new apartments were running wild while their parents were at work. In her words, they were becoming "ignorant little vandals, defacing the walls and stairs" (60). Convinced that these children were neither being cared for properly nor learning what they should at home, Montessori designed the school she had been asked to establish *in* the housing project *for* the housing project children as the kind of home to which the resident poor should aspire. Making it their school by giving them collective ownership (63), she nevertheless modelled it on a version of home many of them did not know.

Montessori's description of what the literal home in the project might one day become captures the spirit of that metaphorical home named school: "It may be said to embrace its inmates with the tender, consoling arms of a woman. It is the giver of moral life, of blessings; it cares for, it educates and feeds the little ones" (*Method* 68-69). Her idealized version of home was based in part, but only in part, on her image of a womb. Like a womb the Casa dei Bambini would provide a safe and secure, supportive and nurturant environment for children. Over and beyond this, the children in the Casa dei Bambini would have a double sense of belonging: they would feel that they belonged to this home *and also* that it belonged to them. Deriving not from possessiveness but attachment — to the school itself, to its physical embodiment, to the people in it — this latter feeling explains the children's zeal in keeping the schoolrooms neat and clean, their pride in showing the school to visitors, their joy in serving each other hot lunches.[2]

One clear implication of Montessori's image of school as home is that the inhabitants of school are to see themselves as a family. When this element of her system is overlooked, Montessori's belief in self-education makes Robert R. Rusk's claim that "the most significant feature of the system is the individualisation of instruction" (306) seem warranted. The conclusions reached in 1914 by William Heard Kilpatrick that Montessori "does not provide situations for more adequate social cooperation" (20) and in 1964 by J. McV. Hunt, a more sympathetic interpreter than Kilpatrick, that her pedagogy underemphasizes "the role and importance of interpersonal relationships" (in Montessori, *Method* xxxiii) also appear so credible that one must either discount the reports of the unselfish behavior of the children in her schools and their genuine concern for each other's welfare or else consider these phenomena to be miraculous. A description like Fisher's of the smiling faces of several children who witnessed one boy's long and ultimately successful struggle to tuck his napkin under his chin and of the way one then patted the napkin "as its proud wearer passed" (25) makes perfect sense, however, if one remembers that they and he are bound together by "domestic affection."

School, Home, and World

Sharing Montessori's belief in the value of domestic life, Fisher understood that the Casa dei Bambini was intended as a surrogate home for children. A home away from home, one is tempted to say, except for the fact that it was situated in the very building in which the children lived and the parents—or at any rate the mothers—were expected to make frequent visits. Foreseeing that one day in the United States women of all classes would be working outside their own homes and that most children would therefore be in need of surrogate homes, Fisher glimpsed the significance for her own country of Montessori's idea. But women at work outside the home is only part of the latter day domestic situation to which the Casa dei Bambini speaks.

Perhaps two million, possibly even three or four million people in the United States today, the great majority of whom live in families with children, are homeless (Kozol). Living on the streets or in rat-ridden, roach-infested shelters, these people can scarcely be said to dwell in a house let alone a home. Telling her audience about the district of Rome in which the Casa dei Bambini was located, Montessori said that children born in this Quarter "do not 'first see the light of day'; they come into a world of gloom... Here, there can be no privacy, no modesty, no gentleness; here, there is often not even light, nor air, nor water!"

(*Method* 52). Describing the Martinique, a once elegant hotel in New York City now littered with garbage and smelling of urine that in 1987 housed 438 homeless families, Jonathan Kozol gives a graphic sense of this world of gloom:

> It is difficult to do full justice to the sense of hopelessness one feels on entering the building. It is a haunting experience and leaves an imprint on one's memory that is not easily erased by time or cheerful company. Even the light seems dimmer here, the details harder to make out, the mere geography of twisting corridors and winding stairs and circular passageways a maze that I found indecipherable at first and still find difficult to figure out. After fifty or sixty nights within this building, I have tried but cannot make a floor plan of the place.
>
> Something of Dickens' halls of chancery comes to my mind whenever I am wandering those floors. It is the knowledge of sorrow, I suppose, and of unbroken dreariness that dulls the vision and impairs one's faculties of self-location and discernment. If it does this to a visitor, what does it do to those for whom this chancery is home? (28)

In the Martinique, where a family of four or even five lives in an unheated room with no chairs, no space to move around in, no stove — indeed, often no food to eat and no clean clothes to wear, there is no Casa dei Bambini. Of the more than 1,400 school-age children living there in 1985, Kozol estimated that over one-third did not usually get to school. Of those who did, many had to travel by bus or subway to outlying districts and even those attending schools nearby fell asleep at their desks and fell behind in their work.

It is not just the homeless who stand to benefit from a Montessorian conception of school, however. In the United States as recently as 1960, 70 percent of all families consisted of children and two parents, only one of whom — the father — worked outside the home (Mintz and Kellogg). By 1987, however, less than 10 percent of families consisted of a male breadwinner, a female housewife, and dependent children (Stacey). One in four children in that year lived in single-parent households and in the majority of two-parent families, both adults went out to work (Schmid). If the concept of school as surrogate home met a need of the poor in the San Lorenzo Quarter of Rome at the beginning of this century, in the United States at century's end it meets a need of almost all.

Fisher's insight into the significance of the Casa dei Bambini deserves closer study than I can possibly give it here. So that history does not repeat itself, however, let us at least ask how it is that she heard

Montessori's message when others did not and why those others were unable to hear either the original message or Fisher's reiteration of it.

An adequate answer to this second question turns on the fact that Montessori's domestic imagery violates this culture's basic expectations about the role of school in society. Implicitly dividing social reality into two parts – private home and public world – we take the function of education to be that of transforming children who have heretofore lived their lives in one part into members of the other part. Assuming that membership in the private home is natural, we see no reason to prepare people to carry out the tasks and activities associated with it. Perceiving membership in the public world as something to be achieved and therefore as problematic, we make the business of education preparation for carrying out the tasks and activities associated with it. Our culture's very conception of education, then, rests on the assumption that domestic life is that which we must learn to go beyond.

Of course almost all of us continue to live in homes and be members of families even as we take our place in the world at large. Yet although to go beyond is not necessarily to leave behind, becoming educated is nevertheless thought of not simply as a process of acquiring new ways of thinking, feeling, and acting. It is also assumed to be a matter of casting off the attitudes and values, the patterns of thought and action associated with domesticity. Considering these latter to be impediments to the successful performance of society's productive processes, we demand that education move us away from home and all it represents even as it equips us for life in the world.

Montessori's intention of bringing home and school into close connection thus conflicts with what appears to us to be the *raison d'être* for a society to educate its young. Writing *as* educators *for* educators, her translators and commentators would not, or perhaps could not, break out of the established framework of thought. When, as Hunt did in his introduction to a 1964 edition of *The Montessori Method*, they acknowledged the existence of Fisher's translation, they reverted quickly to the standard one. Even when their own appreciative readings of Montessori stood to be enriched by an acknowledgement of the homelike qualities of the Casa dei Bambini, these were ignored.

Henry Holmes noted in his introduction to the 1912 edition of the same work that "Montessori children often are in a real social enterprise, such as that of serving dinner, cleaning the room, caring for animals, building a toy house, or making a garden" (xxiii). He did not say, because he did not see, that as domestic activities each of these social enterprises takes on a special shape or that when they are considered together they constitute a special form of life. Martin Mayer, in turn, said in the introduction to a 1964 edition of *The Montessori Method* that whatever we do in response to "the scandal of modern education for slum children" (xxxviii), much of it will have to be "informed by the Montessori spirit, and some of it must employ the Montessori method" (xli). Emphasizing the seldom remembered fact that Montessori placed the Casa dei Bambini in "the model tenement where the children lived" (xxxix), and also made that tenement the Directress' home, he wanted it known that the Montessori system is not reducible to a set of techniques, however valuable they may be. Because he overlooked the ways in which the Montessori spirit is informed by domestic imagery, he conveyed to his readers at best a partial understanding of it.

Envisioning school as an extension of home and a means of strengthening that "temple of domestic affection," Montessori assigns it a societal function as different as can be from the one that almost all her interpreters and critics have taken for granted. The system of education that Kilpatrick said had nothing new in it of importance is, thus, nothing short of revolutionary. To be sure, Montessori was not the first person in the history of Western educational thought to deny a radical separation between school and home.[3] She is the one, however, to insist that the atmosphere and affections associated with home be preserved in school.

In the preface to *A Montessori Mother*, Fisher felt it necessary to make explicit the difference between her own standpoint and that of other commentators:

> This volume of impressions is not written by a biologist for other biologists, by a philosopher for an audience of college professors, or by a professional pedagogue to enlighten school-superintendents. An ordinary American parent, desiring above all else the best possible chance for her children, addresses this message to the innumerable legion of her companions in that desire. (x)

Writing as a mother who did not want to send her own preschool-age children to school in the outside world, and writing for mothers like herself, Fisher was, on the one hand, attuned to Montessori's domestic imagery and, on the other, better situated than her peers to step outside the educational paradigm that controlled their thinking. Had Montessori's more theoretically inclined discussants acknowledged her domestic metaphor and its implications, they would not only have had to rethink the relationship of school and home; they would also have had to reassess the relationship between school and world. Fisher's position made it unnecessary for her to face up to these difficult issues.

Montessori herself did not, to my knowledge, confront them directly. There is ample evidence in *Education for Peace*, however, that she was well aware that school forms people for life in the public world. She might have been reluctant to admit that from the standpoint of maintaining that world a conception of school as home will be considered dysfunctional. Yet she knew full well that a public world hospitable to peace in the positive sense would have to be very different from the one of her acquaintance and that those living in it would have to have been formed by a very different kind of school. Thus, although she did not explicitly formulate a new theory of the relationships obtaining among home, school, and public world, there is every reason to suppose that in her system there is no room for the radical dichotomies so often drawn in both her day and our own between school and home, home and world, world and school.

Romanticism and the Montessori Spirit

"The history of Romanticism is — to a far greater extent than the history of any other artistic or philosophical movement — a history of redefinitions," say Charles Rosen and Henri Zerner (16). Barriers between genres are broken down, they add, as is "the barrier between art and life" (17). Fusing and confusing genres, as according to Friedrich Schlegel's definition of Romanticism the novel does, Montessori proved herself in this respect a true Romantic and an artist among educators. School was to be a home for children. The homes of the poor were to move closer to the ideal home embodied by school. And if positive peace was ever to prevail, the world itself would become "a temple of domestic affection."

Yet if in one way an accurate rendering of Casa dei Bambini strengthens the case that Montessori is a Romantic thinker, in another it weakens it. In a book that attempts to reconcile Romanticism and liberal thought, Nancy Rosenblum distinguishes within "the romantic sensibility" the "militarist opposition to prosaic peace and the law of the heart's opposition to legalism" (6). The content Montessori builds into the term "home" — the domestic form of life the Casa dei Bambini embodies — is fundamentally at odds with both aspects of Romanticism.

"Romantic militarism," says Rosenblum referring to Wordsworth's "Convention of Cintra," "is the invention of sensibilities who usually were not inclined to real aggression, but who imagined war as the prime occasion for perfect freedom and self-expression" (9). Montessori imagined nothing of the sort. Serenity and love, not aggression and war, were to her mind the conditions in which the freedom and self-expression she prized so highly for children would flourish. Whereas in liberal thought liberty is inseparable from legal security and peace, Romantic militarism opposes "the prosaic promises of civil society" (19), Rosenblum continues. Montessori did not make civil society, which in liberal thought stands in opposition to home, the model for school. From the standpoint of Romantic militarism, however, the promises of the model she did adopt are even more prosaic than those of the liberal's public world. Starting as do Romantics from an assumption of individualism,[4] Montessori did not simply purge this position "of its moderating elements" (Rosenblum 10). She endowed it with a domestic dimension that at once nullifies the violence, the unrestrained self-assertion, the heroism that this strand of Romanticism idealizes and nurtures the peaceable qualities and prosaic activities it despises.

Washing and dressing, dusting and sweeping, setting tables and serving meals: these everyday chores are the stuff out of which the practical exercises for children in the Casa dei Bambini were constructed. Equating domesticity with banality and the banal with the boring, Romantic militarism would oppose any system of education that made such activities central. A love shorn of selfishness and possessiveness and purged of passion and transitoriness: this is the relation in which a Casa dei Bambini Directress was to stand to the children and in which they were to learn to stand to each other and to all living things. Glorifying unconstrained expression and extraordinary action, Romantic militarism would consider intolerable the serenity and calm affection embracing the children in Montessori's school.

Rosenblum distinguishes several versions of Romantic militarism, for it is by no means a unified position. While, for example, Wilhelm von Humboldt's emphasis on individuality and spontaneity seems to accord with Montessori's domestic vision, what does not accord is his claim that "the essence of man's value is that he can risk himself, and, when necessary, play freely with his own life" (Rosenblum 14). The attraction of death, or at least of risk to life and limb, is a unifying theme in Romantic militarism, one that contrasts sharply with the Montessori spirit. As the metaphor of a second womb implies, Montessori's hope was to institute an education for our young in which life could flourish. As her lectures to European audiences at a time when war was imminent demonstrate, her object was to prevent adults from waging war by instilling in them as children "a love and a respect for all living beings and all the things that human beings have built through the centuries" (*Peace* 33):

> If man were to grow up fully and with a sound psyche, developing a strong character and a clear mind, he would be unable to tolerate the existence of diametrically opposed moral principles within himself or to advocate simultaneously two sorts of justice—one that fosters life and one that destroys it. He would not simultaneously cultivate two moral powers in his heart, love and hatred. Nor would he erect two disciplines, one that marshals human energies to build, another that marshals them to destroy what has been built. (22)

The psychic transformation Montessori sought would deny the romantic militarist's identification of peace with ennui even as it made extinct his flirtation with death (Martin, *Virtues* 37ff).

The domestic spirit that animates the Montessori system precludes application not just of the Romantic militarist label. Romantic anarchism may not glorify death and danger but it too rejects social conventions (Rosenblum 34). In the works of Friedrich Schiller, for instance, "the law of the heart" stands in opposition to legalism. Yet what are Montessori's practical exercises if not training in those societal conventions that children are expected to learn at home? Striving for boundlessness not order, Romantic anarchism also values spontaneity and impulsiveness not predictability (Rosenblum 45). Yet as designed by Montessori those exercises in domesticity impose an external order on the process of learning even as they make predictable how children will act in society at large. Making "faithfulness to feelings the measure of all things" (Rosenblum 45), this brand of Romanticism in addition emphasizes sincerity and authenticity of the self over that self's ties with others. Yet the family model of human relationships the Casa dei Bambini incorporates constitutes a clear rejection of such "narcissistic self-absorption" (Rosenblum 45).

There is more to Romanticism, of course, than the militarist and anarchist aspects Rosenblum discusses. However, even that most central Romantic component—that authentic experience, self-discovery and wholeness derive from the individual's proximity to nature—is contradicted by the Casa dei Bambini. In Romanticism nature is represented by the open countryside: by mountains, rocks, clouds, flowers, trees, waterfalls. Montessori's school, however, is a creature of the city that in Romantic thought stands in opposition to nature. Geographical considerations aside, from the standpoint of Romanticism

Montessori makes the grievous error of interposing home and family between child and nature. Granted, for Romantics like Rousseau home and family are natural institutions.[5] Nevertheless, they necessarily mediate one's relationship with nature. View school as home and instead of the direct unmediated fusion of human being and the natural world desired by the Romantic, the primary relationship in education is of one human being to another.

A rereading of the Casa dei Bambini casts doubt, then, on Montessori's credentials as a Romantic theorist of education.[6] Yet she valued the child's freedom and spontaneity as few educational thinkers have. She rejected arbitrary distinctions and boundaries as a good Romantic must. And she saw in the child intimations of the man. As if this were not enough to make one uneasy about withholding the label, there is also the matter of joy, something Romanticism values highly and most educational theorizing ignores. Consider Fisher's description of a Casa dei Bambini child working with buttons on a frame who then succeeds in fastening a button on his own shirt: "When the bone disk finally shone out, round and whole, on the far side of the buttonhole, the child drew a long breath and looked up at me with so ecstatic a face of triumph that I could have shouted, 'Hurrah!'" (14). In the context of the Casa dei Bambini this experience of joy is not at all extraordinary: Fisher cites several more examples of it and Montessori presents it as an integral part of children's learning (*Method*; White).

Needless to say, in a Casa dei Bambini joy tends to be a byproduct of quiet concentration rather than the explicit goal of exuberant exertion. The Montessori system whose domestic spirit has eluded her interpreters' grasp thus demonstrates that peace is not intrinsically joyless and that domesticity need not be boring. Revealing that independence can flourish in an atmosphere of family affection, that a homelike environment does not entail passivity, and that the home's initiation into society's conventions is compatible with individuality and self-expression, this system allows us to recognize the false dichotomies upon which Romanticism rests.

The domesticity of the Montessori spirit makes the characterization of her educational thought as Romantic a contradiction in terms.[7] If, however, one rejects the terms according to which Romanticism defines domesticity, it is possible to see Montessori as a special kind of Romantic thinker. Call Montessori a Romantic pure and simple and the spirit of her system — the domesticity embodied in the Casa dei Bambini — is lost to view. Call her a theorist of domesticity and the Romantic cast of that spirit is suppressed. Call her a Domestic Romantic, however, and her celebration of child and home, freedom and cooperation, personal autonomy and social interdependence, individuality and connection to others, work and play, prosaicness and spontaneity, concentration and joy is illuminated; her refusal to accept arbitrary boundaries is respected; and the significance for our own day of her attempt to redefine not just the terminology of education but the terms according to which our young are educated is brought into focus.

Is Montessori the only Domestic Romantic in the history of educational thought or have there been others? The answer awaits detailed discussion of the roles played by home and family in the philosophies of the likely candidates. Supposing she is until now the sole member of the class however, the category is still worth establishing. That early twentieth-century Italian creation of hers, the Casa dei Bambini, holds so much promise for late twentieth-century America, who can say how many Domestic Romantics the future of educational thought will contain.[8]

Notes

1. For accounts of open education see, for example, Featherstone, Nyquist and Hawes, Rathbone, Silberman.

2. Montessori made it clear that in her idealized version of home women were the equals of men. Thus, in the Casa dei Bambini both boys and girls were to carry out these domestic activities.

3. See, for example, Pestalozzi's pedagogical novel *Leonard and Gertrude* and Dewey's *The School and Society*.

4. For a discussion of individualism in Montessori, see Martin (*Virtues*).

5. For critical discussion of this position see Martin (*Conversation*).

6. There are other reasons for doubt too, most notably her scientific approach to education. The question of the adequacy of the Romantic label in the case of Rousseau, Pestalozzi, and Froebel also arises but that discussion must be reserved for another occasion.

7. This is not to say that the lives of those we classify as Romantics did not include domesticity or that domesticity cannot be discerned as a *suppressed* or *repressed* theme in their works.

8. Montessori's invention must of course be adapted to local conditions. It is important, however, that in all contexts a domestic atmosphere be provided in which individuality can flourish lest the practical domestic exercises in which children engage become occasions simply for the imposition of a veneer of middle-class manners and tastes. It is also essential that measures be instituted to allow parents to cooperate with school people in this endeavor. It should be noted that Montessori herself advocated collective ownership of the Casa dei Bambini by parents. I wish to thank Ann Diller, Barbara Houston, Michael Martin, Beatrice Nelson, Jennifer Radden, and Janet Farrell Smith for their helpful comments on an earlier draft of this paper, the John Simon Guggenheim Memorial Foundation for the Fellowship that gave me the time to write this essay, and Radcliffe College for an appointment as Visiting Scholar during that Fellowship year.

Works Cited

Dewey, John. *The School and Society*. 1899. Chicago: University of Chicago Press, 1974.

Featherstone, Joseph. "The British Infant Schools." *Radical School Reform*. Eds. Beatrice and Ronald Gross. New York: Simon and Schuster, 1969.

Fisher, Dorothy Canfield. *A Montessori Mother*. New York: Henry Holt, 1912.

Holmes, Henry. "Introduction." *The Montessori Method*. By Maria Montessori. New York: Frederick A. Stokes, 1912.

Hunt, J. McV. "Introduction." *The Montessori Method*. By Maria Montessori. New York: Schocken Books, 1964.

Kilpatrick, William Heard. *The Montessori System Examined*. Boston: Houghton Mifflin, 1914.

Kozol, Jonathan. *Rachel and Her Children*. New York: Crown, 1988.

Martin, Jane Roland. *Reclaiming a Conversation*. New Haven: Yale University Press, 1985.

Martin, Jane Roland. "Martial Virtues or Capital Vices? William James' Moral Equivalent of War Revisited." *Journal of Thought* 22 (1987):32-44.

Mayer, Martin. Introduction. *The Montessori Method*. By Maria Montessori. Cambridge, MA: Robert Bentley, 1964.

Mintz, Steven and Susan Kellogg. *Domestic Revolutions: A Social History of American Family Life*. New York: The Free Press, 1988.

Montessori, Maria. *The Montessori Method*. New York: Frederick A. Stokes, 1912.

Montessori, Maria. *The Montessori Method*. New York: Schocken Books, 1964.

Montessori, Maria. *Education for Peace*. Chicago: Henry Regnery, 1972.

Montessori, Maria. *The Absorbent Mind*. New York: Dell, 1984.

Nyquist, Ewald B. and Gene R. Hawes, eds. *Open Education*. New York: Bantam Books, 1972.

Pestalozzi, Johann Heinrich. *Leonard and Gertrude*. Boston: D.C. Heath, 1885/1781.

Rathbone, Charles H., ed. *Open Education*. New York: Citation Press, 1971.

Rosen, Charles and Henri Zerner. *Romanticism and Realism*. New York: W. W. Norton, 1984.

Rosenblum, Nancy. *Another Liberalism: Romanticism and the Reconstruction of Liberal Thought*. Cambridge: Harvard University Press, 1987.

Rusk, Robert R. *Doctrines of the Great Educators*. 3rd ed. New York: St. Martin's Press, 1965.

Schmid, Randolph E. "Unmarried US Couples Increase, Top 2.3 Million." *The Boston Globe* (13 May 1988) A6.

Silberman, Charles E. *Crisis in the Classroom*. New York: Random House, 1970.

Stacey, Judith. "Sexism by a Subtler Name? Postindustrial Conditions and Postfeminist Consciousness in the Silicon Valley." *Socialist Review* 96 (1987) 8-28.

White, Jessie. *Montessori Schools: As Seen in the Early Summer of 1913*. London: Oxford, 1917.

Chapter 9

ROMANTICISM AND ALTERNATIVES

IN SCHOOLING

Edgar Z. Friedenberg

In 1967 the journalist and social critic, Peter Schrag, published in *The Saturday Review* an article in which he summarized and appraised the critique of schooling that a number of educationists and anti-educationists had generated during the previous decade, including Paul Goodman, John Holt, Ivan Illich, Jonathan Kozol, Herbert Kohl, George Dennison and myself, among others less persistent. We didn't entirely agree among ourselves, of course; but we did share a certain doctrinal persuasion. Schrag called us "Romantic Critics of Education," and the name stuck.

It stuck well enough to suggest, 20 years later, my inclusion in this collection of essays on *The Educational Legacy of Romanticism*. The legacy has been greatly eroded by inflation and yuppitude; but it seems to be recovering from that and there was something yuppie about it from the beginning anyway: despite liberal enthusiasm, not many poor kids got to go to progressive alternative schools.

This volume may have taken its initiative from "William Wordsworth and the Age of Romanticism" project, but Wordsworth entered and influenced our minds much less directly than William Blake. We did try to sing of innocence and experience but, on the whole, we were untroubled by intimations of immortality. We were also not much influenced by contemporary British efforts at educational reform. They interested us, and we studied their literature and their programs, but British school reform worked on a different operating system incompatible with ours. The problem lay in our contrasting attitudes toward social class which British school reformers acknowledged as an adamant if evil structural fact, while Americans regarded it as a troublesome phenomenon, a source of problems to be attacked by ingenious social engineering within the school system itself. We American Romantics regarded a pamphlet published back in 1932 by

George S. Counts, *Dare the School Build a New Social Order?*, as one of our classics. The British, who were free to be Marxist if this helped them to understand their society, knew it never could.

This is a rather crucial point. A lot of what might be called Romanticism among North American school-reformers was not in any positive sense ideological; it expressed a futile effort to evade ideology. Our social thought was weakened and convoluted, like Ptolemaic celestial mechanics, by our constant efforts to avoid a simpler but politically embarrassing model of how the system worked. We did this by imputing to the schools, and to individual educators, greater autonomy than they actually had, urging them to manoeuvre independent of the larger political and economic forces that constrained them. We recognized and acknowledged these forces, usually with intense and justifiable indignation; but we refrained from exposing their sources in the basic structure of western industrial society.

Our notions that appeared Romantic to Peter Schrag originated in our own false consciousness rather than in historical influences of which we were hardly aware. Yet, I think we do find a consistent reflection of Romanticism in plans for alternative schooling. For a distinctive characteristic of Romanticism has always been the exaltation of the individual in conflict with established social institutions; and Romantic critics have usually been blind to the ways in which their individualism has served to shield the very institutions they attacked, obscuring their understanding and deflecting their aim.

Whether we were influenced by the Lake Poets or reinvented for ourselves some of the values and attitudes that animated them, we certainly shared certain views that distinguished us from the conventional wisdom of our respective times. The most obvious of these was our attitude toward childhood itself. We usually think of Jean-Jacques Rousseau, who died when Wordsworth was eight years old, as the first author to write seriously about the education of children. He is an intellectual forebear of the Progressive Education movement of the 1920s and hence of the romantic critics of the 1960s as well, even though his approach to Emile's education was grotesquely manipulative — indeed, totalitarian. Moreover, he sought to carry the conflict between the individual and society to lengths twentieth-century critics of schooling, however Romantic, would have found shocking and destructive, as he isolated his hypothetical pupil during education to prevent his corruption. But he, like Wordsworth and like ourselves, took childhood seriously as a stage of life and children seriously as persons, at least in the abstract. Although as Professor Rosenberg makes very clear in his contribution to this volume, any resemblance between Emile and a real boy would be an unhappy coincidence.

Writers continued to treat children sentimentally through the nineteenth century as, of course, they still do today in Disneyworld and the republic for which it stands. Yet to us, Blake's line, "For I am black, but, O, my soul is white" is about as embarrassing as the death-scene of Little Nell: Peixote would not have found it sympathetic. But children mattered to Blake and Wordsworth, unlike Rousseau or Boswell, who once horrified Dr. Johnson by asking "If, Sir, you were shut up in a castle, and a newborn child with you, what would you do?" The Romantics never viewed children as raw material to be molded, or blank tablets to be inscribed, or animals to be trained.

The Romantic view of the individual as locked in continual conflict with society—the young Wordsworth fled England for a time to escape its anticipated repression—is reflected in distinctive attitudes toward education. It is the source of our most fundamental opposition to schooling, and our vigilant opposition to the processes by which schooling systematically alienates pupils from their own experience, and represses, ignores, or reinterprets that experience in terms compatible with conventional social demands. This opposition is what we have taken as our core responsibility; and what consistently arouses the fear, mistrust, and often the contempt of school personnel who, understanding full well that their own security depends on managing children and turning out an educated product either acceptable to their community or properly labelled as sources of potential trouble to be avoided, are Romantic critics.

But we have often been unaware of crucial assumptions about the nature of the individual and her relationship to society that underlie our position and tend to limit or distort it. Romanticism tends to assume that what makes each person uniquely valuable is her innate, human potential, and that the best education is that which encourages the fullest possible development of that potential. This doesn't imply, of course, that Romantic critics consider heredity a more decisive influence on individual development than environment. The converse is true, because all human beings, except a few who are obviously biologically damaged, are assumed to be so richly endowed that they might, nurturance and opportunity permitting, have become whatever they wished. Even with the most propitious education most potential must be forfeited, for choices foreclose most possibilities as they open the way to develop

others. But the best schooling makes it more likely that choices and
insights will lead to *coherent* development of the potential abounding in
each child.

What may be misleading about this view is not that it places too much
confidence in people who may simply be born too stupid to learn very
much. There probably *are* very, very few such people. Stupidity itself has
to be learned, and our schools, supported by the family and by certain
forms of religion, do a great job of teaching it. Let us grant at the outset
that just about everybody starts out with brains and vitality sufficient to
reach any human goal: redundancy is the key to success and survival in
evolution as in advertising. The difficulty is more subtle.

The romantic view of human personality, locked in dialectical struggle
with society, rather resembles the proverbial conception of a statue as
something a sculptor liberates from the block of stone in which it is
latent.   Great sculptors liberate profoundly meaningful and perhaps
beautiful statues; derivative sculptors liberate kitsch.   People who
consider honest sculpture obscene break the figure up or disfigure it as it
emerges. But all these depend on a social consensus as to what sculpture
is, and a socially engendered disagreement about what it should be, in
order to get started at all. In a society that does not recognize sculpture
as a form of human expression, there will be no figure to be liberated
from the block.   And, in any case, Pygmalion and Galatea
notwithstanding, the completed statue can only be made of such material
as the sculptor had available and could recognize as appropriate and able
to retain its properties.

Similarly, the Romantic view of the individual presupposes that
society itself recognizes and values, even though it is threatened by,
human personalities that transcend and resist social demands, while
commanding the language and imagery necessary to do so. This is a valid
assumption, by and large, for Western societies, although Clarence
Karier warns us in this volume that it has become very tenuous indeed.

But we tend to reify the personality as it emerges through the
educative — or more precisely, the experiential — process as if it were no
longer made of social stuff and now existed independently of the society
from which it was derived: influenced by it, vulnerable to it, sometimes
overwhelmed by it, but separate from it, as any organism must be from its
substrate. Well, so it does, so we are. But this view of the individual *vis-
à-vis* society has some curious implications for education. It does not
take enough account of the fact that individuality itself, awareness of
oneself as an individual, is a social construct and a much more imposing

construction in societies like our own than in many others. We regard respect for the individual as perhaps *the* basic value of our culture. This value morally distinguishes our culture from, and makes it superior to, cultures we regard as totalitarian; although Anne McWhir, another contributor to this collection, does well to remind us how ready we are to call that individual a monster. Being a creature of my culture, I endorse the supremacy of the individual wholeheartedly. I am not raising the issue here in a spirit of cultural relativism, but because it has some important metaphysical implications, that is, implications affecting one's view of the nature of reality itself.

As Romantics view the task of education as freeing individuals from the shackles of society so that, then, human potential may be most fully developed, we tend to lose sight of the fact that the possibilities have already been socially defined. (They have also been socially *determined* to a degree, but that is a different process, and one we have struggled against more effectively.) To return to the analogy, we, like fairly creative sculptors, already have in mind an extensive set of patterns that might be liberated from the inchoate personality of our pupils—and, being people rather than stone, so do they. But neither of us is fully aware of the degree to which those patterns themselves are social artefacts. We do know this about social roles that are presumably subject to choice, like becoming a doctor or lawyer. We understand that these roles are socially reified and would not exist except by definition and consensus. Some of us understand that this is also true of roles like "criminal" or "terrorist," though our adversaries are likely to freak out at this point in the argument.

But we have trouble thinking clearly about statuses that are perceived as the expression or consequence of natural endowments. Gender, of course, is the most salient of these; and we have begun to acknowledge that masculinity and femininity are largely socially constructed. *Gender*, that is, is socially constructed; although sex apparently is not, except, occasionally, by surgical intervention.

But then sexuality is socially constructed, too. The *feelings* we call sexual may not be so constructed; but the definition of them as sexuality is. The destructive insistence that some parts of the body are dirty and some acts felonies, just because they involve the genitalia—all this is socially constructed and serves obviously oppressive social functions as part of society's power-trip. One thing we Romantics *have* consistently supported is sexual liberation and freedom of sexual expression and choice. But half the battle was lost when these freedoms were called "sexual," whatever that may mean. One thing it surely means is that the neighbors have an acknowledged right to interfere in such matters, however destructively. It's a high price to pay, even for works of art like Benjamin Britten's operas; but without it, they'd have no plot.

The Romantic component of our heritage does indeed align us with those who try, in E. M. Forster's phrase, "to keep open a few breathing holes for the human spirit," and it is especially important that educators do that, for schools are especially stuffy places: it's their business to be. God knows—He is said, in our culture, to be omniscient—I do not disparage this function.   Societies *are* disgustingly, murderously oppressive and deserve far more opposition than they get. The point is not that as critics we are wrong, but that we must never forget that we, too, are part of the program stored in social memory. Romanticism, too, is itself a social construct. We, and the blows we aim against our, and our children's, oppressors, are part of the vast and intricate mechanism of culture's town cuckoo-clock. We always strike late, and afterward, everything goes on much as it had before, until society runs down or goes digital. The citizenry do not listen to us, but if we actually missed an hour, they'd be troubled by our silence. In some clocks, the program calls for us to be slain, but we always come back later. Romantic critics are essential to the illusion of progress. Progress, too, is a cultural conceit; societies that can't conceive of it don't have critics: the role does not exist.   They have crazy people and holy men and witches, but who doesn't?

Inevitably, then, we reify and confirm what we oppose in the process of opposing it. By complaining that the schools deny equality of opportunity, we endorse the specific conceptions of opportunity and equality our society purports to accept. By attempting through education to secure women's rights or gay rights or Black people's rights, we affirm that such people are a part of the natural order and as such ought to be treated as well as, if no better than, anybody else. But no social category is a part of the natural order; there isn't any natural order—though, naturally, most people think there is—and there aren't any natural, or unnatural, people.   It's all politics, really; which is why politics is dreadfully important. Liberal politics started in the Middle East, with Cain's prescient perception that all men are naturally brothers.

An important corollary to the alliance of the Romantic critic with individuals in their struggle with society is our attitude toward nature itself. We reify nature as a basis for exalting individuals, since the individuals are a part of the natural creation. We deny that this individuality, like the social order of which it is an inextricable component, is largely an artefact. It is self-evident, Americans declare, that all men are created equal: the more significant word in this declaration is not *equal* but *created*. Society and its institutions can claim no comparably divine origin.

Alternative education, therefore, has rather consistently shown a bucolic bias. Where feasible, alternative schools have established themselves in rural settings. Conservative boarding schools have, of course, also done so in order to protect their students from the putative evils of urban life and control their movements more completely. But the bucolic bias in alternative schools had a more positive basis: not the evasion of temptation but the quest for a better life-style if not a better life. Even those programs that were established in urban milieux tended to treat the city as a great, complicated farm to be explored at first hand by sharing, so far as possible, in its chores and establishing relationships with its, hopefully, friendly animals. Learning was to be concrete, personal, derived from the senses.

Our insistence that concrete experience form the basis for education opened Romantic critics to the change of being anti-intellectual, which was frequently and vituperatively made. Conventional schooling, I would argue, is far more weakly rooted in intellect than alternative schooling, since it depends so heavily on conventional wisdom and officially certified facts — the kind of thing James Herndon calls Egypt lessons, featuring flax. But it is true that our disdain for the abstract and for forms of understanding not validated through experience has left alternative-school students less committed to the basically urban, impersonal, competitive value-structure that prevails in contemporary life and suffuses the public school system. Alternative schools were, or tried to be, counter-cultural, as had the Lake poets, by and large. But the application of the Wordsworthian idiom to the schools of contemporary urban America might open the way to misconstruction, to recall "Tintern Abbey":

But oft, in lonely rooms, and 'mid the din
Of towns and cities, I have owed to them,
In hours of weariness, sensations sweet,
Felt in the blood and felt along the heart;
And passing even into my purer mind
With tranquil restoration. . . .

To which Coleridge, whom we usually think of as more conversant with these matters, might today respond, "Just say 'no,' William."

Conservative critics of the counter-culture also accused alternative schools of engaging in something worse than anti-intellectual: of teaching our students to be bone-idle and leaving them ignorant. The wave of large-scale, statistical, foundation-sponsored studies that fuelled the back-to-the-basics movement a few years ago and culminated, or came to a head, in Allan Bloom's recent polemic, *The Closing of the American Mind*, implied and sometimes alleged that our pernicious influence on the conventional schools had sapped their discipline, lowered their vitality, and led to widespread illiteracy, innumeracy, irreverence, and, worst of all, humanism. But this does us too much honor, crediting us with being the cause of developments that are deeply rooted in contemporary social change, and of others that never in fact occurred, Americans never having been much fonder of book-learning than they should be. They blame us for inroads on the dominant culture we would have been proud to claim but never achieved.

But it is true that our commitment to the personal, the subjective, and the small, face-to-face social unit tended to leave our students deficient in one crucial respect. Critical as we were of our society, we neglected to provide them with an adequate and comprehensive theoretical base from which that criticism might be justified. It was easy for them and for us to overlook this because the harsh impersonality of the society was so obvious, so painful as to seem to require no explanation. This was just the way it was, just as a life-expectancy of 30 years or so is the way it is for children born in much of what we call the third world. But, in fact, an explanation is required, all the more because our adversaries agreed so insistently that none was needed: Capitalist America was a triumph of nature itself. And we left our students without the means of constructing one. Any explanation that would have made sense would have required more Marxian insights than we could safely permit ourselves or them.

This deficiency has had serious consequences, one of which has been to leave us Romantic critics with excessive optimism about our power to change not only society, but the school system itself. Romantics affirm that individuals, pitting themselves against society, can make a difference; and of course they can. That point is not really debatable. But they can only struggle for those goals that their society permits them to imagine and teaches them to value, and on those terms it puts at their disposal. Even revolution, as Barrington Moore has eloquently argued, is a modern conception; before the eighteenth century, revolts sought to replace bad sovereigns, not unjust social orders—that would have been inconceivable (169-70). As Romantic critics of education in the 1960s, most of us sought to reform the schools, believing this to be possible. Those who did not, and became "de-schoolers," as John Holt did and Ivan Illich always was, seldom achieved a broader social vision. For to eliminate compulsory schooling in North America, and probably a lot of other places, is to create an abhorrent social vacuum that bigots and elitists rush to fill. The public schools *do* perform essential functions in a democratic polity, even though they are repressive and teach bullshit; indeed, perhaps just because they are and do. Pupils learn to deal with this in a place they manage to make their own, within their own distinctive, though derivative, culture. There is *glasnost* as well as peristalsis.

Meanwhile, some of the changes we sought to bring about have developed piecemeal. The schools are more humane than they were 30 years ago; at least, the brutality and violence that occur less frequently stem from official policy. Students acquired significant rights of freedom of expression which the Supreme Court of the United States has recently been busy eradicating; but, meanwhile, such rights have become conventional. There has been significant grade inflation: the curriculum is not being taken as seriously as it used to be.

With the rate of unemployment among youth what it is, and most of the few jobs available being dead-end employment in fast-food outlets, school is as good a place as kids are likely to find. Reforming *it* wouldn't make that much difference; the entire status of youth in society would have to be changed, which would mean fundamental change in society itself. It's about time, but it's tricky, and more than most of us Romantic critics wanted to bite off. *Epater les bourgeois!*, fine. *Ecraser l'infame!*, super. But *écraser la bourgeoisie*? That could lead to big trouble, and having to go through the whole thing again in Japanese.

The limitations of Romantic criticism of the schools become clearer if we contrast the views of Rousseau with those of Charles Dickens. By Dickens' time, the romance of Romanticism had begun to wear off and the dark, Satanic mills had pretty well prevailed in England's green and pleasant land. Schooling has never had a harsher critic than Dickens and for the right reasons.

Dickens did not, however, share with Romantic critics a belief that the right sort of schooling would lead children to develop their innate powers to grow into mature, creative, compassionate people. Such characters hardly occur in his novels: the kind or cheerful ones are even more sickly than the monsters. There are no good schools either, but he never suggests that there might be. The schools, like the courts, the economy, and even the family are institutions that—as W.S. Gilbert said of the House of Peers—are susceptible of no improvement whatever. The children in Dickens' works are doomed, and doomed, at best, to become adult members of a society he delighted to scorn. Dickens' view of society, indeed, is almost the negative, in the photographic sense, of the bucolic view of Romantic criticism.

Is such criticism of social institutions, then, essentially futile? Are Dickens and, worse, Bertolt Brecht, who was both a Marxist and a pessimist, right in portraying social institutions as essentially impervious to criticism and incapable of reform?   Not really, because their relationship to other institutions of society as well as to its members *does* change and so, therefore, does their social role.   I recall here the wonderfully sardonic passage in James Herndon's *How to Survive in Your Native Land* (111-12) in which he compares what is now happening to the schools with what happened to the Church in the past century or so. Neither institution changes much, but its authority diminishes and some of its social functions are taken over by other social institutions, while it remains freer, if somewhat diminished, to serve the people who feel that they need it and still believe in it. It is no longer the central integrating force in its society, but what it loses in authority—and funding—it may gain in authenticity.

Romantic critics have, I think, contributed a little encouragement to this process of de-authorization of schools and other institutions, which is certainly what we meant to do. In the process, we have been and still are blamed for diminishing the educational effectiveness of schooling. But education, in the sense of getting pupils to master the required course of study, has never been a major function of schooling, and the schools have never been very good at it. When they appeared to be, it was because their clientele was disproportionately drawn from children of elites who shared a consensus as to what the basics were and what knowledge was of most worth, and whose socialization at home, wholesome or destructive as the case might be, largely reinforced what the school provided.

As this consensus became diluted and eroded, the major social function of schooling shifted from instruction toward certification. However undependable the school might be as an independent and frequently embattled source of education, it retained its authority to identify and separate winners and losers on terms that reified the strictures of conventional society. It still maintains a virtual monopoly of this function, though challenged by social groups whose increasing political and economic power permit them to insist on the recognition of different norms of achievement. But the function of insuring social cohesion by controlling the meaning of symbols, setting the agenda for public discussion, and instilling the appropriate anxieties and misunderstandings needed to maintain and support the existing social order — Deborah Dooley deals superbly with this process in her contribution to this volume — is falling increasingly to the mass media — the *other* mass media, chiefly, of course, television. I don't think this is a calamity. Neither the schools nor the other media are or can be an independent source of truth or insight; and TV has the advantage of being, superficially at least, more immediately responsive to children's interests, and a source of a somewhat wider variety of role models. Both have a basic dishonesty built into them, which they occasionally transcend, about the world they purport to portray. The kids, be they pupils or viewers, know this quite well.

The great deficiency of the media is not their intellectual inferiority. The poorest television can hardly be more stupid and vulgar than the worst schoolteaching while being less coercive. The best television, like Public Broadcasting's *Frontline*, makes interdisciplinary presentations expressing value judgements in ways that high school and college courses, hobbled by specialization and commitments to ethical neutrality, seldom dare to do.

The worst deficiency of the media is not their banality, which they share with the rest of the culture including the family, but the fact that we view them in isolation. Kids need a safe place to hang out; they need a role and a status to explain to themselves and to others what they are doing there, they need access to adults when certain difficulties arise. The school is the highly imperfect instrument the society provides to meet these ends. "Education" is essentially the pretext that legitimates the status of the young — as students — even as it subordinates them, disparages their power to comprehend their own experience, limits their contact with unauthorized adults from whom, for better or for worse, they might learn a lot more.

Television can't provide any of this. Still, what we need more than better schools, and are just as likely to get, are public places in which the young are welcome to socialize with their elders, get decent jobs working with them, and feel respected for what they already are as well as what they may become. TV supplemented by covertly hostile shopping centres and fast-food outlets is not an adequate substitute. But, then, there is no substitute for decent cultural values, and the institutions that prevail will reflect and reinforce those values, whatever they may be. The most that Romantic poets, or Romantic critics, can do is to show those institutions and the values they express more clearly, in sharp relief. For this relief much thanks; 'tis bitter cold, and we've miles to go before we sleep.

Works Cited

Bloom, Allan. *The Closing of the American Mind: How Higher Education Has Failed Democracy and Impoverished the Souls of Today's Students.* New York: Simon and Schuster, 1987.

Herndon, James. *How to Survive in Your Native Land.* New York: Simon and Schuster, 1968.

Moore, Barrington Jr. *Reflections on the Causes of Human Misery and Upon Certain Proposals to Eliminate Them.* Boston: Beacon Press, 1972.

Schrag, Peter. "Education's Romantic Critics." *Saturday Review* 50 (February 18, 1967): 80-82.

Chapter 10

THE THEORY OF THE SUBJECT
IN CONTEMPORARY CURRICULUM THOUGHT

Madeleine R. Grumet

Perhaps I should begin by apologizing for the title of this paper. It was motivated by an ambition that I now renounce, hoping that I have realized it somewhere else. The "Theory of the Subject in Contemporary Curriculum Thought" promised, I thought, the large, subsuming, but hospitable categorical discourse that men produce. And in constructing the kind of title that men devise for their monologues, I had hoped to bring an air of seriousness, of significance, of matter both to my words and to myself. The title was my defence and my revenge.

Now, almost two years after the conversation with John Willinsky that spawned this false promise, I am taken up with the work of a large, urban school of education. The desire for matter, to matter, is absorbed into the material of this daily work, and writing has fallen back into its previous, its privileged and appropriate relation to what I write about, what we call our material.

The subject who appears in the original title disappears into abstraction, excusing me from speaking through and to my own subjectivity. It is an ironic evasion, considering that for the last decade I have worked with autobiographical texts to identify and justify the epistemological status of an individual's experience of education in curriculum theory and practice. And for years I have been struggling with the Romantic tradition that supports this search for the voice of the subject, both drawn to and repelled by its self-consciousness. Through writing and reading I have played out my ambivalence. Contemporary theories of the text offer elaborate diversions. They invite us to talk about how texts are produced by subjects and in turn produce subjectivity. Displacing Marxist correspondence theories with a discursive model of the immaculate conception, they truly argue that words create consciousness. Experience is reduced to genre as we stroll through our lives narrating someone else's story. What I intend to show is that just as the Romantic poets wrenched themselves away from the dominant discourse of their age in order to construct another possibility for themselves, and then for other selves, so must we, who often think of our own lives in terms of their quest, revise their version of subjectivity.

Harold Bloom defines two stages or modes of energy in Romantic writing — the organic and the creative:

> Prometheus is the poet-as-hero in the first stage of his quest, marked by a deep involvement in political, social and literary revolution, and a direct, even satirical attack on the institutional orthodoxies of European and English society, including historically oriented Christianity, and the neoclassic literary and intellectual tradition, particularly in its Enlightenment phase. The Real Man, the Imagination, emerges after terrible crises in the major stage of the Romantic quest, which is typified by a relative disengagement from revolutionary activism, and a standing aside from polemic and satire, so as to bring the search within the self and its ambiguities. In the Prometheus stage, the quest is allied to the libido's struggle against repressiveness, and nature is an ally, though always a wounded and sometimes a withdrawn one. In the Real Man, the Imagination stage, nature is the immediate though not the ultimate antagonist. The final enemy to be overcome is a recalcitrance in the self, what Blake calls the spectre of Urthona, Shelley the unwilling dross that checks the spirit's flight, Wordsworth the sad perplexity or fear that kills or, best of all, the hope that is unwilling to be fed, and Keats, most simply and perhaps most powerfully, the Identity. (11)[1]

Reflexive Writing

We write, we are told, at the edge of our egos (Showalter). Our thoughts, drawn through our walks to the subway, conversations in the halls, our motions to accept the minutes as read, our requisitions and our petitions, are projected beyond our fingertips, carried by another medium until they are inscribed, printed or illuminated on yet another surface. Reaching beyond our bodies and the daily spaces we inhabit, our written words are always linked to the life of our bodies, to the brightness of the sky, to an autumn chill or an endless fatigue that gathers in the chest and petitions for a cough that never comes. Nevertheless, what we write never exactly coincides with the flow of our perceptions and sensations. Once arranged in language, they assume pattern and purpose; the line of our argument reaches to a significance always located just beyond the edge of the data. Our writing takes us always a little over budget.

In the talk of teaching words flow or trickle, or rush like a cataract, and they carry me with them, like a twig in the current, toward someone else. Nevertheless, it is narcissism that prevails at the word processor. Peering into the dark waters of the monitor, I find flickering images of self-made-word. The hum of its fan is a metabolic murmur and I stroke the monitor, confusing it for the hard drive that holds all my thoughts since 11-7-88 and that I love like I love my own head.

Perhaps one way of conceiving of the distinction between teaching and writing is the distinction between intentional and reflexive thought. In the mode of intentionality we are swept into the objects of our thought. There is no self-consciousness as we run to catch the train, as we turn the page of the novel, as we worry about what we will say when we pick up the phone or start the lesson. Eager as they were to return to nature, our Romantic predecessors did not seek this mute absorption in what is other. Hartman argues that the Romantics never desired a "mere return" to nature, but only a temporary reversion to the undifferentiated phase in their own development in order to recreate the process of their individuation and identity.

Reflexivity always harbors this invitation to revision. Contrary to its reputation, reflexivity is not merely thinking about matters that have to do with oneself. Reflexivity is thought about thought. It is thinking about those thoughts one has had about oneself, or about other intentional objects, that train, that novel read so intentionally I can't remember anything about it, the dreaded phone call or the lesson. Now all writing is not necessarily reflexive in this manner; it is not always this second seeing. Sometimes the import of the text moves with the centrifugal energy of intentionality, flung out from itself toward the object. Then, even though the presentation of the object, let us say, curriculum theory, is influenced by the writer's history and perspective, those influences are muted; they fall into the background and only the object is highlighted. Sometimes the presentation of the object is subordinated to a rhetorical intention, and the real object is the imagined reader and her persuasion or manipulation. Sometimes, the writing merely encodes an old intention and produces a document that is a memorial to something lively long ago.

Writing that is reflexive challenges the writer to turn back on her own previous ideation, to turn it over, take it apart. Then it becomes reading as well. Rooted in the past, turned to the future, this kind of reflexive writing cannot get stuck at either the beginning or the end of time without falling back into the intentional mode, becoming stuck in the past or marooned in the future. Reflexive writing is dialectical in that it requires a re-reading of yesterday and tomorrow from today's position and a deconstruction of the present to reveal its surreptitious commitments to other times and places. The ties to past and present are not ignored; they are interpreted as self-as-written is re-read.

The style and method of a paper of the sort I had anticipated, one that would create the categories and then sort the work of others into them, would for all its Aristotelian elegance contradict what I mean to be its content: the relationship between subjectivity and curriculum. The Aristotelian approach, so present in our reviews of the literature and critiques of each other's work, is rarely reflexive. Under the guise of "objectivity" it hides the interests of the one who categorizes and critiques within an order that legitimizes his desire. Even the most obsessive of us, sorting the silverware once again, spending precious hours when we could be writing, rearranging the objects on the desk, the books on the shelves, is aware that she is struggling to make herself a safe and definitive place where she can hide from the winds of thought.

Curriculum is another shelter. The arrangement of knowledge, of texts, the ordering of the syllabus, class meetings, exams and papers, the articulation of the course of study, requirements for the major, for graduation — for existence — can and will suffice. But it too is bad faith. It collapses the subjects who create and are created by these processes into these categories. Swallowing them into the objects of their thought, it reduces them to their intentionality and denies the reflexive space, the wedge of negation, the possibility of transformation, that, along with Sartre, I call subjectivity.

Romanticism and Curriculum Theory

Romantic poets and philosophers were suspicious of reflexivity but spent their lives wandering through it while warning us away from it. They associated it with the Enlightenment rationalism that entered their culture as the science of society was substituted for its religion, and they longed for a lost world where thought and feeling and nature were one. Lionel Trilling understood the Romantic movement as an attempt to compensate for this loss of religion by providing "a vivid relation to the sentient world," but pointed out that more than they sought religion, the Romantics sought restitution of the power to feel (422).

Terry Eagleton traces the Romantic flight from the anomie and atomism of industrial capitalism, through this search for feeling, to the splitting off of art, and literature from the matters of the mundane world

(18). After the Romantics, he claims, literature becomes synonymous with the imaginary and whatever does not exist:

"Imaginative creation" can be offered as an image of non-alienated labor; the intuitive, transcendental scope of the poetic mind can provide a living criticism of those rationalist or empiricist ideologies enslaved to "fact." The literary work itself comes to be seen as a mysterious organic unity, in contrast to the fragmented individualism of the capitalist marketplace; it is "spontaneous" rather than rationally calculated, creative rather than mechanical . . . . Its task is to transform society in the name of those energies and values which art embodies. Most of the Romantic poets were themselves political activists, perceiving continuity between their literary and social commitments. (20)

Like vines of ivy clinging and curling around the houses of knowledge, these themes of Romanticism — intuition, transcendence, criticism, unity and loss — have crept around our sense of subjectivity in its relation to curriculum. Curriculum is our memorial to an old intentionality. Remembered, resymbolized, a former relation to the world is reviewed and then arranged for someone else. What we have constructed out of our reflection is presented to the young as appropriate and necessary objects of their intentionality. What curriculum theory strives to return to the reception of curriculum is the reflexive moment that was there in its creation.

In the 1970s, what is now known as reconceptualist curriculum theory split into two strands: existentialist and Marxist critiques of schooling. Each critique was motivated to expose the ways that curriculum masked both the intentionality and reflexivity that funded it, hoping to establish the primacy of the subject in the place that had become crowded with the objects of its thought.

Existential theorists sought subjectivity, poking through the rubble of accountability, behavioral objectives, the dominance of behavioral psychology, standardized testing. Seeking a return to sensuous experience, to the passions, terrors and persistent dilemmas of human experience, existential theorists turned to literature, autobiography, and philosophy to address subjectivity. Lonely, opposed, the subject of educational experience, teacher or student, was enjoined to take responsibility for what she made of what schooling had made of her. The social self inscribed in autobiographical accounts, in fiction or research, was an objectification that invited repudiation. Peering into the critical mirror provided by the objectification of her thought, the student was challenged to repudiate that image, and like Sartre's image of a snake wriggling out of old skins, to make herself anew.[2] Phenomenology, the lure of the *lebenswelt* and the texture of the concrete linked the existentialist work to the romance of the object: the "violet by the mossy stone," the song of the nightingale, the Elgin Marbles.

Neo-Marxist curriculum theorists were critical of educational theory that stressed subjectivity of the individual teacher or student. Marxist literary critics had attacked the novel as a bourgeois consolation, designed to compensate the middle class for the loss of enterprise, adventure and feeling in their lives. Autobiographical methods were also charged with replicating the structure of the *roman*, the journey that dramatizes the individual's lonely struggles, alienation and desire for reunion. Studies of life history and educational experience were accused of condoning the retreat to privacy, surrendering the public world and the class struggle to aesthetic and emotional solace. Currently, we find contemporary literary criticism challenging identity itself, impugning the authority of the narrative voice. Deconstruction distrusts the author, claiming that the coherence, momentum and argument of the linear story creates an illusion of individual control and purpose that obscures the confused, accidental and surprising character of everyday life and of the texts that we write about it.

In contrast to the existentialist study of the individual, the neo-Marxist critique of schooling insisted that we investigate the ways that schooling enforces the socialization to the world that Wordsworth, Shelley, Keats and Byron fled. Ethnographic studies of classroom life testified to the correspondence of its routines, discourse and work ethic to the means and relations of production that prevail in the workplace (Carlson). Subjectivity is hard to find in these accounts and is only identified when it is attached to behavior that expresses refusal. "Resistance," expressed in dropping out, acting out, underachievement or the theater of punk performance, becomes the expressive medium of human consciousness in these accounts.

It was Paul Willis' study, *Learning to Labour*, that provided the model for studies that searched out and resymbolized the resentment and refusal of those who stay and fight. Willis was eager to escape the individualism of the Romantic tradition that saw refusal as the act of the yearning individual. He situated negation in the contradictions of working class culture and its masculine ideology to the feminized and middle class culture of the school. And whereas the Romantics had yearned for a total unity where human consciousness participated in a global harmony, Willis eschewed that transcendence and situated unity within the collectivity of male adolescents.

By identifying the class base of the brilliant humor and obstructionism of the "lads," Willis was not associating their power to say no with the exercise of their ontological capacity for negation celebrated in existential theory. Repudiating, as well, the sentimental portrayals of consciousness brought to us by humanistic psychology in which true selves hovered just under the surface of habitual duplicities and collusions waiting for an invitation to burst out and express their authenticity in primal screams, t-groups, and values education, he located negation not in nature, not in persons, but in discourse. Sadly, despite their macho togetherness and theatre of intimidation, Willis' "lads" are no more effective than their brooding precursors, exiled in Italy or moping by the side of the lake. Committed to and trapped in their otherness, their collective voice is as impotent and poignant as the suffering heroes of Byron's sonnets.

Isolated either in existential loneliness or class entrapment, the Romantic heroes of existential and Marxist reconceptualist curriculum theory have failed to make schools the sites of social transformation. Our failure is compounded by the conservative curriculum criticism that has come from Bloom and Hirsch. Estranged from the schools and students in the cities they grew up in, lonely for the intellectual and ethnic communities that inspired them and celebrated their achievements, these scholars have also returned to the themes of Romanticism in their attempts to cure what ails us. They have invoked the Romantic theme that is the most insidious of all, because it appears the most harmonious. They have invoked the myth of return to a culture that is coherent and integrated.

Ironically, it is Romanticism which Hirsch castigates as he denounces the child-centred curricula of Rousseau, Dewey, and the so-called Romantic critics of the 1960s and 1970s. Exposing the emptiness of the skills curriculum, Hirsch calls for curriculum that requires students to know the history, literature, science and politics that constitute our culture. He worries that the curriculum of our schools is fragmented: "It isn't facts that deaden the minds of young children, who are storing facts in their minds every day with astonishing voracity. It is incoherence – our failure to ensure that a pattern of shared, vividly taught, and socially enabling knowledge will emerge from our instruction" (133). He tells us how his father would quote Shakespeare to encourage timely action from his customers:

There is a tide in the affairs of men
Which, taken at the flood, leads on to fortune;
Omitted, all the voyage of their life
Is bound in shallows and in miseries.
On such a full sea are we now afloat,
And we must take the current when it serves,
Or lose our ventures.

If Romanticism repudiates the fragmentation and industrialization of contemporary culture ("the world is too much with us; late and soon/ Getting and spending we lay waste our powers"), Hirsch's own navigation through the arts and sciences merely catches the tide of socialization and expediency. His list of terms, names and allusions that constitute the background knowledge of Western culture collapses critique into collusion.

Bloom, disgruntled and sardonic, could never be accused of collusion, at least not with anyone living. *The Closing of the American Mind* is a memorial to the bitter exile of the Romantic critic as Bloom rails against the accommodations to power and comfort made by the academic disciplines. Reassured by Plato's longing for ideal truth or Rousseau's longing for the state of nature, he yearns to see the ancient divisions between mind and body, male and female, freedom and bondage encoded in our personal identities. He is convinced that these antimonies structure human consciousness and identity, and that knowing is a profound challenge to one's being:

True liberal education requires that the student's whole life be radically changed by it, that what he learns may affect his action, his tastes, his choices, that no previous attachment be immune to examination and hence re-evaluation. Liberal education puts everything at risk and requires students who are able to risk everything. (370)

Bloom seeks the integration of knowing and being because he condemns being to the harsh and excluding commitments that make us crave knowledge of what we have been denied.

Existential, Marxist, or conservative, curriculum theories are all refusals of the common order. They express longing for coherence, for passion, for identity, for nature and spirituality. And they all locate what they seek beyond what goes on in schools. Predicated on loss, these curriculum theories replicate the rupture in human consciousness that strands us on one side, longing for the other.

Romanticism and Feminist Theory

If we return to the terms that Eagleton uses to describe the Romantics — "mysterious, organic, intuitive, transcendental, artistic" — we recognize that they are also the terms that we associate with feminine rather than masculine gender. Object relations theory accounts for this bifurcation by pointing to the different experiences of identification and separation that male and female children undergo when the primary parent of each sex is the mother. Male gender is purchased at the price of the male's repudiation of his earliest identifications. Unfortunately, repression is not neat; so if feeling like mother is repressed, so is feeling the way the world felt then, when it was not yet charted by language and sorted into concepts.

This history of separation that marks the gendered ego of the mother-raised male is swept into a subsuming theory of subjectivity by Hegel and by the German and English Romantic philosophers and poets who follow him. Here is Hegel's version of the Fall:

> The first reflection of awakened consciousness in men told them they were naked .... The hour that man leaves the path of mere natural being marks the difference between him, a self-conscious agent, and the natural world. The spiritual is distinguished from the natural ... in that it does not continue a mere stream of tendency, but sunders itself to self-realization. But this position of severed life has in its turn to be overcome and the spirit must, by its own act, achieve concord once more .... The principle of restoration is found in thought, and thought only: the hand that inflicts the wound is also the hand that heals it. (qtd. in Hartman 81)

In contrast to this portrait of alienated and isolated male subjectivity, women, according to the theory of object relations, may sustain their earliest object relations. Blurred and distant, for they are also situated before speech, these identifications are not antagonistic to their own gender identities and continuity with what has come before and may come again is not only possible but unavoidable. What men cannot remember, women cannot forget.[3] Nevertheless, as Hegel's narrative implies, western culture has chosen to honor male amnesia rather than female memory. Mary O'Brien's brilliant critique of Hegel shows us how only men are seen to have this second nature and it is this second nature that Hegel, Freud and our Romantic friends valorize as the achievement of culture, of maturity, of, finally, men.

If becoming male comes to mean becoming not female, repudiating and repressing the deeply felt and original relations that bind us to life, then the romantic project of restitution becomes the project of the male to reclaim what he has abandoned. The yearnings in existential, Marxist and conservative curriculum theories are poignant echoes of the loss that funds male gender, seeking feeling, integration, continuity that, because they are associated with infancy, with woman, with their own womanliness are terrifying and can be desired only if they are portrayed as other, mysterious, distant, compelling but impossible.

For women the matter is more complex. If the project of male genderization is to switch identity from female to male, the project for women is to retain their identification but to switch the object of their erotic desire from female to male. Men may choose not to be like their mothers, but they may, if heterosexual, choose to desire the female. Women learn to love the one who is not like them. The abandonment of their mother, their first love, supports their differentiation and secures their otherness and independence. Their attachment to the male comes later in their developmental story however, and they are trapped in desiring the one who is different from them but who desires them to be like the one they are turning from. Woman, trying to elude continuity, immanence, transcendence in pursuit of her own autonomy and passage to the public world is desired for those very attributes.

Although object relations theory emphasizes the social and historical relations within which we come to form, rather than attributing our development to an inevitable unfolding of biologically determined preferences, these critical relations develop so early in the life of consciousness (which Freud called the archaic period), that the feelings and fantasies they engender might as well be genes or stones. Although object relations theory, as presented by Nancy Chodorow, offers us little relief from the harsh repressions and denials that genderization entails, the clinical practice of object relations theorists identifies the ways that we use play, literature, culture to mediate between our present and lost selves.[4]

The feminist theory of Julia Kristeva, combining psychoanalytic and literary insights, also offers us a way of thinking about this fissure in the life of consciousness so that it is not a wide divide that separates us from each other by gender, age, class or any of the identifications that constitute the ego. When Kristeva calls for the "demassification of the problematic of difference," she is saying that it is not the difference *between* males and females that we must examine so much as it is difference *within* each of us that needs to be addressed.

Kristeva is convinced that our earliest ways of being in and responding to the world never disappear. She classes the expressive and perceptual modalities that survive from this archaic stage as constituting a semiotic system of meanings that runs through our symbolic discursive systems like a deep current. She encourages us to incorporate the semiotic into our lives rather than splitting it off into fantasy, into regression into Romanticism. The feminist project in curriculum theory is to gather up what Marcuse called "rebellious subjectivity" like pearls from the sea. The yearning, the loss that surrounds whatever has been split off from our lives, demands not only articulation but integration.

Romanticism and Reflexive Reading

I ask my students to write about educational experience. When I first worked this way with William Pinar we invited a coherent narrative, a life-history if you will (Pinar and Grumet). This invitation received, to my dismay, what it sought. Compliant writers selected or created episodes that would bring verisimilitude to an imagined logic for their lives. This is the deadly coherence that Nietzsche warned us about when he condemned the ideal selves upon whom we drape the fabric of our lives (Altieri). I countered this coherence with a request for multiple texts. I now ask the writers to compose three distinct narratives of "educational experience" ("Personal Knowledge"). I ask them to abstain, if they can, from constructing a definition of "educational experience" in the three essays, but to work instead from particular episodes in their lives that they associate with the phrase without determining in advance their rhyme and reason.

Arguing that the truth of autobiography, like that of fiction, resides in its detail rather than its generalization, I ask them to bring forward every physical detail of the account that they can remember, even if it does not seem significant to the meaning of the narrative. Carried in the wake of these details, in the felt texture of the world of memory, in its rhythms and inflections, we find traces of the semiotic disposition that Kristeva has identified. Melodies, and images ripple through the text, reporting the relatedness of the subject to the world, a profound connection that inheres in the text despite the thetic structure of sentences founded on the separation of subject and predicate.

Over and over again undergraduate and graduate students mourn the loss of their innocent vision of the world, often rendering in poignant detail the day that innocence was compromised by the sadistic teacher, the expedient classmate, the dogmatic text. Over and over again they scale mountains, brave tumultuous seas, slick highways, football and hockey fields risking even enough to satisfy Allan Bloom in order to feel and to claim a moment that is vivid. To ask for a narrative is to invite this invention of another world, richer, brighter harder, fuller than the one that generated this discourse. If the writer's task is to write his way out of this world my task has been to read him back in, and to find the places in the text where a lively engagement in the world undermines the futility of the romantic vision.

These instructions have elicited narratives that closely resemble the Romantic journey that Wordsworth describes in *The Prelude*, although the requirement of three stories provides some relief from the trek though the wilderness as other scenarios are chosen. It is important to ask for three stories. Two stories would summon dyadic oppositions and lead us into the romantic schism between presence and absence, loss and reconciliation, industry and fantasy. My goal is to find ways that curriculum can mediate these oppositions, so I ask for three. The three stories that follow present the writing of one student, Katherine Bennett (who has agreed to let me use them in this way) with my reading of them that works to grasp subjectivity and to draw it back from the Romantic horizon to the material world where we live. The journeys that Katherine Bennett makes in each of these stories recapitulate and challenge the legacy of Romanticism.

Late September

Heel, toe. Heel, toe. My brown and white saddlebacks, scuffed from much wear, clicked against the sidewalk. It was a cool but sunny day in the fall of 1968. Because of this, I was wearing two sweaters, one brown wool V-neck and over it, a gray cardigan. The gray one matched my gray and cream plaid skirt. The brown one didn't. After walking heel, then toe, for half a block, the calves of my legs began to ache, so I decided to walk so that my skirt swung back and forth as much as possible. I became so engrossed in watching my skirt that I tripped over a broken piece in the sidewalk. I have no memory of feeling self-conscious, only that my shadow was long upon the sidewalk and the air smelled tangy and fresh.

I arrived at my friend Nancy's house, which always smelled of cats, and rang the doorbell. Nancy opened the door. She was three years older than I, but still my best friend. I asked her if I could borrow "the bike." My parents did not have enough money to buy me a bike and since I had just learned to ride one, Nancy's father had said I could borrow their extra bike as long as I always put it in the garage when I was done. Nancy said, "sure" and that she would go riding with me. We went out to the garage and got the bikes out. My bike was a small, very old bike with wide tires. It was painted a dark gray. Nancy's bike was blue and a little bigger than mine. We proceeded to ride around the block on the sidewalk. We were not allowed to ride in the road yet. I had only recently learned to ride a two-wheeler and I remember the incredible sense of freedom and self-esteem it gave me. The wind would whistle in my ears and blow my bangs away from my face. I felt very powerful and loved. I felt as though people were stopping to watch me ride past and that they were saying things like, "Wow, look at that girl! She must be something if she knows how to ride a two-wheeler." Riding that bike was a very big deal to me.

Nancy and I rode around the block a few times and then rode around a different block a few times. We even stopped at the Elmhurst and bought a piece of gum for a penny. It was Bazooka, so we split it in half at the crease and shared it. Then we read the comic and the fortune which said, "Good things come to those who wait." I remember feeling very independent and mature. I thought that everyone would think that I was really grown-up, seeing that I was riding a bike to the store. There were always a lot of bikes at the store, belonging to "big kids," who were probably getting ice cream or something. Now I was one of them. As I reflect back on this moment, I wonder what this urge to grow up means. Why do children wish for the burden of responsibility, the complications of relationships, the crushing disappointments? As a child, I had no idea of these things. I only saw freedom, like the bright light at the end of a tunnel. I wonder what I would have done had I known that, as an adult, I would wish again for the simplicities of my childhood; the haunted houses, the Mother-may-I?'s, the fighting to stay up late and the homework.

Nancy and I walked our bikes across the street and then rode down the sidewalk toward her house. When we reached it, I started to put my bike in the garage but Nancy said just to leave it in the front yard. I protested, "But your father always said to . . ." Nancy said, "Oh, he won't care. It's only for a few minutes." I left the bike in the front yard and we went into the house and went "down cellar" to play a game. The cellar had a painted cement floor, was very damp and smelled also of cats. Nancy and I decided to play a game of Candyland but I remembered that it was time for dinner. I went out the back door and through my backyard to my house. I told Nancy that I would be back later.

After I had eaten my dinner, I walked down the sidewalk to Nancy's house again. When I came in sight of the yard I remembered that I had left the bike out, but it wasn't there. As I reached the front walk, Nancy's father came out the front door. He was a big man, 6′ 2″ and about 275 lbs. He always wore green work pants and a white T-shirt. He always had a big lump of tobacco in his cheek; however, he had never been known to spit. The nice, friendly Mr. Reitnauer was gone for the moment. When he saw me, he began yelling and screaming at me about the bike being left in the yard. I was so mortified and embarrassed that I didn't even hear what he said. My eyes were locked on the big lump of tobacco in the side of his cheek, which kept going up and down as he yelled. Finally, I could hear again. Mr. Reitnauer was saying that I could never ride the bike again. My dreams of freedom and adulthood were shattered. I began to cry, turned and ran home as fast I could.

The journeys of the Romantic poets are recapitulated in this first narrative as the child's and the adult's visions are intertwined, each shaping the other. The childhood that is remembered is movement resymbolized. She doesn't just run to Nancy's house but improvises on her own movement, heel toe, heel toe, skirt swishing, and she is rebuked for the reflexivity when she trips on the pavement. Reflexivity is not experienced as separation, though, for she reports no memory of self-consciousness. Her image is her shadow long upon the sidewalk and the air smelled tangy and fresh. Being in the world and thinking about being in the world are intertwined.

Bike riding is another matter. Somewhat removed from the ground, heel toe, skirt swishing gives way to freedom, but this freedom is again escorted with attachments. This is not the solitary ride. She is with Nancy, the older girl. They break the Bazooka bubble gum at the crease. Pink, and soft, it is an oral memento of bubbling babiness, of a pliable mother/baby body that they share. The fortune cautions them to wait and she worries now that she rushed through these years desiring a false freedom. The Romantic image of the light at the end of the tunnel appears, but the light is misleading as it illuminates this false freedom. Childhood's constraints, binding and terrifying as they were then, are all impositions from outside and less binding than the constraints that bind her as an adult. The romance of freedom that Katherine has borrowed from the older girl turns out to be the property of the father. He grants it and takes it away. The romance of the free child gives way to guilt and fear and disgust as she faces the tobacco-chewing menace whom she has offended.

Late Spring

"Mom, Michael's hanging in the lilac tree by his foot!" I can hear myself yelling these words, over and over again, like they were the last sane words that would ever come out of my mouth. There was no answer, no rush of my mother out the back door to save my youngest brother, who was very accident-prone.

It was May 19, 1968 and I was eight years old. Michael was five and Joe, six. I called to my mother again but she still didn't answer. I went into the house and through the kitchen door. There were still dishes on the counter and in the sink. My mother was in the dining room, just hanging up the phone. She was crying. I had never seen my mother cry. She said, "Katie, don't take it too hard..." Just then my father drove in the driveway. My mother went out the front door and I, out the back. I looked up the driveway and saw my father get out of the car. He was crying too. He took my mother in his arms and led her to Harriet's porch next door. Harriet was an elderly lady who was very close to my parents. They all sat on the porch steps together. I went back out to the lilac tree where my brother was still hanging. Somehow, Joe and I got him down. I told my brothers what I had seen and speculated that probably John Horey had died. He was my mother's ex-boss who had leukemia.

A few minutes later, Harriet came out back and asked us if we wanted to go get some ice cream. We all said "yes" and got in her car. She took us to the Elmhurst and I got a chocolate cone. Joe and Mike started talking about Mom and Dad crying when we drove into the driveway. I reiterated my statement about John Horey. Harriet shut the car off and said, "Kids, your grandma died." There was a moment of silence and then I said, "Which one?" Harriet said, "Your grandma Strong." I felt a rushing, roaring sound in my ears, like a big jet was flying overhead. All of a sudden, I didn't want my ice cream anymore. I took it into the house and when I saw my mother coming down the stairs, I started to cry, but she wouldn't let me. She said, "Don't cry". She took my ice cream and threw it away for me. She said we would have to pack to go to my Grandma's house right away.

The next thing I remember was the three of us kids sitting in the back seat of the car. Joe and I had windows. Michael said, "I don't know why everybody's crying. Just because some old lady died." I slapped his face very hard and said, "Now you are." But, he didn't.

It was a two-hour drive to the farm. We all were very quiet. Even Mom was not crying. Before we pulled into the driveway, my mother told us not to cry in front of my aunt Linda. My aunt was 25 years old and had been helpless from birth due to cerebral palsy. My grandmother had taken care of her for her whole life. We all knew she had been completely dependent on my grandmother.

When I got out of the car and saw the back door, I remembered that the last time I had seen my grandmother, she was standing there waving to me. I had picked some cherry blossoms from the orchard and laid them on the step for her. She had given me a pink corsage for Easter.

We walked into the entryway and up the stairs to the kitchen. My Uncle Jimmy was lying on the floor by the refrigerator, under some folding chairs. I thought he might be dead too, but no one said anything.

My Aunt Linda was lying in the sofabed in the living room. My mother hugged her and asked me to read her a story. I read her a story about Winky the Cow. She seemed to enjoy it. I remember thinking that she was more like a child now than I was. My mind puzzled over this. How could a grown-up act like a child and a child be like an adult? I didn't know what was going on, but I just did what my mother told me. As I recall, this was my first taste of adulthood and I did not like it.

The passing of the generation brings the child to adult decorum. Grandmother leaves a space that Katie begins to fill. In the first story she is helpless in the face of separation. For a while Mr. Reitnauer fills her vision: "Finally I could hear again. Mr. Reitnauer was saying that I could never ride the bike again. My dreams of freedom and adulthood were shattered. I began to cry, turned and ran home as fast as I could." In this story she doesn't run away. It is she who gets Michael down, who slaps him for disrespect, who reads to her Aunt Linda.

The story is heralded by Michael's inversion, hanging upside down by his foot. "Mom, Michael's hanging in the lilac tree by his foot." These are identified as Katie's last sane words before her world also turns upside down and she faces the loss of her grandmother and of her childhood. Transcendence does not come on the roar and curl of the tides. Its rushing roar is like a jet in her ears. The adults around her collude in extending her childhood. They feed her ice cream instead of truth. Nevertheless, the imposition of this loss is mediated by her own activity, not imposed, but chosen. It does not descend around her as the "shades of the prison-house begin to close around the growing boy." This loss is not presented as an ontological or social shade that falls around her, closing her off to the world. On the contrary, through maternal designation she, the eldest daughter is chosen to substitute for her grandmother, even while Uncle Jimmy lies on the floor near the refrigerator. She, who exchanged flowers with her grandmother now exchanges childhood for adulthood, and separation from her grandmother slides into continuity as Katie assumes her labor and her capacity to care.

Late Summer

It was Sunday, September 1, 1985. I have two vivid memories of that day, like two pictures, juxtaposed. One memory concerns the daughter, who, at the crucial moment, was lying inside a tent in the Adirondack Mountains, making love to a man she had been seeing only three weeks. The other memory concerns the father, who, at the crucial moment, was lying on the dining room floor in his boxer shorts fearing that death was finally upon him and seeing the bright sunshine illuminating his slippers, which were five feet away, in front of the bathroom door. He had just been wearing them.

The Daughter

The daughter and her boyfriend had pitched the tent at 3:00 a.m. using light from the car headlights. It was a cold, clear night in Cranberry Lake. The moon was so full and bright that no stars were visible. The daughter was listening to an oldies show on the car radio.

She had left her husband of three years two months before, on Independence Day, and had started seeing the boyfriend six weeks later. Fearing the reaction of her family to her having a boyfriend too soon, she had told only a close friend, in passing, where she was going.

Among the memories of this night were the crickets, the moon, the warmness of the sleeping bag and the fear of bears.

They awoke to a very hot tent at 9:00 a.m., dressed and made breakfast. After eating and cleaning up, they retired to the tent until about 11:30, at which time they tried to start the car. Unfortunately, the battery was dead from the previous night's tent-pitching. After an hour or so, a Ranger finally showed up to jump the battery. The Ranger was an inept sort who almost put the exhaust pipe of his truck through the tent. Later, they laughed about it like two people do who are still getting to know each other. They decided to take a nap and got back into the tent.

The daughter awoke to the sound of someone calling her name. It was a man's voice from outside the tent. She got out and found a State Trooper. He told her to call her mother's house. He had a card in his hand and had written on it, "mother heart attack." The daughter screamed, "My mother had a heart attack?!" The daughter and her boyfriend ignored the trooper and got into the car. They drove to a phone near the campground's entrance. Her mother's friend answered the phone and said that her father had had a heart attack and to come home right away. The daughter said that she was five hours from home. She asked if he was dead. The friend said, "Just come home."

The Father

The father arrived home at 5:00 a.m. and made love to his wife. He had arisen at 10:45, after the mother had left for Mass. The mother was angry at the 16-year-old son because he had refused to go to church. The son was in bed. At 11:00, the son heard someone calling for help as if in a dream. He struggled to wake up and finally realized that the call was coming from downstairs. He ran downstairs to find the father lying on the dining room floor. He was wearing his boxer shorts. His slippers were five feet away, lying in a patch of sunlight in front of the bathroom door. The father told the son to call an ambulance and he did. He then lay down on the floor next to the father. The father asked him if his heart was still beating. The son listened and said yes. The father said that he was sorry for the things he had done and said, "I never meant to hurt anybody." He said, "Tell everybody that I love them."

The ambulance came and put the father on a stretcher. He yelled, "Quit pissing around with the belts and get me to the hospital!" The father was in a lot of pain, but when they gave him oxygen, he felt better.

When the mother drove up to the house, the son was standing in the street, holding his shoes. They went immediately to the hospital but were too late to see the father alive.

What of the significance of the slippers and the boxer shorts? What about the daughter who was making love? What if she had been sewing or reading? The daughter wants to ask someone about this but doesn't know how to explain the memory of these things. The daughter wants to know what the slippers represent and why a father has to die wearing a pair of boxer shorts.

Now our author has become a narrator. She will not claim this story as hers. She has sought romance. She makes love to a man she has chosen when the moon is bright and the sky is clear. Is it for romance that she has abandoned her husband and her father? Wrenched out of nature, she wishes later that she had been reading or sewing, suitable Victorian defences against her desire, as her father died.

In this last story she bares her sole, as others are unshod. She launched the trilogy in her scuffed brown and white saddlebacks, clicking against the sidewalk. The middle narrative starts with Michael caught by his foot in a tree. And in the last story Michael (or is it shoeless Joe) stands in the street, holding his shoes and we do not know whether those are the shoes of his father or his own. If they are his father's shoes and Michael has them, how can she step into them as she did her grandmother's? The empty slippers of her father are bathed in sunlight. Is that the bright light at the end of the tunnel that she mistook for freedom? The author resists romance with irony in the first two stories but surrenders to her father's vulnerability in the third, repudiating her own independence. If romance hinges on the father, on his separation, on his quest for reunification, if we are all arranged on the set to effect and applaud his reconciliation, what parts shall we play given this denouement? His story stops at those slippers. Will hers?

Whereas the literary genre of romance was originally associated with tales of medieval chivalry, contemporary notions settle for a narrative whose scene and incidents are far from ordinary life. When romance becomes the standard for meaningful action we learn to devalue local knowledge, local courage and domestic power. Romance is the myth of meaningful action that escorts the masculine journey of separation and repudiation. It poses a dilemma to a young woman who addresses the question of meaning in the construction of her own narratives.

We read against the romance, and as we reclaim the freedom and power that romance gives away to the future – to the fathers – we begin to construct a narrative for human action that celebrates the dignity of daily life. Literate educators are trapped in the narratives that dominate our self-understanding. Power gets attached to authority owned by others, freedom located in places we can't reach. We read and re-read our stories so that we do not become the medium for romantic myths of human action that fling value and significance over the wall that separates what is possible and within reach from what is inaccessible, always desired and denied. Curriculum theory that empowers students and teachers must do more than castigate those self-interested authorities and mark those distant places in eloquent but plaintive critiques. It must create schools where freedom and responsibility are not merely concepts in critical thinking exercises but realized in the creative and continuous construction of curriculum and community.

Notes

1. In "The Internalization of Quest-Romance" Bloom identifies these pairs: "Orc and Los in Blake, Prometheus bound and unbound in Shelley, Hyperion and Apollo in Keats, the Child and Man, though with subtle misgivings, in Wordsworth" (11).

2. Both of these images, the critical mirror and the snake appear in Jean-Paul Sartre's autobiography, *The Words*.

3. This theme is developed in the last chapter of my book, *Bitter Milk: Women and Teaching*, which is entitled, "The Empty House: Furnishing Education with Feminist Theory."

4. Nancy Chodorow's emphasis in *The Reproduction of Mothering* is sociological. She points to the economic structures that establish women as primary parents and urges their transformation so that both parents will be significant in the child's initial attachments. On the other hand, Atwell has explored Winnicott's psychological realization of how the individual uses imagination to mediate the harsh separation or overdetermined attachments that gender has required: "Rejecting an overdependence on the id-instinct theories of Freud because they do not emphasize human experience in the world, Winnicott sought to understand how the self uses culture to achieve identity. His psychology of children's creativity turns away from the pursuit of an inhuman, impersonal reality called the id, which Freud designated as primitive drives lurking beneath a civilized exterior. Instead, Winnicott focused on how humans, from infancy, use their cultural environment to create their identity and make sense of their lives" (Atwell 41).

Works Cited

Altieri, Charles. "Ecce Homo: Narcissism, Power, Pathos and the Status of Autobiographical Representation," *Boundary II* 9.3-4 (Spring 1981).

Atwell, Wendy. "An Application of Reader Response Theory and Object Relations Theory to Three Secondary English Teachers' Reading Experience and Their Literature Curriculum." Diss., University of Maryland, 1988.

Bloom, Allan. *The Closing of the American Mind.* New York: Simon and Schuster, 1987.

Bloom, Harold, ed. *Romanticism and Consciousness.* New York: W.W. Norton, 1970.

Carlson, Dennis. "Updating Individualism and the Work Ethic: Corporate Logic in the Classroom." *Curriculum Inquiry* 12.2 (1982): 125-160.

Chodorow, Nancy. *The Reproduction of Mothering.* Berkeley: University of California Press, 1978.

Eagleton, Terry. *Literary Theory.* Minneapolis: University of Minnesota Press, 1983.

Grumet, Madeleine. *Bitter Milk: Women and Teaching.* Amherst: University of Massachusetts Press, 1988.

Grumet, Madeleine. "The Politics of Personal Knowledge." *Curriculum Inquiry* 17.3 (1987).

Hartman, Geoffrey, H., "Romanticism and 'Anti-Self-Consciousness'," in Bloom, *Romanticism and Consciousness.* 70-86.

Hirsch, E. D. Jr. *Cultural Literacy: What Every American Needs to Know.* Boston: Houghton Mifflin, 1987.

Jardine, Alice and Harry Blake.. *Feminist Theory.* Eds. Nannerl O. Keohane, Michelle A. Rosaldo, and Barbara C. Gelpi. Chicago: University of Chicago Press, 1981.

Kristeva, Julia. *Revolution in Poetic Language.* New York: Columbia University Press, 1984.

Marcuse, Herbert. *The Aesthetic Dimension: Toward a Critique of Marxist Aesthetics.* Boston: Beacon Press, 1977.

O'Brien, Mary. *The Politics of Reproduction.* Boston: Routledge and Kegan Paul, 1981.

Pinar, William and Madeleine Grumet. *Toward a Poor Curriculum.* Dubuque, Iowa: Kendall/Hunt, 1976.

Sartre, Jean-Paul. *The Words.* Tr. Bernard Frechtman. New York: George Braziller, 1964.

Showalter, Elaine. "Feminist Criticism in the Wilderness," in *Writing and Sexual Difference.* Ed. Elizabeth Abel. Chicago: University of Chicago, 1982.

Trilling, Lionel. *Matthew Arnold.* New York: Harcourt Brace Jovanovich, 1977.

Willis, Paul. *Learning to Labour.* Lexington: D.C. Heath, 1977.

Chapter 11

AN EDUCATION IN ROMANTICISM
FOR OUR TIME

Johan Lyall Aitken

The ancient golden longing of romance is manifest in our young as the twentieth century wanes and the twenty-first looms. We say that the sixties are over, implying that the "spontaneous overflow of emotions," the Romantic and revolutionary time we had of it then, are gone forever and some new day of law, order, and conformity has been ushered in. The euphoria, or what we remember as euphoria, may be missing but many responses from that decade seem to continue, perhaps with diminished hope but certainly not without fervor. In European and North American universities there still seem to be fewer docile citizens among the student body than among the beleaguered professoriate. At my own university, with overcrowded city conditions, there is new student unrest and much of it is expressed in Romantic rhetoric visualizing a "better world." We may be witnessing the last hurrah of the Romantic longing for peace within and paradise without. I believe it is more likely, however, that the continuing legacy of the Romantics, made new, is keeping divine discontent alive. Daniel Stempel refers to the *violent discontinuity* of the period from 1790 to 1830, and as all accounts of that time indicate, the Bastille was only one of the many edifices, concrete and metaphorical, being stormed. The determination to storm the Bastille, if institutional structures become too cumbersome, too impersonal, too alienating, wells up whenever the Romantic spirit can no longer endure the agonizing split between subject and object.

As teachers, administrators, publishers, parents, we need to get in touch with the intimations of Romanticism in our students and so gauge whether or not the time is ripe for a revival of the Romantics in education, and if so, what forms it might take. We must listen to the lyrics of our students' music as well as to its beat, catch the muddled messages of the "language of their clothes" (Lurie), acknowledge the authentic elements in their turbulence over the plight of our planet, understand their search for intimacy and respect their sometimes desperate efforts to revivify or replace through art, music, and drugs the gods they now find alien or remote. If we attend to these portents, we find indications of a romantic world view often combined with an intensely romanticized picture of the individual. It could be argued that this view, operating in opposition to the dominant, reactionary view of yuppyism, is simply a counter-culture of misfits and malcontents. It might as easily be claimed, however, that counter-cultures have always been composed of Romantics. "A book which does not include its opposite or counter-book, is considered incomplete" (Borges 29). So with educational theories and approaches. If an education in the Romantics reaches the counter-culture in our classes, the effort to teach the Romantics will be worthwhile. My own hunch is that the bewilderment and need for connections that the "counter-group" displays may well be felt as strongly by their conformist classmates. In any case, if the "purpose of education is to make one maladjusted" (Frye, "Elementary Teaching and Elemental Scholarship," in *The Stubborn Structure* 95), an education in Romanticism and its ways of knowing should accelerate the process.

It is clear that, as Lovejoy once observed, "there is no Romanticism, there are only Romanticisms." However, a consideration of the legacy of that cluster of artists referred to as *the* Romantics, those larger-than-life figures whose names conjure up a way of knowing and seeing, provides our first point of entry into this unwieldy topic. It is no accident that present-day theorists must seek recourse to the Romantics.

> Subjectivity—both its psychological and discursive forms—is experienced by Wordsworth as a problem that at once disturbs and shapes the form of his work.... While the pretext of Wordsworth's poem, *The Prelude*, is that becoming depends on "returning," in actuality it depends upon the visionary and linguistic powers of his imagination as they work in the present moments of writing. It is in these moments that the poem's subject is produced and invented. (Jay 82)

Not only was the self-reflexive writer unabashedly in the work but the reader was free to take possession of the text as well. Eliot, as we know, was to make short work of this happy state. For him it was an indefensible approach to text by critic, author, and reader. Uncomfortable with Coleridge's show of emotions, he unequivocally states that "a literary critic should have no emotion except those immediately provoked by a work of art—and those are, when valid, perhaps not to be called emotions at all." In denouncing Coleridge for being "philosophic," Eliot continues, "It is one more instance of the pernicious effect of emotion" (12-13). The painful separation between subject and object, healed in part by the Romantics, again dominated our approach to the material world. Recent critical theory and thinking have acknowledged once again what the ancients always knew, that we think in our hearts and that it is only the humble, halting reader who makes human sense of any text. "In literature it is only necessary to outline the steps. Let the people dance!" (Kerrigan in Borges 10).

We can no longer be satisfied with what the *great men* have seen in the *great poets*. The vigorous task of reconstruction or production of meaning is now incumbent upon the reader. In Wordsworth's "Tintern Abbey," "the reader must take the situation which the opening lines force him to construct not as an external framework but as the proleptic assertion of the major thematic structure; the imagination's assimilation of and response to particulars of the world" (Culler 167). Students of the Romantics are now required to embrace *strenuous liberty*, as they are no longer expected to simply consume meaning but actively to produce it.

How do the Romantics, our modal grandparents, *fit*, in thought and expression, our present tensions and longings? Our lives and cravings, aesthetic and otherwise, are not parallel, far less some sort of cyclical repeat of theirs but as Stempel observes, "emergence springs from inheritance; it does not repeat it" (90). It is this relatedness — not forced but simply *there* — that provides whatever "sudden rightness" there may be to the study of the Romantics in our time. A number of teachers have pointed out that the lyrics of current rock music have remarkable affinities to the imagery of nature and the dreams of a better world that run rampant, of course, in *the* Romantics. There is certainly a preponderance of gardens and roses, valleys and violets, nostalgia and rainbows. The contemporary rock group called "U-2," for example, is typical of many in which the Romantic rhyme, rhythm and dream of harmony, intended to carry us away on some rapturous Mendelssohnian wings of song, abound. There are many correspondences which can engender dialogue between *then* and now. We need to educate Rita and Richard concerning some of the possibilities embedded in the term, *Romanticism*. We can encourage them to recognize its four centres of gravity: in history — the period from around 1790-1830, in the creative arts at all times but with upsurges at various points, in those specific artists belonging to the *school* of Romanticism such as Keats, Shelley, Coleridge and Wordsworth and, as the students already know, in sexuality.

Individualism and the Child

The individual, particularly in the form of a young child, takes on a special importance in Romanticism. Romantic novelists often gave distinctive names to their characters so that Jane Eyre and Heathcliff remain in our memories as individuals, not simply as types. In fact we may feel that we know their individual rhythms, as Henry James called them, as well as we know those of our *real life* intimates. Wordsworth's Lucy and Michael are not generic names: They remind us that "attention must be paid" (a Romanticism of our own century) which is a dominant Romantic theme. "Oh, the difference to me!" Human life, always considered cheap by the marketplace, is redeemed by the Romantics. The individual child becomes the incarnation of this Romantic view of humanity. The birth and death of children, both common occurrences of the time, are emphasized and idealized. Childhood is seen as a condition of innocence and our source of hope rather than as a manifestation of original sin or miniature adulthood. Children are remarkably "inmates of this active universe." The child, trailing clouds of glory, is an apt symbol of the Romantic ideals of simplicity, innocence, wisdom and an innate harmony with the natural world. When child encounters adult, the untainted state of innocence collides with the "heavy weight of this unintelligible world" of experience. The child, for Wordsworth, symbolizes his aesthetic to be "materially different" from the "gaudiness and inane phraseology of many modern writers." In fact, the characteristics which Wordsworth attributes to late eighteenth-century writing often resemble those assigned to the adults in poetry. Children, characteristically, see beyond the conventions of their time. How often do adults, speaking of the arms race, for example, and our penchant for *overkill*, mutter that a child can see what inane nonsense it is — only adults can be persuaded by such false logic and the seductive urge towards self-destruction. Our adolescents teeter between bravado and despair as they behold a mushroom in their sky. Wordsworth's language, of course, was never as simple as he claimed. Nevertheless, his poems about children are frequently akin to verse designed for the young in rhyme and rhythm:

I have a boy of five years old;
His face is fair and fresh to see;
His limbs are cast in beauty's mould,
And dearly he loves me.

("Anecdote for Fathers")

Similarly, Coleridge in "Dejection: An Ode" begins with a quotation from "the grand old ballad of Sir Patrick Spence." His imitation of the ballad form renders his poetry childlike because for one thing, the ballad-makers, like children, do not have a strong sense of causality. Childhood as the source of morality and creativity is celebrated by the Romantics. We echo their sentiments in the films of Spielberg and, *in theory*, through our educational theorists. The sanctity of the moral force of childhood is expressed by G. K. Chesterton who remarks that children, being innocent, seek justice while we, being fallen, crave mercy. The dependence upon childhood for creativity is remarked by George MacDonald, who should know: "The child within us must not die but be reborn again and again." Both Wordsworth and Coleridge congratulate themselves upon having retained something of their childhood selves in their adult lives and both identify in their memories of childhood, and their desire to return to it, the source of their poetic power:

> Wordsworth, first and greatest of the theorists of childhood launched by the Romantic movement, takes us into the mystery of the fact that culture and being act on each other to make both the individual and his world. As Wordsworth notes, the shaping or fiction-making spirit may be thoroughly suppressed as well as cultivated by circumstances. Indeed, suppression, abatement, what Ted Hughes calls "the lobotomy of the national imagination" seemed to him then as to us now just a more likely consequence of the child's assimilation of the culture than that the spirit should be kept "pre-eminent till death." Wordsworth's great poem, however, was written in the effort to show how the pre-eminence might be sustained in the teeth of the recurrent tendency of the social world to regulate and distinguish and straighten out, against which he affirmed the blessedness of uncertainty, richness, over- and undergrowth, the incorrigible beauty of unplanned and untheoretic life. (Inglis)

Many writers recognize childhood as the inexhaustible source motivating their art and providing its substance. The influence of the child's relationship to nature upon the creative powers of the mature adult is central to the Romantics' vision of their work. Such a conception would have seemed completely foreign to an earlier age, yet, in spite of its innuendoes and multiple possibilities, we could scarcely imagine schooling that did not, at least as policy, laud and honor the creativity of the child and the teacher who encourages this creativity.

The *incurably* romantic view is evident in the following excerpts from an educational report:

> The needs of the child are simply stated. Each and everyone has the right to learn, to play, to laugh, to dream, to love, to dissent, to reach upward, and to be himself. Our children need to be treated

as human beings — exquisite, complex, and elegant in their diversity. They must be made to feel that their education heralds the rebirth of an *Age of Wonder*. Then, surely, the children of tomorrow will be more than we are, and better equipped to search for truth, each in his own way. (Hall and Dennis 47)

The authors go on to claim that each will have learned with Don Quixote, in *Man of La Mancha*:

> To dream the impossible dream,
> To fight the unbeatable foe,
> To bear with unbearable sorrow,
> To run where the brave dare not go.
> To fight the unrightable wrong,
> To love the unchaste from afar,
> To try when one's arms are too weary,
> To reach the unreachable star.

An attentive reading of these lyrics reveals not only the excruciating excesses of Romanticism but the intolerable pressure these excesses place upon any reader who takes them seriously. Small wonder that depression and suicide are common when we *begin* by tilting at windmills. Mere mortals cannot attain the larger-than-life stature of the Romantic hero and we are doomed to failure if we try. This is one reason to encourage students to deconstruct Romantic heroics. It is still possible, fortunately, to drink deeply of the primary sources, the Romantic poets themselves, who have never been out of print and are no longer quite so out of fashion. They lament as well as rhapsodize and they recognize that agony, or at least a sense of loss, is likely to follow ecstasy. The poets spoke not only of passion and love after all but of its "sad satiety." We know that the *accidents of birth* — genes, geography, and gender along with the forces of politics, history, economics, and the social order — dictate and determine almost everything. But it is upon that tiny left-over wisp of freedom-to-exist, through choices and actions, that we bet our lives and dare them to have meaning. Sentimentality aside, we cling to the notion that in the child lies our only hope of a transformed society. Yet, as a society, we give little recognition to primary teachers, inadequate care to the very young, and little genuine respect to those who nurture them. Perhaps the inflated rhetoric of the Romantically idealistic educator can be more readily tolerated when viewed against the backdrop of an adult world that does not make its young a high priority.

The plight of the individual lost in society's shuffle is felt throughout the educational system. As Edgar Friedenberg states in his contribution to this collection, students have a few basic needs that are not always

met: "Kids need a safe place to hang out: they need a role and a status
to explain to themselves and each other what they are doing there. They
need access to adults when certain difficulties arise." The impact of what
Industry, that contemporary giant, wants education to accomplish comes
in a direct line from the Industrial Revolution and its influence is
immense in our technological time. But a Romantic voice continues to
be heard in the land as professors such as Bill Harvey question their
educational role: "At some stage, we educators used to be proud of
turning out what I call the critical, articulate citizen. Now we have to
produce somebody who's going to make the president of The Bay [a
department store] happy. I'm not convinced that's my purpose and goal
in life" (8). While Bill Harvey in spite of himself employs metaphors of
the factory, he retains the ideal of an individual who is critical of language
and culture, who has an individual will and a distinctive human voice. We
recognize that while a Whitmanesque song of myself can become almost
as tiresome as the "Me Generation," the value of individual human
life – the pearl beyond price – is a Romantic value for which, in our age,
we yearn. Recourse to Blake may help for the *potential of the individual*
was something he understood. In *Songs of Innocence and Experience* the
grim incarnations of the first stanza are in sharp contrast to the infinite
human possibilities implied in the second.

> Cruelty has a Human Heart,
> And Jealousy a Human Face;
> Terror the Human Form Divine,
> And Secrecy the Human Dress.
>
> ("A Divine Image")

> For Mercy has a human heart,
> Pity a human face,
> And Love, the human form divine,
> And Peace, the human dress.
>
> ("The Divine Image")

Liberty and Revolution

A second correspondence between then and now can be seen in the
Romantics' preoccupation with liberty and revolution. These relatively
modern words are beacons for a portion of the youth of each generation
and they are often combined with an escape to, or a communion with,
nature. Freedom is often a state that existed in the past (memory) or, it
is believed, will exist in the future (desire). Like Marxism, Judaism, and
Christianity, there is either a lost paradise to which we long to return or a

promised land at which we never quite arrive. The West Wind is uncontrollable, the Skylark flies higher still and higher, and Faust will, for as long as possible, brook no limitations. "We must be free or die." Perhaps the Now Generation is weary of "looking before and after and pining for what is not." Freedom, of course, is not the freedom to abandon responsibility and learning. When Wordsworth suggests that he and Dorothy go outdoors and, just once, leave their books behind, it is clearly an extravagant exception. The diaries and letters of the Wordsworths reek of routine and inner control over mind and body. This self-control brings one kind of freedom: An escape from the world of commerce brings another: "The world is too much with us; late and soon / Getting and spending, we lay waste our powers ("Sonnets"). Wordsworth's insistence, in poems such as "Simon Lee," "She Dwelt Among Untrodden Ways," "The Brothers" and "To A Highland Girl," that no human value can ever be placed upon rank, class or wealth, gives him automatic credibility with many students. The schizophrenic attitudes which prevail in our own society toward money, power, and politics help the Romantics to appeal to many students:

> The Romantic era is more likely to capture the interest of minority students, especially black students, than is any other period of English literature. Its appeal springs from that revolutionary zeal and enthusiastic idealism which at once arouse a response in students eager to connect poetry with politics and the social order. Of the major Romantic poets Wordsworth offers the greatest scope for discussion since he, more than any previous writer, probes the inner significance of ordinary happenings in ordinary lives. It is, then, Wordsworth the liberal thinker, supporter of the French Revolution, and poet of common humanity and of the common human experience whom I first introduce to students in a historically black college when I teach a survey of English literature course.... Too often they tend to look at English writers as distant figures whose works have little immediate relation to modern life. I try to counter this impression by showing Wordsworth as a moral poet whose work reflects a passionate belief in human rights and human dignity. (Mellown 33-34)

There is nothing straightforward in our attitudes toward wealth or our attachment in a material world to things. Wordsworth, in possession of what we rather quaintly call *independent means*, decried the materialism of his contemporaries: "The wealthiest man among us is the best." As we know, Wordsworth saw the greed for gain sapping energy that might have been devoted to what he considered our proper human business — the contemplation of nature and a life of freedom and moral purpose. He saw the structures of society militating against individual freedom, choice and even duty, that "stern daughter of the voice of God."

As the journals of Dorothy Wordsworth, that largely unacknowledged collaborator, make plain, she was free to make detailed diary entries and William was free to make whatever use of them he chose. She, in turn, was free to feel honored and *useful*. She was free to iron while he was free to read. The Wordsworths, even in their *ménage à trois*, had no monopoly on this kind of division of labor or of recognition! Nor do they yet. Such Romantic imprisonment, however, is more likely to be understood by today's student particularly if that student is female. The ideal woman — in Wordsworth's terms "nobly planned, to warn, to comfort, and command" or "a creature not too bright, or good, for human nature's daily food" — seems to put women, however idealized, in circumspect and circumscribed occupations ("She was a Phantom of Delight"). "Her heart" had jolly well better be "in her house," as was the heart of Michael's wife, or she may come to grief ("Michael"). Feminist readings of the Romantics are essential and some of these have already led to the discernment of what Nina Auerbach has called *Romantic Imprisonment*. Throughout much poetry of the Romantics one only escapes from bondage to enter, usually willingly, into another form of it. The bars are words and in Jameson's phrase, the name of the prison house is *language*. If we encourage students to pull and tease apart the deep meanings as well as the surface messages of the seductive language of Romanticism we will have been of service. They need freedom to take what is of use to them and to let the rest go.

Romantic Love

The experience of romantic love, while often available only outside marriage, reveals another correspondence between *then* and *now*. As we try desperately to romanticize the beloved, we are heirs of the courtly love tradition as well as of the nineteenth century's strange mix of piety and passion. As a character in *Paint Your Wagon*, a fifties musical, announces after the first night with the wife he purchased from a Mormon with a surfeit of such riches, "It was so good I almost forgot she was my wife." And an audience in 1989 still laughed heartily. An emphasis on curriculum, as Friedenberg reminds us, is becoming less important in spite of the admonitions of Bloom and Hirsch. At such a time of opportunity it seems unfortunate that young adult romances, such as the *Sweet Valley High* series which by 1986 had sold 15.5 million copies, and the "romance" (no longer mystery) of Nancy Drew which is running a close second, are so cleverly marketed that they have become the *new curriculum* for many young women (Basler). Romance will clearly out and we abdicate if we do not provide our female readers with more nutritious fare in a genre they clearly admire.

A return to the satisfactions celebrated by Wordsworth seems unlikely. It is impossible, however, to see one's own time with any clarity and "without the ideal enunciated by romance — a stable, continually evolving, passionate relationship — life is too many TV dinners alone, too many one-night stands" (Ignatieff 20). The glorification of the individual hails from the Romantics and even in the social sciences, where the needs of the group usually precede those of the individual, its impact continues to be felt:

> Love is that elusive knowledge Roland Barthes called *the impossible science of the individual*. Indeed, in the face of the incessant blather, silliness, and confusion of modern commercialized discourse — the radios blaring away about love and sex, and hopelessly confusing the two — it becomes an essential activity of the intelligence to safeguard the meaning of the romantic tradition (the integrity of love poetry, for example) so that our children can still grow up hearing the dream speaking from its source.... The romantic utopian, child of individualism, is always threatened by the rapacious progress of individualism itself. What is threatened is love's long association with human continuity and permanence, love as a shared experience of time past, and as a joint commitment to time future. Even the experience of falling in love is retrospective, a coming to terms with feelings, that were at the time more tumultuous than self-aware. As Proust said, all paradise is recollected paradise; this means that love is lodged not so much in the heart as in memory. (Ignatieff 20-21)

For the Romantics, "memory and imagination seem to offer, not perhaps an escape from time, but a kind of circumscribed freedom within it. It is by memory and imagination that we perceive and measure time" (Baker 15). A modern education in the Romantics, then, might fulfill the barbaric cry of relevance and also liberate the genuine mythology of love and memory from its perverted and dislocated forms. What Wordsworth refers to as "the luxury of our imaginations" is a necessity for students moving toward another century needing at least as urgently as in any time preceding them to sort out the language and meaning of sexuality and its connections to that even more elusive and confusing conception — *love*.

Nature and Immortality

Preoccupation with nature and the brevity of this "corporeal frame" are Romantic concerns of our time. We have inherited a number of stances toward nature: nature as mother, the sustainer who "never did betray the heart that loved her," nature in accord with our moods or at ironic variance from them, nature as indifferent or alien, nature malevolent as in *Tess of the D'Urbervilles* or simply nature "red in tooth and claw." Although unlike other species we cannot survive in nature and must live out our brief, bright hour in a culture of some sort, we are tempted in our time, recognizing our literal dependence upon it, to join in a cosmic dance with the rest of nature, trying to become a part of what we behold and to reunite consciousness with that which it is conscious of. Gone is the notion that we are central to the proceedings on planet earth except perhaps as rapists and murderers. The fields and the beasts of the fields get on better without us. In Timothy Findley's novel, *Not Wanted On The Voyage*, the overture made by laughing, gregarious porpoises to frightened pugilistic humans puts us in our place — and it is a far from flattering one. Little children are curious about all aspects of nature including their own bodies. Adolescents, obsessed with their romantic, if forlorn, hope to save nature from the rape of the elders can hark back with benefit to "nature's beauteous forms" as the English Romantic poets described them. The elders themselves can receive succor from the seeming consistency of seed time and harvest in a world in which there are no other constants. Finally, the Romantic in each of us may find no morality in the "vernal woods" but continue to feel toward nature that ancient tension between connection and alienation. It is intriguing that Marion Montgomery describes this dilemma in the case of Wordsworth as his devotion to his "false Beatrice." However, M. Enani points to the false note in this Wordsworthian call to connection: "It is no use singing the praises of nature and the greatness of continuity...when inner discontinuity has set in emotionally and intellectually" (14).

The longing to be refreshed by nature, "to one who has been long in city pent" (Keats, Sonnet X), is the feature of the Romantics best known in popular culture. Where is the sense of community in a place where one huddles with his fellows "to make money from each other," the city of getting and spending? How much have the Romantics influenced us to see the city increasingly as a place of decay and nature as both an escape from alienation and as the site for what we whimsically call *self-discovery?* Many young people flee the city with some Thoreauesque hope of simplification. Others, dependent upon it, yet resist and resent it, singing and writing of their disenchantment with the Metropolis and their longing for fresh air, fresh water, open space and what they call *peace*, the most elusive goal of all. The lure of suburbia, the call of cottage country are not only the dislocation of the classical and biblical myths to return to the garden, they are Romantic in their origins and language. The dehumanizing of the industrial and technological revolutions hurl us backwards toward ancient gods but the myths and gods of our classical past do not always speak to our children and they must, like the Romantic poets, create their own efficacious symbols.

We try to find assurance of some kind of continuity in the lyrics of Dylan Thomas, the Shelley of our turbulent time: "Though the lovers be lost, love shall not; / And death shall have no dominion." The decline of a belief in an after-life, in the sense of some continuation of individual consciousness, places new strains on time present. Wordsworth says that "there are in our existence spots of time," that is, the past is present. Once one acknowledges human consciousness as an integral element of space-time, the whole matter is transposed from a mathematical to a poetical affair. Other living creatures, however, seem spared the special human suffering of a mind whose perception may seem immune from change but which is lodged in a human body. As Wordsworth points out in 'The Fountain," our pain issues not from what is lost but from what is retained. The Romantic yearning is around us and within as we seek for meaning "in the very world, which is the world of all of us — the place where in the end/we find our happiness or not at all" (Wordsworth, "The French Revolution"). Wordsworth's "intimations of immortality" are of an immortality in the world of all of us, through art, through our "little unremembered acts of kindness and of love" and of course, through our identity with the natural world when we too are "rolled round in earth's diurnal course / With rocks, and stones, and trees" ("A Slumber"). We may, with the little girl in "We Are Seven," wish to believe that we are united with our brothers and sisters whom the adult world considers dead:

'Twas throwing words away; for still
The little Maid would have her will,
And said, "Nay, we are seven."

As Wordsworth's longer poems suggest, neither point of view is sufficient by itself. In "Intimations of Immortality," the child already has the adult world thrust upon him. The echo of Jaques' famous speech in *As You Like It* postulates that the child on the adult world stage is learning to become artificial and hypocritical:

The little Actor cons another part
As if his whole vocation
Were endless imitation.

Finally, we perceive limitations of immortality which, until they are finally accepted, put an immense pressure upon us to stay the fears that we "may cease to be" with frenzied activity and corporate delusion. The Romantics redefine immortality as we must do for ourselves in our own time but perhaps an education in them can help us bridge that agonizing split between subject and object which alone can bring us into harmony with both material and natural worlds. In speaking of this union of subject and object, Frye reminds us that metaphor "arises in a state of society in which a split between a perceiving subject and a perceived object is not yet habitual, and what it does in that context is to open up a channel or current of energy between human and natural worlds... the sense that all humanity is linked in a common identity, both with itself and with nature, is much more taken for granted in the world than it was thirty years ago" ("Expanding").

Discourse and Writing

An education in the Romantics helps us enter into a dialogue about discourse itself. The Romantics saw themselves not only as the "unacknowledged legislators of the world" but as heroes of new thought and perception. However, by the time their work was studied in schools, constraining and inflexible interpretations inhibited much of the possible transfer of their exuberance to their readers. As we have seen, post-structural thought and deconstruction have given teachers the freedom to view texts through apertures denied us under new criticism. We can muse about collaboration between Coleridge and Wordsworth, between Hazlitt and Keats, and most notably between Dorothy in her notebooks and William in his poetry. Shelley's ego and conception of genius are no longer outside the poem any more than the long length of Wordsworth's life and Keat's aborted one are beyond our consideration when we read their work. Biographical criticism, author's possible intentions, conscious or unconscious, acknowledged or tacit—are all fair game. How much more stimulating for our students!

When Keats feared an early death, his terror was founded. When Shelley repeatedly eloped, his life and letters were philosophically conjoined. When Coleridge experienced altered states of awareness, his writing soared. Many students will see the connection here even if their own experience has not resulted in immortal verse. When domestic exigencies such as illness or marriage in Wordsworth's life are recorded in poetry, students can examine the objectifying and healing power of writing. The apparent *closure* or what Kermode terms the "sense of an ending" that many Romantic writers provide can be examined in contrast to more recent writing in which no attempt is made at resolution or even the illusion of closure and the reader is not only required to produce meaning in the body of the text but to write, in Blau Du Plessis's words, "beyond the ending" as well. As Stephen Sondheim says in the musical *Into the Woods*, "and they lived happily ever after: maybe."

Twenty years ago Northrop Frye wrote about the restoration of Romanticism as part of the literary tradition:

> The anti-Romantic movement in criticism which in Britain and North America followed the Hulme-Eliot-Pound broadsides of the early twenties, is now over and done with, and criticism has got its sense of tradition properly in focus again. (*English Romanticism* v)

Now, as the nineties dawn, the only point remaining upon which we have any certitude is that there is no single *proper focus* toward a sense of tradition or toward the texts of literary theory itself. As we saw earlier, there is a great deal of dialectical thinking and posing going on concerning *which comes first*—the individual or her biological, communal, and social context. Binary oppositions abound: independence and dependence, freedom and imprisonment, the solitary reaping of knowledge and collaborative learning, the natural world and the mechanistic thought of technology. As academics and educators we are now repulsed by the notion of *proper* stances or responses to texts. Coincidentally, post-structural and deconstructive approaches, even if well on their own way to a new orthodoxy, do allow for a happy rediscovery and reconstruction of that revolutionary and manic depressive movement that occurred between 1790 and 1830 and which, even when under eclipse or erasure, has continued to bother and disturb us. In addition to opening the discourse, we remember that "deconstruction as an analytical mode means disturbing the poem according to its own fault-lines" (Hartman, "Reading" 215).

A further connection between contemporary literary/linguistic theory and Romantic practice is the primacy of writing. A recent obsession with the oral rendering of poetry and the emphasis upon *hearing* the sound of human voices in response and rebellion to electronic devices and media is welcome and salutary as far as it goes:

> Wordsworth has often been enlisted into the ranks of those who see poetry as primarily oral. This view looks upon written language as a copy of living speech. Some passages by Wordsworth seem to affirm this view, but in fact Wordsworth's thinking on this matter is more complicated. . . his poetry was in fact written down. (Miller 79)

His celebrated *recollection* involves sufficient distance from immediate experience to allow it to be recorded in a *secondary present*. This may be what Hillis Miller calls a "representation of a representation." Derrida's insistence on the primacy of writing is reminiscent of Wordsworth's "fascination with all kinds of written language":

> This includes not only the "Books" that are the overt title and subject of Book V of *The Prelude*, but also many other forms of inscription — epitaphs, monuments, memorial plaques, signs, and so on. One of Wordsworth's earliest poems is called "Lines Left Upon a Seat in a Yew-Tree, Which Stands Near The Lake of Esthwaite, On A Desolate Part of the Shore, Commanding a Beautiful Prospect." The "Essays upon Epitaphs" investigate that kind of poetry which is inscribed on stone to mark a grave. One section of the collected poems is called "Epitaphs and Elegiac Pieces." Another is called "Inscription." The latter group contains short poems with titles like the following: "Written with a Pencil upon a Stone in the Wall of the House (an Out-house), on the Island of Grasmere," "Written with a Slate Pencil on a Stone on the Side of The Mountain of Black Comb," "Written with a Slate Pencil upon a Stone, the Largest of a Heap Lying Near a Deserted Quarry, Upon One of the Islands at Rydal." These titles almost longer than the poems they name, are striking in the extreme circumstantiality of detail with which they identify the act whereby the poem was given physical existence. The exact place, the stone, the act of writing, the tool used for the inscription — all are described with precision. This precision suggests that the most important aspect of these particular poems may be the act of writing them. In that act a mute stone becomes the bearer of marks speaking a silent message to any passerby. Such poems are by their titles so wedded to the stone on which

they were written that one wonders if they can survive being copied in the book in which we read them today. Their "primary" existence was not as living speech but as marks made with a slate pencil on a particular place. (Miller 80)

Wordsworth's understanding of the nature of writing and its identification with reading as a single activity anticipate contemporary theory (Scholes). The Romantics' preoccupation with the survival of writing and art is of their time and of our own.

The longing for individual continuance through works of art is combined with the knowledge that while art may be longer than life, it is yet fragile and in jeopardy. Art goes far beyond "carving one's initials on a block of ice on a hot July day" but the generating impulses and the fear of ultimate futility have affinities. As our historic buildings crumble from acid rain, as the paper deteriorates at an alarming rate in our books, and as the mounts of our paintings and lithographs eat away at the works they surround, we, like the Romantics, may feel the earth of our aesthetic heritage slipping away beneath us. Like the Romantics we have a growing distrust of history, yet their history and our present purpose may fold into each other to the benefit of both:

> ... the scene of writing becomes for the poem both locus and theater, a site where the language of imagination struggles with the perception of fact, where neither can alone resolve the poet's dilemmas, and where those dilemmas deepen as history and present purpose fold into each other. (Jay 91)

Collaboration between *them* and *us* may form a fundamental aspect of a modern education in the Romantics now that we are free to *be in the text*:

> That poetry *thinks* does not seem to be a startling proposition; but that Romantic poetry thinks, that its visionariness is a form of conceptual mediation, has been a hard-won discovery of recent years. (Hartman, *Criticism* 86)

In the universe of discourse, we find unexpected affinities and serious endorsement for the writing act itself. Montgomery sagely refers to our time "as the most autobiographical century of our literature" (13) and on this reflective journey she traces the stream that flows through Joyce, Eliot, Pound, and Hemingway as flowing in part from Wordsworth: and our writers such as Eudora Welty, Margaret Laurence, and Dylan Thomas share the same heritage.

Education: Romantic Visions and Revisions

Let us return to Romanticism's four centres of gravity. In the first place there is that remarkable period between 1790 and 1830 which we can revivify in our Arts, History and English classes encouraging students, in the spirit of that age and this, to interrogate all texts, including (if we are sufficiently brave), the teacher as text. In the second place we can help students recognize and participate in a Romantic breakaway as they discover their own new directions in the arts as all art has elements of rehearsal and performance. Picasso's celebrated rehearsal and the pop song writer's insistence that "long before I met you, I loved you so" speak of the same phenomenon — placing experience in the context of memory and desire. The young will make it new for their time and in so doing, may be empowered by the knowledge that they are following in a rebellious and honorable tradition. Some of them, at least, sense with Blake that if they are not to be enslaved by the system of another, they must create their own.

There are many testimonials such as Muriel Mellown's to the effectiveness of teaching *the* Romantic poets in the last days of the twentieth century. That it may be done, how it may be done and the satisfactions for all concerned are outlined in S. Hall's *Approaches to Teaching Wordsworth's Poetry* as well as anywhere. In spite of these testimonials and many others, and in spite of current literary theory's striking interest in exploring the Romantic *school* of poetry, we must admit that many students will never feel the Romantic longings and ways of understanding our world and our place in it by direct contact with Shelley, Keats, Coleridge or Wordsworth. I would go further and say that many of the "clean new breed" of teachers possess neither competence nor desire to share much capital "R" Romantic poetry with their students. But hit and miss may be sufficient. The enthusiasms of a teacher who chooses to teach *the* Romantics will be Romantically contagious. For others the Romantic way of looking can be found anywhere from sixteenth-century dramas and nineteenth-century novels to a Romantic revival in our own time, a point amply demonstrated by Kieran Egan's contribution to this collection. The point is to tap into the authentic romance that idealizes the beloved person, place, occasion or world, making it holy without sentimentalizing it and helping students to distinguish between the genuine and the fake.

The fourth centre, the one of sexuality, is where we all begin. As Blake shows us, it is the source of our creativity and if we repress it too much, it will turn destructive and blow up the world. Such is the dynamic of Romanticism. The feminist, Jane Rule, and the masculinist, Robert Bly, both focus on the *rich particular* of song or story rather than upon *a thousand case studies*. However they are perceived politically, both are

Romantic to the core. Rita and Richard are the young and the restless. We owe them some Romantic visions and the opportunity to write their own revisions and their own versions of what Henry James called, because he had no choice in a priggish age, the "great world renewal." We cannot engage in the romantic psychic and emotional acrobatics of *The Man of La Mancha* but we can, with Shelley's *Prometheus Unbound* "hope til hope creates from its own wreck the thing it contemplates." For an education in Romanticism in our time, such hope must suffice.

Works Cited

Auerbach, N. *Romantic Imprisonment: Women and Other Glorified Outcasts*. New York: Columbia University Press, 1985.

Baker, J. *Time and Mind in Wordsworth's Poetry*. Detroit: Wayne State University Press, 1980.

Basler, B. "A Sleuth's Newest Venture." *The New York Times*, 26 October 1986, p. 21Y.

Blake, W. *The Complete Writings*. Ed. Geoffrey Keynes. London: Oxford University Press, 1966.

Borges, J. L. *Ficciones*. Intro. Anthony Kerrigan. New York: Grove, 1962.

Burns, R. *Poems and Songs*. Edited by J. Kinsley. London: Oxford University Press, 1969.

Cappon, A. P. *Action, Organism and Philosophy in Wordsworth and Whitehead*. New York: Philosophical Library, 1985.

Chapman, R. *Linguistics and Literature*. London: Edward Arnold, 1973.

Clark, C., ed. *Home at Grasmere*. Harmondsworth: Penguin, 1960.

Cook, E. *et al.* (eds.) *Centre and Labyrinth: Essays in Honour of Northrop Frye*. Toronto: University of Toronto Press, 1983.

Culler, J. *Structuralist Poetics*. London: Routledge and Kegan Paul, 1975.

Eliot, T. S. *The Sacred Wood*. London: Methuen, 1957.

Enani, M. M. *Dialectic of Memory: A Critical Study of Wordsworth's Two-Part Prelude*. Cairo: Egyptian State Publishing House, 1981.

Fotheringham, J. *Wordsworth's "Prelude" as a Study of Education*. London: Horace Marshall, 1899.

Frye, Northrop. "Expanding the Boundaries of Literature." Unpublished paper in Mind and Matter Lecture Series, Toronto, 1985.

_____. *The Secular Scripture: A Study of the Structure of Romance*. Cambridge: Harvard University Press, 1976.

_____. *The Stubborn Structure: Essays on Criticism and Society*. London: Methuen, 1970.

_____. *A Study of English Romanticism*. New York: Random House, 1968.

Garvin, H. R. (ed.) *Romanticism, Modernism, Postmodernism*. London: Associated University Press, 1980.

Hall, E. and L. Dennis. *Living and Learning: The Report of the Provincial Committee on Aims and Objectives of Education in the Schools of Ontario*. Toronto: Newton Publishing, 1968.

Hall, S. (ed.). *Approaches to Teaching Wordsworth's Poetry*. New York: The Modern Language Association of America, 1986.

Hartman, G. H. *Saving the Text*. Baltimore: The Johns Hopkins University Press, 1981.

_____. *Criticism in the Wilderness: The Study of Literature Today*. New Haven: Yale University Press, 1980.

_____. "Reading Aright: Keats' Ode to Psyche." *Centre and Labyrinth*: *Essays in Honour of Northrop Frye*. Ed. E. Cook. Toronto: University of Toronto Press, 1983.

Harvey, Bill. "A Renaissance Man for Our Time." *Vic Report* (1988/89): 8.

Ignatieff, Michael. "Lodged in the Heart and Memory." *London Times Literary Supplement*, April 15-21, 1988.

Inglis, F. *The Promise of Happiness*. Cambridge: Cambridge University Press, 1981.

Jay, Paul. *Being in the Text: Self-representation from Wordsworth to Roland Barthes*. Ithaca, NY: Cornell University Press, 1985.

Keats, J. *The Complete Work of John Keats. Volume 1*. New York: Thomas Crowell & Company undated.

Lurie, Alison. "Sex in Fashion." *The New York Review of Books*, 22 October 1981.

Mellown, Muriel. "Teaching Wordsworth to Minority Students,"in Hall, *Approaches to Teaching Wordsworth's Poetry*.

Miller, Hillis. *The Linguistic Moment*. Princeton: Princeton University Press, 1985.

Montgomery, Marion. *The Reflective Journey Toward Order*. Athens: University of Georgia Press, 1973.

Natoli, Joseph (ed.) *Tracing Literary Theory*. Chicago: University of Illinois Press, 1987.

Schauber, E. and E. Spolsky. *The Bounds of Intepretation*. Stanford: Stanford University Press, 1986.

Scholes, Robert. *Semiotics and Interpretation*. New Haven: Yale University Press, 1982.

_____. *Textual Power: Teaching English and Literary Theory*. New Haven: Yale University Press, 1985.

Shelley, P. B. *Selected Poetry and Prose*. Ed. K. N. Cameron. New York: Rinehart, 1956.

Stempel, Daniel. "History and Postmodern Literary Theory," in Natoli, *Tracing Literary Theory*.

Thomas, Dylan. *Collected Poems, 1934 to 1952*. London: Dent, 1952.

Wordsworth, W. *The Poems, Volume II*. Ed. J. O. Hayden. New Haven: Yale University Press, 1977.

_____. *The Prelude 1799, 1805, 1850*. Ed. J. Wordsworth, M. H. Abrams and S. Gill. New York: W.W. Norton, 1979.

_____. *Selected Poems and Prefaces*. Ed. J. Stillinger. Boston: Houghton Mifflin, 1965.

Chapter 12

WOMEN'S WRITING AND THE RECOVERY

OF THE ROMANTIC PROJECT:

LESSONS FOR CONTEMPORARY

WRITING PEDAGOGY

Deborah A. Dooley

> plain and ordinary things
> speak softly
> Adrienne Rich, "From an Old House in America"

The first day in a freshman writing class is inevitably one in which the sound of an anxious and expectant silence deafens real speech. The first spoken words are often a recitation of the syllabus: papers to be written, books to be read, first words then sentences then paragraphs to be understood, then forms of writing to be mastered, a jargon to be learned like those in all the other college classrooms. Next to the mathematics class, writing class is probably the place of more anxiety than any other college classroom; the place where mistakes will be corrected with varying degrees of embarrassment to corrector (teacher) and correctee (student); where inevitably some hidden fault will come to light, no matter how hard its author tries to cover her confusion; a place of many assumptions about what should be known before we come — or worse — what has never been known and seemingly never will, with being and knowing playing hide and seek on expectant faces, suspicious (and rightly so) that despite all the talk about process (*being* in relation to *experience*) the grade is an evaluation of a product (what is known) pure and simple.

Is it any wonder, then, that following the first, tentative written piece, dashed off in varying degrees of hurry and confusion (often the "writing sample") the students will turn from the peer group sharing each other's work toward the place in the room where the teacher stands: "Is this right?" "Am I right?" "Is this what you want?" "How many pages should it be?" "Is this too short?" "Is this long enough?" "My teacher said that you should always/never do it this way." Clearly, there is a silent, conspiratorially enforced agreement: this will never be the place of "plain and ordinary things." Thus, the anxiety as these students sense that they are somehow broken writers who have come to the college writing class, with understandably varying degrees of desire, in one last effort to be "fixed."

The effort to separate process and form (or content), the ecstatic and the rational, the natural and the human, the private and the public, the reproductive world of conceiving, gestating, nurturing children and the productive one, is a hallmark of the separation of ontology from epistemology, of being from knowing. The relationship of these two worlds of experience, or better, the recognition that being and knowing are dialectical processes informing our experience of one world, is crucial to making art (the "piece" is, after all, an intersection of many kinds of knowing-in-the-world and being-in-the-world). This recognition is crucial to making meaning in a written text. In short, the piece gives speech to what both William Wordsworth and Adrienne Rich think of as "plain and ordinary things" and in so doing, as utterance, connects us to them and enables us to "compose" our brokenness. In composing the text, we compose the self, as well.

In re-thinking the art of writing and the art of teaching writing, the feminist movement's revisioning activity can make a radical contribution. To explore that contribution, it is finally not necessary — and not the project of this paper — to ask if women's writing is "different" in some particular way. But it is my project to look at three dimensions of some women's writing that I know in light of their efforts to recover, to re-address and to re-integrate the work of Romanticism which writers like Matthew Arnold and T. S. Eliot strove so hard to repudiate. The first dimension includes the writer's definition of the object; the second incorporates the writer's sense of the perceiving subject's relations *with* (not to) it; and the last entails the nature of knowing/being expressed in the written record of that seeing-in-relationship.

My thesis is that as the Romantic experiment failed and as efforts to repress the questions it raised and to repudiate the relationships it deemed important intensified, the 19th century experienced a gradual, horrifying numbness: the "denaturing" of experience marked by a growing rift between human and natural, human and human, between aspects of the self, between knowing and being, between the song and the text.[1] If our connection with the world and with each other is broken, and if significant aspects of the self are repressed, the text that explores and constructs meaning will be broken, too. Women's literature records the effort to come to terms with this actual — and literal — brokenness. Consequently, I believe that we can learn a great deal from their work.

Finally, I propose that as teachers of writing in the 20th century, what we are facing in our students' texts are the consequences of that brokenness. If we must discover a new form to reconstruct meaning from brokenness, as teachers of writing, we must also find new forms to help students re-establish the relationships that Romantic writers understood and attempted to forge in their texts as crucial to a fulfilled authentic life, and new forms for making meaning of the learning process, as well. So pedagogical and, if you will, "aesthetic" questions are never mutually exclusive; both practices — the pedagogical and the aesthetic — remain rooted in *ethos*, in questions about how to live authentically.

Where have students learned this sense of brokenness, and how have we come to suggest to them — and perhaps believe ourselves — that the writing class is higher education's last-stop repair shop? In part, it is because they come convinced that they have no story to tell. In part, it is because of the failure of Wordsworth's triumphant experiment "to ascertain how far the language of conversation in the middle and lower classes in society is adapted to the purposes of poetic pleasure" ("'Advertisement' to the *Lyrical Ballads*" 116) — an experiment about language, but really an experiment about connecting people to their world and to one another. And in part, it is because the potential fruits of his experiment were finally buried under an enervating avalanche of competing cultural demands upon writers and their work and upon the reading/listening public, an avalanche unleashed, or at least hastened along, by the growth of the modern city.

In his book, *The Singer of Tales*, Albert Lord reflects on the oral impact of the urban experience: "If the way of life of a people furnishes subjects for story and affords occasion for the telling, this art will be fostered. . . . The songs have died out in the cities not because life in a large community is an unfitting environment for them, but because schools were first founded there and writing has been firmly rooted in the way of life of the city dwellers" (cited in Neisser, 247). During the nineteenth and the early part of the twentieth century, English and American people found themselves coming to terms with city life as a reality and as an image — or better, an icon — of the impact its technology would have on their lives. In Byron's *Don Juan*, there is London:

> A mighty mass of brick, and smoke, and shipping,
> Dirty and dusky, but wide as eye
> Could reach. . .
> A wilderness of steeples peeping
> On tiptoe through their sea-coal canopy.
>
> (10.1-6)

For Wordsworth, it is a "monstrous ant-hill on the plain / Of a too busy world":

> A work completed to our hands, that lays
> If any spectacle on earth can do,
> The whole creative powers of man asleep!
>
> . . .
>
> What a shock
> For eyes and ears! what anarchy and din,
> Barbarian and infernal, — a phantasma,
> Monstrous in colour, motion, shape, sight, sound!
>
> (*Prelude* 7.679-688)

In Dicken's *Martin Chuzzlewit*, it is "this crowd of objects" (162) and in *Bleak House*:

> Smoke lowering down from chimney pots, making a soft black drizzle, with flakes of soot in it as big as full grown snow flakes — gone into mourning, one might imagine for the death of the sun. . . . Fog everywhere. Fog up the river, where it flows among green aits and meadows; fog down the river, where it rolls defiled among the tiers of shipping and the waterside pollutions of a great (and dirty) city. (1)

For Eliot, it is simply "Unreal" (*Wasteland* 60); for Conrad, surreal: "Then the vision of an enormous town presented itself, of a monstrous town more populous than some continents and in its man-made might as if indifferent to heaven's frowns and smiles; a cruel devourer of the world's light. There was. . . darkness enough to bury five million lives" (*Agent* xii).

In the midst of the city that had so powerfully gripped the imagination of these Romantic and Victorian writers stood the Crystal Palace, a paradox of steel and glass erected in 1851 on the green in Hyde Park, an industrial exhibit hall which rapidly became the pervasive symbol of their worship of progress. But the psychological reality was a pervasive sense of their own brokenness. Wordsworth would write in his Preface to the *Lyrical Ballads*:

For a multitude of causes unknown to former times are now acting with a combined force to blunt the discriminating powers of mind, and unfitting it for all voluntary exertion to reduce it to a state of almost savage torpor. The most effective of these causes are the great national events which are daily taking place, and the increasing accumulation of men in cities.... (128)

The early part of the century had witnessed a Romantic revival of the lyric whose singers sought with varying degrees of success to make the subject into an image through which their transcendence of brokenness might be achieved. So Tintern Abbey and the natural landscape that surrounded it became for Wordsworth not only a reminder that a certain kind of childhood vision—when their "colors and their forms, were then to me/An appetite, a feeling and a love" (79-80)—was to be repudiated by the adult mind, but became as well vehicles for an extraordinarily abstract (and one might say finally highly suspect) feeling of "connection" to "humanity":

> I have learned
> To look on nature, not as in the hour
> Of thoughtless youth; but hearing oftentimes
> The still, sad music of humanity,
> Nor harsh nor grating, though of ample power
> To chasten and subdue. And I have felt
> A presence that disturbs me with the joy
> Of elevated thoughts; a sense sublime
> Of something far more deeply interfused,
> Whose dwelling is the light of setting suns
> ... and in the mind of man.
>
> (88-99)

Romantic poetry often begins in specificity—a ruined abbey, daffodils, a nightingale, an urn—but end with the object-made-image—thus somehow no longer itself—and inevitably, with the lament of Keats ("Cold Pastoral!") who, entombed in his hedgerow, recognized the failure, or at least the unbearable transiency, of this project of transcendence: "Was it a vision, or a waking dream?/Fled is that music: —do I wake or sleep?" ("Ode to a Nightingale," 79-80).

It is not surprising, then, that by mid-century, the voice of Arnold would be heard claiming, emphatically and repeatedly, a new project: the effort "to see the object in itself as it really is" ("On Translating Homer") as he rode the railroad through England for thirty-five years, inspecting schools and producing several volumes of essays and annual reports on the problem of education in England and on the continent.

Like Arnold, his fellow Victorians were, early in their careers, obsessed with form as a means of managing a psychically unmanageable content, and their poems were a poignant lament over their disconnection from history, from other persons, from nature, from the imaginative faith of their Romantic predecessors and from themselves. It is, after all, not an accident that the Romantic lyric gave way to the dramatic monologue, a poem of implied, not actual, conversation, and a poem of intellectual relativism that was the form perfected by this latter part of the nineteenth century. Defeated by his inability to fulfill his own classical prescription that poetry should "inspirit and rejoice the reader," Arnold concludes the Preface to his *Poems, 1853* with a resounding exhortation to formal excellence:

> ... if it is impossible for us, under the circumstances amidst which we live, to think clearly, to feel nobly, and to delineate firmly; if we cannot attain to the mastery of great artists — let us, at least, have so much respect for our art as to prefer it to ourselves. Let us not bewilder our successors: let us transmit to them the practice of poetry, with its boundaries and wholesome regulative laws, under which excellent works may again, perhaps, at some future time, be produced, not yet fallen into oblivion through our neglect, not yet condemned and canceled by the influence of their eternal enemy, caprice. (1:15)

The ultimate terror of this self-exploration was, of course, solipsism, which Arnold called in the 1853 Preface "the great disease of modernism, the dialogue of the mind with itself." While his classicism calls him to epic, his inherently Romantic legacy makes him, at his best, a lyric poet, but one frightened by what his poetic self-confession may reveal. It is, in fact, only quite late in his career that Arnold can put aside his terror of the emotional anarchy that the Romantic exploration of the feeling self seems to threaten and celebrate the vital promise offered by their "lyrical cry" ("On Translating Homer" 1:209). While his "Scholar Gipsy" was "born in days when wits were fresh and clear" (201), his nostalgically Romantic, Victorian consciousness experienced itself, "With its sick hurry and its divided aims" (204), "Wandering between two worlds, one dead,/The other powerless to be born" ("Stanzas from the Grand Chartreuse," 85-86). And in "The Buried Life" he stutters rhetorically:

Only — but his is rare —
When a beloved hand is laid in ours...
When our world-deafened ear
Is by the tones of a loved voice caressed
... then he *thinks* he knows

The hills where his life rose
And the sea where it goes

(77-98, emphasis added)

Arnold's legacy in the twentieth century is Eliot's "Prufrock," who "dares" not even "think he knows," and the "objective correlative," a catchphrase that seeks to achieve the same promise as Arnold's "imaginative reason," that is, appropriate connection of the feeling subject to an object "in itself, as it really is." Eliot's work demonstrates a visceral struggle with the problem of integrating feeling and the necessity to provide an "objective" description of experience. And it reflects the failure of William Blake's triumphant proclamation that imagination itself might "buil[d] Jerusalem/In England's green and pleasant land" ("Preface," from *Milton* II: 15-16). The increasing isolation of the writer from nature and from human relationships paralleled the increasing separation of the minister from his flock and the increasing unease of the believer whose "apology" for faith became often an apology for his life itself; thus, the dogmatic faith to which Eliot appealed complemented Newman's *Apologia* for his early conversion, an explanation for an act of faith that he entitled "Pro Vita Sua." And what was the male teacher who so often enacted the role of minister to do when he found himself increasingly without his docile flock of believers? This question may well explain the brutality of nineteenth-century schools as Dickens and others have so graphically represented them.

Disconnection, the denaturization of the lived experience, had inevitably to be accompanied by a devaluing of the feminine — life — principles, of "woman," and of individual women in the culture. This devaluing was acted out in the creation of forms (the Victorian "Angel in the House" and her whalebone corset not the least of these) which could capture and possess her energy and her potency, thus mastering and sanitizing (dreadful corruption of the word) a terrifying array of natural processes, not the least of which are conception, birth, and the nurturing of children, through mastering her. Many "forms" were erected in the conventional ground of language itself. Pregnancy was called her "confinement"; working women who married were abruptly and immediately "retired" to the home to await the birth of children without any cultural ritual to ease that drastic change of lifestyle; "rest" cures for "hysterical" symptoms focused on eliminating factors that had caused them — underlying disturbances of her reproductive organs and functions — and were conducted with the demand for complete control by male physicians whose nurses dispensed milk diets and douches while he himself prescribed aliments and nutriments, the potables heavily laced with alcohol. Massive furniture, some of it heavily and elaborately carved, crowded every room, its weight and mass bringing a kind of solid security in a rapidly changing world as well as a massive cleaning problem. Multiple patterns covered walls, drapes, and rugs as though to fill up every possibility of empty space. The nursery was removed to the top of the house. In *Jane Eyre*, only the attic, where Rochester's nymphomaniac wife was kept and from which her mad laugh echoed, was at further remove from the everyday work of the household. As Charlotte Perkins Gilman's short story, "The Yellow Wallpaper," recording her own "rest cure" reveals, more than one attempt was made to confine women there with their children and to use infantilization itself as a primary means of control leading to the Victorian sexual fascination for the child-woman.

And gradually, relentlessly, writers in the latter half of the century, their texts strewn with broken-hearted lovers, tell stories of efforts — largely unsuccessful — to bind up and thus to control those daemonic and ecstatic elements that were the great fascination of an earlier Romantic generation. It is a tribute to the power of this Romantic inheritance that despite relentless efforts at repression, this feminine energy will not be contained. The child Jane throws herself furiously against the locked doors of her dead stepfather's blood-red bedroom and they do not yield, but she is delivered unconscious from this room, reborn in the identity of a confirmed defiance that causes Jane the woman to refuse Rochester's efforts to dress her as his doll, and infuses her refusal to return to him until his dreadfully maimed state guarantees her mastery of their married life together. Rochester's wife emerges from her attic and the fire of her unbounded rage burns down his house and wreaks upon him a terrible, castrating revenge. Keats' sinuous Lamia and Coleridge's Christabel find expression in Tennyson's Vivien and Rossetti's often halo-bound recreations out of myth and literature. Yet despite her reduced social status at court, the prostituted equality of her sexuality and the pitiful tenor of her jealousy, Vivien works her magic, entombing Merlin for eternity like no mean Circe. And the sinuous hands of Rossetti's women along with the sheer mass of their hair and torso threaten always to burst from the confinement of his frames. In short, as Nina Auerbach argues of texts whose women are apparently more submissive (the saintly child Helen is clearly Jane's foil in this regard), these women's stories are the fulfillment of "a vital Victorian mythology whose lovable woman is a silent and self-disinherited mutilate, the fullness of whose extraordinary and dangerous being might at any moment return through violence. The taboos that encased Victorian woman contained buried tributes to her disruptive power" (8). Again, "Burne-Jones and his Victorian associates force us to look into the serpent-woman's face and to feel the mystery of a power, endlessly mutilated and restored, of a woman with a demon's gifts" (9). Seeking to master nature, we confront increasingly the fact that we have instead unleashed a monster — many monsters, in fact. But the warnings of these consequences were present already in nineteenth-century images of women over whom for centuries patriarchal cultures had sought control as part and parcel of this ongoing obsession for mastery over life and thus, over death.

Madeleine Grumet, writes that women's project is "recovering our possibilities, ways of knowing and being in the world that we remember and imagine and must draw into language that can span the chasm that presently separates what we know as our public and private worlds" (xii). The irony of this project of women's writing is that it involves first a return through memory to a time and culture that is not "illiterate" as it is typically described, but "pre-literate," to an oral tradition when the word is conceived as "utterance," the "outering" of self in order that the self can find a creative and fluid intersection with an ongoing cultural tradition. This is, of course, what the Romantic lyric, which is first and foremost a song, was about. In women's writing, this has often involved the recovery of personal history, partly yet significantly of what Virginia Woolf called "thinking back through the mother," a task that every woman writer must inevitably do at some point — or at many points — in her ongoing process. Secondly, it involves the rediscovery and the reaffirmation of the senses and the sense of time, of history, that are the hallmarks of this time of life and this relationship to language. Just as there is an oral tradition emerging from the pre-literate period in the history of a culture's literature, a period when "composition and performance are two aspects of the same moment" (Lord 244), so too is there a pre-literate period in the history of an individual's struggle toward written language and the sense of fixity and "conventionalization" that the mastery of written language inevitably brings (cf. Ong).

In their effort to move back behind erected linguistic conventions that have fixed their identity in a language foreign to their experience and a linearity foreign to their understandings of time and space, these women, too, seek a return to a kind of Romantic consciousness in which being and knowing — composition and performance — are at least dialectically understood if they can no longer in a literate society be conceived as one. Pre-literate men, bards, troubadours, and their Romantic legatees sang the poetry that shaped and was shaped by culture, but lost the song when their literacy became obsessed with fact, with linearity, with progress defined only as a relentless hurtle toward technocracy.[2] Reminding us of what we had lost and seeking a way to recover it in song was pre-eminently Romantic work, with Blake's *Songs of Innocence and Experience* among the first of these efforts. Women writers, like their Romantic counterparts, seek the recovery of this oral tradition, not its formed or formal but its forming possibilities and its connection to mythic time, seeking the song as utterance, mediating as it does between the image and the object, the moment of relation and the many moments that become history, seeking what Rich calls "the thing itself and not the myth" ("Diving into the Wreck" 1.63). They are both willing, and in fact recognize the need, to suspend fact for facticity, expecting to find and articulate not "truth" but "truth-in-relation," and to "know" it by its "being" there in relation to them.

Despite current cultural pressure to make students write in conformity to accepted standards, the first battle of the writing classroom is, ironically, against the conventionalization of language. This is, it seems to me, a renewed Romantic battle in the oral tradition particular to the project of women's literature, and their work in this regard can be significantly instructive to writing pedagogy. Its aim is to help students discover, to hear, or perhaps best, to overhear their own voice — one that many writing teachers I know will lament as absent from students' texts for a very long time — and once they have overheard it, in Eliot's phrase, to "dare" to trust what they have overheard.[3]

This work is crucially about memory, a chief fascination for Romantic and Victorian alike (although each group regarded its activity and its fruits very differently), and it is about discovering techniques that can link sensation to experience and to feeling, leading ultimately, as Robert Langbaum describes the Romantic understanding of these, to self or what Keats called Soul, to identity and the continuity of self over time, and, I would argue, to voice emerging from a written text. For self and therefore voice, in my view, is dependent on the capacity to do exactly what Grumet describes: to remember ways of knowing and being in the world, the childlike and the playful not the least of these, to imagine the possibilities for other ways of knowing and being, and to have the capability of calling them into language. Tracing nineteenth-century understandings of "self" through Locke, Hume, and chiefly, Wordsworth,

Langbaum argues that for Hume the self is the produce of memory: "The self is a retrospective construction of the imagination, and for this reason 'memory not only discovers identity, but also contributes to its production.' Only through memory can we create the self by seeing continuity between past and present perceptions. . . . Memory above all will remain the creator, the artist-fabricator of self" (27).

This movement backward in order to go forward is, as Langbaum notes, a chief characteristic of Wordsworth's "processive self"; it is also a hallmark of the personal narrative work of countless women writers, and it spills richly over into their fiction, as well. The object-relation happens by remembering it and imaginatively recreating it, and in this relationship the self is formed and transcended at the same time, a circular, or perhaps better, spiralling evolution both celebratory of – and dependent upon – a faith in the relational possibilities of human experience.[4]

Yet while the object-made-image is a rich means for tapping into archetypal dimensions of the human self and of human experience, the risk is always that the object will become disconnected from its reality as a thing in the world. This is one dimension of the kind of solipsism most feared by the Romantic generation, and it underlies Keats' lament about the veracity of his own ecstatic experience as the nightingale flees from his hedgerow.

Often the inability of contemporary students to grasp multiple levels of meaning that attach to image and symbol as they are claimed and elaborated by individual writers and cultures causes them to be labelled "literalist." But as legatees of the romantic struggle with the same issue, they are finally, it seems to me, certainly not literal – and this is the problem – they are simply not connected to the object at all. How, then, does the writing teacher help these students to begin to make connections? I suspect the answer is not to forget, as Wordsworth felt he had to, the time of "thoughtless youth," but to begin to remember it. These memories and imaginings are first called into language – first given voice – in song. This is where the troubadours began; this is where the Romantic poets began, and this is where many contemporary women writers begin as well. "[S]uch a price/The Gods exact for song/To become what we sing," Arnold had written in "The Strayed Reveller" which is richly reminiscent of Keats. "I do not believe in separation," says Bernard in Virginia Woolf's *The Waves*, "The human voice has a disarming quality – (we are not single, we are one)" (221).

In an important sense, students' questions – "Is it right?" "Is it long enough?" "How do I do that?" – suggest the extent to which we have communicated to them a false linearity in the writing process (first we compose it, then it is read, usually in silence, by the teacher at her desk, to determine if it is 'right'). This sense of fixed forms has to be learned and imitated rather than seen as a fluid process to be entered into, and a sense of their role as mere transmitters of cultural convention overcomes opportunities to be as creative voices to be added to the chorus of those who have come before. Writing so often with a frightened sense of how their texts will look (rarely sound) to their teacher-audience, students lose both a sense of ownership of their work (words pass through them but do not come from and so do not belong to them) and a validation of their own voices. Thus the brokenness of their relationship to fact, of facticity. These voiceless students simply never tell their own stories because they never feel invited, in the world of school, to tell them, nor have they inherited the tools that would make the telling possible. How few of our students feel able to risk the act, or to pay what Arnold calls (and Woolf demonstrates) is the price — in self-exposure, in effort, and in time — to be genuinely connected to the object. And how often have they learned from the academy a false sense of appropriateness that has negated their experience and in some cases invalidated the fullness of experience itself?

It was the urge to invite back into their songs all kinds of experiences that had been proscribed by past formal constraints that gave impetus to the Romantic movement. This same impetus informs women's writing — and should inform contemporary teaching as well. Woolf's poet, Neville, one voice of the six who compose the single, collective narrator of *The Waves*, speaks about experience in a way that prescribes how her prose poem is to be read — or better, how it is to be listened to — and what the nature of the relationship between person and person, person and world, person and self or selves, reader/listener and narrator must be:

> Certainly, one cannot read this poem without effort. The page is often corrupt and mud-stained, and torn and stuck together with faded leaves, with scraps of verbena or geranium. To read this poem one must have myriad eyes.... One must put aside antipathies and jealousies and not interrupt. One must have patience and infinite care and let the light sound, whether of spiders' delicate feet on a leaf or the chuckle of water in some irrelevant drainpipe, unfold too. Nothing is to be rejected in fear or horror.... One must be skeptical, but throw caution to the winds and when the door opens accept absolutely. Also sometimes weep; also cut away ruthlessly with a slice of the blade

soot, bark, hard accretions of all sorts. And so (while they talk) let down one's net deeper and deeper and gently draw in and bring to the surface what he said and she said and make poetry. (313-14)

"My mother always sang to her children," Eudora Welty has written, overhearing her mother's storytelling voice in the dark. "Long before I wrote stories I listened for them. Listening *for* them is something more acute than listening *to* them" (12). "Writing is to start," writes Chantel Chawaf, "It is always to push the beginning further back, because in language nothing of the body, nothing of the woman has, as yet, been integrated.... Everything starts from the body and from the living, from our senses, our desires, our imagination" (qtd. in Makward 96). "I learn," May Sarton writes, "by being *in relation to*" (107).

Journal-writing, telling one's story to oneself, is one means of creating facticity, the relation of persons to the facts of their experience, remaking as it does so our sense of time and of our "place" in it. While it is clearly not song, journal-writing is a personal narrative which is undisputedly a significant one for women participating in some of the rich possibilities of its roots in oral narrative. Like the lyric, its impulse is inherently conversational: as a conversation with the self, it offers to its composer/performers the opportunity to circle back upon our experiences and ourselves, revising, reseeing both. Rereading each successive diary entry, we may circle back not upon recorded experience *per se*, but on a sometimes continually varied series of fixed texts that record our memory of the experience reproduced there. Composing the narrative, in act, we compose ourselves; like the way an oral poet learns his song, one comes to it "little by little" (Lord 250).

In 1918, Nelly Ptaschkina wrote of herself: "Two Nellys live in me. Sometimes I would like to know which is the real one. When I am in that other world, 'that' Nelly seems the real one; when I am back again in my ordinary everyday one it is 'this.' In fact, they complete each other and make up the real one" (Moffat and Painter 59). Joanna Field speaks about her diary work in *A Life of One's Own*: "I seemed to have two quite different selves, one which answered when I thought deliberately, another which answered when I let my thought be automatic. I decided to investigate further the thought of the automatic one, to ask it questions and write answers without stopping to think" (Moffat and Painter 352). Anne Frank's journal is a series of letters written to an alter-ego she calls Kitty: "I hid myself within myself... and quietly wrote down all my joys, sorrows, and contempt in my diary" (Moffat and Painter 35-36).

Whether it is introduced as a book for free-writing, pre-writing, reaction, focused reflection, description or dramatization, and if its use is not distorted by an over-zealous writing teacher anxious only to help her students find material to write about, the journal can be a safe place where conversation can begin. The risk is solipsism; the promise, the beginning of overhearing one's own voice. Because its truth is "my story," truth-to-me, as a form it can validate the kind of "playing around" with experience that schooling's passion for order and form so frequently condemns, and it can be a place where the re-signifying process that marks feminist work with language can begin. It validates chaos as a means of making order. And in the guise of a linear record of time, it allows participation in a circular, recursive temporality so fascinating to the Romantics that is at the heart of "composing" anything, including ourselves. Virginia Woolf writes of this need to be open to experience in her journal:

> ... there looms ahead of me the shadow of some kind of form which a diary might attain to. I might in the course of time learn what it is one can make of this loose, drifting material of life; finding another use for it than the use I put it to, so much more consciously and scrupulously in fiction. . . . The main requisite, I think, is not to play the part of censor, but to write as the mood comes or of anything whatever; since I was curious to find how I went for things put in haphazard, and found the significance to lie where I never saw it at the time. (Moffat and Painter 227)

Like her Romantic predecessors, what Woolf explores is her own creative process — her journals are the ground of her fiction-making — and in the dialectic between journal-writing and fiction-writing, Woolf explores consciousness itself. Her particular interest is an inherently Romantic one: her work is an extended inventory of the objects and relations of her life in memory, but she seeks them less as images through which the transcendent can occur than as things themselves which are part and parcel of the "moments of being" punctuating the organic and orgasmic movement of her text. Woolf's texts are the songs of many voices all of which are her own. More than any other twentieth-century writer she seems to have grasped the capacity to become one with the object. Her effort is to reclaim the landscape out of which the colors and the voices of her experience are born, reclaiming not fact, but facticity, and negating the kind of portraiture in which writers "collect a number of events, and leave the person to whom it happened unknown" (*Moments of Being* 69).

Like Blake's *Songs* and Wordsworth's *Prelude*, much of women's writing is a retrospective effort to reclaim their own childhood with their mothers in order that they might reclaim both their children and themselves: "Many bright colors; many distant sounds; some human beings, always including a circle of the scene which they cut out: and all surrounded by a rest space—that is a rough visual description of childhood" (*Moments of Being* 79). This world begins in the nursery; like her Romantic predecessors, Woolf seeks first to reclaim not solely childhood, but the childlike connection to the object:

> ... without stopping to choose my way, in the sure and certain knowledge that it will find itself—or if not it will not matter—I begin: the first memory.
>
> This was of red and purple flowers on a black ground—my mother's dress; and she was sitting either in a train or in an omnibus, and I was on her lap. I therefore saw the flowers she was wearing very close; and can still see purple and red and blue, I think, against the black; they must have been anemones, I suppose. Perhaps we were going to St Ives; more probably, for from the light it must have been evening, we were coming back to London. But it is more convenient artistically to suppose that we were going to St Ives, for that will lead to my other memory, which also seems to be my first memory and in fact it is the most important of all my memories. If life has a base that it stands upon, it is a bowl that one fills and fills and fills—then my bowl without a doubt stands upon this memory. It is of lying half asleep, half awake, in bed in the nursery at St Ives. It is of hearing the weaves breaking, one, two, one, two, and sending a splash of water over the beach; and then breaking, one, two, one, two, behind a yellow blind. It is of hearing the blind draw its little acorn across the floor as the wind blew the blind out. It is of lying and hearing this splash and seeing this light, and feeling, it is almost impossible that I should be here; of feeling the purest ecstasy I can conceive.
>
> .   .   .   .
>
> Those moments—in the nursery, on the road to the beach—can still be more real than the present moment. (64-66)

In her struggle for identity, Woolf's Rhoda begins with a lament—"I have no face"—but she ends with the intuition that identity is about relationship, about facticity: "Alone, I often fall down into nothingness. I must push my foot stealthily lest I should fall off the edge of the world into nothingness. I have to bang my hand hard against some door to call myself back to the body" (223). To her own mother, Virginia Woolf writes an incessant elegy in diaries, autobiographical fragments and in many fictional works:

> What one would not give to recapture a single phrase, even! or the tone of the clear round voice... past as those years are her mark on them is ineffaceable, as though branded by the naked steel, the sharp, the pure. Living voices in many parts of the world still speak of her as someone who is actually a fact of life... as of a thing that happened, recalling, as though all around her grew significant, how she stood and turned and how the bird sang loudly, or a great cloud passed across the sky. Where has she gone? What she said has never ceased. (36, 39)

Later she would reflect of her mother that "she was keeping what I call in my shorthand the panoply of life — that which we all lived in common — in being" (83).

The willingness — in fact, the inevitability — of becoming and confronting a "divided self" is a central theme of women's journals. Its pervasive expression, crossing cultures, generations, and historical periods, suggest these writers' connections to personal, cultural and historical pasts — in particular to childhood and to the metaphoric childhood of the beginning writer's discovery of process — that can facilitate the reconnection of the knowing subject and the object-in-relation-to-which she knows. Dividedness need not be, although it often becomes, brokenness. This was perhaps one of the most significant, though perhaps the least heralded, discoveries of the Romantic period — a dialectical consciousness (innocence/experience; imagination/reason; past/present; clod/pebble; tiger/lamb) that became the excited fascination of a Romantic generation and the despair of their Victorian descendants. Understood and affirmed as both the blessing and the curse of memory, that sense of being "two selves," private and public, childlike and adult, deviant and appropriate, can create a rich, dialectical tension out of which much creative activity is born. Most importantly, it can be a basis for validating other kinds of knowing central to the world of imaginative play, and to the activity of composition which is the writer's work, and life's work.

In his essay, "On Memory and Childhood Amnesia," Ernest Schachtel suggests that we do not remember very early childhood (the pre-Oedipal period) because "the categories (or schemata) of adult memory are not fit to preserve these experiences and enable their recall" (192). The average adult's post-childhood memory is "fairly continuous":

> Its formal continuity in time is offset by barrenness in content, by an incapacity to reproduce anything that resembles a really rich,

full, rounded and alive experience. Even the most 'exciting' events are remembered as milestones rather than as moments filled with the concrete abundance of life. Adult memory reflects life as a road with occasional signposts and milestones rather than as the landscape through which this road has led. (193)

Schactel's description of adult memory's sterility is an appropriate one for so many "voiceless" and "landscape-less" student papers of which I have spoken earlier, and once again much that he argues can be traced to another—far more negative—confluence than Welty recognizes in exploring her own creative process. Nineteenth-century literature is a poignant record of the culture's repudiation of women, but also of children, from Blake's lament for the London chimney sweeps crying "'weep, 'weep" to Dickens' fictional excoriation of his society's literal and metaphoric orphaning of its sons and daughters. The term "childlike" comes into the language in the short-lived Romantic attempt to preserve and validate certain kinds of imaginative ways of seeing and knowing that they perceived as central to making art. But working against the continued affirmation of children and child-like ways of seeing and knowing and being are the tide of technology, its insistent emphasis on linear time, descriptions, processes; the conventionalization of language and the intolerance of deviance imperative to making and measuring "progress"; the anxious sense of the speed of time; the increasing formalization of education and its appropriation by the public domain; and the devaluing of leisure and of play. And so the proverbial village idiot found himself institutionalized as a ward of the state and the child, dressed like a miniature adult, was remanded to the custody of the nursery, the boarding school or the factory, all of which served to separate mothers and children, and served, as well, the industrial machine. Schachtel recognizes the profound irony in this process:

It is safe to assume that early childhood is the period of human life which is richest in experience. Everything is new to the newborn child. His gradual grasp of his environment and of the world around him are discoveries which, in experiential scope and quality, go far beyond any discovery that the most adventurous and daring explorer will ever make in his adult life. . . . Education and learning, while on the one hand furthering this process of discovery, on the other hand gradually brake and finally stop it completely. There are relatively few adults who are fortunate enough to have retained something of the child's curiosity, his capacity for questioning and for wondering. The average adult "knows all the answers," which is exactly why he will never know even a single answer. (195)

The typical freshman writing classroom, to pun on Schactel's term, is a place of many brakes, and many breaks. At worst, it is jammed with squirming bodies, shifting, whispering, doodling, staring off disconnectedly into dead space, wandering in late, leaving early, without books or with the wrong books, having read stories for "the facts" or not at all, docile recorders of everything heard from the teacher, carefully avoiding a record of student comment lest they become confused. The overwhelming temptation is to urge students to "grow up" and demonstrate that they are "serious learners" with an interest in the world and their own development. Yet what we need to urge is that they grow "back" or "down" so that they can grow out into the world, becoming playful learners capable of climbing behind the conventional structures and significances of language to discover their own voices and the multiple means, beyond the five-paragraph essay, by which facticity allows experience to be ordered, engaged and celebrated.

Schactel's description of contemporary disengagement from experience, the matter-of-fact absence of facticity, is a paradigmatic record of nineteenth-century literature's thematic threnody, but it is also a record of the twentieth-century classroom and its legacy of brokenness. In light of this discussion of the disconnection from pre-Oedipal childhood, his food metaphor is a paradoxically rich one:

> To have been there, to be able to say that one has been present at the performance, to have read the book even when one is unable to have the slightest personal reaction to it, is quite sufficient. But while Midas suffered tortures of starvation, the people under whose eyes every experience turns into a barren cliché do not know that they starve. Their starvation manifests itself merely in boredom or in restless activity and incapacity for any real enjoyment. (194)

And it is recorded in the literal self-starvation of hundreds of thousands of contemporary women, some of whose journal-reflections are collected by Geneen Roth in her book, *Feeding the Hungry Heart*.[5]

Another Victorian legatee, E. M. Forster, began his wonderful novel, *Howard's End*, with the epigraph, "Only connect." The writing classroom must become the place and the time where the means of fulfilling Forster's great urging can genuinely be explored. The writing teacher's task is not, then, to demand specificity in students' writing, but to help them discover the tools to recover their own experience; it is not to teach language conventions but the suspension of them in order that language might be remade, experience revisited and significance revised to express the individual writer's connection to fact. It is the work of empowerment.

When my students come to their first writing class, and we have chatted awhile, named each other and told an uncomfortable story or two about ourselves, I ask them to come back with two books, a writing book and a drawing book. The work of the first week is to subvert the word, of the second, to subvert the sentence, of the first month to allay anxieties by talking about and playing with revision — recovering sight and coming to understand how it gestates insight. Frederick Franck's *Zen of Seeing* inspires the first few days, sending students out beyond the classroom walls, instructing them to make space around them, to focus on whatever is immediately before them, to sit for a time before it, eyes closed, then to open them, and to draw, focused on the object, not the drawing, never lifting the pencil, "let[ting] the hand follow what the eye sees" (xv). Sharing their drawings anonymously, little by little students are drawn toward the kind of empathy that enables them to climb behind the labels for things and experience themselves as connected to what they have drawn. My students read some of what Franck writes; we talk a bit about insight, about significance-meaning-making:

> Seeing and drawing can become one, can become SEEING/DRAWING. When that happens there is no more room for the labelings. . . . Every insignificant thing appears as if seen in its three dimensions, in its own space and its own time. Each leaf of grass is seen to grow from its own roots, each creature is realized to be unique, existing now/here on its voyage from birth to death. No longer do I "look" at a leaf, but enter into direct contact with its life-process, with Life itself, with what I, too, really am. . . . Their growing is my growing, their facing I share. Becoming one with the lilies in SEEING/DRAWING, I become not less, but more myself. For the time being the split between Me and not-Me is healed, suspended. (Franck 7)

Little by little we move toward words, but our pre-writing exercises do not end in sentences. Semantic networks become the means of exploring the apparently random associative fibre-optics of memory, of leaping synaptic gaps and figuring out why. Word pictures lead to mind-pictures; free-writing is yet another resource to inventory experience, to recall smell, taste, touch, sight, sound. Sentences begin in a journal, and these pieces are shared aloud if the writer so chooses; the sounds and rhythms of their own words and other's words can be heard and savored. Communities of writers are formed in smaller groups, part of the larger collective that begins to define itself is the risking experience of hearing and being overheard, of listening and being listened to. In this community, each person's work becomes everyone's work, originality resides in the uniqueness of the stories, the pictures, the experiences, the insights, not merely in the words. Multiple drafts in response to multiple readings and listenings battle back the tyrannical permanence of the word, integrate revision from before the beginning to after the end, and enforce a potent sense of the connotative nature of language and the interpretive activity of knowing. Finally, if it all works, there emerges gradually through the ritual of reading, writing, story-telling, listening, in the dialectic of public and private, a sense of the sacred, of something holy, whole, healthy, of being participating in Being as in Annie Dillard's conception of insight. May Sarton's *Journal of A Solitude* is a rich reflection of what every Romantic poet seems eventually to have discovered—the song as utterance becomes, inevitably, prayer:

> I suppose that the only prayer—reached only *after* all pleas for grace or for some specific gifts have been uttered and laid aside—is: "Give me to be in your presence." ... Simone Weil says, "Absolute attention is prayer." And the more I have thought about this over the years, the truer it is for me. I have used the sentence often in talking about poetry to students, to suggest that if one looks long enough at almost anything, looks with absolute attention at a flower, a stone, the bark of a tree, grass, snow, a cloud, something like a revelation takes place. Something is "given," and perhaps that something is always a reality *outside* the self. We are aware of God only when we cease to be aware of ourselves, not in the negative sense of denying the self, but in the sense of losing self in admiration and joy.[6] (99)

Despite her professed atheism, like Franck and Sarton, Woolf too shares this sense as a consequence of becoming one with the object, not an outcome but an expression of this intense experience of fusion:

> I was looking at the flower bed by the front door; "That is the whole," I said. I was looking at a plant with a spread of leaves; and it seemed suddenly plain that the flower itself was a part of the earth; that a ring enclosed what was the flower; and that was the real flower; part earth; part flower.
>
> . . . .
>
> I feel that I have had a blow; but it is not, as I thought as a child, simply a blow from an enemy from behind the cotton wool of daily life; it is or will become a revelation of some order; it is a token of some real thing behind appearances; and I make it real by putting it into words. It is only by putting it into words that I make it whole; this wholeness means that it has lost its power to hurt me; it gives me. . . a great delight to put the severed parts together. . . From this I reach. . . a constant idea of mine, that behind the

cotton wool is hidden a pattern; that we — I mean all human beings — are connected with this; that the whole world is a work of art; that we are parts of the work of art. *Hamlet* or a Beethoven quartet is the truth about this vast mass that we call the world. But there is no Shakespeare, there is no Beethoven, certainly and emphatically there is no God; we are the words; we are the music; we are the thing itself. And I see this when I have a shock. (*Moments of Being* 71-72)

Being and knowing — what Woolf calls "telling the truth about my own experience as a body" ("Professions for Women" 62) — come together in community, when "performance and composition" are one: every writer, every singer, has an audience. But the last paradox, the lesson so difficult for the socially passionate nineteenth-century novelists to learn (busy as they were about the work of repudiating Romantic individualism in the name of social responsibility, busy as they were at imposing upon life a sequential march from cradle to grave), was that the ground of community is solitude, and solitude is constructed upon the sense of being "composed," of being "at home" with oneself. I suspect this same difficulty confronts the contemporary student; I am certain this same difficulty confronts the contemporary teacher.

Denise Levertov sings this last message that was, finally, the intent of my own first reflection:

I sing those messages
you've learned by heart. . .
You hear
yourselves in them,
self after self. Your solitudes
utter their runes, your own
voices begin to rise in your throats.

("Poet and Person," 7-12)

Towards the end of *The Waves*, Bernard confronts the despair in what he calls "the contribution of maturity to childhood's intuitions — satiety and doom; the sense of what is inescapable in our lot; death; the knowledge of limitations; how life is more obdurate than one had thought it" (363). We cannot help but hear the voice of Keats in this. But Woolf causes Bernard to answer the despair, although the response can by no means be any Wordsworthian conception of joy. The ecstasy is of a different order altogether: it is about wresting meaning from experience through utterance.

Some people go to priests; others to poetry; I to my friends, I to my own heart, I to seek among phrases and fragments something unbroken — I to whom there is not beauty enough in moon or tree; to whom the touch of one person with another is all, yet who cannot grasp even that, who am so imperfect, so weak, so unspeakably lonely. There I sat.

. . . .

But if you hold a blunt blade to a grindstone long enough, something spurts — a jagged edge of fire; so held to lack of reason, aimlessness, the usual, all massed together, out spurted in one flame hatred, contempt. I took my mind, my being, the old dejected, almost inanimate object and lashed it about among these odds and ends, sticks and straws, detestable little bits of wreckage, flotsam and jetsam. I jumped up, I said, "Fight." "Fight," I repeated. It is the effort and the struggle, it is the perpetual warfare, it is the shattering and piecing together — this is the daily battle, defeat or victory, the absorbing pursuit. The trees, scattered, put on order; the thick green of the leaves thinned itself to a dancing light. I netted them under with a sudden phrase. I retrieved them from formlessness with words. (361; 363-64)

Without a knowledge of brokenness, connectedness cannot be understood. Without the experience of connectedness, our students' texts will be forever broken. These are the lessons Adrienne Rich explores in her search "for the thing itself." This is the legacy that Virginia Woolf, that journal-makers, their work deeply embedded in the Romantic tradition, seek to learn in the effort "to become the thing" — to become themselves. This is the dialectic of the writing classroom's project.

Notes

1. In one sense, of course, the Romantic experiment succeeded: its proponents did offer us an alternative, "holistic" vision counter to the "broken" one which I propose as that which marks the modern and post-modern periods. Nevertheless, the very fact that virtually every successive generation of poets from Tennyson and Arnold to Eliot and Stevens and beyond finds itself struggling to come to terms with that vision of one hundred and fifty years ago suggests to me that it has indeed *not* been integrated into the collective psyche, and in that sense I stand by my argument of its failure.

2. Despite the predominance of men among the group of troubadours, Judy Chicago's research team found that "Of the one hundred known minstrels between 1150 and 1250, twenty were female" (*The Dinner Party*, 141).

3. In her essay on French feminist theory, Domna Stanton paraphrases the work of Julia Kristeva, whose work is perhaps the most helpful in addressing this question of voice: "All subjects articulate themselves through the interaction of the semiotic and symbolic modalities, Kristeva insists, but the first of these has been consistently repressed by the Logos because it is experienced as a threat. Only the eruption of the semiotic into the symbolic can give reign to heterogeneous meaning, to difference, and thus subvert the existing systems of signification.... In much of women's writing, she discovers that "the notion of the signifier as a network of distinctive marks is insufficient, because each of these marks is charged over and beyond its discriminatory value as a carrier of signification, by an instinctual or affective force which, strictly speaking, cannot be signified but remains latent in the phonic invocation or the inscribing gesture.... Poetic language has always shared analogous traits" (73-87).

4. "For Wordsworth the self is memory and process—the memory of all its phases and the process of interchange with the external world. The movement of thought into sensation and back again corresponds to the circular movement of self into nature and back again and to the circular movement from the subjectively individual to the archetypally objective phases of identity and back again. Each circular movement, which could be conceived as starting from outside as well as inside, is a new creation, a new confirmation, of self—and is impelled by joy" (Langbaum 46).

5. This collection of Roth's own and other women's journal entries regarding their struggles with eating disorders is a powerful statement of the body-mind-spirit connection at the heart of the Romantic argument, and of the consequences when our sense of that connection is lost. While the need for nourishing food is a real and desperate one, Roth, as a therapist, views the symptoms of eating-disordered women as a manifestation of the longing for satisfying (loving) relationships—with themselves and with other persons.

6. This notion of prayer may, but need not, be understood in a Judeo-Christian or formally religious sense; it is an "attention to" to use Weil's word, or a "mindfulness of" to use the Buddhist term, that which is intimately a part of and yet powerfully transcends the self—a moment when epistemology and ontology come together. And so are Wordsworth's poems to daffodils and clouds, and numerous moments in the sonnets when his apostrophe turns to God or Shelley's to the skylark, or in the vision of Coleridge's Mariner.

Works Cited

Arnold, Matthew. *The Complete Prose Works of Matthew Arnold*, Vol. 1, 2. Ed. R. H. Super. Ann Arbor: University of Michigan Press, 1962.

Auerbach, Nina. *Woman and the Demon: The Life of a Victorian Myth*. Cambridge: Harvard University Press, 1982.

Chicago, Judy. *The Dinner Party*. Garden City: Anchor Books, 1979.

Conrad, Joseph. *The Secret Agent*. Garden City: Doubleday, 1953.

Dickens, Charles. *Bleak House*. Eds. George Ford & Sylvere Monod. New York: W. W. Norton, 1977.

_____. *Martin Chuzzlewit*. New York: Scribner & Sons, 1905.

Eisenstein, Hester and Alice Jardine (eds.). *The Future of Difference*. New Jersey: Rutgers University Press, 1980.

Eliot, T. S. *The Complete Poems and Plays, 1909-1950*. New York: Harcourt Brace, 1962.

Forster, E. M. *Howard's End*. New York: Vintage Books, 1921.

Franck, Frederick. *The Zen of Seeing*. New York: Vintage Books, 1973.

Grumet, Madeleine. *Bitter Milk: Women and Teaching*. Boston: University of Massachusetts Press, 1987.

Langbaum, Robert. *The Mysteries of Identity*. New York: Oxford University Press, 1977.

Levertov, Denise. *Candles in Babylon*. New York: New Directions, 1982.

Lowry, Howard Foster. *The Letters of Matthew Arnold to Arthur Hugh Clough*. Oxford: Clarendon Press, 1968.

Makward, Christine "To Be or Not to Be... A Feminist Speaker," in Eisenstein and Jardine.

Moffat, Mary Jane and Painter, Charlotte. *Revelations: Diaries of Women*. New York: Vintage Books, 1974.

Neisser, Ulrich, ed. *On Memory Observed: Remembering in Natural Contexts*. New York: W. H. Freeman, 1982.

Ong, Walter. *Orality and Literacy: The Technologizing of the World*. New York: Routledge Chapman and Hall, 1982.

Rich, Adrienne. *Diving into the Wreck*. New York: W. W. Norton, Inc., 1973.

Roth, Geneen. *Feeding the Hungry Heart*. New York: Signet, 1982.

Sarton, May. *Journal of A Solitude*. New York: W. W. Norton, 1973.

Schachtel, Ernest. "On Memory and Childhood Amnesia" in *On Memory Observed: Remembering in Natural Contexts*. Ed. Ulrich Neisser. New York: W. H. Freeman, 1982.

Scholes, Robert and Kellogg, Robert. *The Nature of Narrative*. London: Oxford University Press, 1966.

Stanton, Domna. "Language and Revolution: The Franco-American Dis-Connection," in Eisenstein and Jardine, 73-87.

Welty, Eudora. *One Writer's Beginnings*. New York: Warner, 1983.

Woolf, Virginia. *Moments of Being: Unpublished Autobiographical Writings*. Ed. Jeanne Schulkind. New York: Harcourt Brace Jovanovich, 1976.

Woolf, Virginia. "Professions for Women," in *Women and Writing*. Ed. Michele Barrett. New York: Harcourt Brace Jovanovich, 1979.

Woolf, Virginia. *The Waves*. New York: Harcourt Brace and World, 1931.

Wordsworth, William. *The Prose Works of William Wordsworth*. Vol. 1. Eds. J. B. Owen & Jane Worthington Smyser. Oxford: The Clarendon Press, 1974.

Chapter 13

AUTOBIOGRAPHIC PRAXIS AND

SELF-EDUCATION:

FROM ALIENATION TO AUTHENTICITY

Richard L. Butt

When I was asked to contribute a paper[1] for this book on the autobiographical impulse and Romanticism, I felt challenged, threatened, supported and encouraged simultaneously. I do not have a literary background; I fear it is a particular weakness in my life. In a positive sense, the topic is appropriate and timely for me for a number of reasons. I saw, in this task, the chance to engage in a particular preoccupation of mine, that of integration, synthesis or a search for synergy. I have been waiting for the right moment to bring together bits and pieces of my autobiography into a more coherent form. This may well be, as Madeleine Grumet notes in her contribution to this book, one male's search for integration as a result of the echoes of loss within the oedipal relationship; but rather than a terrifying struggle, I see it as a joy to bring together the things within myself. As well, though I am not versed in the Romantics, I think my life history reflects elements of the Romantic story. It also strikes a very strong harmonic link with the Romantic roots of progressive education through the claiming, expression, education and making of the self and community through individual and social action.

I currently am working with experienced teachers to provide a way in which they can take charge of their own personal and professional development. In order to do this I have evolved a form of *collaborative autobiography* through which we help each other write our own stories as persons and as teachers. I participate fully with them, in a graduate course, as a co-learner; their personal quest is also mine. We get to know ourselves and our peers better. We claim our strengths and attempt to understand our weaknesses. In this way we can take more responsibility for our professional lives and can counteract the alienating technical rationality of the school system. We evolve our life stories at the risk of the tyranny of coherence that Madeleine Grumet writes of in her paper. But, in the first assignment particularly, I really encourage an expression of the incoherence of our working lives — the negativity — in order to try to get to "exaltation beyond despair." Our stories, as well, contain the problematics of our lives. What coherence, with respect to self, we do obtain is a necessary first step in the personal ownership of our stories.

Through telling my story in this paper I hope to show how I came to the pedagogy of collaborative autobiography and how the course facilitates the autobiographical impulse. As Ann Berthoff said at the colloquium for this book, "It is a history of the process that I am part of." In a sense it is a story of the struggle to become literate, to join the conversation, but in a way which joins theory and practice. We have so many discourses and dialects that we need to work towards a more universal language that rejoins the person to both the work, *and the world*, as well as providing a voice that is understood. I think stories can do that; they are not atheoretical but can express both lived reality and personal, moral, and social theory. In the realm of education, these stories can cut through the technical paraphernalia and speak equally to parents, teachers, pupils, scholars, and administrators with both individual and collective voices.

My story, however, might be seen as naïve in several ways — romanticized in the worst sense — and perhaps solipsistic. Yet the "I" in this story is not just me. The lived realities and ideas are not just mine but ours. They belong to my students — teachers with whom I learn; they also belong to my colleagues, at the colloquium, who created this book. This story, or any story of progressive education, is naïve, however, with respect to its Romantic roots and as a number of papers in this book clearly show, the link between Romanticism and progressive education is problematic. Progressive education, however, does have a coherent ontological, epistomological, and axiological base which includes elements of the Romantics' thinking (Butt, *Conceptual System*). The Romantics did acknowledge the child, but were not quite able to bring him and her in from the cold state of abstraction and isolation. Later progressives, however, did bring Rousseau's child into the warm reality of the home in order to play, learn, and create herself; as Jane Roland Martin points out in the title of her paper on Maria Montessori, it can be "Romanticism domesticated."

The philosophical base for progressive education as drawn from the Romantics, appears to be a myth in both the illusory and exemplary senses. It is, however, a *positive* myth whose invention takes only those parts of Rousseau and other Romantics that go beyond their struggle and preoccupation with manipulation and control to the real self-initiated child. Through my story, I will try to show how *teachers* can become self-initiated — how I arrived at collaborative autobiography as an emancipatory form of self- and peer-related pedagogy. My story will examine my current pedagogy — how I think and act in my current context first. I will then delve into my personal and professional past in an attempt to reveal how I came to be that way. I will conclude with a view of a positive future for the legacy of Romanticism within post-modern progressive education.

Teaching with Collaborative Autobiography

The purpose of the graduate course which uses collaborative autobiography as its main pedagogy is to help school improvement through teacher development. Teachers are faced with an avalanche of other people's ideas, materials, curriculum prescriptions and tests of accountability which may or may *not* take account of classroom reality, pupil needs, and the teacher's style. Research on change has underlined that teachers need to make sense of these impositions in their own way, to take ownership, adapt and elaborate prescriptions to suit their own classroom contingencies. In this way, not only is teacher alienation minimized but also materials can be transformed through the teacher's pedagogical style into actions that are useful, valuable and motivating for pupils. In order to be able to take up the challenge of authentic teaching and self-initiated professional development, however, it is essential for the teachers to know themselves as explicitly as possible. In order to pursue this goal through the graduate course, I ask teachers to respond to five assignments through autobiographical writing. A minor assignment asks for a brief education or career profile — a *curriculum vitae* — as a broad introductory context for our mutual deliberations. Teachers are then asked: "What is the nature of your working reality? What and how do you teach in that context? If that is how you teach, how did you come to be that way? What is your disposition towards these three autobiographical pieces — how do you wish to be in the future?" The nature of the course is described in detail elsewhere (Butt, "Teacher's Biographies"). Here, however, it is important to note that there are a number of conditions essential to the climate of our interactions that facilitate the autobiographical impulse. Firstly, we are all regarded as learners and teachers, including myself; I also present my own autobiographical writing — risking myself along with classmates. We try to create a climate of trust, support, frankness and honesty to encourage sharing and disclosure. Direct personal criticism is not, then, encouraged; our job is to engage in questions and dialogue so that we can better understand each other's perspective. It is made very clear, however, that each of us has direct control over what we choose to disclose. By the end of the semester, through various autobiographical drafts, oral presentation, dialogue, learning from each other's stories, and elaboration of our own narratives, we have some fairly explicit ideas of who we are as unique persons and professionals and some sense of an agenda for the future. We also are able to identify some commonalities that exist across our lives as a collective form of teachers' knowledge.

I think it is clear that I favor self-education which is achieved through concrete personal experience and social interaction. This experience is of contexts and activities that are relevant — real exemplars, as far as possible, of the life-space within which the learning is to be manifest. Realness also applies to keeping things all of a piece, not separating bits out. I try to provide each student with the opportunity to express what he or she feels, thinks, intends, in response to the context and interaction, both in intellectual terms and in action, as they move from dependence to independence, autonomy and authenticity. During the course, I evaluate the students' work, rather than their lives, using a ten-point approach that I have worked out which includes an assessment of the quality of expression, clarity or organization, creativity, coherence, internal consistency, and how well the writer has conveyed the context and experience of teaching.

So far we have spoken mostly of individuals. Teaching, however, is a relational activity. Even though each of my students is his or her own best *expert* with respect to the personal professional knowledge they hold and are developing, the next best expert is someone in the same situation — a peer. Their co-learners are closest to them. The expertise of co-learners can be tapped through group co-operation and collaboration — in teaching each other and in co-designing (as far as possible) the course. I also am a teacher learning to teach — a co-learner. I participate in activities with my students and try to think and risk myself as they do. Being a co-learner within a community breaks open, somewhat, the vertical professor-student relationship to a more collegial forum. This can ameliorate dysfunctional aspects of power relations in "pedagogy" that cause alienation and inauthenticity. There are seeds, then, of authentic self-education leading to a non-oppressive relationship. We attempt to create, and help each other create, our own teaching selves; in a critical sense we desocialize ourselves from our institutionalized biographies and the alienation and oppression that that brings. My prime interest becomes, then, liberation and emancipation through both individual *and* collective action. The common factor that runs across my diverse research and teaching within the non-abuse of science, multiculturalism, professional development and curriculum change is an interest in emancipatory forms of learning, teaching and research. Several themes emerge from the description of how I work:

1. I try to dwell in the learner's place with them (not above them).

2. I try to help us address our mutual concerns and questions.

3. I try to share and portray my continuing struggle to become a teacher with my students, to make my concerns, needs, and thinking visible for them in the hope that they will do likewise so we can help each other.

4. I regard the knowledge we need for authentic teaching as a form of personal knowledge that is both quite unique to each teacher but which also possesses commonalities with other teachers. This represents a collective form of teachers' knowledge.

5. I think that the best way to evolve this sort of knowledge is through the self-education of personal and social experience, and reflection on, and the expression of, one's own style of teaching.

6. I think pedagogical theory, which is relational, is something that you must be able to *live* as well as think — theory and practice being different aspects of the same thing — praxis. I, therefore, have to practice what I preach as a professor/teacher.

7. I try to risk myself as my students do by engaging, as far as possible, in the same activities that they undertake.

8. I prefer to think of myself as a co-learner with them, in the same boat, in order to make our pedagogical relationship as horizontal and collegial as possible.

9. I try to involve my students in a gradually increasing way, in co-designing their own course.

10. I try to have us live through changes instead of just talking about them.

Working Class Roots

If this is the way I currently teach, then, how did I come to be this way? What key choices did I make along the way? What particular people, events, and contexts, in both my personal and professional life, disposed me to become the way I am?

I came from a working class background in England. Our family lived in "council houses"—what North Americans call low-income housing—throughout my life. The first one I can remember was a bit of a slum. It had no hot water or bath. We repeatedly boiled the kettle to fill a zinc tub in front of the living room coal fire for the kids' weekly dip. Our next house had a bath but it was still difficult to get hot water, though it was new, clean, and relatively more spacious. The lack of heat upstairs meant I had to leap from warm clothes, immerse myself in hot water, and leap out again into layers of towels. Similar leaps into and out of bed were required in the winter when we might have ice on the inside of our windows. Things did improve over time, however.

My mother came from what we might call a country peasant background. Her parents and eight children lived in what earlier was a converted cow barn. Later it was one of those quaint English thatched cottages. Her father worked as a husbandsman—a lay vet—for local gentry. It was said that animals he couldn't cure with his knowledge and poultices couldn't be cured. In payment for his services he was often given the choice of money, kind, or the key to the cider barn; he often took the key. Cider takes its toll and he died at a relatively young age. These circumstances contributed to my mother leaving the country to go into domestic service in London at the age of fifteen. Those who have seen the television series *Upstairs—Downstairs* will have an idea of what downstairs is like!

My father was the son of a foreman of a cuff and collar works in Gloucester, England. It was one step up, so to speak, from the shop floor and the gutter. Grandad had come to Gloucester from Somerset, with the man who financed and owned the factory, to be his right-hand man with the workers. He provided my dad's family with a really comfortable house to live in. The family tale is that the cuff and collar works did very well under the direction of my grandfather and his benefactor, except when my father's sister (my very kindly aunt) lead the women on strike!

The owner made a number of promises to my grandfather in gratitude for his loyalty, hard work, and success; he was to have the house and be given some form of part-ownership in the factory. The promise of these rewards were well believed by my grandfather since his friendship with the owner was close. His potential benefactor would visit him at the house when he was ill — arriving by horse-drawn hansom cab, scattering farthings on the street for the children as he left. He lived in a large mansion by the park. My father and his siblings were often instructed to call (by the front door, mind you, not the back) whereupon the housekeeper would feed them all up to the hilt and then load them up with leftovers to take home to the family.

In a very unfortunate turn of fate, however, his potential benefactor died suddenly, having neither made his gifts nor written his wishes into his will. The owner's relatives claimed the house, much to the devastation of my grandfather. This proved to be a turning point for the worse in his life. Following his tragic and untimely death my grandmother and the family were left to fend for themselves through some times of extreme difficulty and poverty.

Class Consciousness

Our family life was, I suppose, difficult (as compared to the standards of other classes), though not as deprived as in my father's time. We didn't want for food, though, or good parenting and support. Although later on I learned that we were supposed to be "culturally deprived," I didn't experience it in the way that liberals might label it. I experienced, firstly, a significant *difference* between myself and other children of more wealthy backgrounds. As time passed, however, this became more consciously associated with superordination or class prejudice: the fact percolated through that, due to my origins, I was being regarded as somewhat inferior. That was quite shocking to me, as the full implication became clear.

Class consciousness gradually crept up on me, starting in childhood and proceeding through adolescence. Going to infant school at age five, I noticed how most of my fellow pupils spoke weirdly. I said to my mother, "Ey mum, they talks funny. They all sez whartah — posh-like. It's wadher init?" in my best Gloucestershire dialect. She said not to worry and that I would be all right. It took me but a few days to discover that it wasn't they who talked "weird," but "us kids" who came from a small pocket of working-class families in a middle-class suburb.

A little later I witnessed the continuing kindness of Mrs. Emery who lived in a big house across our back fence. She used to give my mother bundles of cast-off clothes from her children. My mother was grateful — so were we — we didn't have the embarrassment of wearing homemade clothes to school. Dad, on the other hand, was angry with hurt feelings — at being an inadequate provider and at accepting charity. I remember the clothes I wore to school. Do you think school uniforms even out economic differences in pupils' appearances? They don't. Besides the earlier indignity of wearing baggy homemade short trousers, I remained the only boy in grade seven who also still wore short trousers to school. My royal blue school blazer was worn until it was faded, sleeves half way up my long arms with leather elbow patches which were removed to put on the next jacket. My school cap from the first form at grammar school was still perched on top of my head like a pimple, many sizes too small, years later. Most of my fellow pupils had new uniforms each year.

In my first year in the grammar school, I was a year younger than most of my peers. As you might imagine, with my socio-economic status, my forte was not the written and spoken word. One signal achievement, however, was a nine out of ten for my first poetry assignment in the first grade of grammar school. That was almost unheard of in the punitive marking system that was used. Poetry gave me the freedom to express what was most pressing; I can still remember the first four lines of my "Ode to a City's Dawn":

Oh dawn when the streets are still cold and wet,
And the early bustle hasten to work,
While in other regions of the town,
Blinds there are still drawn down. . .

I could name class consciousness. Later in my adolescence, when quite mature, independent, and with some *savoir faire*, I recall various girl friends, mostly of middle class backgrounds, being glad of my company. But they either did not take me home to visit or, if they did, their parents emanated the essence of luke-warm politeness that encouraged me like a wet blanket. They didn't want to fan any relational flames to life!

Knowing Your Place

I suppose the most irksome phrase working class people had internalized together with our "appropriately lower self-concept" went something like "it's not your place to do so and so." As an inferior working class person you should *know your place* — your subservient role — in the hierarchical pecking order! Encountering that notion anywhere, any time, from anyone would make me red with anger.

Probably the most vivid story I can tell that portrays "knowing your place" relates to my parents and the low-income house we lived in for twenty-one years. One local municipal authority decided to give tenants the opportunity to buy the houses they had occupied for some time. The selling price of houses included a pro-rated reduction depending on how long a tenant had lived in the house. My parents' house was very inexpensive; some $10,000 fifteen years ago. They looked at it—the mortgage payments and taxes—and were elated to think they could afford it. The dream of having a house might come true!

The longer they thought about it, however, the more they were convinced there were hidden costs—interest rates would be raised too high—or there was some other "catch" to it. They didn't buy it; psychologically, it was just not proper for people in *their place* to have a house! Had they just talked to me in Canada.... Class repression left my father yelling his anger loudly; my mother, experiencing the double jeopardy of class and chauvinism, spoke volumes in her long-suffering silence.

During my adolescence, as with many children, I was not too enamoured of my parents and their station. In turn, my father disliked education because it created a gap between us. For a while, then, I was ashamed of the fact that my mother was a cleaning lady and that my father drove a lorry. Nor did I like the fact that he noisily slurped his tea out of the saucer or that he gobbled his hot meals down with a slopping noise. I was also upset that my father never came to my school. Later, of course, I was to appreciate that my father's job didn't permit him time to eat his mid-day meal at a leisurely pace; the quickest way to cool tea was in the saucer—so he could get back to the job. Working six or seven days a week including overtime, left little energy or time for him to visit my school. My mother as well worked hard, in the home and at her job, in order to give her three kids a decent home and life.

At a certain point, however, this shame regarding my working class roots turned gradually to pride. I think it was at the point when I realized how independent I was compared to my middle class peers. At that time, I was able then to see the positive side of how I grew up—to see the value of persistence and striving against the odds to survive. Even the food we ate (complemented by inexpensive school meals for the kids)—the heart, chitlins, stew, liver, kidneys and tripe—the awful offal—I now see as nutritious food, full of vitamins. (Nowadays, however, they are full of chemicals.) I can remember buying my first real steak in a restaurant at seventeen; being asked, to my astonishment, which type I wanted—sirloin, filet or T-bone? I didn't know there was more than one type!

Making Your Place

At around thirteen, I think it was, my parents talked to me about the fact that I would have to get a job for pocket money and to help buy my own clothes. They could provide me with board and lodging but, especially if I wanted to stay on at school, I would have to fend for myself. During the next few years, I worked at paper rounds, picked fruit, dug ditches and was a lorry driver's mate with my father on his truck. With an extension ladder, a bucket, a chamois and scrim, I started my own window cleaning round that lasted the weekend. Through my latter teens I was a semi-professional musician playing jazz and beat when the Beatles were emerging. All of this I enjoyed immensely. Both the money and the sense of autonomy and independence made it worthwhile. I hasten to add, however, that this feeling was contingent on not having to do any of this for the rest of my life! I had seen and felt what that type of work had done to my father – not just the labor but the stab of servility and helplessness.

In the sixth form at school, when we had long discussions about the meaning of life, we discovered that the amount of freedom and independence working class boys had exceeded that of our middle class friends. We realized, then, what gifts fending for ourselves had given us. Our middle class friends were still very much tied, in terms of behavior and activities, to their parents' choices and decisions – if they wanted pocket money and other such things. I certainly was not.

This independence, autonomy, and authenticity grew out of other sources as well, some of them painful. At thirteen I was totally and completely confused, functioning somewhere in between the tough street values of the neighborhood, the working class disposition of my father, the pseudo-aristocratic values of my mother which she had picked up while in domestic service, and the values of the British grammar school. I could not completely reject or accept any of them, so I was forced to choose my own, while learning to understand and adapt to different value contexts. This could be seen as the start of a decidedly individualistic and existential bent, on my part – the creation of personal values and choices. I think it started, however, in a visceral, emotional and symbolic way much sooner.

The Pile-Up

The pile-up is the central symbol of how I understand my life – a most frighteningly vivid memory from my childhood. I can remember around age eight or nine being grabbed by older and bigger acquaintances and friends from our working class neighborhood. They yelled, "Grab 'im quick; we 'aven't done 'im yet—it's time!" I was petrified. I had seen what had happened to the other boys before. Small and skinny, I struggled briefly, before realizing the futility. They pinioned me face down flat on the grass. One by one they piled on top of me. As many as fifteen or twenty bodies must have lept on the pile, yelling and laughing, as I screamed in pain and fear. With my nose flat to the ground, breathing was hardly possible, especially with the weight on my chest. I could not move an inch. Individual impacts grew less and the total crush grew worse as each additional body lept on the pile. I felt absolutely, totally, completely, helpless. My disembodied screams mingled with their laughter to a certain point, at which they lessened, as I began to pass out. That was the time when the pile knew to unfold. Willing hands picked me up and brushed me down at this passing of the test. This was accompanied by the sense that I should now feel *better*.

Surprisingly, I experienced this not so much in terms of being oppressed by my peers—of blaming them—but as a lack of personal control over my own life. What had I done to get myself into that situation? I was determined to figure out what I could do to avoid or control those sorts of situations. I attributed responsibility to myself. I think the experience had introduced me to existentialism in a concrete, physical and emotional way. Regardless of this, however, the pile-up does symbolize, for me, hierarchy and oppression, both by others and ourselves (working class kids subjugating themselves). I find myself fascinated by the not so ironic fact that I chose to be in the middle of the quintessential physical pile-up: I played hooker in the middle of a rugby scrum for twenty-five years! I don't think it was completely fortuitous; I enjoyed the challenge of attempting, with others, to control that morass of sixteen bodies. One motivation for me to work hard, persist, and strive in my life has been the challenge that I might not be able to overcome. This is especially true if someone else said or implied that I couldn't do it: it produced anger, energy and an "I'll show you" disposition.

Early Schooling

While my self-concept was certainly helped and honed by my life experiences as I grew up, school played a very significant and positive role. I started nursery school at age three in 1946. Nursery schools had been started in working class areas so that women could go to work and help with the war effort while the men were away fighting. They helped children learn and develop in physical, emotional, social, and cognitive ways through play, interaction, and the expressive arts. The available materials and experiences far surpassed what we had at home. The philosophical underpinnings which had been drawn from Rousseau and others were implemented by well-educated women who directed and taught, helped by working class mothers whose natural child-centredness complemented the pedagogy. I can remember looking forward to these days of activity and fun. I distinctly remember, as well, the small folding canvas beds in which we all took our afternoon naps.

Fortunately for me, the infant school I attended next followed much the same philosophy with, however, much more structure and purpose to play, materials and activity. This was *informal* or *open* education at its best. We could pursue what we wanted within the organized environment in a thematic, rather than subject-oriented, way. I can actually remember my culturally biased thoughts. I enjoyed all of the activity, play, and fun but wondered when we would have to sit in our desks and learn something! Our teachers were wonderful, positive, and encouraging people, who helped us do what *we* wanted to do, while they enabled us, in turn, to learn what they knew we should. I can remember reading and writing and expressing myself a lot through various media. I was really motivated because it was directly related to my interests and activities.

Jane Roland Martin's contribution to this book has allowed me to relive aspects of my infant school which were very much like Montessori's *Casa dei Bambini*. It was a children's house and home in every sense of those words; every physical, moral, emotional aspect of it was geared to our natures as children. I can still feel the importance of that environment to me and the sense of self the activities I chose gave to me. I was particularly reminded of the domesticity of the infant school, the explicit image of family that was encouraged there. Those images were particularly played out in the way we were taught to help each other and with the routines of the classroom through the rotating system of monitors. Family lunches were especially enjoyable, with children of all ages and one adult at each table. We all helped each other with the chores all the time. Boys and girls worked equally at all tasks — this was one difference from our working class homes. The link between home and school, however, was very intimate — parents, especially mothers who could spend the time, were in the classroom as we came to school and as we went home, as well as at lunch with us, or as volunteers. Contrary to the class system, the school and its staff held our working class homes, families, and parents in high regard. What is interesting to note is that some of the stronger images that come through teachers' autobiographies with respect to their classrooms are related to home, haven and family (Clandinin; Butt, Raymond and Yamagishi; Butt, Raymond and Ray).

There is another part of my life that acted as a positive bridge between home and school that might have been unique to our little pocket of working class kids. We always had access to nature, either through the natural environment or through gardening. We lived close to the edge of the city. Within easy reach of the expeditions of small groups of children lay farms, brooks, fields, and hills. Ever since I can remember we wandered—exploring nature in our little groups. The symbols were the brook and the hill. We spent timeless hours catching and keeping tadpoles, frogs, minnows, and sticklebacks. We birdnested, found foxes' dens, owls' pellets. We picked wildflowers and blackberries for our mothers. We swung on ropes, made hide-outs, forts, dared each other to jump, got our boots wet in the brook or fell in completely. We explored freely and learned from observation and activity in the natural classroom. This natural focus carried right through early and middle adolescence when we teased and courted members of the opposite sex.

At home one of the times I shared with my father was in our flower and vegetable garden. By age five I was planting potatoes with him. He taught me how to grow everything; his teaching style, however, was quite demanding and direct. Even when I was over twenty years old, I sometimes failed to plant the potatoes to his satisfaction.

What occurs to me now is that this was a particularly strong link between home and school. Nature—working with the outdoors, plants and animals—formed a very large part of our curriculum. Think of how knowledgeable and affirmed we downtrodden kids felt in the midst of this. When school brought all of nature into the classroom and also explored out into it—it gave us ways of finding out, of exploring and symbolizing both in the artistic sense that Diane Korzenik describes in this book, and as junior scientists and writers. These new understandings we then took on our expeditions with us.

Junior school (age 9-11) was similar in tone; we still maintained a very high proportion of individually or group chosen projects. As compared to infant school, however, which used vertical family grouping and the integrated day approach to curriculum, junior school was organized into grades and the more traditional school subjects although nature study and geography were integrated into environmental studies. There was, as well, a form of streaming across the three classes at each grade level.

Nevertheless, teachers were still very supportive, encouraging, and helpful; their methods of classroom management were not at all harsh.

In the final grade of junior school, we were prepared for what used to be the most ominous of all hurdles in Britain—the 11-plus examination. We were tested on Maths and English to sort out who would attend the Grammar School, a potential route to university and for the professions, and who would be sent to a Secondary Modern School. In the latter schools, pupils were "occupied" until fifteen or sixteen when they departed to seek menial work or, at best, an apprenticeship to a trade.

Even though I was from the wrong side of the tracks and supposedly deprived, I had managed to make my way up through the streams in Junior School to reach the top class. I was still, however, weak in writing ability—the other subjects made up for it, particularly science and maths. I can recall earning a prize for progress and effort. I was invited into the headmaster's office to choose a book as my prize. My eyes immediately fell on some beautiful leather-bound books. I looked quickly—I saw and wanted *Treasure Island*. All of this had occurred prior to the headmaster asking me formally to look. When he did, I blurted out, *"Treasure Island!"* He looked perturbed: he had, he explained, been in the middle of letting me know that I could only pick from a certain selection of books. The leather-bound section was for the top prize winners only, an echelon I had not yet reached. He asked me to pick another. I did, almost blindly, covertly tearful, and crestfallen. When I walked on to the stage to collect my book at prize-giving the same feelings returned. I reluctantly began to open the wrapping. What I saw was not the paper cover of the book I had eventually chosen but a mottled leather surface—I had been given *Treasure Island*! I was so happy. Later, a smiling headmaster explained that one of the "top" prize winners would rather have another book, leaving a spare leather-bound title, which just happened, he said with a wink, to be *Treasure Island*. I'm positive that spurred my reading; it certainly was the first book of that length I read from cover to cover.

I think that my early nursery schooling gave me the *head start* that I needed, coming from the background that I did. It provided material, an expressive environment, and interactions that I otherwise would not have had at home. Infant school carried on from there, providing me with choices, decisions and options for self-learning that emphasized personal experiential knowledge. This, combined with teachers who constantly trusted, encouraged, and supported me helped offset the lower future-focused role image that "knowing your place" in the working class might have brought. It helped break the ghetto cycle of self-oppression. The very nature of the curriculum legitimized our home and personal experiences; the interactive pedagogy paradoxically bypassed my lack of literacy (learning through experience). It gave me reason, motivation and desire to express myself through speaking and writing. I also wanted to learn more through listening and reading. It enabled a really positive personally-owned self-concept to develop. This climate, however, did not continue in high school.

Grammar School

Despite my background, relatively poor English skills and the trauma of the test, I did pass the 11-plus. I think I must have made it by the skin of my teeth, since I was placed in the bottom stream of four classes in the equivalent of grade 7. I think my maths pulled me through plus the fact that Gloucester, my home town, had a higher percentage of Grammar School places than other jurisdictions (thank God for geography). I should hasten to add though, in my favor, that I was one year younger than the average age of my class.

My first day was traumatic. As compared to the cuddly, warm, and informal elementary schools that I had attended, most of the all-male teachers at the all-boys grammar school wore formal gowns and barked at us in classrooms with traditional rows of desks. I can still remember trembling as we lined up outside the classroom door on that first day, having our home room teacher shout our family names, in what, I thought, was a most abusive way, and point to a desk where we were to sit — in alphabetical order. We soon found, though, the humanity, the hidden warmth, the twinkle in the eye, of certain teachers.

Yet the structure was lots of homework, formal discipline, strict rules, harsh punishments, and a prefect system to enforce order outside the classroom. Being in the bottom stream did concern me; the bottom of the pile again. I responded, as usual, and dug my way out through determination and hard work. After one term and the Christmas exams, I found myself promoted to Form One Upper, the top stream, which was due to be accelerated by completing four years of work to the "O" level G.C.E. examinations in three. This required a tremendous pace and lots of demanding work, quite a challenge bearing in mind my age. Eventually, I was able to respond with relative success, not without some cost, I think, at being pushed so hard. Both my wife and I were accelerated at school and we both feel we could have done better without acceleration; there were costs we could have avoided. The question is, though, what contributed to my relative success?

My elementary schools were characterized by positive reinforcement, warm, caring and supporting teachers; the tone of grammar school was characterized by teachers who were strict, organized, and who had high expectations. Even if the grammar school erred on the side of punitiveness, it was generally fair. These two types of teachers are those found in the literature that learners characterize as "good" — from whom they learned different but worthwhile things. I had, then, perhaps a synergistic combination. I think, as well, that having been able to evolve a very positive self-concept and self-learning skills in elementary schools enabled me to withstand and even benefit from the high demands, discipline and rigor of the grammar school. Had the reverse occurred, I'm not sure I would have made it! The two school environments also reflected and reinforced, perhaps, my two main motivations — an environment of *support and encouragement for personal knowledge and the challenge of being at the bottom of a pile-up* of streaming, the oppressive discipline, and the punitive marking schemes. I think, as well, that the elementary school provided a strong beginning for my disposition to be androgynous.

At the colloquium held for the contributors to this book, Roy Graham suggested another way of looking at my schooling. He saw my elementary schooling as feminine and my secondary education as masculine. These flavors of schooling were, of course, reinforced by my parents. My mother's support and unconditional love matched well with the elementary school and gave me, perhaps, many of my more "feminine" qualities which are quite dominant in many contexts — intuition, expressed caring, sensitivity, provision of warmth and encouragement and the like. My relationship with my father, quite understandably typical of most working class fathers and eldest sons, was "challenging!" It matches up more with the grammar school. It was a testy relationship despite the fact that he always did want us to be pals. Apart from the usual competitiveness between working class fathers and eldest sons, in particular, the values I was evolving through my life — the values of the schools I went to — were quite different from his. He saw education as taking me away from him; he, therefore, derided it. We did have windows of relationship, though, through the garden, sports — he always came to watch me play — and through pride in hard physical labor when we worked together on his lorry. A later symbolic act that showed that he had seen the worth of education was the appearance of an oak desk in my bedroom to study at while in college; something he had "purloined" from work!

There were two other avenues of success in grammar school. One related to specialization in science—the other, sports. In the stark disciplined halls I think we searched for any hint of positive feedback! In grammar school we specialized in some eight or ten subjects at a very early stage. I achieved better marks in the Maths and Sciences and related subjects, so I dropped English Literature, Geography, History and anything else that, in retrospect, required superior language skills. I took Maths, Physics, Chemistry, Biology, Woodwork, English, which was compulsory, and French, which I needed for university. I passed most of them at the ordinary level of G.C.E., after which for sixth form I took Pure and Applied Math, Physics, and Chemistry. The point, here, is that the symbolism of science and maths was an emancipatory route for me. I started on an equal basis with my peers in that realm, whereas in language I was behind by dint of my background. Later I was able to move outwards from science as I worked on my language skills.

There is another element to success here that links to my culture and elementary school. Nature linked very well to the sciences, also many of the subjects I succeeded in and chose to pursue were *practical* and *hands-on*. In the sciences, fifty percent of our time was spent in experimentation. In these subjects, experience and practice were linked with writing and reading—it was Piaget continued. Woodwork and art were practical and expressive respectively. This emphasis on the concrete and action was carried through in the other reinforcing activity—sports—which, for me and many others, made school palatable and kept us sane. I was generally good at a number of things but I specialized in rugby in the winter and pole-vaulting in the summer. Sports—rugby, cross country running and pole-vaulting—were personal, practical and related to the outdoors. I represented the school on some very successful teams. I represented my district at rugby and earned two silver medals at the English schools championships in pole-vaulting. I received lots of praise for these efforts. Once again the ingredients were a tough challenge, lots of hard work, and support, encouragement and positive feedback. The hard training and play also were confluent with class influenced persistence and a work-hard, play-hard, theme which still characterizes my life. I think the sense of physical efficacy was most important to me, as was the reinforcement of my class-conflicted ego. The admiration these achievements produced did shore up the self-esteem of a working class lad. For a number of years, however, it did lead to approval- or admiration-seeking behavior which does obstruct authentic personal growth.

The Fall

Life looked pretty full and good in the sixth form: fair but not outstanding achievement academically (I needed to work harder), success and admiration from sports, and financial independence from my jobs. Playing as a semi-professional musician in jazz bands and beat groups was particularly enjoyable and lucrative; it formed another important element of my life — too important, as I was to discover later.

I took my "A" Level G.C.E.s and passed two with reasonable grades. I applied to University and got a place to read chemistry, I think more on the basis of my sports prowess than on my grades. I approached my Local Education Authority about a grant to attend University. They assured me that anyone who has been accepted to University would be given a grant. This was a dream come true for a working class lad. But wait — I still had a year to play with if I wished. Yes, assured of the place and the grant, I could stay on for another year at school to improve my grades. I could enjoy sports — especially have another crack at the English Schools' pole-vault record. I probably would have a chance at the gold! I stayed on at school an extra year.

During my third year in the sixth form I played hard at sports, the band and at all sorts of social activities. Coming up to the English Schools' Athletics Championships I was doing well — vaulting higher than ever — at 17 I was second in the British under-19 rankings. I was really trying hard, too hard. On one particular vault, at a record height, I got my run-up wrong. At top speed I planted the pole in the box, but it tore me off the ground before I was ready. I instinctively drove down hard with my left leg, hit thin air instead of the ground, then my foot did hit the ground. This pattern of resistance was the opposite to that of the normal pole vault take off. It ripped and damaged almost every muscle and tendon in my left thigh and rear. The physical pain almost matched the emotional agony of not being able to pole-vault for the year, of missing my chance to compete for the gold medal at the All England Schools championships.

Worse was to come. Lulled by the certainty that I had a place at University and that I would have the necessary financial support, I did not work excessively hard at my studies. Instead, I allowed myself to be distracted by sports, music and my social life. I did improve my grades, but not much. I returned to my Local Education Authority to confirm that I would be going to University in the autumn and could I have my money, please? The officer informed me (words like massive pieces of concrete tumbled down on me burying me in the worst pile-up ever — as my life collapsed around me) that the rules had changed. Grants were competitive now, not automatic on getting a university place. I had not won the competition. I had no grant. I could not go to university!

Even my mother, who had given my unconditional love and acceptance throughout my life, compounded the hurt. She had told all the neighbors that I was going to university. Her worry was what would she tell them now. Just thinking about the problem made me fall apart; I was extremely depressed. Playing in band was about the only thing that took me out of myself. I needed to block it all out, so I got a job on Gloucester's docks — unloading grain from ships, and loading lorries with sacks of agricultural products. I worked twelve hours each day and weekends when I could. Physical work, and the tiredness it produced, helped me not think about failing to get to university, and obscured the pain. Very gradually, throughout the next several months, I recovered and was able to contemplate creating some sort of future again. I liked the people with whom I worked on the docks, Irishmen, transients, and ex-criminals. They looked after each other and me. When I started working, though I was strong, they made me watch how they lifted, carried and moved heavy loads. Only after several days of observation, did they let me try — they supervised, corrected and helped — so that I could get the hang of things. You had to lift properly, look after each other and work together as a team; otherwise someone could get hurt.

Eventually, though, I reluctantly took my leave to go to work as a research officer at the Coal Research Establishment where Jacob Brunowski was the director. Again, I liked the way the workers helped each other and worked together. I was particularly impressed with the team approach that scientists used to investigate problems. We all got together, exchanged ideas and results; everyone had a chance to speak, from the Ph.D.s to the lowly bottle-washers. I was astounded that suggestions I made were taken seriously and tried out. This contrasted, so graphically, with my experience with the vertical and oppressive class system. This supportive environment and the intellectual satisfaction of research provided a time for me to heal from the trauma I had just experienced. Playing in the band also provided positive feedback. We all, by now, had left home and were sharing the same apartment. I knew, however, that I did not want to become a professional musician. I also knew I didn't want to work in a lab for the rest of my life. Even though it was collaborative, test tubes and equipment were not for me; I needed a more people-oriented profession. During the despair and nothingness of my adolescent anomie and fall, I had been reading Sartre's existentialism, and lived some of it in the sub-culture of jazz clubs. It was, however, too morbid for me. My other experiences with the sense of self that came from working together with others, collaborating and supporting each other, countervailed and pointed me towards more humanistic existentialists and an optimistic view of life. I spent six months pondering what type of life would provide a collaborative people-oriented context. At the end of that time I decided to go into teaching.

Teachers' College

I applied and was fortunate to be accepted at St. Paul's College, a Church of England teacher education institution in Cheltenham. I carried with me a sense of commitment and vocation to what I thought was a humanistic pursuit. I was influenced by my own child-centred elementary education. My sense that the teachers did work in a very collaborative way — including the headmistress — was accurate and well characterized by my own schools. I realized later, however, that this was the exception. I wonder now, if, being faced with tough times, I was returning to some sort of educational womb, where I might be safe, where the progressive embryo might still be taken care of.

Despite many teachers' assertions that their own teacher education was useless in preparing them for teaching, I thought that St. Paul's did an excellent job. Our first two weeks were spent in small tutorials rediscovering ourselves as children and adolescents through literature like *Catcher in the Rye* and through our own reflections. We went out on one month's teaching practice immediately and taught in an elementary school; the emphasis was on understanding children. We did four in-depth child studies during this time, including home visits for one of them. The program consisted of a constant interaction of field work and tutorials, where we combined the intellectual, the practical, and the experiential. One particularly powerful experience was that of group teaching practice, in which eight students and one tutor co-planned, co-taught and evaluated a unit in a classroom. This individual experience of a common activity heightened the degree to which collective exchanges could aid both intellectual, practical, and professional growth. In my specializations, science and education, we did lots of personal explorations and individual projects, culminating in an independent honors study. In science we studied both man-made systems and nature as well. Science and science education, for me, has always been like that pursued by Rousseau's Emile — activity and discovery of personal knowledge through experience. (I still remain puzzled by the attack on science and the empirical-analytic paradigm, although I see the criticism correctly levelled at scientism, behaviorism, logical positivism, and other abuses of science by politicians and industrialists.) The most pervasive influence, however, on my disposition towards teaching was the progressive approach to education both preached and practised by the college. This evolved for me not only out of science education, but out of the practical and intellectual emphasis on the child and child growth, readiness, and development. In the field, our observational visits and placements included a significant exposure to informal education. This certainly reinforced the naturally exploratory pedagogy I had grown up with both in school and through my many personal adventures with nature as a child.

Teaching, Study and Research in Canada

After completing a year of teaching, I decided in 1967 to emigrate to Canada. I had a three year teaching certificate, but no degree, and at that time it would have been difficult to pursue one in England. Canada offered that chance, plus adventure and an excellent salary (I was paid less than a garbage collector in England). What I did not consciously realize, however, was that Canada's open society would give me such great opportunities for personal and professional development. I experienced hardly any class system; I felt I had escaped it completely. The school system at the secondary level was less punitive and more reinforcing; so was university, I discovered when I studied part-time. Everything appeared to me to be encouraging and supportive; in retrospect, it was like having a lead weight lifted from my shoulders. If you did well, people were generous with praise; there was a "you *can* do it" attitude. It did not matter what "station" in society you came from, how rich you were, who your parents were — if you could do the job, that was all that counted. If you did it well, you got the credit. I discovered later, of course, that oppression manifests itself, if not so much through a socio-economic class system, through an ethnic structure and, of course, in gender-related ways.

There is, however, one significant reversal. Teachers in Canada are oppressed in one particular way. Within the classrooms in England, when I taught there, the teacher, particularly at the elementary level, was very autonomous with respect to both curriculum and pedagogy, requiring much in the way of curriculum development at the classroom level. I was also involved in teaching Nuffield Junior Science, providing experience of a very teacher-oriented project. Teaching in Canada, however, with detailed prescribed curricula and required texts, provided quite a contrast, as did the attempt to implement PSSC Physics, BSCS Biology, and Chem-Study, all of which I taught during the curriculum reform era. I experienced, first hand, the classroom constraints that teachers faced while trying to implement these new programs. The teacher was treated as something to fix — a technician — not an autonomous authentic professional.

Later, as a graduate student, I was involved in a province-wide assessment of the implementation and effects of an inquiry-oriented junior high school program which used both quantitive approaches, classroom observation, and personal interviews with teachers. As we observed and assessed the degree of implementation, we became vividly aware of three things: (1) the possibility that curriculum evaluation studies might appraise non-events, (2) the richest understanding of the quality of the program and reasons for its implementation or non-implementation came from our interviews and conversations with teachers, and (3) from our data on degree of implementation, those teachers who were in some way modifying and adapting the program to suit classroom contingencies had the highest degree of implementation. The central role of the teacher in curriculum implementation and elaboration, as well as the potential of understanding this process through qualitative explorations of the personal perspectives of teachers, were highlighted. This contributed to my decision to work in classrooms with teachers on a school-by-school basis, during a ten year period, to learn about teachers' classroom realities and how we might approach change from a teachers' perspective. School- and classroom-based approaches appeared to facilitate a realistic and successful approach to classroom and curriculum change (Butt, "Transitional Curriculum").

As opposed to top-down ways of attempting to implement change, school/classroom-based approaches created a relationship between reformers (outsiders) and the teachers (insiders) whereby (1) teachers were regarded as experts in their own classroom reality and outsiders were students of that reality, (2) outsiders could provide, as participant/observers, some ways in which teachers could reflect on what they were doing, and offer other ideas, and (3) jointly insiders and outsiders could consider how these ideas might relate to, and practical for, classroom issues and concerns (Butt and Olson). We were successful in implementing a child-centred pedagogy in science eduction in a number of schools using this approach. We noted that the more self-initiated each teacher was, both in terms of the initial motivation for change and as projects evolved, the more quickly and more successfully new ideas were implemented. As well, the more we could relate the project to the needs and interests of the teacher, *as a person*, the better the project proceeded. This approach was used even to the extent of building a curriculum that, while serving pupil, parent, and pedagogical interests, was elaborated from teachers' personal interests in science.

Intertwined with these experiences, however, was another practical link back to my earliest years. In my doctoral program at the University of Ottawa in curriculum I pursued, quite predictably, a view of curriculum that emphasized the personal. My dissertation was to develop a conceptual theory for open or informal education (Butt, "The Open Classroom"). In a time when progressive education was being misinterpreted in North America, when it was coming under attack both in Britain through the "Black Papers," and in North America, through the back-to-basics movement, I wanted to contribute to a clearer understanding of what informal education meant. I examined the philosophical and psychological roots of informal education, the practical folklore that surrounded it and empirical research—all as potential sources of a theory of informal education. This work included Comenius, Rousseau, Pestalozzi, Froebel, Montessori, Tolstoy, and Dewcy, as well as developmental, humanistic, and existential psychologists' work.

The study emphasized, for me, the themes of *individualism* and *activity* within collaborative work of the pupils with each other and the teacher. They attempted, in pursuit of authenticity, to help each other and themselves to implement their own intentions, through an ever-evolving web of choices, decisions, and actions. Teachers attempted to create a classroom and school climate that was warm, encouraging, and trusting, within which activity facilitated both teacher and pupil intentions. This certainly presents a different view of how to maximize "time-on-task" through interest, motivation and engagement, rather than just through managerial manipulations found in traditional teacher-effectiveness research.

I could, of course, relate this study back to my own experience of the informal classroom. I also brought it forward with me to my emerging study, through autobiography, of the teacher *as person* in applying the notions of informal education to how teachers, through experience learn to become teachers. Paralleling these influences from my personal life, my research and my doctoral work was a continuing association with the Reconceptualist curriculum theorists. Their work gave significant initial form to the scholarly framework from which my colleague, Danielle Raymond, and I began to use teacher autobiographies in understanding how teachers develop their own personal professional knowledge and how we could, through collaborative autobiography, help them take their own development further.

My early experiences within the class structure of England lie at the heart of my personal knowledge. I experienced it as an *oppressive pile-up*. The successful self-initiated ongoing process of liberation I experience as the positive core of my life. It's an *existential* response towards authentic personal growth, towards self-literacy so that I can join the social conversation with equals. I responded to other tests in my life in a similar way, I suppose, as challenges to prove myself worthy; this combined with external support and encouragement, where it existed, generated the commitment, motivation, drive and persistence to accomplish difficult goals against the odds. The cycle of challenges, support and encouragement, and the process of commitment, effort, and achievement generally brought success, internal gratification, and external approval and acceptance. This affirmed and reinforced my own efforts, my emerging self, self-esteem and self-concept — a self-concept conflicted by a sense of class-inflicted inferiority. So whereas I was building my self-concept in a positive sense through intrinsic means, paradoxically, I still sought external approval of that self. My biggest challenge during young adulthood and later was to gradually transcend this paradox from external approval to more self-approval.

As a result of this cycle of activity, in large measure self-chosen, in life and school, I gained personal knowledge through experiential learning. Probably, the most important affirmative experience was the integrating link between life and school experiences. The themes of practical activity, nature, sports, individualism were integral bridges between life and school. School valued and legitimated life but also built upon it through the symbolization and the abstraction of experience; it provided the chance to induce thinking and reflection on experience leading to true education in the Deweyian sense. I was able, then, to bring together theory and practice, to be intellectual about the practical, and to live praxis. A last and dominant meta-theme is, of course, integration, synthesis and synergy — not only of themes but of people. The tendency to bring things together also evolved out of an empathy for others and the experience of Montessori's children's family, the teams of rugby, the groups of the band and docks, collaborative activity of the scientific team and in college; collaborative groups of men! This leads perhaps to my simultaneous pursuit of both individualism and a collaborative community, a synergy of the existential and social — hence collaborative autobiography as a means of personal and collective emancipation. These biographical patterns and themes make it possible to comprehend my interest and involvement in progressive education at all levels and the interest in helping others and myself in overcoming oppression, in respect to the environment, multiculturalism, the alienation in the school system or any other pile-up for that matter.

The Future: A Romantic Renaissance?

Given the past and the current way I am teaching, doing field work and conducting research, what do I intend to do in the immediate future? Following ten years of school-based research and developmental activities with teachers during the 1970s and early 1980s, I "withdrew" from the field in order to reflect on the personal meaning that teachers bring to their teaching and the way they experience classroom reality. Ironically, this "withdrawal" took me to the centre of the teacher and the classroom. I did this in order to understand better ways of approaching teacher development and school improvement, believing there is a strong imperative to change curriculum content and pedagogical approaches to enable our children to meet the pressing needs of individual, social, and environmental futures. This led to my current work in collaborative autobiography which I will continue.

What I also have begun to do now, however, is to re-enter schools. My intention is to take what I have learned about teacher knowledge and its development back into the school. With my colleague, David Townsend, I wish to use collaborative autobiography as the foundation for a new integrative school-based approach in staff development. This approach will also take into account what we have learned about change, curriculum implementation, peer supervision, team building, and Frierian approaches to adult education (Butt and Raymond, "Teacher Development"; Butt and Townsend).

With my colleagues, there are other elements we can integrate into this endeavor to produce a synergistic effect on the school. One of our main sites will be the Blood Indian reserve where we can assist with the development of schools which the band has just taken over from the federal government. This also affords us the chance to get involved in community development and the evolution of a positive future-focused role image with our native people.

The strong positive and mythic base of progressive education that was derived from Romanticism can be elaborated further through existential, developmental, and humanistic psychology (with all its bumps and warts) into a modern theory of progressive education (Butt, "The Open Classroom"). The weaknesses of aspects of this theory, however, have been revealed by modern educational critics. How the research pedagogy of collaborative autobiography evolved and how it can be used for staff and teacher development in schools might provide insights into how the theory of progressive education might involve a post-modern integration of contemporary sociological, feminist, neo-Marxist, psychoanalytic, literary, phenomenological and existential theory. Some of these have been integrated into educational projects which are progressive and Romantic in tone, through reconceptualist, literary, and feminist work, and, indeed, through the projects of liberation theology. Indeed, Madeleine Grumet's book, *Bitter Milk*, can be viewed as one such endeavor in the theoretical realm. What is also important to note, is that the original, somewhat naïve political and social consciousness of the Romantics that took a back seat in earlier forms of progressive education, as Friedenberg points out in this book, is avoided in most modern work.

In the end, and somewhat predictably in terms of my biography, I suppose I want also to move beyond polemic arguments for and against using either existential or structural frames in understanding our own and others lives; we need to use a form of learning which creates a synergy of both. Humans living and learning can then be seen, at least in significant measure, as agents of their own destinies within a dynamic interplay of socially, culturally, structurally, and politically deterministic contexts. One cluster of biographical work, besides collaborative autobiography, that looks particularly at the collective through a series of individual life histories can be found in the work of a group of scholars, originating from Britain (Butt and Raymond, "Teacher Development"; Ball and Goodson; Goodson; Hargreaves; Sikes; Woods; Woods and Sikes). Many aspects of the practical and intellectual promise of a renaissance and evolution of Romantic progressive education and the problematics involved are revealed by the papers in this book, as well as some well germinated seeds of post-modern theory of progressive education.

What I have tried to do with this chapter is to celebrate the Romantic roots of progressive education and to provide a platform from which one can elaborate a post-modern view of self-education. Self-education through experiential learning over time is an autobiographic conception of education. Awakening the autobiographical impulse to facilitate the explicit description, interpretation, and reflexive analysis of experience serves to heighten the previously unconscious, sub-conscious, or preconscious process of self-education. Facilitating the autobiographical impulse must then be a profound form of individual education; collaboration among individuals who share and facilitate each others' stories provides an equally profound form of social education. Self-education must, however, go on to the expression of thought in action, with others, to create an authentic community.

This view of reflective thought and action and the acting out of one's own story can be construed as *autobiographic praxis*. This emancipatory process can counteract varying forms of alienation — alienation from the self through lack of authenticity, or from reality and others through narcissism, structural determinism and other forms of oppression, and specifically through the patriarchical authoritarianism of some traditional forms of education. This post-modern elaboration of an essentially Romantic view of self-education can be a synergy of social, structural and political views of becoming emancipatory and authentic. I have attempted to achieve this both through theoretical discourse and through telling my own life-story using the framework from a graduate course in collaborative autobiography. Writing the paper has helped me understand where I have been, where I am, and where I wish to go. I hope it helps others also.

Note

1.   This work was supported in part by a grant from the Social Sciences and Human Research Council of Canada. I am indebted to John Willinsky, and the University of Calgary Humanities Institute, for the opportunity to participate in the symposium and to my fellow participants for the insights that occurred during our collaborative endeavors. I am grateful to Donna Obermeyer for her patience and persistence deciphering my handwriting and typing multiple drafts of this paper.

Works Cited

Ball, Stephen J. and Ivor F. Goodson. *Teachers' Lives and Careers*. London: Falmer Press, 1988.

Butt, Richard L. "The Development of a Conceptual System for the Open Classroom." Diss. University of Ottawa, 1978.

Butt, Richard L. "Classroom Change and Scientific Literacy." *Curriculum Canada III*. Ed. J. Lerthwood and A. Hughes. Vancouver: University of British Columbia, Centre for the Study of Curriculum and Instruction, 1981. 90-108.

Butt, Richard L. "The Transitional Curriculum." *Educational Leadership* (1981, November): 117-119.

Butt, Richard L. and John Olson. "Dreams and Realities: Approaching Change Through Critical Awareness." *Curriculum Canada IV. Insiders' Realities, Outsiders' Dreams: Projects for Classroom Change*. Eds. Richard L. Butt, John Olson and J. Daignault. Vancouver: University of British Columbia, Centre for the Study of Curriculum and Instruction, 1983. 1-16.

Butt, Richard, L. "Arguments for Using Biography in Understanding Teacher Thinking." *Teacher Thinking*. R. Halkes and John Olson. Lisse, Holland: Swets and Zietlinger, 1984. 95-102.

Butt, Richard, L. "An Integrative Function for Teachers' Biographies." *Re-interpreting Curriculum Research: Images and Arguments*. Eds. Geoffrey Milburn *et al*. London: Falmer Press and Althouse Press, 1989.

Butt, Richard L. and Danielle Raymond. "Arguments for Using Qualitative Approaches to Understanding Teacher Thinking: The Case for Biography." *Journal of Curriculum Theorizing* 7:1 (1987): 62-63.

Butt, Richard L. and Danielle Raymond. "Teacher Development through Collaborative Autobiography." A paper presented at the International Conference on Teacher Development. Toronto: Ontario Institute for the Study of Education, 1989.

Butt, Richard L., Danielle Raymond, and L. Yamagishi. "Autobiographic Praxis: Studying the Formation of Teachers' Knowledge." *Journal of Curriculum Theorizing* 7:4 (1988): 87-164.

Butt, Richard L., Danielle Raymond, and Ray (pseudonym). "Biographical and Contextual Influences on a Teacher's Thoughts and Actions." In *Teacher Thinking and Professional Action*. Proceedings of the 3rd ISATT Conference. Leuven, Belgium: University of Leuven, 1986: 306-328. Ed. J. Lowyk.

Butt, Richard L. and David Townsend. "Collaborative Autobiography and Action Research: An Integrative Model for School-Based Staff Development." Jasper, AB: CACS Invitational Conference on Collaborative Action Research, 1989.

Clandinin, D. Jean. "Personal Practical Knowledge: A Study of Teachers' Classroom Images." *Curriculum Inquiry* 15.4 (1985): 361-385.

Egan, Kieran. *Primary Understanding*. New York: Routledge, 1988.

Egan, Kieran. *Romantic Understanding*. New York: Routledge, forthcoming.

Goodson, Ivor. "Life Histories and the Study of Schooling." *Interchange* 11.4 (1980/81): 62-76.

Grumet, Madeleine. *Bitter Milk: Women and Teaching*. Amherst: University of Massachusetts Press, 1988.

Hargreaves, Andy. *Two Cultures of Schooling: The Case of Middle Schools*. London: Falmer Press, 1986.

Sikes, P.J. "The Life Cycle of the Teacher." *Teachers' Lives and Careers*. Eds. Stephen Ball and Ivor Goodson. London: Falmer Press, 1985. 27-60.

Woods, P. "Conversations with Teachers: Some Aspects of the Life History Method." *British Educational Research Journal* 2.1 (1985): 13-26.

Woods, P. and P.J. Sikes. "The Use of Teacher Biographies in Professional Self Development." *Planning Continuing Professional Development*. Ed. F. Todd. London: Croom Helm, 1987.

Chapter 14

RECAPITULATING ROMANTICISM

IN EDUCATION

Kieran Egan

My aim for this paper is to expose some correlations between features of Romanticism and the intellectual lives of early adolescents today, and then to give reasons why we should see a significant causal component in these correlations. This is a somewhat slippery enterprise, as Romanticism is not the kind of beast whose features can be confidently described, and the psychological language in which adolescents' intellectual lives are commonly characterized does not readily cohere with that used about Romanticism. Also, any causal connection, it will be immediately obvious, cannot be straightforward. Even so, I will plunge in and try to show that the connections drawn are based on something more interesting than invented similarities of language.

The causal connection will not be stretched directly between Romanticism and modern students. Rather each of these will be seen as effects of some other cause, but the character of Romanticism will be seen as further affecting, or conditioning, the characteristics of modern adolescents' intellectual lives. That other cause is the two-fold technology of the intellect — writing and printing. As my purpose is also to show how one can best recapitulate features of Romanticism in modern students' intellectual lives, I will conclude with a planning framework that teachers might use in order to achieve this end fairly routinely.

It is relatively easy to list some of the characteristics of Romanticism in a way that hints at correlations with early adolescents' intellectual lives: Romanticism involves a delight in the exotic and a revolt against the conventional, in the powers of imagination and an intoxication with the sublime in nature, in intense inquiry about the self and a resistance to conventional order and rationality, in glorification of power and transcendent human qualities, and so on. While the glorification of transcendent human qualities, to take one example, might find an outlet in many Romantics' fascination with the career of Napoleon and in modern adolescents' fascination with a pop star or football player, we can recognize something similar in the glorification of the chosen object and the identification with him or her. What underlies each is what we rather vaguely and diffusely recognize as a Romantic orientation to the world. In Romanticism and in early adolescence, there are exemplified features of what I will call Romantic understanding. Romantic understanding seems to me one of the few, very general, coherent forms of understanding developed in Western cultural history. Well, these are very general terms. What follows is an attempt to drag them down to earth somewhat.

Romance and Romanticism

"Romanticism" is a twentieth-century term for a set of somewhat distinctive characteristics particularly evident in the work of a group of writers at the end of the eighteenth and the beginning of the nineteenth centuries. That their writings were received enthusiastically by a significant part of the literate population at the time suggests that whatever attitude of mind is expressed in these writings was quite widely shared. Related characteristics are evident in contemporary paintings, sculptures, music, and in the enthusiastic responses of many to the French Revolution and then to the career of Napoleon. A part of Romanticism was the conviction that new and powerful ways of making sense of reality were combining with new ways of truly expressing that sense, that immensely complex problems about our place in the world were being in some new fashion addressed and resolved.

The form of understanding that I am calling Romantic is not, however, unique to Romanticism. One of the reasons it is so difficult to provide a generally convincing account of Romanticism as a movement is that it is very difficult to identify anything that is unique to it. The more precisely one tries to describe some distinctive feature, the easier it becomes to point to examples of that feature in other times and places. Even if Romanticism is the fullest instantiation of what I am terming Romantic understanding, we find adumbrations of it throughout cultural history. The sense of romance is evident in much Greek classical writing, informing, for example, Herodotus' *Histories* — in which brave little Athens, on behalf of freedom and democratic virtues, spearheaded the victorious battle against the vast and despotic Persian empire. The emphatic response of so many Europeans to the career of Napoleon is echoed precisely in Arrian's account of the career of that earlier law-less hero, Alexander. If we note the characteristic interest of Romantic writers with dreams, we will be hard put to distinguish this from the similar interest we see in Elizabethan and Jacobean dramatists.

It is common to try to highlight the distinctive qualities of Romanticism by contrasting them with the neo-classicism of the preceding Enlightenment, which aimed to reintroduce classical rigor and reason into all areas of life. We are encouraged to see profound differences between succeeding generations here, to see, say, Wordsworth as representing a new freedom from the rigid conventions of neo-classical forms and a new incorporation of everyday language into poetry which achieves sublime effects. In part this real difference in style is exaggerated by Romanticists' own rhetoric, as when Coleridge insists on the new exploitation of the imagination and talks disparagingly of those "who have been *rationally* educated, as it is styled. They were marked by a microscopic acuteness; but when they looked at great things, all became and blank & they saw nothing—and denied (very illogically) that anything could be seen" (in Potter 355).

The Romantic rhetoric, so quick to declare a revolution in consciousness, tends to suppress the continuities evident in their work with that of the neo-classical Enlightenment. Our use of categories which have been mainly deployed to define contrasts tends to hide the sense in which Romanticist writings may be seen rather as the fulfillment of trends evident during the earlier period. Marilyn Butler, for one, would dispel the Romantic sense of a dramatic break with tradition:

> It is easy to miss Wordsworth's representativeness as it is to miss Blake's. Both are often taken to be initiating a new artistic tradition, rather than joining an established one. Yet the fact is that Wordsworth was brought up in the mainstream of Enlightenment culture, and he realized its potential better than any poet anywhere, with the possible exception of Goethe. (57)

One way of establishing a uniqueness for Romanticism is to establish a canon of Romantic writers and focus on their individual works. These indeed are unique. But it quickly becomes clear that this merely moves the problem once we try to find common elements among the works of the canon that are not present elsewhere. Then we are forced to recognize Romanticism as a continuation of the neo-classical Enlightenment, which in turn continued and elaborated ideas and forms of expression from the Renaissance. The Renaissance, the Enlightenment, and Romanticism all body forth significant features of Romantic understanding, and my focus here is on Romanticism, not because it represents a distinct kind of understanding from those evident in the earlier periods, but because it represents some of its central features in a fuller form. Lovejoy has also argued for a historical continuity that should caution us against looking for radical breaks:

> If...we recognize the shift from uniformitarian to the diversitarian preconception [as] the most significant and distinctive feature of the Romantic revolution, it is evident that there had always been present in the Platonic tradition a principle tending towards Romanticism, and that this had been enunciated with especial clarity and insistence by the philosophers and moralists and philosophic poets of the so-called Age of Reason. (297)

So the differences among the cultural eras of modern Europe are of less interest to me here than certain common features which develop through the period, culminating in Romanticism. I realize that this might seem a touch cavalier when so much scholarly effort goes to etch the differences among these periods, particularly between the Enlightenment program of reason-guided reform and Romanticism's reaction against it. But it is a matter of the level of the phenomena on which one focuses:

> At first sight nothing could be more sharply opposed to Romanticism [as neo-classicism], yet some of the most characteristic elements in the classical revival can just as easily be described as Romantic—the attraction of the primitive and of simplicity, the appeal to the emotions in painting, the ecstatic language in which Winckelmann wrote about Greece, Piranesi's exaggeration of the scale of Roman ruins the admiration for the sublime. (Bullock, 75)

Having noted this, let me focus briefly on just three characteristics commonly associated with Romanticism, each of which seems central, in ways I will explore later, to a Romantic orientation towards the world. First, there was felt to be a new access to nature and reality. The excitement of Romanticism was not due simply to a sense of the imagination being freed, but rather to its freedom being of a kind to enable its exploiters to explore afresh the reality of human experience and the natural world, uncluttered by the artificial conventions of eighteenth-century neo-classicism. William Blake expressed it in terms of the need to cleanse the gates of perception; Shelley saw the poet's proper task as lifting the veil from the hidden beauty of the world and showing the familiar in all its strange wonder. It is the everyday detail of the world, often at a purely descriptive level, that fills much of the most distinctively Romantic art and literature: "Romantic art is not 'romantic' in the vulgar sense, but 'realistic' in the sense of the concrete, full of particulars" (Barzun 26).

As in the earlier outburst of romantic energy during the Renaissance, which in part involved a revolt against the ossified scholasticism of the late Middle Ages, so the movers of Romanticism looked back to the earlier liberation of spirit they saw in, or projected into, myth and popular fantasy. The resistance to "classical" reason led many to a fascination with the exotic and mysterious, to fantasy and the "irrational" myths of the ancient world and contemporary "savages." This attraction towards the extremes of experience and reality, then, is a second commonly observed feature of Romanticism I will draw on.

A third characteristic of Romanticism is the ambivalence caught in the figure of the hero: "The writers who achieved the greatest popular success in the late eighteenth and early nineteenth century were those who created simpler, more colorful imaginative worlds, dominated by heroes of superhuman effectiveness" (Butler 2). The ambivalence is due to the recognition of the constraints of reality along with the desire to transcend them. The hero is constrained by reality like the rest of us, but manages somehow to overcome the constraints that hedge us in. The career of Napoleon fascinated most Romantics because of his force of will that transcended what seemed politically and militarily possible. The Byronic hero is another example of the cult of heroism that grew up during the period.

Some Characteristics of Students' Imaginative Lives

I want to argue that the characteristics of Romanticism touched on above are recapitulated — or recapituable — first in the oral culture of childhood and second as a consequence of the internalizing of literacy by early adolescence. Part of an explanation for such a recapitulation might be found in Vygotsky's argument that social functions later become internalized as psychological processes. Let me first simply suggest correlational echoes, although I have pursued these relationships in some detail elsewhere (*Primary Understanding*; *Romantic Understanding*). I will focus on the case of early adolescents and discuss only analogues of the three characteristics of Romantic imagination touched on above.

If one considers the kinds of films or reading material that seem commonly to be found most engaging to early adolescence, there is evident a significant difference from the fantasy or fairy-tales that commonly engage younger children. Crucial is their concern with reality. Even the wilder super-heroes, like the Hulk or Spiderman, or even Superman, require an aetiology that links them with some possible, however implausible, reality. Superman is not accepted, as is

Cinderella's fairy godmother, without our knowing about his birth on the dying planet Krypton and his being launched into space by his father, Marlon Brando, and of his arrival in Kansas to the care of Mr. and Mrs. Kent, and so on.

If we consider further the kind of material about the real world that students around this age seem most readily engaged by, it is either the fan magazine, covering pop-stars or sports heroes, or material such as is compiled in *The Guinness Book of Records*. That is, the attraction to reality is hardly to its everyday aspects, but rather to its extremes, to exotica and the bizarre. The student's imagination grappling with reality is more attracted to who or what is the biggest, the smallest, the fastest, the slowest, the fattest, the thinnest, the hairiest. It is the mysterious, the strange, the weird, the wonderful that engages the student's imagination.

Another common feature of students' imaginative engagements during this time of life is the development of obsessive interests in something in particular, or in a hobby. Typically students are drawn to exhaustively collect or master something in detail, or find out everything about something. It may be a pop-music group, cathedrals, castles, a football team, the kings and queens of England, costume through the ages, steam trains, shells, spiders, whatever. One explanation of these kinds of obsessive interests in some detailed activity is an echo of the previous item. With the discovery of an autonomous real world there comes the need to explore its extent and scale. One can do this by discovering its limits and extremes, and one can relatedly explore some aspect of it in exhaustive detail. By discovering something exhaustively one gets some security and also some sense of the scale of things in general. Simply as a strategy for exploration these are perfectly sensible procedures. They also reflect prominent features of that imaginative exploration of reality during Romanticism: the intense interest in details of the world and in the exotic and extreme features of the world and of experience.

The third characteristic also echoes a common aspect of the Romantic imagination, what I shall call the association with transcendent human qualities. The everyday autonomous world is somewhat threatening to the immature ego; the student is very much immersed in it but relatively powerless to affect it, subject to routines and activities decided on by others — parents, teachers, etc. A common response to this situation is to associate with those qualities that seem best able to transcend the threats of the everyday world. Most commonly those qualities are identified in a hero or heroine. As in Romanticism, the association with an heroic figure—whether Superman, pop-stars, sports heroes, Rambo, Crocodile Dundee, Mad Max, Harriet the Spy, Mother Teresa, Alfred E. Neuman, or Albert Einstein—allows the imagination to both acknowledge constraints of the real world and to associate with some means of transcending those constraints. Whether the association is merely passive, or whether the student tries more actively to follow the transcendent path laid out by the heroic figure by adopting, or trying on, a role, the result is some taste of power or control or security or confidence—if things go well. This process of association is one that overlaps with Erikson's developmental task of integrating ego identity.

Another common means of internalizing the heroic figure is to keep a diary. The secret diary, with elaborate locks, enables one to gain some power over the everyday world. The diary is often associated with spying—the possession of secret knowledge. This can be culled—parents often discover to their dismay—from overheard family conversations, telephone calls, chats with neighbors, captured and transformed into scarlet dramas in the pages of (most commonly) daughters' diaries. It is not I think coincidental that Romanticism saw the virtual birth and very rapid proliferation of the autobiography (Susanna Egan).

I should note some reservations about focusing on the hero. Voltaire said, "I don't like heroes; they make too much noise." Progressive voices today are concerned that the very idea of the hero gives a false view of the world and experience to the young, and tends to imply an élitist sense of society. Typically heroes have been males whose powerful wills are seen to cause events, leaving the masses as mere fodder while turning economic, social, and normal psychological processed into irrelevancies before the gleaming force of transcendent power. Girls, it is sometimes claimed, have not had the same vast array of heroes available to respond to, nor have they been taught to respond to heroes as boys have. On the other hand, some "traditional" voices in education call for heroes as role models, as it were, to attract students to the old virtues which the hero embodies. It is not in this sense that I see the hero as having an educational role.

The sense of the hero I am using here does not refer to the traditional, autonomous, white male. Rather the hero represents an intellectual capacity to highlight and vivify particular features of the world and experience. The highlighting or "heroizing" could be performed on a pop-star, football team, institution, idea, or anything in the universe. By heroizing an institution—say the United Nations Organization—one creates as it were a kind of fiction, which places the institution centrally in some implied story or general scheme.   My concern here is not the particular objects chosen in the past or present for this kind of treatment, but rather the fact that it is an intellectual capacity we seem to develop with a particular urgency during early adolescence (a theme given detailed treatment in chapter four of my *Romantic Understanding*).

Technologies of the Intellect

I want to argue that aspects of romance such as those discussed above, whether in Romanticism or the intellectual life of early adolescence, are in very large part a product of writing and print.   The implications of writing and print have been the subject of considerable research in recent decades, and I will draw liberally on that work.

Before the invention of writing, people knew only what they could remember.   Consequently, in order to preserve whatever knowledge, lore, and customs that were important, oral cultures prized highly those techniques invented to better aid memorization.   These included such things as rhyme, rhythm, meter, and formulae.   Perhaps most important of the technical inventions that aid memory was the story.   Indeed, it seems reasonable to see the story form as one of the most important of all cultural inventions or discoveries.   Once knowledge was coded in stories it was made much more easily memorable.   Once the coded forms included vivid images and events within stories it was yet more memorable.   Evoking, stimulating, and developing the capacities which made grasping these images within stories was crucial to the socialization or education of the young in oral societies.   Given our tendency to deprecate memorization in education today, it is salutory to realize that it was the need to remember that seems to have given birth to the imagination.

With the invention of writing many of the techniques invented to support memorization began to lose their social importance.   Once writing became common some rather different intellectual capacities were evoked, stimulated and developed.   The recent research into the transition from orality to literacy has been useful not simply in exposing something of the implications of writing but in exposing something of orality as well.   In the common earlier view, orality represented a mass of confusion or diseases of language which the clear light of Greece swept away.   It is becoming increasingly clear that orality, and its ubiquitous myths, employs a set of complex techniques for making sense of the world and experience that are very effective if one lacks the technology of writing. In an oral environment the economy of the mind inclines us to develop particular sense-making techniques, and in a literate environment some others become more readily evoked. Here I will not try to rehearse the work on literacy of Havelock, Ong, Stock, Goody, Olson and others, but draw on it to focus on one kind of change stimulated by writing in ancient Greece — the development of a sense of history.

If one accumulates written records, after many years one has a new kind of access to the past than that common in oral cultures. The human memory cannot store all the details of the past, and oral cultures tended to have a couple of kinds of reference to the past. The most sacred accounts are usually of the actions of gods or sacred ancestors "in the beginning," and the accounts are of their making the world as it is today. The sacredness of the story carries a warrant for the prevailing state of affairs — clan relationships, economic activities, property rights, and so on. A second kind commonly is made up of genealogies, sometimes augmented by heroic stories. The genealogies also carry warrants for current power relationships, property entitlements, and so on. These references to the past in oral cultures, however, are subject to change; and their changes reflect changes in current power relationships, or those due to natural catastrophes or migrations or the results of battles. The oral memory is subject to what has been well called "structural amnesia" (Horton), and one of its functions is to "obliterate history" (Eliade) in our sense of recording what actually happened — *wie es eigentlich gewesen war*, in Ranke's celebrated phrase. The past in oral cultures serves present social purposes, and reflects them entirely.

Once writing becomes common people can keep all kinds of records, as occurred at the hands of those writers we group together as *logographoi* in early classical Greece. Some centuries later their work was described by Dionysius of Halicarnassus:

> Some of them wrote Hellenic histories, and some barbarian histories. They did not write connected accounts, but broke them up instead according to peoples and cities, treating each separately, but with one aim in view — to make generally known whatever local records had survived, whether of peoples or cities, and whether lying about in temple precincts or anywhere else, without adding anything to what they found, or leaving anything out. Mythological material, acceptable because of its antiquity, was included, and also some dramatic tales, quite silly from a modern point of view. (qtd. in Brown 829)

Once one has collections such as these written down, it is inevitable that one will compare them and try to coordinate them. The need to coordinate diverse activities in an increasingly complex society tends to lead to forms of time measurement that are "disembedded" from the activities themselves. Once diverse written pasts of various families and cities became available for inspection (Drews, Pearson, Vernant), the need to coordinate them similarly led to a disembedding of the past from the particular accounts. Family genealogies that traced ancestry to gods in four generations needed coordinating with those that claimed seven mortal generations since the time of the gods. And these in turn required more radical coordination with the experience of travellers like Herodotus who encountered in Egypt long lists of mortal generations of high priests stretching far back into a past which the Greeks' accounts had populated only with gods.

Coordinating different pasts led quickly toward history, toward the attempt to record what actually happened, regardless of one's present interests. This is something that remains notoriously difficult for even the most austere historian. But the disembedding of the past from the self-glorifying or interest-justifying stories of particular families and cities created a temporal extension of experience. Trying to coordinate what records and claims were available led to logical procedures for assessing the truth-value of such records and claims, and consequently to a skeptical stance before them. The mental stance is well expressed in the opening fragment from the *Genealogies* of Hecateus of Miletus: "The stories of the Greeks are many and, in my opinion, ridiculous."

Once one had begun to develop a generally coordinated sense of the past, and had begun to develop the techniques of criticism, skepticism, and inquiry, one might set about the kind of enterprise Herodotus took on. He wrote primarily to be heard, so he was also going to use the "oral" techniques that would delight the ears of his audience, and he did it with such success that the Athenians gave him a prize of ten talents for reciting his *Histories* (Hartog 275).

One of the consequences of writing is a reduction in the anxiety of forgetting, which thus allows us to preserve endless details, and allows us then to deploy these to charm our audience or readers, so long as they can be coherently fitted into our overarching story or history. So the fact that the Egyptians shaved off their eyebrows at the death of their cats is interesting to one's audience and can be included in Herodotus' narrative if he can neatly slot it into his description of the Persians' previous enemies. The effect is a little like putting the contents of the *Guinness*

Book of Records into a coherent story. The reader is kept alert and fascinated by the exotic detail bound within an epic true story which glorifies the hearers and the heroic city with which they identify. Such a narrative clearly embodies the Romantic characteristics sketched earlier: it is concerned with particulars of what is real, it is full of exotic detail, and so on.

A. N. Whitehead observes that "Romantic emotion is essentially the excitement consequent on the transition from the bare facts to the first realizations of the import of their unexplored relationships" (18). Herodotus wrote precisely at the point when coordination of sets of bare facts were yielding the first realizations of the import of their unexplored relationships. His Romantic exuberance at the wonders and diversity of the world make his text so accessible and enjoyable. After those first realizations come the interest in spelling out systematically those unexplored relationships, and a different kinds of more "scientific" history writing is born, in the Greeks' case most notably by Thucydides. But the Herodotean kind of historiography, recording the sparkling details of the world within an epic story form, is one that we find constantly recurring in Western cultural history, and it is a form of understanding history made possible by the technology of writing.

The related technology of the intellect is the printing press. One of the problems in tracing consequences of print on cognition is due to the fact that it "is difficult to observe processes that enter so intimately into our own observations" (Eisenstein 6). Print enters into our observations as a result of its cumulative effects since our culture entered the Gutenberg galaxy. Ong claims, echoing McLuhan, that "typography was interiorized in the Western psyche definitively at the moment in Western history known as the Romantic movement" (1977, p. 283). What does this mean? And how did it happen?

Some consequences of print are relatively easy to observe—though sometimes their cognitive effects remain rather elusive. During the half century after Gutenberg's press began operating early in the 1450s, more books were produced than from all the scriptoria of Europe and the Roman Empire since the first years of the Common Era. While the first printed books often looked very like scribal products, there was a revolution in scale. Eisenstein shows that in 1483 the Ripoli Press charged three florins per quinterno for setting up and printing Fincino's translation of Plato's *Dialogues*. The going scribal rate for the same work was one florin per quinterno. At the end of their work the scribe produced one copy, the press 1,025 copies.

One consequence of this revolution in productivity, evident early in the next century, is the possession of libraries. Erasmus and Montaigne both had at hand a range of works which no medieval scholar could have hoped to encounter. The medieval scholar who wished to consult a variety of books had to be ready to travel (Waddell). This "novelty of being able to assemble diverse records and reference guides and of being able to study them without having to transcribe them" had profound effects according to Eisenstein (255). She argues persuasively that the revolutionary ideas of the century following this remarkable proliferation of printed material, such as those of Copernicus and Galileo, were not so much a product of new data being discovered but rather of scholars suddenly having access to a wide range of data and diverse commentaries on them. Such discoveries were a part of "the ferment engendered by access to more books," a ferment which we perhaps cannot easily recapture because we take access to huge data resources so much for granted (Eisenstein 43).

In an oral culture much intellectual effort has to go to the preservation of the society's hoard of knowledge. A scribal culture, too, is subject to constant decay of knowledge. The materials written on were perishable, subject to worm and fire (and, as Umberto Eco suggests, eating) and the less dramatic wear of time and use. And, significantly, texts were subject to copyists' corruptions, whether by a scholar copying a work he was studying and interpolating ideas of his own or replacing sections or the inevitable errors of scriptoria where a tired copyist only half-hears what was read. While print initially and in abundance reproduced the corrupted texts it inherited from scriptoria while adding its own corruptions, what it ensured, particularly through the print-shops as competitive centres of entrepreneurial activity and scholarly concourse, was the beginning of the reversal of the corruption. Texts quickly appeared with "errata" slips which were sent to subscribers across Europe. New and improved editions appeared, outpacing the worm. The apparatus of editorial and textual scholarship, that reached a peak of immense refinement by the nineteenth century, began its career.

The process of scribal corruption which was reversed by the printing press gave way not just to less corrupt editions but also to a process of increasing security and accessibility of knowledge. This process continued through the establishment of reliable maps of earth and heavens, to more reliable ancient texts available in abundance and new departures in European scholarship, to the "scientific revolution" and the founding of the Royal Society. It reached one culmination in what we still call, though no longer without a tincture of irony, the Enlightenment, and most visibly in that great Enlightenment project, the *Encyclopédie* of Diderot and d'Alembert. All knowledge was to be brought together, arranged alphabetically, and made accessible to anyone.

The *Encyclopédie* both exemplified and supported a kind of confidence and sense of security in knowledge. This had two sides, at least. On the one side was a proto-positivist confidence in the advance of knowledge. On the other, represented well by Diderot's own particular genius, was the confidence to doubt. McLuhan and Ong argue that the security of knowledge storage exemplified by the *Encyclopédie* and later similar compilations represented a culmination of a long process through a new technology: "The store of knowledge accumulated in print was no longer managed by repetitive, oral techniques, but by visual means, through print, tables of content, and indices" (297). Never before had the store of knowledge been held so securely and so accessibly. Not only could one afford to be more confidently skeptical, but one could more steadily contemplate precisely the areas one did not know about, the mysterious, strange, and exotic. While there was anxiety about preserving the knowledge one had, the security and leisure to explore the mysterious could be only a flickering impulse. By the end of the eighteenth century, it became a central feature of an emerging Romanticism.

While at one level the fascination with the mysterious was somewhat trivial, echoed today in the fascination with stories of the "Bermuda Triangle," there was also a level, represented by the leading Romanticist poets, which was concerned to point out that the confident advance of knowledge was only in very limited areas. The most important parts of our lives, the day to day sense we make of them, were left largely untouched and unenlightened. Indeed, the confidence of propagandists for the Enlightenment was seen as quite misplaced.

McLuhan and Ong see Romanticism as the intellectual partner of the Industrial Revolution. This may appear a surprising partnership, as we tend to think of Romanticism as a kind of reaction against the "satanic mills" of the new industries. But together they exemplified confidence in the conquest of nature, practically and theoretically:

> Romanticism appears as a result of man's noetic control over nature, a counterpart of technology, which matures in the same regions in the West as Romanticism and at about the same time, and which likewise derives from control over nature made possible by writing and even more by print as means of knowledge storage and retrieval. (Ong 20)

I think this way of putting it perhaps underestimates the sense in which Romanticism represents also a new participation in nature via the imagination and many of the techniques of orality. Romanticism's confidence and exuberance seems due to its reliance on the technologies of writing and print and its successful coalescing of their cognitive consequences with those that played and continued to play so vital a role in oral cultures. The danger represented by the "control over nature" was one's alienation from it: "Little we see in Nature that is ours; / we have given our hearts away, a sordid boon!" In oral cultures, by use of the techniques that the Romantic poets were busily harnessing, people were less forlorn than their literate descendants alienated from a nature rich in meaning:

> Great God! I'd rather be
> A Pagan suckled in a creed outworn;
> So might I, standing on this pleasant lea,
> Have glimpses that would make me less forlorn;
> Have sight of Proteus rising from the sea;
> Or see old Triton blow his wreathed horn.

(Wordsworth, Sonnet 33)

An achievement of Romanticism lies in its discovery of a key to harmony and balance in our cultural lives. A prime instrument is the vivified imagination and an important agent is the natural world to which the imagination can give proper access. In the terms I have used above, Romanticism relies on the security of knowledge storage provided by print in order to point to some of the deficiencies of the kind of knowledge that can thus be stored, and to some of the dangers of relying too confidently on that knowledge and the forms of thought it evokes, stimulates, and develops. But the security of knowledge storage also supports the confidence to look into the mysterious and exotic features of experience and of the world. Wordsworth declares his subject to be those mysterious places, the human heart and mind. The transcendent in nature, and in human achievement, can be seen within the everyday. We are to see the world afresh, as though newly made for transcendent acts each morning.

Conclusion

I have suggested some correlations—which could be greatly multiplied—between characteristics of Romanticism and the mental lives of early adolescence. And I have argued that these Romantic characteristics are consequences or implications of the technologies of writing and of the printing press. Romance appears in Western cultural history as a consequence of the invention of the phonetic alphabet and has been, as it were, cemented into a permanent feature of Western culture by the security of knowledge made possible by print.

Saying that characteristics of romance became permanent features of Western culture during the period of Romanticism is a very vague way of putting it, of course. I do not mean to suggest that these features are automatically "internalized" by anyone who attends the normal kind of educational institutions that are supposed to initiate the young into the Western cultural tradition. Rather that they have become pervasive features of our culture, such that it is relatively easy for people to recreate for themselves what required rare individual geniuses to generate. Romanticism has become a permanent constituent of Western culture in the sense that the characteristics of romance that flickered into life intermittently after literacy became common, were given so powerful, compelling, and satisfying instantiation that they remain almost inescapable for anyone becoming literate today. While almost inescapable, we do need to be very much clearer about these characteristics of romance. It is indeed far from automatic that students will recreate them in their richest forms. Our failure to escape them may mean only that we engage their debased or trivialized forms, such as we see commonly in TV shows and other popular media.

What I am suggesting is that the transition to literacy in Western culture is a long process that reaches one kind of culmination in Romanticism. One of the consequences of literacy, I am suggesting, is this sense of Romanticism — a kind of excitement that comes with initial contact with an area of knowledge that is made in such a way as to hint at, give an engaging sense of, unexplored realms full of potential riches and pleasure. In our educational development there are other forms of understanding besides the Romantic, and these can coalesce with it and, in a sense, control Romantic exuberance. But the common characteristics of early adolescents' mental lives that seem to be Romantic in this sense are not, I think, random or due to some natural developmental process. They are rather a consequence of reaching a particular stage in the transition to literacy in a print-saturated environment. Their common Romantic orientation to the world and to experience is due to their internalizing or recreating two related technologies that profoundly affect cognition.

It is a period for the young of potential intellectual excitement if we properly take advantage of it, and enable students to use it to explore the world and experience, romantically. Literacy and print create a kind of cultural predisposition in the West for students to make sense of the world through a Romantic understanding. So how might we teach in such a way as to take advantage of it? One may move from some of the characteristics of Romance touched on above in the direction of a framework that could be used by teachers in planning units and lessons designed to evoke, stimulate, and develop students' Romantic engagements with the world and with a range of human experience. As there is not space here to elaborate this framework with examples, as I do in *Romantic Understanding*, I will simply conclude with a set of questions, the answers to which should provide a lesson or unit outline designed to engage students' Romantic understanding, and encourage them thereby to recapitulate Romanticism in their own education.

The Romantic Model
Taking a Romantic Perspective
1.   Identifying Romantic Qualities: What characteristics are brought to mind by looking at a particular topic in a Romantic way? What transcendent human qualities are most prominently embodied in the topic?
2.   Identifying Romantic Associations: What aspects of the topic can most engagingly attract students' Romantic associations? What transcendent human qualities are most accessible?

Organizing the Content into a Story Form
1.   Providing Access: What content, distant from students' everyday experience, most vividly exemplifies the Romantic qualities of the topic with which the students can associate?
2.   Organizing the Unit/Lesson: What content best articulates the topic into a developing story-form, drawing on the principles of Romance?
3.   Pursuing Details: What content can best allow students to pursue some aspect of the topic in exhaustive detail?

Conclusion
What is the best way of resolving the dramatic conflict on which the unit/lesson is articulated? How does one tie together a satisfactory ending to the Romantically important features of the topic?

Evaluation

How can one know whether the topic has been understood and the appropriate Romantic capacities have been stimulated and developed?

Works Cited

Barzun, Jacques. *Classic, Romantic, and Modern*. Boston: Atlantic—Little Brown, 1961.

Brown, T. S. "Herodotus and his Profession." *American Historical Review* 59 (1954): 4.

Bullock, Alan. *The Humanist Tradition in the West*. London: Thames and Hudson, 1985.

Butler, Marilyn. *Romantics, Rebels, and Reactionaries*. Oxford: Oxford University Press, 1981.

Drews, Robert. *The Greek Accounts of Eastern History*. Washington, D. C.: Center for Hellenic Studies, 1973.

Egan, Kieran. *Primary Understanding*. New York: Routledge, 1988.

Egan, Kieran. *Romantic Understanding*. New York: Routledge (forthcoming).

Egan, Susanna. *Patterns of Experience in Autobiography*. Chapel Hill: University of North Carolina Press, 1984.

Eisenstein, Elizabeth L. *The Printing Revolution in Early Modern Europe*. Cambridge: Cambridge University Press, 1983.

Eliade, Mircea. *Cosmos and History*. New York: Harper and Row, 1959.

Erikson, E. H. *Childhood and Society*. New York: Norton, 1963.

Goody, Jack. *The Domestication of the Savage Mind*. Cambridge: Cambridge University Press, 1977.

Goody, Jack. *The Interface between the Written and the Oral*. Cambridge: Cambridge University Press, 1987.

Hartog, François. *The Mirror of Herodotus*. Trans. Janet Lloyd. Berkeley: University of California Press, 1988.

Havelock, Eric. *Preface to Plato*. Cambridge: Harvard University Press, 1963.

Havelock, Eric. *The Muse Learns to Write*. New Haven: Yale University Press, 1986.

Horton, Robin. "Tradition and Modernity Revisited." *Rationality and Relativism*. Ed. Martin Hollis and Steven Lukes. Oxford: Blackwell, 1982.

McLuhan, Marshall. *The Gutenberg Galaxy*. Toronto: University of Toronto Press, 1962.

Lovejoy, Arthur O. *The Great Chain of Being*. Cambridge: Harvard University Press, 1936.

Olson, David R. "The Cognitive Consequences of Literacy." *Canadian Psychology* 27 (1986): 109-121, 196.

Ong, Walter J. *Rhetoric, Romance, and Technology*. Ithaca: Cornell University Press, 1971.

Ong, Walter J. *Interfaces of the Word*. Ithaca: Cornell University Press, 1977.

Ong, Walter J. *Orality and Literacy*. London: Methuen, 1982.

Pearson, Lionel. *Early Ionian Historians*. Oxford: Clovendon Press, 1939.

Potter, S. (ed.) *Selected Poetry and Prose of S. T. Coleridge*. London: Nonsuch, 1933.

Stock, Brian. *The Implications of Literacy*. Princeton, New Jersey: Princeton University Press, 1983.

Vernant, Jean Pièrre. *The Origins of Greek Thought*. Ithaca: Cornell University Press, 1982.

Vygotsky, L. *Mind in Society*. Eds. M. Cole, V. John-Steiner, S. Scribner, and E. Soubermann. Cambridge: Harvard University Press, 1978.

Waddell, Helen. *The Wandering Scholars*. Harmondsworth: Penguin, 1954.

Whitehead, A. N. *The Aims of Education*, 1929. New York: Free Press, 1967.

INDEX

adolescence, 94, 103, 287-294, 300-302
Agassiz, Louis, 103
Alteri, Charles, 199
American Psychological Association, 103
Arnold, Matthew, 232, 235-237
Atwell, Wendy, 208n4
Auerbach, Nina, 238
autobiography, 194, 199-200, 239, 244-248, 250-252, 259-261, 282-283, 293

Baker, J., 220
Ball, Stephen, 282
Ballauf, Theodor, 116
Balser, B., 220
Barnes, Dorothy, 44
Barnes, Douglas, 44
Barth, Karl, 71n1
Barthes, Roland, 220
Barzun, Jacques, 2
Beaumont, Lady, 44
Beekman, Ton, 117
Beets, Nicolas, 117
Berthoff, Ann, 34
Blackburn, Gilmer, 111n3
Blake, William, 1, 3, 68, 82, 89n17, 177, 237, 247, *Songs of Innocence and Experience*, 217, 240
Bloom, Allan, 182, 196, 200
Bloom, Harold, 47, 190, 208n1
Bly, Robert, 227
Bollnow, O. F., 116, 121, 125-126
Borges, J. L., 212
Brannon, Lil, 51n1
Brecht, Bertolt, 184
Brereton, John C., 71n2
Britton, James, 51n2
Brontë, Charlotte, 214, 238
Brontë, Emily, 214
Bullock, Allan, 290
Burke, Edmund, 82-83
Burne-Jones, Edward Coley, 239
Burnet, James, 89n12
Burns, Ralph, 111n1
Butler, Marilyn, 289, 291
Buytendijk, Frederick, 118
Byron, Lord, 233-234

Carlson, Dennis, 194
Caudwell, Christopher, 36, 38
Chandler, James, 12, 38
Chawaf, Chantel, 243
Chesterton, G. K., 215
Chicago, Judy, 253n2
childhood, 215, and writing, 225, 232
Chodorow, Nancy, 198, 208n3
Clandinin, Jean, 269
Clark University, 103
Clarke, Isaac Edwards, 143
Coates, Wilson H., 111n3
Coleridge, Samuel, 1, 2, 34, 39, 45, 56-71, 214, 289, and Eliot, 212-213, on fancy, 57-58, 62-63, on imagination, 56-58,
Conrad, Joseph, 234
Counts, George, 175-176
Culler, Jonathan, 213
Culture Criticism, 119

Danner, H., 116, 124, 135
de Selincourt, Ernest, 11
de Saussure, Ferdinand, 62
Delacroix, Eugene, 148
Dennis, L., 216
Derbolav, Josef, 116
Derrida, Jacques, 123, 225
Dewey, John, 33, 144, 173n3
Dickens, Charles, 183-184, 234, 237, 247
Diderot, Denis, 88n6, 89n13, 299
Dillard, Annie, 250
Dilthey, Wilhelm, 116-117, 119, 124, 130, 133
Dilthey-Nohl School, 117
Dionysius of Halicarnassus, 295
Drews, Robert, 296

Eagleton, Terry, 192
Eco, Umberto, 298
education, and nature, 22, New Literacy, 33-35, 40, 49-51, social class, 21
Egan, Susanna, 293
Eicher, Hans, 2
Eisenstein, Elizabeth, 297-298
Eliade, Mircea, 295
Eliot, T. S., 212, 234, 237, 240

Laing, R. D., 15
Langbaum, Robert, 240-241, 253n4
Langeveld, Martinus Jan, 117, 121, 123, 125, 128, 131-132
Lecercle, J.-L., 29n15
Lessing, Doris, 45
Levertov, Denise, 251
Levin, Susan, 36, 44
Linschoten, Jan, 117
Lippitz, W., 135
Litt, Theodor, 116, 131, 133-134
Lord, Albert, 233, 239, 243
Lovejoy, Arthur, 2, 212, 290
Lurie, Alison, 211

MacDonald, George, 215
Macherey, Pierre, 39
Mann, Horace, 143
Marcuse, Herbert, 199
Marxism, 176, 189, 194-196
Maxwell, J. C., 51n5
Mayer, Martin, 167
McGann, Jerome, 38
McLuhan, Marshall, 297, 299
Mellown, Muriel, 218, 227
Miller, Hillis, 225-226
Milton, John, 74, 81-84, 86
Mintz, S., 165
Moers, Ellen, 78
Moffat, Mary Jane, 243-244
Mollenhauer, Klaus, 117, 135
Montessori, Maria, 159-174, and design of school, 163-168, in relation to open education, 161
Montgomery, Marion, 221
Moore, Hannah, 73
Moore, Barrington, 182
Mosse, George, 111n2

Napoleon Bonaparte, 288, 291
Newman, John Henry, 237
Niebuhr, Richard, 71
Nietzsche, Friedrich, 123
Nin, Anais, 45
Nohl, Herman, 116-119, 121, 130, 134
Noordam, N. F., 129
Nyquist, Ewald B., 173n1

O'Brien, Mary, 197
Ogden, C. K., 61-62, 71n3
Olson, John, 278

Ong, Walter, 239, 297, 299

Paine, Thomas, 88n5
Painter, Charlotte, 243-244
Parker, Francis Wayland, 141-142, 144-156
Pearson, Lionel, 296
Peirce, C. S., 62-66, 69
Pestalozzi, Johann Heinrich, 125, 173n3
Petersen, Peter, 116
Pinar, William, 199
Plato, 15, 28n3, 30n16, 62, 64, 103
pragmatism, 63
Prelude, 45-48, 51n5
progressive education, 2, 34, 38, 144, 175-176, 258, 282
Proust, Marcel, 220
Ptaschkina, Nelly, 243

Ranke, Otto, 295
Raymond, Danielle, 269, 280-282
rhetoric, 62-63
Rich, Adrienne, 232, 240, 252
Richards, I. A., 56, 61-66
Robinson Crusoe, 20
Romanticism, defn., 2, 212, 287-291, French, 12 (and see Rousseau), German, 55-56, 93-94, 105-109, 116-124, and anti-intellectualism, 181, and art, 147-151, 155-156, militarism, 168-170, childhood, 177, on nature 77-78, 81, and Marxism, 36, and Nazism, 93-94, 105-109, 119-120, personality, 178-179, and the poet, 36-38, and race, 101, romantic education critics, 175-180, 182-183, 195, and writing, 232-233, 244-245
Roosevelt, Franklin Delano, 98
Rosen, Charles, 148, 150, 168
Rosenblum, Nancy, 168-170
Ross, Dorothy, 106
Rossetti, Dante Gabriel, 238
Roth, Geneen, 248, 253n5
Rousseau, 85, 125, 128, and authoritarianism, 94-95, and B. F. Skinner, 22-24, and Wordsworth, 11-12, *Confessions*, 17, 19, 28n3, 74, 85, 88n2, 88n3, *Discourse on Inequality*, 12, 75, 78-79, 81, 88n7, 89n20, 90n22, *Emile*, 3, 5, 13-30, 277, *La Nouvelle Heloise*, 16-22, on art, 148-151, 154, 155, on nature, 12-13, 19, 22-23, *Social Contract*, 15, 17
Rule, Jane, 227

Also published by Wilfrid Laurier University Press
for The Calgary Institute for the Humanities

THE EDUCATIONAL LEGACY OF ROMANTICISM
Edited by John Willinsky

Essays by: Aubrey Rosenberg, Ann E. Berthoff, Clarence J. Karier, Diana Korzenik, Edgar Z. Friedenberg, Johan Lyall Aitken, Richard L. Butt, John Willinsky, Anne McWhir, Max van Manen, Jane Roland Martin, Madeleine R. Grumet, Deborah A. Dooley, Kieran Egan

1990 / pp. xiv + 310 / ISBN 0-88920-996-0

SILENCE, THE WORD AND THE SACRED
Edited by E. D. Blodgett and H. G. Coward

Essays by: David Atkinson, Robin Blaser, E. D. Blodgett, Ronald Bond, Joseph Epes Brown, Harold Coward, Monique Dumais, David Goa, Stanley Hopper, Doug Jones, Smaro Kamboureli, Rudy Wiebe

1989 / pp. xii + 226 / ISBN 0-88920-981-2

THE EFFECTS OF FEMINIST APPROACHES
ON RESEARCH METHODOLOGIES
Edited by Winnie Tomm

Essays by: Margaret Lowe Benston, Naomi Black, Kathleen Driscoll and Joan McFarland, Micheline Dumont, Anne Flynn, Marsha Hanen, Jeanne Lapointe, Hilary M. Lips, Pamela McCallum, Thelma McCormack, Rosemary Nielsen and E. D. Blodgett, Lynn Smith

1989 / pp. x + 259 / ISBN 0-88920-986-3

RUPERT'S LAND
A Cultural Tapestry
Edited by Richard C. Davis

Essays by: Richard I. Ruggles, Olive P. Dickason, John L. Allen, Clive Holland, Sylvia Van Kirk, James G. E. Smith, Robert Stacey, Irene Spry, Fred Crabb, Edward Cavell, R. Douglas Francis, Robert H. Cockburn

1988 / pp. xii + 323 / ISBN 0-88920-976-6

THINKING THE UNTHINKABLE
Civilization and Rapid Climate Change
Lydia Dotto

Based on the Conference
Civilization and Rapid Climate Change
University of Calgary, August 22-24, 1987
1988 / pp. viii + 73 / ISBN 0-88920-968-5

GENDER BIAS IN SCHOLARSHIP
The Pervasive Prejudice
Edited by Winnifred Tomm and Gordon Hamilton

Essays by: Marlene Mackie, Carolyn C. Larsen, Estelle Dansereau, Gisele Thibault, Alice Mansell, Eliane Leslau Silverman, Yvonne Lefebvre, Petra von Morstein, Naomi Black

1988 / pp. xx + 206 / ISBN 0-88920-963-4

FRANZ KAFKA (1883-1983)
His Craft and Thought
Edited by Roman Struc and J. C. Yardley

Essays by: Charles Bernheimer, James Rolleston, Patrick O'Neill, Egon Schwarz, Ernst Loeb, Mark Harman, Ruth Gross, W. G. Kudszus

1986 / pp. viii + 160 / ISBN 0-88920-187-0

ANCIENT COINS OF THE GRAECO-ROMAN WORLD
The Nickle Numismatic Papers
Edited by Waldemar Heckel and Richard Sullivan

Essays by: C. M. Kraay, M. B. Wallace, Nancy Moore, Stanley M. Burstein, Frank Holt, Otto Mørkholm, Bluma Trell, Richard Sullivan, Duncan Fishwick, B. Levy, Richard Weigel, Frances Van Keuren, P. Visonà, Alexander G. McKay, Robert L. Hohlfelder

1984 / pp. xii + 310 / ISBN 0-88920-130-7

DRIVING HOME
A Dialogue Between Writers and Readers
Edited by Barbara Belyea and Estelle Dansereau

Essays by: E. D. Blodgett, Christopher Wiseman, D. G. Jones, Myrna Kostash, Richard Giguère, Aritha van Herk, Peter Stevens, Jacques Brault

1984 / pp. xiv + 98 / ISBN 0-88920-148-X

IDEOLOGY, PHILOSOPHY AND POLITICS
Edited by Anthony Parel

Essays by: Frederick C. Copleston, Charles Taylor, John Plamenatz, Hugo Meynell, Barry Cooper, Willard A. Mullins, Kai Nielsen, Joseph Owens, Kenneth Minogue, Lynda Lange, Lyman Tower Sargent, Andre Liebich

1983 / pp. x + 246 / ISBN 0-88920-129-3

DOCTORS, PATIENTS, AND SOCIETY
Power and Authority in Medical Care
Edited by Martin S. Staum and Donald E. Larsen

Essays by: David J. Roy, John C. Moskop, Ellen Picard, Robert E. Hatfield, Harvey Mitchell, Toby Gelfand, Hazel Weidman, Anthony K. S. Lam, Carol Herbert, Josephine Flaherty, Benjamin Freedman, Lionel E. McLeod, Janice P. Dickin McGinnis, Anne Crichton, Malcolm C. Brown, Thomas McKeown, Cathy Charles

1981 / pp. xiv + 290 / ISBN 0-88920-111-0

CRIME AND CRIMINAL JUSTICE IN
EUROPE AND CANADA
Edited by Louis A. Knafla

Essays by: J. H. Baker, Alfred Soman, Douglas Hay, T. C. Curtis and F. M. Hale, J. M. Beattie, Terry Chapman, André Lachance, Simon N. Verdun-Jones, T. Thorner and N. Watson, W. G. Morrow, Herman Diederiks, W. A. Calder, Pieter Spierenburg, Byron Henderson

1985, Revised Edition / pp. xxx + 344 / ISBN 0-88920-181-1

SCIENCE, PSEUDO-SCIENCE AND SOCIETY
Edited by Marsha P. Hanen, Margaret J. Osler, and Robert G. Weyant

Essays by: Paul Thagard, Adolf Grünbaum, Antony Flew, Robert G. Weyant, Marsha P. Hanen, Richard S. Westfall, Trevor H. Levere, A. B. McKillop, James R. Jacob, Roger Cooter, Margaret J. Osler, Marx W. Wartofsky

1980 / pp. x + 303 / ISBN 0-88920-100-5

THE NEW LAND
Studies in a Literary Theme
Edited by Richard Chadbourne and Hallvard Dahlie

Essays by: Richard Chadbourne, Hallvard Dahlie, Naïm Kattan, Roger Motut, Peter Stevens, Ronald Sutherland, Richard Switzer, Clara Thomas, Jack Warwick, Rudy Wiebe

1978 / pp. viii + 160 / ISBN 0-88920-065-3

RELIGION AND ETHNICITY
Edited by Harold Coward and Leslie Kawamura

Essays by: Harold Barclay, Harold Coward, Frank Epp, David Goa, Yvonne Yazbeck Haddad, Gordon Hirabayashi, Roger Hutchinson, Leslie Kawamura, Grant Maxwell, Cyril Williams

1978 / pp. x + 181 / ISBN 0-88920-064-5